# Modern Catholic Family Teaching

**Other Titles of Interest from Georgetown University Press**

*Modern Catholic Social Teaching: Commentaries and Interpretations, Second Edition*
Edited by Kenneth R. Himes

*Beyond Biology: Rethinking Parenthood in the Catholic Tradition*
By Jacob M. Kohlhaas

# Modern Catholic Family Teaching

*Commentaries and Interpretations*

EDITORS

Jacob M. Kohlhaas
Mary M. Doyle Roche

Georgetown University Press
Washington, DC

The publisher is not responsible for third-party websites or their content. URL links were active at time of publication.

Library of Congress Cataloging-in-Publication Data

Names: Kohlhaas, Jacob M., editor. | Roche, Mary M. Doyle, editor.
Title: Modern Catholic family teaching : commentaries and interpretations / Jacob M. Kohlhaas, Mary M. Doyle Roche, editors.
Description: Washington, DC : Georgetown University Press, 2024. | Includes bibliographical references and index.
Identifiers: LCCN 2023029839 (print) | LCCN 2023029840 (ebook) |
    ISBN 9781647124328 (hardcover) | ISBN 9781647124335 (paperback) |
    ISBN 9781647124342 (ebook)
Subjects: LCSH: Catholic Church—Doctrines. | Families—Religious aspects—Catholic Church.
Classification: LCC BX2351 .M54 2024  (print) | LCC BX2351  (ebook) |
    DDC 233—dc23/eng/20231204
LC record available at https://lccn.loc.gov/2023029839
LC ebook record available at https://lccn.loc.gov/2023029840

♾ This paper meets the requirements of ANSI/NISO Z39.48-1992 (Permanence of Paper).

25 24        9 8 7 6 5 4 3 2    First printing

Printed in the United States of America

Cover design by Nathan Putens
Interior design by BookComp, Inc.
Cover image by Naomi Gerrard. The image used here is an early version of the artist's work *Family Dynamics*.

With gratitude and admiration
to our colleagues in the field,
especially members of the
College Theology Society
where this project began.

# CONTENTS

# PREFACE

For over a century, Catholic magisterial teaching on the family has existed side by side with the expanding body of social ethical thought known widely as Catholic Social Teaching (CST). Magisterial documents on the family have often paralleled those of CST in their composition, concerns, and social assumptions. However, they have not generally been treated by either the magisterium or academics as a parallel body of Catholic moral thought. Whereas CST is widely acknowledged as a developing tradition of theological reflection in conversation with social, political, and economic developments, Catholic teaching on the family has generally been presented as stable, unchangeable, and concerned only with rearticulating objective truths about marriage, the family, sexuality, relationships, and the human person in changing contexts.

Consequently, whereas numerous academic volumes critically explore the content, development, and future trajectory of CST as an unfolding moral tradition, parallel presentations of documents related specifically to the family are relatively sparse. The volumes that do exist tend to be apologetic in their outlook and fail to critically explore whether the representation of this tradition of moral thought within magisterial documents themselves does full justice to its diversity and development over time. As this volume will demonstrate, while many of the documents of CST address family life (e.g.,

*Gaudium et spes*, 47–52), there is also a significant library of documents that takes family and family life as its primary focus and has the potential for similar academic richness if it is more critically and concertedly explored.

By naming modern Catholic magisterial teaching related to the family as Catholic Family Teaching (CFT), this volume claims this historically developing moral tradition as worthy of critical study in a parallel fashion to CST. Throughout this volume, essays by a wide array of theologians offer various perspectives on primary texts that demonstrate the potential of this approach for understanding and making this tradition widely available for academic study. To accomplish this aim, the present volume is inspired by and may serve as a companion to the edited volume *Modern Catholic Social Teaching: Commentaries and Interpretations* (Georgetown University Press, 2005).

It may be too early in this endeavor toward a new way of understanding to name precisely the relationship between CST and CFT. Both are developing documentary traditions within the realm of social ethics such that, in some ways, CFT may be thought of as a species of CST. However, CFT also encompasses significant teachings in sacramentality of marriage, interpersonal morality in the realm of sexual ethics, and more concerted formulations of theological anthropology utilized in support of specific moral norms and possibilities. Consequently,

CFT and CST may alternatively be thought of as parallel traditions, given the similarities among the documents' chronology and shared vision of the family as a social unit. However, this fails to account for the many ways in which CFT and CST often intersect, with some documents rightfully belonging to both traditions. This project has gathered scholars who attend to the dynamism at the intersections of these traditions and also maintain the critical and creative tension in the bonds joining this living double helix.

It is our sincere hope that through this volume, students and scholars of the Catholic moral tradition may come to appreciate, understand, and critically investigate CFT in new and more profound ways. We offer this volume as an invitation to engage more intentionally in a field where more is possible than has often met the eye.

# ABBREVIATIONS

| | |
|---|---|
| *AC* | *Apostolica constitutio* |
| *AD* | *Arcanum divinae sapientiae* |
| *AL* | *Amoris laetitia* |
| *AM* | *Africae munus* |
| *CC* | *Casti connubii* |
| CDF | Congregation for the Doctrine of the Faith |
| CFT | Catholic Family Teaching |
| *ChV* | *Christus vivut* |
| CRP | Considerations Regarding Legislative Proposals to Give Legal Recognition to Unions between Homosexual Persons |
| CST | Catholic Social Teaching |
| *CV* | *Caritas in veritate* |
| *DCE* | *Deus caritas est* |
| *DIM* | *Divini illius magistri* |
| *FC* | *Familiaris consortio* |
| GIRM | *The General Instruction of the Roman Missal* |
| *GS* | *Gaudium et spes* |
| HS | Hebrew Scripture |
| *HV* | *Humanae vitae* |
| *LE* | *Laborem exercens* |
| *LG* | *Lumen gentium* |
| LTB | Letter to the Bishops of the Catholic Church on the Pastoral Care of Homosexual Persons |
| LTF | Letter to Families |
| *MD* | *Mulieris dignitatem* |
| MF | Male and Female He Created Them |
| NFP | natural family planning |
| *NL* | *Nimiam licentiam* |
| NT | New Testament |
| OCM | *The Order of Celebrating Matrimony* |
| PCPM | Pontifical Commission for the Protection of Minors |
| *PH* | *Persona humana* |
| *RC* | *Redemptoris custos* |
| *RN* | *Rerum novarum* |
| *RF* | *Relatio finalis* (2015) |
| *SC* | *Sacrosanctum concilium* |
| SCC | Some Considerations Concerning the Response to Legislative Proposals on the Non-Discrimination of Homosexual Persons |
| *ST* | *Summa Theologiae* |
| *UP* | *Ubi primum* |
| USCCB | United States Conference of Catholic Bishops |
| WMOF | World Meeting of Families |

# INTRODUCTION

# A Documentary Approach
# to Catholic Family Teaching

JACOB M. KOHLHAAS AND MARY M. DOYLE ROCHE

## FAMILY AND SOCIETY TODAY

For ages it seems, parents have often been inundated with rhetoric that casts the future of children and families in doubt. Whether this comes through religious or political leaders, the social media of the day, or partisan journalism, parents frequently encounter messaging along the lines of *our children are being corrupted by forces of evil; we cannot sit idly by while the truths we know in our hearts, that all people know in their hearts, are maliciously attacked; we must act against these evils to save our children, to save ourselves, our faith, and our country, from inevitable destruction.* The opening of the twenty-first century is no aberration in the way that seismic economic shifts, encounters with new cultures, and violent conflict at national and international levels provided pretext for fearmongering around the security of the family. A brief snapshot of recent developments shows no indications of a calmer social climate or cooler heads prevailing anytime soon.

In the United States, the governor of Iowa recently praised a crowd of politically conservative mothers for their "refusal to stand quietly by while we've seen the radical left treat our kids like their personal property. . . . They think that patriotism is racist and pornographic library books are education. . . . They believe

that the content of our character is less important than the color of our skin. They believe children should be encouraged to pick their gender, and parents—well, they're just in the way."[1] Meanwhile, the governor of Florida has been openly preparing for a presidential bid by waging war on "woke" education, going so far as to block an advanced placement high school course in African American history and to stack a small state college's board to enact ideological change.[2] At the same time as forces on the political Right rally their legislative power to confront what they have identified as destructive left-wing ideology, many on the Left portray these efforts as themselves the ideologically driven destruction of established and valued social practices. All partisans, it seems, see their children's and families' futures crumbling before their eyes; they just happen to diametrically disagree on what is progress and what is misguided ideology.

Meanwhile, Francis, the eighty-six-year-old pontiff encumbered with an ailing knee, recently traveled to South Sudan and pleaded for peace in the decade-old civil war between the Muslim North and the Christian South. His clarification shortly before the trip, that homosexuality itself is not a sin and should not be criminalized, fueled fears among some African Christians that the pope had departed

1

from the clear message of scripture and natural meaning of the family. In alarmist responses, the distinctions utilized by Francis (and most of the Western world) between sin and criminality as well as among sexual orientation, sexual activity, and marriage went little acknowledged, while the perceived assault on African Christian values and cultural indoctrination took the fore.[3]

Francis and the Catholic hierarchy, however, are no innocent victims in the political weaponization of fears related to children and the family. Arguably, the most socially alarmist statement from a Vatican dicastery in recent memory was approved by Francis through the Congregation for Christian Education in 2019. Titled "Male and Female He Created Them," the statement opens with a condemnation of social developments in the understanding of gender and sexuality that echoes the rhetoric of socially abrasive political and religious leaders and declares an "*educational crisis*" in the field of sexuality whereby curricula are composed with "an anthropology opposed to faith and to right reason" through the "ideology" of "gender theory" that seeks to eliminate the "anthropological basis of the family."[4] Far from unprecedented, such stoking of fear over children, education, and the future of the family against what is portrayed as active, intentional, and organized maliciousness is deeply rooted in modern Catholic teaching.

## THE RHETORIC OF CATHOLIC FAMILY TEACHING

Leo XIII's inaugural encyclical, *Inscrutabili Dei consilio* of 1878, inveighed against the evils of society and offered an assessment of contemporary family life that drew on established rhetorical patterns that still echo to this day. Lamenting the present crisis of the family, he offered a return to authentic Catholic doctrine as the only solution:

Now, the training of youth most conducive to the defense of true faith and religion and to the preservation of morality must find its

beginning from an early stage within the circle of home life; and this family Christian training sadly undermined in these our times, cannot possibly be restored to its due dignity, save by those laws under which it was established in the Church by her Divine Founder Himself. Our Lord Jesus Christ, by raising to the dignity of a sacrament the contract of matrimony, in which He would have His own union with the Church typified, not only made the marriage tie more holy, but, in addition, provided efficacious sources of aid for parents and children alike, so that, by the discharge of their duties one to another, they might with greater ease attain to happiness both in time and in eternity.[5]

Here and in other documents, Leo XIII sets up a declension narrative, a remarkably common and effective rhetorical strategy. The essential elements of such narratives include a present crisis that has emerged from the deterioration of an idealized past. In Christian contexts, this assessment is usually joined to a call for renewal through a return to earlier moral purity before the opportunity is lost.[6] In Catholic magisterial documents on the family from the modern period into the early twentieth century, the identified crisis tended to revolve around intrusions of secular state authority in regulating aspects of marriage that were held as properly subject to ecclesial authority alone. Fears of the results of such incursions included relaxed morals that would lead to increased sexual sin and the spread of divorce.[7] Confidence in the objectivity of Catholic doctrine, male authority, and Western cultural superiority informed the contextual backdrop for such warnings.[8]

Throughout this period, ecclesial interpretations of scripture proved remarkably adaptive in meeting the needs of the particular declension narrative being offered. The Holy Family provides an excellent example of this flexibility, as seemingly against the odds it is commonly held up as a model for thoroughly modern visions of the family. Before and after Leo XIII, virtues were commonly ascribed to the Holy Family that contradict or fill silences in biblical testimony. In a near reversal of Joseph's silence, Mary's voice, and Jesus's disparagement of family ties in scripture, Leo XIII writes of Joseph's "vigilance" and "fatherly protection," Mary's "love, modesty, and spirit of submission and perfect faith," and the child Jesus as a "model of obedience."[9] Pius XI repeated this interpretation so that women of his day "who, weary of children and the conjugal bond, have debased and violated the duties that were imposed on them" might look to Mary's example and "be induced to shame for the disgrace inflicted on the great Sacrament of Matrimony."[10] And bizarrely given belief in Mary's perpetual virginity, Pius XII employed the Holy Family as a model for strengthening married persons' appreciation of "the glorious burden of numerous children."[11]

## ENGAGING, LAMENTING, AND RETELLING OUR STORY

Stories shape human realities that, in turn, shape the types of stories that are valued and retold. A significant motivation behind this volume is to call attention to the ways in which the story commonly repeated about Catholic teaching on the family fails to give full justice to the complexities, diversities, and developments found within the documents themselves as well as the documents' own limitations in taking global, honest account of the conditions and experiences of families. CFT, as a body of teaching, is uniquely prone to narrative forms that both hide the tradition's actual responsiveness to theological and sociohistorical contexts and elide the need for more earnest assessments of the complexities of social developments and the dynamics of family systems and experiences.

Recognizing these limitations, this volume presents itself as an invitation to discover the depth and potential of a documentary heritage that offers much theological value despite its rather obvious and perennial limitations. CFT is marked as much by tragic failings on behalf of the faithful and the institutional church to live up to its ideals as it is by the internal limitations of the tradition itself. Responsible

reception of this heritage includes acknowledging the deep-seated Eurocentrism and European cultural supremacy that especially marked its early documents and encouraged neglect of the full geographical, cultural, and racial diversity of the Catholic faithful. In so doing, such horrors as the destruction of enslaved families and the forced removal of indigenous children from their families' homes continued despite being absolutely inimical to the vision of family offered within the documents.

More recently, the global sexual abuse crisis within the Catholic Church has become painful public knowledge. Incidents of sexual abuse, some of which were concerted and organized among offenders, appear to have peaked alongside CFT's shift toward emphasizing sexual ethical norms. Despite this, reports were not acted on swiftly or systemically. Upon greater social acknowledgment of the depth of the crisis, many vocal Catholic leaders tenuously turned to blaming the evils of the world beyond the Catholic Church as the true source of such internal corruption.

Responsible reception of this history is difficult. The late recognition and protracted ineffective responses to the sexual abuse crisis represent both a failure to live up to the ideals of CFT and the formation of its own rhetorical strategies that for over a century had pointed blame externally while shielding even basic self-criticism. Today, Catholic parishes are leaders in the institutional protection of children, but Catholics have hardly begun to remember honestly let alone come to terms with the church's complicated and often grim historical association with colonialism, slavery, and the treatment of indigenous populations. Meanwhile, many social developments that are almost universally regarded as positive have come about in the face of ardent opposition in CFT. These advancements include coeducation for male and female students (including advanced education for women), women's rights to hold and advance in a career and to positions of public authority, and the value of ecumenical and interreligious association. Far from a once-and-for-all set of truths handed directly from the mouth of Christ to the Roman pontiffs and often despite its own insistences, the story of CFT is wrapped up in ever-changing social realities. CFT is a heritage shaped by both a will for a better world and the self-interests and limited vision of its authors, its teaching can provide a framework for family flourishing but often contents itself with a model of the family that is tragically too narrow to address many needs, and it contains the possibilities for boldly discovering the grace of God in human experiences but is often far more wary of the power of evil to corrupt our wills and interpretations. Receiving this tradition is a complex responsibility but nonetheless a responsibility to which you, the reader, are invited to participate.

## CONTENTS

The contributors to this volume come from a variety of disciplinary perspectives within academic theology, including ethics, systematics, history, and biblical studies. They also represent a range of methodological approaches, such as feminist and liberationist methodologies, and include scholars at different stages of their careers and from different institutional settings, cultural backgrounds, and geographical locations. Contributors are also invariably influenced by their own family experiences. Many contributors are married and have children, while others are single or committed to celibacy through ordination or religious life. The diversity and intersectionality among contributors are intentional, though we readily acknowledge that one volume cannot fully capture the enormously rich tapestry of existing perspectives. We hope that this endeavor will provide a model of international, intergenerational, and intersectional collaboration that honors difference and builds solidarity.

To accommodate differences while providing a level of consistency throughout the volume, the editors have utilized some common standards while attempting to preserve the distinctiveness of each contributor's approach. For example, chapters in the second part of the volume are all structured in three parts (context,

commentary, and interpretation) even as individual authors have managed these areas differently. The volume also utilizes gender-inclusive language throughout but does not change direct quotes. If an interpretive question arises regarding a magisterial document, the reader is advised to refer to the original language of the text (typically Latin or Italian) when possible, as this often preserves gendered intentions that are obscured in English.

The chapters in Part I lay the foundation for the textual analyses that follow. Part I adopts a hermeneutical approach to CFT that mirrors academic approaches to CST in its attention to scripture, natural law, and ecclesial traditions as key sources for critical theological and ethical reflection. Biblical scholar Andrew Massena explores the ways in which CFT documents incorporated scripture and the possibilities for historical critical approaches to contribute to its future. Ethicist Craig Ford Jr. deftly explores the often neuralgic subject of natural law, offering directions for a way forward. Ecclesiologist Annie Selak helps us to navigate the terrain of a church that is at once an intimate community and a complex institutional bureaucracy. Moral theologian Matthew Sherman brings us up to speed on the seeds of CFT prior to the modern period. Theologian Jacob M. Kohlhaas offers a crucial intervention in reckoning with the inescapable presence and impact of racism and Eurocentric reasoning in the Catholic Church's teaching on family life.

Part II: Commentaries and Interpretations, takes a deep dive into teachings promulgated from the late nineteenth through the early twenty-first centuries. Systematic and moral theologians reflect on a range of documents in chronological order that represent teachings with differing degrees of magisterial authority. The authors also provide a window into the liturgical and pastoral contexts in which the faithful participate and contribute to this evolving tradition. Angela Senander offers another critical intervention that confronts the global clergy sexual abuse crisis that has seriously undermined the moral authority of the hierarchy in the arena of family life.

The editors' primary goal was to collect a wide array of academic voices to illuminate the importance of recognizing CFT as a documentary tradition. As such, aside from a critical, informed academic lens, the volume does not propose a normative way of receiving this tradition but instead invites engagement. To facilitate engagement beyond the text, the endnotes of each chapter favor stable online versions of documents (typically via the Vatican's website) to make accessing primary texts as direct as possible. Individual chapters have also been kept to a modest length to allow for ease of use within classroom settings.

This volume is an initial introduction that offers a variety of perspectives that may be critically engaged and developed in future work. These are not the final words on the documents but instead are particular perspectives offered to facilitate further engagement. We hope the reader will find in these chapters the inspiration to raise new questions as we learn together how to better understand and respond to God's will in our efforts to realize human flourishing specifically through families.

## NOTES

1. Grant Gerlock, "Reynolds Pledges to Follow School Choice with Push for Transparency Rules in Public Schools," Iowa Public Radio, February 3, 2023, https://www.iowapublicradio.org/state-government-news/2023-02-03/iowa-governor-kim-reynolds-school-choice-parents-rights-book-challenges.

2. *Morning Edition*, "Fla. Gov. DeSantis Is Now Looking to Overhaul the State's Colleges and Universities," National Public Radio, February 1, 2023, https://www.npr.org/2023/02/01/1153150917/fla-gov-desantis-is-now-looking-to-overhaul-the-state-s-colleges-and-universitie.

3. See Philip Pullella and Waakhe Simon Wudu, "Pope Francis Wraps Up South Sudan Trip, Urges End to 'Blind Fury' of Violence," Reuters, February 5, 2023, https://www.reuters.com/world/africa/pope-francis-wraps-up-south-sudan-trip-urging-an-end-violence-2023-02-05/; and Edward Pentin, "Pope Francis Flies into African Storm over His Call to Decriminalize Homosexual Relations," *National Catholic Register*, January 31, 2023, https://www.ncregister.com/blog/pope-ap-comments-ahead-of-africa-trip.

4. Congregation for Christian Education, "Male and Female He Created Them," February 2, 2019, 1–2, http://www.educatio.va/content/dam/cec/Documenti/19_0997_INGLESE.pdf.

5. Leo XIII, *Inscrutabili dei consilio* (April 21, 1878), 14, https://www.vatican.va/content/leo-xiii/en/encyclicals/documents/hf_l-xiii_enc_21041878_inscrutabili-dei-consilio.html. Leo XIII's later encyclical on marriage, *Arcanum*, is almost entirely structured as a declension narrative. Characteristically, historical complexities, contradictions, or potential embarrassments are glossed over or presented as the unfolding of God's plan in God's own due time, while the church's own agency is unwaveringly aligned with advancing God's will in a world that is nearly constantly obstructing or avoiding its realization.

6. Pius XI is particularly alarmist in his assessment of an impending crisis in Venezuela, writing that "if God no longer reigns in the family and no longer showers down his blessings with the Sacrament of Matrimony, the union is ruined, mutual duties between parents and children diminished, public morals themselves are in danger! It is inevitable that after having put aside the commandment of God and His Church, everything collapses and all is in confusion: justice, charity, the union of the classes." Pius XI, "Quad novas" (April 25, 1923), in *Matrimony*, Selected and arranged by the Benedictine Monks of Solesmes, trans. Michael J. Byrnes (Boston: St. Paul Editions, 1963), 216–17.

7. See Leo XIII, *Ci siamo* (June 1, 1879), in *Matrimony*, 131.

8. See, e.g., Leo XIII, *Arcanum divinae sapientiae* (February 10, 1880), 11, 19, https://www.vatican.va/content/leo-xiii/en/encyclicals/documents/hf_l-xiii_enc_10021880_arcanum.html.

9. Leo XIII, *Neminem fugit* (January 14, 1892), in *Matrimony*, 177.

10. Pius XI, *Lux veritatis* (December 25, 1931), in *Matrimony*, 293. This encyclical is available in Italian and Latin at Hole See, vatican.va.

11. Pius XII, "The Family, Cell of Society" (June 26, 1940), in *Matrimony*, 312.

PART

I

Foundations

# CHAPTER

# 1

## Scripture and Catholic Family Teaching

ANDREW MASSENA

In his commentary in *Modern Catholic Social Teaching*, John Donahue observes that Catholic Social Teaching (CST) has relied heavily on natural law, and to a far lesser extent CST has drawn on scripture, typically interpreted through the patristic tradition. Consequently, CST and Catholic biblical studies have run on parallel tracks for much of the last century. But in 1943 with the promulgation of *Divino afflante Spiritu*, the Catholic Church accepted modern biblical scholarship and its methods. These were affirmed again in 1965 with *Dei verbum*, which called the Bible "the soul of sacred theology."[1]

The documents of Catholic Family Teaching (CFT) covered in the present volume use scripture generously. These documents contain 1,583 scriptural citations out of 3,547 total citations, making 44.6 percent of the citations scriptural.[2] *Amoris laetitia* has the most scriptural citations, with 275 out of 684 total, followed by *Mulieris dignitatem*, with 267 out of 384, and *Africae munus*, with 163 out of 414. *Humanae vitae* represents a turning point. Of the papal documents included in this volume, those written before 1968 average 25 scriptural citations, or 41.2 percent of all citations. After 1968, documents average 143.4 scriptural citations, increasing to 46.1 percent of all citations.

In agreement with Donahue's assessment of CST documents, under John Paul II, CFT began to cite scripture more and drew more on the fruits of modern biblical scholarship.[3] For example, *Mulieris dignitatem* (1988) was the first to identify Genesis 1 and 2 as two different creation accounts; it also acknowledges the original Hebrew, noting a wordplay in Genesis 2:23 when the man calls the woman '*iisah* (woman) because she was taken out of '*is* (man). This same document initiates the placement of scriptural citations in text instead of endnotes, rendering them more obvious. A year later, *Redemptoris custos* (1989) was the first to engage in a synoptic gospel comparison.[4] More recently, *Amoris laetitia* (2016) makes reference to the "priestly tradition," sources in the Pentateuch, including Genesis 1, written by the "Priestly" author sometime after 587 BCE. Notably among recent popes, Benedict XVI's documents do not make obvious use of modern biblical scholarship.[5] Nor do they cite scripture as frequently: while John Paul II and Francis average 59.7 percent and 42.7 percent, respectively, Benedict XVI averages only 31.9 percent. However, given how often magisterial documents are criticized for proof texting, more does not necessarily mean better.

In his assessment of CST, Donahue argues that it would be more accurate to say that rather than proof texting the church has used scripture as "a moral reminder" to motivate people to action and as intertextual references, meaning that the church's interpretations draw on a tradition that has made associations between various texts and doctrines. To Donahue, this contrasts with proof texting, which possesses no tradition of interpretation behind it or "intrinsic connection" between a text and the position it supports.[6] CFT's use of scripture generally falls in line with this assessment, though proof texting does still occur. One example is in *Divini illius magistri* 68–69. Here, coeducation of children is rejected as being against God's will and the natural order. The encyclical cites Matthew 18:7—"Woe to the world because of these scandals!"[7]—as a call to vigilance against coeducation. However, in what precedes (Matt. 18:1–7), the disciples ask Jesus who is greatest in the kingdom of God, to which he responds that they must become *like* children to enter the kingdom. He then warns against putting stumbling blocks before his disciples.[8] Certainly, connecting this warning to coeducation is a stretch.

CFT documents clearly favor the New Testament (NT). There are 1,130 NT citations versus 427 from the Hebrew Scriptures (HS) and 26 from the Deuterocanon. Perhaps surprisingly, 1 Corinthians 13, Paul's exposition on love, is not the most commonly cited pericope (in fact, a robust interpretation of 1 Corinthians 13 does not appear until *Amoris laetitia* 89–119). Instead, Genesis 1:26–2:24 leads with 124 citations, followed by Ephesians 5:21–33 (47 citations), and then Matthew 19:1–12 (40 citations). The documents treat Genesis 1:26–2:24 as thematically centered on theological anthropology, Ephesians 5:21–33 as centered on marriage, and Matthew 19:1–12 as centered on divorce.[9] These three popular texts exemplify the ways in which interpretations within CFT have developed over time while speaking to some of CFT's dominant topics.

The following sections identify CFT's most significant interpretations of these texts in turn. Because interpretations are often repeated, this section concentrates on the first appearance while identifying important later interpretive developments. The interpretations of each text are then brought into conversation with modern biblical scholarship.[10]

## GENESIS 1:26–2:24

Biblical scholars today see the first two chapters of Genesis as containing two accounts of humanity's creation. Genesis 1:26–31 recounts the simultaneous creation of humanity as male and female in the image of God, while Genesis 2:4–24 speaks of man being formed from the earth and woman emerging from man.[11]

*Arcanum* 5 does not explicitly cite Genesis 2:7–18 but reads the text through the lens of Matthew 19:5–6, which it uses to articulate "the never-interrupted doctrine of the Church" in six crucial points: (1) God created Adam; (2) God created Eve as a companion; (3) God instituted marriage;[12] (4) the purpose of marriage is unity and procreation;[13] (5) marriage is monogamous, not polygamous; and (6) in marriage, man and woman become "one flesh," thus making the bond indissoluble.

Citing Genesis 1:27, *Familiaris consortio* 22 states that creating humanity as "male and female" gives equal dignity to men and women. *Mulieris dignitatem* III.6–7 acknowledges that calling woman a "helper" in Genesis 2:18 can give the impression of subordination but stresses that she is man's "helper" in helping subdue the earth and in procreation. Helper also means companionship, which requires *mutual* help: neither can live alone without the other.[14] Reading Genesis 2:18–25 in light of Genesis 1:26–27, *Mulieris dignitatem* states that as a "unity of the two" man and woman reflect the image of God, who is triune. John Paul II's "Letter to Women" 7 develops this idea, citing Genesis 1:27; 2:18, 20: "Womanhood expresses the 'human' as much as manhood does, but in a different and complementary way." "Considerations Regarding Proposals to Give Legal Recognition to Unions between Homosexual Persons" I.3 takes this line of reasoning further: the complementarity between man and woman in Genesis 1:27–28 is also sexual; man and woman were created only for heterosexual

sexual expression. The same document uses Genesis 2:24 to establish marriage as exclusively between a man and a woman.

Interpreting Genesis 1:27 as articulating gender complementarity has support among biblical scholars. Victor Hamilton and John Goldingay each see Genesis 1:28 as referring to humanity's role in procreation, which implies sexual complementarity.[15] Walter Brueggemann argues that 1:27's use of "created *him*" and "created *them*" indicates that male and female are fully the image of God not on their own but instead only together.[16] In contrast to Brueggemann, Gordan Wenham argues that 1:27 bestows God's full image in each individual through three clauses placed in apposition. The first two are chiastic and center on men being in the image of God. The third affirms that women are *also* in God's image.[17] Wenham furthermore argues that being in God's image means being God's representatives on Earth, a view common to the ancient Near East.[18]

Wenham does see gender complementarity in the second creation account of Genesis 2:18, where God finds that man needs a "helper"[19] or, more specifically, a "helper matching him" (עֵזֶר כְּנֶגְדּוֹ). This may suggest complementarity. If the helper were exactly like the man, the term כמוהו would be used instead of עזר. The term עזר most commonly refers to God's aid but does not signal that the helper is superior, only that the one needing help cannot achieve success independently.[20]

Historically, Christianity tended to read Genesis 2:18ff as promoting the superiority of men over women.[21] In contrast, *Mulieris dignitatem* and subsequent documents have remarkably viewed Genesis 2:18ff as affirming fundamental equality. This egalitarian interpretation can be traced to the pioneering work of Phyllis Trible, a feminist biblical scholar who first challenged patriarchal readings of Genesis 2:18ff in 1973.[22]

No comparable shift has occurred with interpreting Genesis 2:24 to exclusively support heterosexual marriage. However, Megan Warner has recently proposed an alternative view.[23] Warner argues that Genesis 2:24 and other texts, such as Ruth and Ezra-Nehemiah, were written during the postexilic Persian period and were focused on the pressing issue of intermarriage between Jews and non-Jews. Warner's argument is based in a word study of עזב (forsake) and דבק (stick). When referring to relationships between individuals, the latter is exclusively used in the HS in the context of intermarriage.[24] Warner finds in Genesis 2:24 an etiological description of intermarriage as a phenomenon so powerful that it can bring men to forsake their parents' authority and engage in exogamy.[25] While affirmations of gender complementarity and heterosexual marriage may be found in Genesis 2:24, they are not the only possible meanings and may not be the original.[26]

## MATTHEW 19:1–12

Jesus's teaching on divorce appears in Matthew 19:1–12 during a discourse with the Pharisees (it also appears earlier in Matthew 5:31–32, but the latter is preferred by CFT documents).[27] Jesus quotes Genesis 2:24, where a man and woman joined together are considered "one flesh." The Pharisees then ask why Moses gave instructions on divorce, to which Jesus replies, "Because of the hardness of your hearts Moses allowed you to divorce your wives, but from the beginning it was not so. I say to you, whoever divorces his wife (unless the marriage is unlawful) and marries another commits adultery" (Matt. 19:8–9).

*Arcanum* 5 cites Matthew 19:5–6 to argue that marriage is indissoluble: husband and wife are "one flesh" and cannot be separated. *Arcanum* 6 then cites Matthew 19:8 to argue that divorce was a concession from Moses to address the people's "hardness of heart"; God's original intent, however, was indissolubility. *Arcanum* 8 explains that Jesus "perfected the Mosaic law," returning marriage to its original state. The document then quotes Matthew 19:9: "I say to you, that whoever shall put away his wife, except it be for fornication, and shall marry another, committeth adultery; and he that shall marry her that is put away committeth adultery."[28] Half a century later, *Casti connubii* 20 added that since God authored marriage and Christ restored it, no human law can supersede the doctrine of scripture preserved in the "constant tradition" of the church.

*Mulieris dignitatem* VI.20–22 first comments on Matthew 19:10–12, which, it argues, supports virginity for both men and women who are called by God and shows "the superiority of virginity over marriage." But *Amoris laetitia* 159, drawing on a statement from John Paul II in 1982 (six years before *Mulieris dignitatem*), argues that neither marriage nor celibacy is superior.[29]

Matthew 19:9's so-called "exception clause," μὴ ἐπὶ πορνείᾳ, translated in the New American Bible Revised Edition as "unless the marriage is unlawful" and in the New Revised Standard Version as "except for unchastity," has garnered the most attention among biblical scholars, who do not universally agree on the translation of πορνείᾳ.[30] According to Ulrich Luz, πορνείᾳ "refers to every form of inappropriate sexual activity on the wife's part, especially adultery."[31] But as Donald Hagner points out, a growing number of scholars translate πορνείᾳ as "incestuous marriage," or those forbidden relations referred to in Leviticus 18:6–18.[32]

Raymond Collins lists twelve different potential meanings of μὴ ἐπὶ πορνείᾳ. Among them, μὴ ἐπὶ πορνείᾳ ("except for unchastity") could modify ἀπολύσῃ ("dismisses"), meaning a person can dismiss (i.e., separate from) his or her spouse for unchastity, but the two are not divorced. Neither can they remarry. Another option, going back to Erasmus, is that μὴ ἐπὶ πορνείᾳ ("except for adultery") modifies both ἀπολύσῃ ("divorce") and γαμήσῃ ("marries"), meaning one can divorce an adulterous spouse and then remarry.[33] Catholic biblical scholars have tended to hold the first position while Protestant scholars tend to hold the second, but recent scholarship does not always follow denominational lines.[34] Curtis Mitch and Edward Sri, on the one hand, argue that Jesus "revoked the legal allowance for divorce altogether. Because the one-flesh union between husband and wife is an unbreakable union in the eyes of God, it follows that divorce and remarriage are equivalent to adultery." The

only exception is an invalid marriage.[35] Craig Blomberg, on the other hand, argues that the position of μὴ ἐπὶ πορνείᾳ in the sentence, syntactically speaking, modifies both "divorce" and "remarriage." Thus, a man can divorce and remarry if his partner was unfaithful.[36]

Amid this debate, Douglas Hare points to a critical and often overlooked issue: in Matthew 5:32, a man who divorces his wife *causes her* to commit adultery. Hare explains that this comes from the assumption that a divorced wife will be in a socioeconomically perilous situation and will be forced to remarry. If the divorced wife was faithful, then only in her remarriage will she have committed adultery, because she remains bound to her first husband. But it is the husband's blame, as he forced her into this position. Jesus's concern, then, is with the socioeconomic safety of faithful wives. This concern is completed in 19:9 by teaching that a husband who divorces a faithful wife and then remarries also commits adultery.[37] Whatever significance might be derived from 19:9, the importance of protection for a faithful wife (and, by extension, a faithful husband) should not be lost.

## EPHESIANS 5:21–33

Ephesians 5:21–33 contains the (in)famous household code along with the marriage analogy of husband and wife to Christ and the church. Verses 22 and 23 frequently receive the most attention: "Wives should be subordinate to their husbands as to the Lord. For the husband is head of his wife just as Christ is head of the church, he himself the savior of the body."

*Arcanum* 9 draws on Ephesians 5:32 to argue that Christ "raised marriage to the dignity of a sacrament" and that marriage is "an example of the mystical union between Himself and His Church." In this way, marriage is indissoluble. The document then cites Ephesians 5:25–32, which discusses how husbands should love their wives as Christ loves the church. *Arcanum* 11 states that husbands are "the chief of the family and the head of the wife." Because woman came from man and not the other way around (a reference to Genesis 2:18ff), she is to "be subject to her husband and obey him." The document clarifies that the wife is not a *servant* but instead is a "companion." In this way, her honor and dignity will be preserved in her *obedience* to her husband. *Casti connubii* 27 provides further clarifications. A woman need not obey her husband if doing so violates "right reason" or her dignity. Moreover, in exceptional cases if a husband becomes negligent in his duties, the wife must head the household. The document cites *Arcanum* 11 to reinforce its argument.

A notable shift occurs in *Gaudium et spes* 48–49. Here, the model in Ephesians 5:25 of Christ loving the church and giving himself over on its behalf is evoked, but instead of applying it only to the husband, *Gaudium et spes* 48 applies this model to *both* husband and wife: "the spouses may love each other with perpetual fidelity through mutual self-bestowal." This interpretation is more fully developed in *Mulieris dignitatem* VII.24, which states that the language of wives being subject to husbands was "profoundly rooted in the customs and religious tradition of the time" in which Ephesians was written (i.e., the first-century Roman and Jewish context) and that the author transforms this language to mean a "*mutual subjection out of reverence for Christ*' (cf. Eph 5:21)."[38] The document then makes absolutely clear that while the church is singularly subject to Christ, this aspect of the analogy does not extend to husbands and wives, who are to be *mutually* subjected to each other. *Africae munus* 52 quotes Ephesians 5:25 and 5:28 in calling on men to love their wives but makes no reference to subjection. In fact, *Africae munus* 57 emphatically states that men and women are equal. The 2015 Synod on the Family's *Relatio finalis* 48 quotes Pope Francis and goes even further, calling the analogy between Christ and church and between husband and wife "imperfect." Without adopting this exact language, *Amoris laetitia* 156 subsequently affirms an egalitarian reading of Ephesians 5:21–33.

Many have pointed out that the Catholic understanding of "sacrament" is not found in Ephesians 5:32.[39] The Greek word μυστήριον was translated in various Latin translations as *sacramentum*, which can mean "mystery." Augustine read a Latin translation of Ephesians that used *sacramentum* and understood this as an outward sign of an invisible reality, carrying with it an unbreakable bond. This influenced medieval theologians to see marriage as a sacrament,[40] which was adopted at the Fourth Lateran Council in 1215.[41] Andrew Lincoln argues that μυστήριον in 5:32 is most likely in reference to the relationship between Christ and the church, which was once hidden but is now revealed in Christ.[42] While Ephesians does not presume marriage as sacramental in nature, Lincoln states that it could certainly be seen as laying the groundwork for future articulations.[43]

As for the household code, many scholars argue that its origins are in Roman codes (e.g., Musonius, Plutarch), which drew on Aristotle who in turn drew on Plato. Other scholars argue that the code was influenced by Hellenistic Judaism (e.g., Philo, Josephus), also influenced by Aristotle. Lincoln suggests that the NT household codes are not directly dependent on any single code. According to Greco-Roman beliefs, proper maintenance of the household was paramount to the political and social order; the codes ensured that each person acted according to his or her nature. Any disruption was considered a threat. Many biblical scholars speculate that Galatians 3:28—which says there is no longer male and female—encouraged women in the early church to pronounce radical freedom from Roman patriarchy. It is thought that as more people joined the Jesus movement and as more Romans became aware of the movement's existence and its perceived perversions of social order, the household code was adopted to avoid tension with the broader Roman society.[44]

The most significant shift in *Mulieris dignitatem* and succeeding documents is reading Ephesians 5:21 as part of 5:22–33.[45] This enables these documents to de-emphasize or reinterpret the singular subjection of women to men in favor of *mutual* subjection. Whether this reinterpretation is exegetically sound is debatable.[46] For example, according to Margaret MacDonald, the author's instruction that a wife must submit to her husband ἐν παντί ("in everything") in 5:24 "is a very strong plea reinforcing the patriarchal authority of the husband."[47]

The decision in *Mulieris dignitatem*, the *Relatio finalis*, and *Amoris laetitia* to read Ephesians 5:21–33 as expressing mutual submission is striking, as these documents mark a clear transition from the interpretations of previous CFT documents and also draw on historical criticism to argue this perspective. *Mulieris dignitatem*, the *Relatio finalis*, and *Amoris laetitia* acknowledge that there is nonegalitarian language reflected in Ephesians 5:22–23, but in the words of *Amoris laetitia* 156, "our concern is not with its cultural matrix but with the revealed message that it conveys." This explanation reveals an appreciation of the distance between the first-century NT world and the present and an effort to ascertain timeless truth from a culturally conditioned text, a move many biblical scholars have advocated.[48]

## FUTURE DIRECTIONS

The use of scripture is generous across these CFT documents, but certainly more could be done. John Paul II's increased use of texts, along with his engagement with modern biblical criticism, has brought important and sophisticated exegesis to the documents, but the continuation and trajectory of this development is not guaranteed.

One of the most glaring imbalances at present is the heavy use of the NT over the HS and Deuterocanon. While this is understandable, it unintentionally gives the impression that the HS and Deuterocanon have little to say about family even though the exact opposite is true. The HS alone is filled with a wealth of resources on marriage and family, many of them being stories about husbands, wives, and their families.[49] Commenting on CST, Donahue writes, "Whatever the intellectual power and depth of papal teaching, the encyclicals rarely touch the lives of everyday Catholics. If Catholic social teaching is to form people's consciences, inspire their imaginations, and shape

their lives, it must weave biblical theology into its presentation."[50] The same can be said for CFT. This can be accomplished particularly well with biblical stories, which have the profound capacity to shape and inspire. And as David Garland and Diana Garland argue, one need not turn exclusively to stories of righteous families for instruction or inspiration. It is frequently the stories of families caught in entanglements, betrayal, and covenant breaking that elicit some of the most profound inspiration and guidance.[51] To really understand biblical stories, though, requires knowledge of the biblical commandments. Biblical stories not only presume an understanding of commandments but also often comment on the implications and practice of them. The stories of Ruth and Tamar provide strong examples. Ruth was a Moabite who lost her Israelite husband but remained committed to her mother-in-law, Naomi. Tamar was a Canaanite who faced precarity after her husband, Er, the eldest son of Judah, passed away (see Gen. 38). Both stories require knowledge of several biblical commandments for a fuller appreciation of their messages; moreover, both can speak to a variety of modern issues, not just loyalty and obligation toward family members but also protection of wives and widows (a vibrant theme in the HS) and the acceptance of exogamy.[52]

CFT documents *have* engaged several NT stories. *Christus vivut* 22–33 explicates Jesus's childhood, *Mulieris dignitatem* reflects on Mary, and *Redemptoris custos* reflects on Joseph. This is certainly welcome, but because there is so little information in scripture on the Holy Family, the documents harmonize the gospels to construct a portrait.[53] Allowing each gospel to speak on its own terms enables the reader to understand the unique message of each gospel writer.[54] In addition, investigating the three-stage formation of the gospels would further aid the reader in understanding the meaning of each text.[55]

Paramount also to not just stories but also any adoption of scriptural texts is an appreciation of the changes that have occurred in conceptions of the family over the last few thousand years. With the exception of *Africae munus* 47, there is a presumption in CFT documents that families are nuclear.[56] Absent any specific proviso, this encourages a reader to superimpose modern assumptions about nuclear families onto scripture. This can profoundly distort the meaning of the text. Acknowledging the historical context not only increases understanding of a biblical text but also, as in the case of *Mulieris dignitatem* VII.24 and its exegesis of the household code of Ephesians 5:21–33, can lead to important new interpretations. There are in fact diverse biblical conceptions of family,[57] as scripture spans thousands of years of history filled with cultural changes and shifts.[58]

### Family in the Hebrew Scriptures

Commenting on the HS, Daniel Block emphasizes that Israel understood itself as "one large extended kinship group" (אם in Hebrew), descending from one ancestor. Each household was a member of a clan, which in turn was a member of a tribe. The Hebrew term for "family" is בת אב, translated literally as "father's house." The average size of a family was between fifteen and twenty-five people, composed of three to four generations and centered on first-degree relatives but including multiple wives as well as concubines and slaves.[59] The father was the head of the household, and he was *ideally* "neither despot nor dictator"; after all, in order to thrive he and his family were mutually dependent on each other.[60]

Upon marriage, women left their family to join their husband's.[61] Both Proverbs 2:17 and Malachi 2:14 speak of marriage as a covenant, though the wedding was a civil affair. One of the main goals of a father was procreation—to grow the family through childbirth—hence the purpose of multiple wives and concubines.[62] This, consequently, meant that though companionship was an important part of marriage, a wife's greatest asset to the family was bringing children into the world, especially male children.[63] Children were a sign of God's blessing, as God was seen as responsible for all births. Children brought joy and, in a mostly agrarian society such as Israel, served as a source of (much-needed) labor.[64] The desire for children

was also due to high child mortality rates. The birth of a child was no guarantee that the child would live to become an adult, as approximately half of children died before turning ten.[65] Male children extended the father's line and were seen as a continuation of the father; children also looked after parents in their old age.[66] As Leo Purdue states, families were run by an "ethic of solidarity" whereby communal needs were greater than those of the individual.[67]

### Family in the New Testament

The political, economic, and cultural world in which the NT was written was the Roman Empire. Roman conceptions of family were, broadly speaking, similar to HS understandings. For example, the vast majority of people in the empire lived in an agrarian context.[68] The father was the *paterfamilias*, the head of the household, having dominion over all his children (and slaves).[69] This power, however, manifested in distinct ways in Roman society. Upon marriage, a woman was still under her father's *potestas* (rule). Consequently, the husband had no legal authority over her (e.g., she could divorce him), but being in the same home as her husband probably brought her under his dominion in practical terms.[70] Multiple scholars over the last few decades have argued that Roman families were essentially nuclear.[71] However, this was almost certainly not the case in Roman Egypt[72] and possibly not in the Roman west either.[73]

The gospels' assumption is that a typical οἶκος (household) was multigenerational, consisting of parents, children, and grandchildren.[74] Ephesians 5:21–33 is a multigenerational household code for husbands, wives, parents, children (both minors and adults),[75] and slaves. NT household codes can be contrasted with other NT statements that observe (or even prescribe) separation from one's family to join Jesus's followers.[76] Both positions on family, Carolyn Osiek observes, have parallels in Hellenistic philosophical traditions[77] and may have been intended for different audiences, one for families who followed Jesus and the other for individuals who had left a disapproving family.[78] Typical of most ancient literature, children are not prominent in the NT; neither are elderly people, who typically only received attention in ancient literature if they wielded social power.[79]

### Speaking to the Present

One can clearly see a great gulf between the biblical contexts and the present. Leo Purdue argues that certain biblical teachings on family (e.g., gender roles, the purpose of marriage) cannot simply be extracted from their thick social, cultural, economic, and political environment and inserted into a new discrete modern context. Purdue instead proposes discerning the "theological, ethical center" from which biblical teachings on family are derived and using this as the primary guide.[80] But whether there is a "center" to biblical theology has been long debated.[81] The debate notwithstanding, a necessary and worthwhile exercise is detecting the particular theology or value that underlays each scriptural teaching on family. Is a teaching after preservation, protection, liberation, maintenance, etc. of someone or something? How does it go about this in its culturally conditioned historical context? One can then discern how that scriptural teaching might be analogized and applied to contemporary circumstances.[82] Tensions between modern biblical scholarship and traditional interpretations will arise. In these instances, reflexively ignoring or explaining away the findings of a critical method in favor of a traditional interpretation is problematic, and often it is precisely this tension that facilitates opportunities for salutary interpretations to come to the fore.

## NOTES

1. See Vatican II, *Dei verbum* (November 18, 1965), 24, https://www.vatican.va/archive/hist_councils/ii_vatican_council/documents/vat-ii_const_19651118_dei-verbum_en.html.

2. These figures count all references made by the documents except for *Sacrosanctum concilium* and *Gaudium et spes*, which count only sections dealing

directly with CFT (i.e., *Sacrosanctum concilium* 77–78; *Gaudium et spes* 12, 26, 32, 48–52). The figures do not include addresses by Pius XII included in this volume (chapter 10).

3. John R. Donahue, "The Bible and Catholic Social Teaching: Will This Engagement Lead to Marriage?," in *Modern Catholic Social Teaching: Commentaries and Interpretations*, 2nd ed., ed. Kenneth R. Himes et al. (Washington, DC: Georgetown University Press, 2018), 11–12, 35.

4. John Paul II, *Redemptoris custos* (August 15, 1989), 2, https://www.vatican.va/content/john-paul-ii/en/apost_exhortations/documents/hf_jp-ii_exh_15081989_redemptoris-custos.html, states, that to better appreciate the annunciation of Jesus's birth in Matthew 1:18, one must compare the parallel account in Luke 1:26–32.

5. An exception might be Benedict XVI, *Caritas in veritate* (June 29, 2009), 48, https://www.vatican.va/content/benedict-xvi/en/encyclicals/documents/hf_ben-xvi_enc_20090629_caritas-in-veritate.html.

6. Donahue, "The Bible and Catholic Social Teaching," 13.

7. The translation is *Divini illius magistri*'s.

8. The "little ones" in Matthew 18:6 is a metaphor to describe Jesus's disciples. See Daniel J. Harrington, *The Gospel of Matthew*, Sacra Pagina (Collegeville, MN: Liturgical Press, 2007), 264–67.

9. The vast majority of documents cite only one or a few verses. However, Genesis 1:26–2:18, Ephesians 5:21–33, and Matthew 19:1–12 are treated as pericopes, thematic units with a cohesive integrity.

10. This section engages both Catholic and Protestant biblical scholarship. Ecumenism has been a mainstay in biblical scholarship since Vatican II. See Shawn W. Flynn, "The Hope of Catholic Biblical Interpretation: Progress and Gaps in the Manifestation of Scripture since Vatican II," *New Blackfriars* 96, no. 1065 (September 2015): 584–85.

11. This depends in part on whether one understands האדם to be a man from the beginning or an androgynous being.

12. Cf. Pius XI, *Casti connubii* (Deceumber 31, 1930), 5, https://www.vatican.va/content/pius-xi/en/encyclicals/documents/hf_p-xi_enc_19301231_casti-connubii.html, which is the first to cite Genesis 1:27–28 and 2:22–23 to establish this point.

13. Cf. *Casti connubii* 8, 11, which is the first to cite Genesis 1:28 to establish this point.

14. Within the early documents of CFT especially, mutuality and interdependence do not imply equality. Instead, hierarchical complementarity is the norm. See chapter 10.

15. Victor P. Hamilton, *The Book of Genesis: Chapters 1–17*, New International Commentary on the Old Testament (Grand Rapids, MI: Eerdmans, 1990), 138; and John Goldingay, *Genesis*, Baker Commentary on the Old Testament (Grand Rapids, MI: Baker Academic, 2020), 37.

16. Walter Brueggemann, *Genesis*, Interpretation (Atlanta: John Knox, 1982), 34.

17. Gordon J. Wenham, *Genesis 1–15*, Word Biblical Commentary (Waco, TX: Word Books, 1987), 33.

18. Wenham, *Genesis 1–15*, 30–32.

19. All translations are in the New American Bible Revised Edition unless otherwise noted.

20. Wenham, *Genesis 1–15*, 68.

21. See Kristin E. Kvam, Linda S. Schearing, and Valarie H. Ziegler, *Eve and Adam: Jewish, Christian, and Muslim Readings on Genesis and Gender* (Bloomington: Indiana University Press, 1999).

22. Phyllis Trible, "Eve and Adam: Genesis 2–3 Reread," *Andover Newton Quarterly* 13, no. 4 (March 1973): 251–58.

23. Megan Warner, "'Therefore a Man Leaves His Father and His Mother and Clings to His Wife': Marriage and Intermarriage in Genesis 2:24," *Journal of Biblical Literature* 136, no. 2 (2017): 269–88.

24. Warner, "'Therefore a Man Leaves His Father and His Mother and Clings to His Wife,'" 279.

25. Warner, "'Therefore a Man Leaves His Father and His Mother and Clings to His Wife,'" 272.

26. Literature on biblical views of homosexuality abound. For diverse opinions, see Daniel A. Helminiak, *What the Bible Really Says about Homosexuality*, Millennium ed. (Tajique, NM: Alamo Square, 2000); and Innocent Himbaza, Adrien Schenker, and Jean-Baptist Edart, *The Bible on the Question of Homosexuality*, trans. Benedict M. Guevin, O.S.B. (Washington, DC: Catholic University of America Press, 2012).

27. It has often been assumed in Christian interpretation that the Pharisees/Jews were opposed to Jesus and sought to entrap him and that Jesus was hostile toward the Pharisees in particular and against Torah/Judaism in general. For examples in CFT documents, see Leo XIII, *Arcanum* (February 10, 1880), 6, 8, https://www.vatican.va/content/leo-xiii/en/encyclicals/documents/hf_l-xiii_enc_10021880_arcanum.html; and John Paul II, *Mulieris dignitatem* (August 15, 1988), V.12, V.14, https://www.vatican.va/content/john-paul-ii/en/apost_letters/1988/documents/hf_jp-ii_apl_19880815_mulieris-dignitatem.html. As Ulrich Luz rightly points out, Matthew was "not concerned with the historical schools of Pharisees at the time of Jesus" but instead was concerned with a group perhaps descended from the Pharisees of Jesus's time. See Ulrich Luz, *Matthew 8–20*, Hermeneia (Minneapolis: Fortress, 2001), 488–89. Douglas Hare aptly writes, "We must disabuse ourselves of the opinion once popular among commentators that the Pharisees are here trying to expose Jesus as a teacher who annuls the law of Moses. We are indebted to modern Jewish scholars who have shown that Jesus' view, while distinctive, would not have been regarded as a challenge to the Torah." See Douglas R. A. Hare, *Matthew*, Interpretation (Louisville: John Knox, 1993), 220.

28. The last clause—"and he that shall marry her that is put away committeth adultery"—does not appear in many manuscripts. See Luz, *Matthew 8–20*, 486n3.

29. *Amoris laetitia* 159n166, refers the reader to Catechesis (April 14, 1982), 1: *Insegnamenti* V/1 (1982), 1176.

30. W. F. Albright and C. S. Mann, *Matthew*, Anchor Bible (Garden City, NY: Doubleday, 1971), 226.

31. Luz, *Matthew 8–20*, 492.

32. For a list of scholars, see Donald A. Hagner, *Matthew 1–13*, Word Biblical Commentary (Dallas, TX: Word Books, 1993), 124.

33. Raymond F. Collins, *Divorce in the New Testament* (Collegeville, MN: Liturgical Press, 1992), 199–205.

34. E.g., Luz, a self-identified Protestant, follows the position that Jesus prohibits any remarriage. See Luz, *Matthew 8–20*, 494–96.

35. Curtis Mitch and Edward Sri, *The Gospel of Matthew*, Catholic Commentary on Sacred Scripture (Grand Rapids, MI: Baker Academic, 2010), 241–42.

36. Craig L. Blomberg, "Marriage, Divorce, Remarriage, and Celibacy: An Exegesis of Matthew 19:3–12," *Trinity Journal* 11, no. 2 (Fall 1990): 178.

37. Hare, *Matthew*, 221.

38. The translation and the emphasis are in *Mulieris dignitatem.*

39. See, e.g., Markus Barth, *Ephesians*, Anchor Bible (Garden City: Doubleday, 1974), 744–49; and Andrew T. Lincoln, *Ephesians*, Word Biblical Commentary (Dallas, TX: Word Books, 1990), 381.

40. Joseph Martos, *Doors to the Sacred: A Historical Introduction to Sacraments in the Catholic Church*, updated ed. (Liguori, MO: Liguori Publications, 2014), 433–34.

41. On this topic, see Barth, *Ephesians*, 642–43.

42. Lincoln, *Ephesians*, 381. Cf. Barth, *Ephesians*, 642.

43. Lincoln, *Ephesians*, 363.

44. Lincoln, *Ephesians*, 357–60. See also Margaret Y. MacDonald, *Colossians and Ephesians*, Sacra Pagina Series (Collegeville, MN: Liturgical Press, 2008), 338; and Craig S. Keener, *Paul, Women, and Wives: Marriage and Women's Ministry in the Letters of Paul* (Peabody, MA: Hendrickson Publications, 1992), 139–48. Cf. Frank Thielman, *Ephesians*, Baker Exegetical Commentary on the New Testament (Grand Rapids, MI: Baker Academic, 2010), 368.

45. See, e.g., Lincoln, *Ephesians*, 352. But cf. Peter Gurry, "The Text of Eph 5.22 and the Start of the Ephesian Household Code," *New Testament Studies* 67, no. 4 (October 2021): 560–81.

46. See, e.g., Keener, *Paul, Women, and Wives*, 168–70. See also Lynn H. Cohick, *The Letter to the Ephesians*, New International Commentary on the New Testament (Grand Rapids, MI: Eerdmans, 2020), 352, 361–62, 367.

47. MacDonald, *Colossians and Ephesians*, 328. See also Lincoln, *Ephesians*, 366.

48. See, e.g., MacDonald, *Colossians and Ephesians*, 341; Lincoln, *Ephesians*, 392–93; and Keener, *Paul, Women, and Wives*, 185–86, 209–11.

49. Some HS stories are acknowledged in *Christus vivut* 6–11 but only in a cursory way.

50. Donahue, "The Bible and Catholic Social Teaching," 13.

51. David E. Garland and Diana R. Garland, *Flawed Families: How God's Grace Works through Imperfect Relationships* (Grand Rapids, MI: Brazos, 2007).

52. For an analysis of biblical commandments and justice toward wives and widows in Ruth, see Georg Braulik, "The Book of Ruth as Intra-Biblical Critique on the Deuteronomic Law," *Acta Theologica* 19, no. 1 (1999): 1–20. For an analysis of Tamar on the same topics, see Garland and Garland, *Flawed Families*, 103–24.

53. For example,, in *Christus vivut* 28, reference is made to Jesus being a carpenter's son in Matthew 13:55 and a carpenter in Mark 6:3. The document supposes that this is why people were astounded by Jesus in Luke 4:22. Luke does not mention Jesus or his father as a carpenter.

54. The importance of this is spelled out in Pontifical Biblical Commission, *The Interpretation of the Bible in the Church* (April 15, 1993), I.A.1, https://www.vatican.va/roman_curia/congregations/cfaith/pcb_documents/rc_con_cfaith_doc_19930415_interpretazione_it.html.

55. For an introduction to the three stages of gospel formation, see Raymond F. Brown, *An Introduction to the New Testament* (New York: Doubleday, 1997), 107–11.

56. See, e.g., Leo XIII, *Rerum novarum* (May 15, 1891), 12–13, 42, https://www.vatican.va/content/leoxiii/en/encyclicals/documents/hf_l-xiii_enc_15051891_rerum-novarum.html. This presumption is persistent. See also, e.g., Francis, *Amoris laetitia* (March 19, 2016), 9, https://www.vatican.va/content/dam/francesco/pdf/apost_exhortations/documents/papa-francesco_esortazione-ap_20160319_amoris-laetitia_en.pdf.

57. There are many sources on marriage and family in the Bible. See, e.g., Leo Perdue, Joseph Blenkinsopp, John J. Collins, and Carol Meyers, eds., *Families in Ancient Israel* (Louisville, KY: Westminster John Knox, 1997). Its companion is Carol Osiek and David L. Balch, *Families in the New Testament: Households and Household Churches* (Louisville, KY: Westminster John Knox, 1997). On divorce, see David Instone-Brewer, *Divorce and Remarriage in the Bible: Social and Literary Context* (Grand Rapids, MI: Eerdmans, 2002). On children, see Kristine Henriksen Garroway, *Growing Up in Ancient Israel: Children in Material Culture and Biblical Texts* (Atlanta: SBL Press, 2018); and Margaret Y. MacDonald, *The Power of Children: The Construction of Christian Families in the Greco-Roman World* (Waco, TX: Baylor University Press, 2014).

58. Moreover, as Daniel Block underscores, there is only limited archaeological evidence, and

the biblical material is diverse in genres and views, often referring to people, circumstances, and events long after they occurred. See Daniel I. Block, "Marriage and Family in Ancient Israel," in *Marriage and Family in the Biblical World*, ed. Ken M. Campbell (Downers Grove, IL: InterVarsity, 2003), 34.

59. See Block, "Marriage and Family," 35, 38, 40.

60. Block, "Marriage and Family," 43–44.

61. See Block, "Marriage and Family," 44–46, 61–69.

62. Polygyny and concubinage may have been limited to the wealthy. See Leo G. Perdue, "The Israelite and Early Jewish Family," in *Families in Ancient Israel*, ed. Leo G. Purdue et al. (Louisville, KY: Westminster John Knox Press, 1997), 185.

63. See Block, "Marriage and Family," 72.

64. Ninety percent of Israel lived in an agrarian setting. See Purdue, "The Israelite and Early Jewish Family," 166.

65. Purdue, "The Israelite and Early Jewish Family," 171, 182, 189.

66. See Block, "Marriage and Family," 80–81, 94; and Purdue, "The Israelite and Early Jewish Family," 170–71.

67. Purdue, "The Israelite and Early Jewish Family," 167.

68. Peter Garnsey and Richard Saller, *The Roman Empire: Economy, Society, and Culture*, 2nd ed. (Oakland: University of California Press, 2015), 133.

69. Garnsey and Saller, *The Roman Empire*, 160–61.

70. Garnsey and Saller, *The Roman Empire*, 154–55, 158–59.

71. This was first argued in Richard Saller and Brent Shaw, "Tombstones and Roman Family Relations in the Principate: Civilians, Soldiers and Slaves," *Journal of Roman Studies* 74 (1984): 124–56.

72. See Sabine R. Huebner, "Household Composition in the Ancient Mediterranean—What Do We Really Know?," in *A Companion to Families in the Greek and Roman Worlds*, ed. Beryl Rawson (Chichester, UK: Wiley-Blackwell, 2011), 77–78.

73. See Huebner, "Household Composition in the Ancient Mediterranean," 83–89.

74. Adriana Destro and Mauro Pesce, "Fathers and Householders in the Jesus Movement: The Perspective of the Gospel of Luke," *Biblical Interpretation* 11, no. 2 (2003): 221–22.

75. See Margaret Y. MacDonald, "Reading the New Testament Household Codes in Light of New Research on Children and Childhood in the Roman World," *Studies in Religion* 41, no. 3 (2012): 382–83.

76. Osiek, "What We Do and Don't Know about Early Christian Families," in *A Companion to Families in the Greek and Roman Worlds*, ed. Beryl Rawson (Chichester, UK: Wiley-Blackwell, 2011), 77–78, 199.

77. Greco-Roman parallels to the NT household codes have been discussed above. For Greco-Roman parallels to familial separation in Mark, see Stephen P. Ahearne-Kroll, "'Who Are My Mother and My Brothers?' Family Relations and Family Language in the Gospel of Mark," *Journal of Religion* 21, no. 2 (August 2015): 166–80.

78. Osiek, "What We Do and Don't Know about Early Christian Families," 200.

79. See Osiek, "What We Do and Don't Know about Early Christian Families," 204.

80. Leo G. Perdue, "The Household, Old Testament Theology, and Contemporary Hermeneutics," in *Families in Ancient Israel*, ed. Leo G. Perdue et al. (Louisville: John Knox Press, 1997), 244–54.

81. For further discussion, see Gerhard Hasel, *Old Testament Theology: Basic Issues in the Current Debate*, 4th ed. (Grand Rapids, MI: Eerdmans, 1991).

82. Here, I am in agreement with Luke Timothy Johnson on the use of historical criticism to illuminate the biblical text. See Luke Timothy Johnson and William S. Kurz, *The Future of Catholic Biblical Scholarship: A Constructive Conversation* (Grand Rapids, MI: Eerdmans, 2002), 16–18.

# CHAPTER 2

# Natural Law in Catholic Family Teaching

CRAIG A. FORD JR.

One could maintain that the relationship between natural law and Catholic Family Teaching (CFT) is analogous to the relationship Aristotle articulated between form and matter. In CFT as in other Catholic moral teaching, natural law operates as a central animating principle, giving official teaching its particular coherence. However, natural law is also a tradition of moral reasoning and is precisely not—despite some presentations—a list of permissions and prohibitions based on a normative concept of nature. To the extent that this fact is accepted, one can admit and appreciate diversity in judgments made on the basis of natural law according to various interpretative traditions. Hence, natural law arguments advanced by the Catholic magisterium within CFT, inasmuch as they are internally uniform, constitute only one potential synthesis relating natural law to the family. This chapter explores both the synthesis found in official teaching and the broader theological tradition.

An important consideration at this point asks what specifically delimits CFT as a coherent body of teaching. Certainly this hinges on the concept of the family, but theological descriptions vary. Emphasizing functionality, for example, Lisa Cahill defines the family as an "organized network of socioeconomic and reproductive interdependence and support grounded in biological kinship and marriage."[1] The Pontifical Council for the Family describes the family as "a natural society, [which] exists prior to the State or any other community" based in the "complementarity between a man and a woman" celebrated in marriage. This society forms a "community of love and solidarity, which is uniquely suited to teach and transmit cultural, ethical, social, spiritual and religious values." Distinctively, the family unites generations to help each other "grow in human wisdom and to harmonize the rights of individuals with other demands of social life."[2]

Though not typically remembered for its original misogynistic overtones, the Christian family as "domestic church"—an image both romantic and evangelical—rose to prominence in Catholic teaching particularly under John Paul II.[3] This conception recognizes the family as "an intimate community of life and love" destined to share in God's kingdom.[4] The distinctly Christian mission of the family is to establish a "civilization of love."[5] John Paul II's social vision of the family is grounded exclusively in monogamous, heterosexual marital relationships that, through the procreation and rearing of children, establish families as the "first and vital cell of society" with the mission of "humanizing and personalizing society . . . by making possible a life that is properly speaking

20

human, in particular by guarding and transmitting virtues and 'values.'"[6]

These perspectives reflect something of the diversity of conceptions of the family in the Catholic imagination and suggest that CFT is not united around a singular concept but instead is characterized by overlapping domains of concern. The family, variously conceived, is the nucleus where the embodied, spiritual, and social aspects of the human person are nurtured. Consequently, CFT is unified by its aim to rightly develop these dimensions of the person as encountered through that nucleus, utilizing natural law as a structuring principle in its response.

## THOMAS AQUINAS'S NATURAL LAW THEORY

The most authoritative articulation of natural law within the Catholic tradition belongs to Thomas Aquinas (1223–1274). Indebted to Augustine's understanding of the origin of moral law as God's will promulgated in eternal law, Thomas described eternal law as "the very idea of the government of things in God, the ruler of the universe."[7] This eternal law is the exemplar of natural law, which Thomas understood as the rational creature's (i.e., the human being's) participation in (or right understanding of) moral law (*ST* I–II 91.2, resp.). Indebted also to Aristotle, Thomas understood morality chiefly as the discernment of what allows the human being to flourish and thereby achieve true happiness (*ST* I–II 3.2; I–II 5.8). This led Thomas to conclude that natural law commanded development in the virtues (*ST* I–II 94.3; I–II 5.5; I–II 61–62). Two other sorts of law, divine law and human law, aid in illuminating the requirements of natural law. This first is revealed by God so that "[human beings] may know without any doubt what [they] ought to do and what [they] ought to avoid" (*ST* I–II 91.4), and the second is promulgated by a lawful authority and, importantly, cannot rightly contravene natural law (*ST* I–II 96.4).[8]

Thomas also articulated the foundation of what natural law commands, otherwise known

as its primary precepts. The first is what human beings share with all living beings: the desire for self-preservation. The second is shared with other animals: sexual desire and procreation. And the third is distinctively human: to know the truth and to live in society (*ST* I–II 94.2). Given the primary precepts' generality, they are not particularly action-guiding. This is why discerning the secondary precepts of natural law (i.e., the application of natural law in a specific situation) is comparatively more difficult (*ST* I–II 94.2, resp.). Hence, the virtues are necessary guides for determining appropriate action in a given situation. Indeed, it is no accident that scarcely more than seven articles in *Summa Theologiae* are devoted to natural law, while nearly 70 percent of Thomas's moral theology is devoted to the virtues.[9]

Thomas's moral epistemology posits that we come to learn natural law through our inclinations, that is, through the desires that we have as creatures to obtain the goods that enable our flourishing.[10] Despite these natural desires, sin constitutes a very large impediment to right action. Sin variously affects reason's ability to know the true good to be pursued and the will's ability to desire the good rightly in a given situation (*ST* I–II 75.3). In other words, because of sin, human beings fail to act according to God's will as disclosed by natural law and rightly realized by the virtuous person (*ST* I–II 21.1; I–II 94.3). Therefore, God's grace is necessary and "assists us" in realizing that law that is our true good (*ST* I–II 90, proem). For Thomas, grace abounds. It is manifested in our natural inclinations as created beings (*ST* I–II 93.2, 93.6), and it strengthens the operation of our reason and our will toward the supernatural end of eternal friendship with God. This is nothing less than our salvation: to respond in love (*caritas*) to the God whose prior love not only allows us to be God's creatures but also raises us beyond our natural capacities in order to become God's own friends. Thus, grace perfects nature (*ST* I 1.8, ad 2), and natural law, Thomas writes beautifully, "is nothing else than an imprint on us of the divine light" (*ST* I–II 91.2, resp.).

As the natural law tradition entered modernity, two important trajectories emerged: one that would result in a purely "scientific" understanding of nature, and another that would bring about the rise of natural rights. Both trajectories remain consequential for contemporary traditions of natural law moral reasoning.

## NATURAL LAW, LAWS OF NATURE, AND MAGISTERIAL CFT

The roots of a scientific understanding of nature trace to the fourteenth century and helped tie the notion of natural law to the closely related concept of the "laws of nature." For Thomas and medieval thinkers in general, these two concepts were virtually united in the notion of eternal law. Defining eternal law as "Divine Wisdom, as moving all things to its due end" (*ST* I–II 93.1), Thomas maintained that all of creation was directed "by inclination" toward its own fulfillment. For Thomas, all creation—from inanimate objects to "irrational" living creatures to human beings—is spontaneously moved toward becoming the best sorts of created things they can be, though specifically human fulfillment requires the right use of intellect and will assisted by God's grace (*ST* I–II 91.2).

Eternal law, which Thomas could replace with "providence,"[11] can assume a moral-political face (via natural law and human law) or can have more of a "causal" face, especially as this relates to inanimate and celestial objects, which operate as if "on their own" in their development toward God's will. After Thomas, natural philosophers and eventually scientists commented on the regular, observable movements of objects in the universe, attributing their motion to God's ordained power expressed as law.[12] Modernity moved one step further and, by focusing on the physical laws themselves, made attribution back to God superfluous. This shift reverberated in natural law morality. Christian natural lawyers did not follow their secular counterparts in asserting the nonexistence or irrelevance of God but nevertheless constructed theologically neutral accounts of natural law. Especially in the seventeenth century, moralists embraced the Enlightenment mode by offering accounts of natural law that were theoretically accessible to all through common reason without explicit recourse to religious principles. Hugo Grotius—widely regarded to be the founder of modern international law—argued that natural law would bind regardless of God's existence, as its norms were "established by reason and are universal."[13]

One distinguishing feature of this approach to natural law moral reasoning was the minimal significance given to human experience as a source of ethical insight. As the Catholic tradition entered the nineteenth and twentieth centuries, for example, the manualist tradition, which continued to codify moral theology by applying universal principles to individual cases through deductive reasoning, would rise to prominence.[14] This pattern would extend with respect to CFT as well, beginning with the domains of sexuality and gender. The Congregation for the Doctrine of the Faith's 1975 document *Persona humana* makes this connection clear. The CDF states, "In moral matters man cannot make value judgments according to his personal whim: 'In the depths of his conscience, man detects a law which he does not impose on himself, but which holds him to obedience.... For man has in his heart a law written by God. To obey it is the very dignity of man; according to it he will be judged.'"[15] This view of natural law functions both epistemologically and soteriologically to warrant teachings that have been reiterated and developed over subsequent decades: that human sexuality is inherently conjugal or fundamentally oriented toward marriage; that marriage only validly exists between a man and a woman; and that marriages and "each and every" sexual act therein must remain "open" to procreation.

John Paul II was the most prominent defender of these theses on human sexuality as they emerged and developed following Vatican II. Supported by Genesis 1:27, "God created mankind in his own image; in the image of God he created them; male and female he created them,"[16] John Paul II argued that all humanity is marked by the "primordial duality" of masculinity and femininity. According to this essentialist view of gender, there are two and only two ways of being a human being according to

God's creation. This inherent, natural human duality is embodied in every particular human being, each born either male or female and expressing their maleness or femaleness through their identity as man or woman.[17]

For John Paul II, these two ways of being a person image the Trinity and together may form a "communion of persons" that constitutes a unity in and through their differences. This relationship of unity-in-difference between man and woman is expressed in the concept of complementarity. Established on such a meta-physical foundation, the two genders evidence their complementarity through their personal and physical differences.[18] Consequently, there exists both a "masculine" and a "feminine" way of being in the world corresponding to the divine plan. This is spelled out very clearly, albeit one-sidedly, in John Paul II's identifi-cation of the "feminine genius," which under-writes women's essential vocation as nurturers, either biologically as mothers or spiritually as virgins,[19] though women's spiritual mother-hood notably excludes access to ordained min-istry.[20] In contrast, men are always expected to be fathers either biologically or spiritually.[21]

Again using Genesis, John Paul II pre-sents gender complementarity as essential to the sacrament of marriage, which unites the differences of man and woman in "one flesh" (Gen. 2:24). The sacramental reality of the spousal union finds its physical counterpart in the sexual act, and their spiritual imaging of the Trinity becomes complete when the sexual act results in the creation of a child, a new life. In this way, the sacramental bond of the married couple becomes the context for the creation of a family, just as at the dawn of creation the com-munion of persons within the Trinity served as the context through which the one God cre-ated the human family.[22] Through procreation, "the family, as a community of persons, is . . . the first human 'society.'"

It arises whenever there comes into being the conjugal covenant of marriage, which opens the spouses to a lasting communion of love and of life, and it is brought to completion in a full and specific way with the procreation

of children: the 'communion' of the spouses gives rise to the 'community' of the family.[23]

As such, the family's primary mission is human-izing both its members and the society in which it exists.[24] Families are called to preach the gos-pel in a way that is appropriate and thus become the "domestic church" in its contemporary understanding.[25]

This account of the relationship between gender, sexuality, marriage, and procreation is also allied with numerous prohibitions for acts that diverge from its normative pattern, including any intentional action to prevent fertilization (aside from periodic abstinence) and attempts to effect fertilization outside of the sexual act (such as in vitro fertilization). The shared rationale is that such acts separate the procreative and the unitive end of the marital sexual act and are therefore wrong.[26] This same rationale condemns same-sex sexual acts, which are described as neither procreative nor genu-inely unitive, as they lack complementarity.[27]

Recently, magisterial teaching has main-tained that persons identifying as transgender or gender-nonconforming act wrongly when they engage in processes of gender transition, defined broadly as any action by which some-one take steps to concretely present themselves as a gender not assigned at birth. Rationales that normalize or promote gender transition are derided as promoting gender ideology, which constitutes "a radical break" with the natural and exclusive complementary of male and female. The Congregation for Catholic Education laments that

Human identity is consigned to the indi-vidual's choice, which can also change in time. These ideas are the expression of a widespread way of thinking and acting in today's culture that confuses "genuine freedom with the idea that each individual can act arbitrarily as if there were no truths, values and principles to provide guidance, and everything were possible and permissible."[28]

Gender transition is regarded as immoral because it challenges gender essentialism and is thereby understood as pitting human freedom against God's divine plan.

As stated above, this particular moral synthesis found in CFT shares the trajectory of a natural law interested in discovering moral regularities that can be applied down to individual cases with minimal recourse to human experience. CFT's marked emphasis on divine revelation and use of analogies to the Trinity to spell out the requirements of natural law have enabled this process. Arguments for conclusions similar to those reached by the magisterium have also been put forward by certain Catholic philosophers. However, instead of appealing to divine revelation, they seek justification on metaphysical grounds.[29] The paths may appear different but are formally identical: both base moral norms on grounds prior to any human experience. Lived human experience receives normative significance only on the back end insofar as it aligns with conclusions already deduced.[30]

## NATURAL LAW, NATURAL RIGHTS, AND REVISIONIST APPROACHES TO CATHOLIC FAMILY TEACHING

Thanks to the work of thinkers such as Brian Tierney, we know that the notion of natural rights has its roots in medieval natural law. Previously, the notion of right (*jus*) was tied to the virtue of justice as its object, that is, the just thing itself. Importantly, the object of justice was believed to inhere in moral situations such that wrongful acts were not defined by their unfair impact on the freedoms of others but instead by the fact that they did not rightly realize the virtue of justice.[31] The idea that rights inhere in the moral subject emerged in a fourteenth-century dispute between William of Ockham and Pope John XXII in which Ockham claimed that in Eden, Adam and Eve had a natural right to the use of the vegetation for sustenance.[32] By the seventeenth century, accounts of natural rights were famously defended by Thomas Hobbes and John Locke, who believed that natural rights descended

from the primary duty of self-preservation in the anarchic state of nature.[33] The following century, Immanuel Kant argued that morality required that all persons treat others as ends and never (merely) as means.[34] In the twentieth century, this view of rights was spelled out in an entirely secular form in the United Nations' "Universal Declaration of Human Rights."[35] On the eve of Vatican II, Pope John XXIII used the declaration as a framework for defining Christian recognition that each person is made in the image of God while invoking the theological natural law tradition as its epistemic grounding.[36]

What made this integrative achievement between natural law and human rights both possible and notable was the church's recognition that meaningful moral insights existed beyond its borders in the wider world.[37] Specifically, this was made possible by understanding the human rights tradition, broadly conceived, to represent a cumulative storehouse of inductive knowledge concerning human dignity and respect for it. Drawing inspiration from Thomas's theological method, which sought to harmonize and integrate the latest scientific insights with those of the existing Christian tradition, this trajectory in natural law moral reasoning placed divine revelation in conversation with human experience as it is represented both scientifically and via the experiential knowledge of communities.

This is the approach of the revisionist school of natural lawyers whose epistemological orientation is inductive and thereby allows for developments in understanding human flourishing over time. From these convictions, revisionists have questioned many aspects of CFT. Feminists in particular have argued that views of the "feminine genius" may more accurately reflect the patriarchal domination of women than divine will.[38] Others have questioned accounts of gender complementarity and, informed by the experiences of same-sex couples, made space for the moral legitimacy of intimate nonheterosexual relationships.[39] Still others are asking why the notion of family must be tied so closely to heterosexual marriage when it seems that children thrive not because of their caretakers' genders but instead because they are good parents, irrespective of gender.[40] Based on the insights of queer theory and the experiences of LGBTQ+ people, revisionists have also sought to celebrate the journey that transgender and gender-nonconforming people make toward personal wholeness precisely as an aspect of growing in their relationship with God.[41]

## CONCLUSION

The genius of Thomas's particular synthesis of natural law was his harmonization of natural law's potential knowability by all human beings, via natural inclinations, with its compatibility to a life lived in obedience to Christian accounts of human flourishing, via the graced development of virtue. The current contours of CFT stand as a synthesis relating Thomas's second and third precepts of natural law (regarding sexual desire and procreation and truth and social life, respectively) with a particular account of how these are rightly lived. Insofar as this is the case, CFT finds its footing in natural law. As John Paul II writes, the truth about human sexuality and gender identity—and, by extension, the family—can be accessed through a law on the heart "written by God."

This chapter has examined two traditions of natural law thinking. One, exemplified by magisterial CFT, emphasizes disclosure of natural law through divine revelation and metaphysical argument promulgated by the Catholic Church's leaders. The other, exemplified by revisionist natural law theologians, emphasizes an approach to natural law foregrounding human experience in the continued discernment of natural law.

Today, the documents of CFT remain characterized by diversity in their applications and use of natural law, even as John Paul II's singular papacy exerts an exceptionally pronounced influence. The views and methodologies of this living tradition's contemporary interpreters, many of whom are presented in the following chapters, exhibit even greater plurality. Those favoring a deductive approach emphasizing the clear norms and dictates of divine revelation favor the synthesis as it now stands in contemporary teaching. Others favoring a more inductive approach that integrates human experience alongside other sources in the discernment of natural law look to the potential for continued development.

## NOTES

1. Lisa Sowle Cahill, *Family: A Christian Social Perspective* (Minneapolis, MN: Fortress Press, 2000), x.

2. Pontifical Council for the Family, "Charter of the Rights of the Family" (October 22, 1983), A–F, https://www.vatican.va/roman_curia/pontifical _councils/family/documents/rc_pc_family_doc _19831022_family-rights_en.html.

3. See, e.g., John Paul II, *Familiaris consortio* (November 22, 1981), 21, https://www.vatican .va/content/john-paul-ii/en/apost_exhortations /documents/hf_jp-ii_exh_19811122_familiaris -consortio.html. The image seems to originate from John Chrysostom, who writes, "Govern your wife, and your household will thus be put in order. Listen to what Paul says: *If they want to know something, they should ask their husbands at home* [1 Cor. 14:35]. If we administer our own households in this way, we will be suitable also to govern the church. For the household is a little church." "Homily 20" in *On Ephesians*, cited in Cahill, *Family*, 57–58.

4. John Paul II, *Familiaris consortio*, 17; cf. 50, where the family is described as "an 'intimate communion of life and love,' at the service of the Church and of Society."

5. John Paul II, "Letter to Families" (February 2, 1994), 15, https://www.vatican.va/content /john-paul-ii/en/letters/1994/documents/hf_jp-ii _let_02021994_families.html.

6. John Paul II, *Familiaris consortio*, 42–43.

7. Thomas Aquinas, *Summa Theologiae*, trans. Fathers of the English Dominican Province (New York: Benziger Bros, 1948), I–II 91.1, resp. (hereafter cited as *ST*).

8. Thomas helps solidify the tradition of civil disobedience within natural law tradition, a thread of the tradition that would be famously invoked by many Christians including Dr. Martin Luther King Jr., who cites Thomas Aquinas in his argument for

disobedience to racially discriminatory laws. See Martin Luther King Jr., "Letter from a Birmingham Jail [King, Jr.]" (1963), https://www.africa.upenn.edu /Articles_Gen/Letter_Birmingham.html.

9. Nicholas Austin, SJ, *Aquinas on Virtue: A Causal Account* (Washington, DC: Georgetown University Press, 2017), xvi–xvii.

10. Jacques Maritain writes that knowledge through inclination is "obscure, unsystematic, vital knowledge by connaturality or congeniality, in which the intellect, in order to bear judgment, consults and listens to the inner melody that the vibrating strings of abiding tendences make present in the subject." Jacques Maritain, *Man and the State* (Washington, DC: Catholic University of America Press, 1951), 91–92.

11. "Since, therefore, as the providence of God is nothing less than the type of the order of things towards an end, as we have said; it necessarily follows that all things, inasmuch as they participate in existence, must likewise be subject to divine providence" (*ST* I 22.2, resp.).

12. God's ordained power refers to all of the things God actually willed with respect to grace, morality, and nature, whereas God's absolute power refers not only to what God actually willed but includes those states of affairs that God could have hypothetically willed. This distinction sought to explain the regularity of laws in the universe while preserving God's omnipotence. See Francis Oakley, *Natural Law, Laws of Nature, Natural Rights: Continuity and Discontinuity in the History of Ideas* (New York: Continuum, 2005), 52–62.

13. Stephen J. Pope, "Natural Law in Catholic Social Teachings," in *Modern Catholic Social Teaching: Commentaries and Interpretations*, ed. Kenneth Himes et al. (Washington, DC: Georgetown University Press, 2004), 48. Even though Grotius is credited with introducing a secular natural law tradition, he personally regarded the prospect of God's nonexistence as impossible. See also Oakley, *Natural Law*, 63–68.

14. See James Keenan, SJ, *A History of Catholic Moral Theology in the 20th Century: From Confessing Sins to Liberating Consciences* (New York: Continuum, 2010), 3–58.

15. Congregation for the Doctrine of the Faith, *Persona humana* (December 29, 1975), sec. III,

https://www.vatican.va/roman_curia/congregations /cfaith/documents/rc_con_cfaith_doc_19751229 _persona-humana_en.html, quoting Vatican II, *Gaudium et spes* (December 7, 1965), 16, https://www .vatican.va/archive/hist_councils/ii_vatican_council /documents/vat-ii_const_19651207_gaudium-et -spes_en.html.

16. From the New Revised Standard Version. All biblical citations come from this edition.

17. John Paul II, *Familiaris consortio*, 6. See also John Paul II, "Letter to Women" (June 29, 1995), 7, https://www.vatican.va/content/john-paul-ii /en/letters/1995/documents/hf_jp-ii_let_29061995 _women.html, which states: "Woman complements man, just as man complements woman: men and women are *complementary*. Womanhood expresses the 'human' as much as manhood does, but in a different and complementary way."

18. John Paul II, *Familiaris consortio*, 8.

19. John Paul II, *Mulieris dignitatem* (August 15, 1988), 19–22, https://www.vatican.va/content/john -paul-ii/en/apost_letters/1988/documents/hf_jp-ii _apl_19880815_mulieris-dignitatem.html.

20. John Paul II, *Ordinis sacerdotalis* (May 22, 1994), 4, https://www.vatican.va/content/john -paul-ii/en/apost_letters/1994/documents/hf_jp-ii _apl_19940522_ordinatio-sacerdotalis.html. See also Congregation for the Doctrine of the Faith, *Inter insignores* (October 15, 1976), https://www.vatican .va/roman_curia/congregations/cfaith/documents /rc_con_cfaith_doc_19761015_inter-insigniores _en.html. These teachings have been upheld by Pope Francis. For his comments on gender complementarity and essentialism, see Francis, *Amoris laetitia* (March 19, 2016), 172–77, 286, https://www.vatican .va/content/dam/francesco/pdf/apost_exhortations /documents/papa-francesco_esortazione-ap_2016 0319_amoris-laetitia_en.pdf. Drawing a distinction between the "Petrine" and "Marian" principles of leadership, Francis maintains, "And why can a woman not enter ordained ministry? It is because the Petrine principle has no place for that. . . . Therefore, that the woman does not enter into the ministerial life is not a deprivation. No. Your place is that which is much more important and which we have yet to develop, the catechesis about women in the way of the Marian principle." See Francis's interview "Pope Francis Discusses Ukraine, U.S. Bishops and More," *America*

(November 22, 2022), https://www.americamagazine.org/faith/2022/11/28/pope-francis-interview-america-244225. Francis draws his meditations on the Marian and Petrine principles from John Paul II, "Letter to Women," 12.

21. John Paul II, "Letter to Women," 11.

22. "The 'communion' of persons is drawn in a certain sense from the mystery of the Trinitarian 'We,' and therefore 'conjugal communion' also refers to this mystery. The family, which originates in the love of man and woman, ultimately derives from the mystery of God." John Paul II, *Familiaris consortio*, 8.

23. John Paul II, "Letter to Families," 7.

24. John Paul II, "Letter to Families," 13.

25. John Paul II, "Letter to Families," 3.

26. For the prohibition on contraception, see Paul VI, *Humanae vitae* (July 25, 1968), https://www.vatican.va/content/paul-vi/en/encyclicals/documents/hf_p-vi_enc_25071968_humanae-vitae.html. For the prohibition on in vitro fertilization, see Congregation for the Doctrine of the Faith, *Donum vitae* (February 22, 1987), 6, https://www.vatican.va/roman_curia/congregations/cfaith/documents/rc_con_cfaith_doc_19870222_respect-for-human-life_en.html.

27. See Congregation for the Doctrine of the Faith, "Letter to the Bishops of the Catholic Church on the Pastoral Care of Homosexual Persons" (October 1, 1986), https://www.vatican.va/roman_curia/congregations/cfaith/documents/rc_con_cfaith_doc_19861001_homosexual-persons_en.html; and Congregation for the Doctrine of the Faith, *Considerations Regarding Proposals to Give Legal Recognition to Unions between Homosexual Persons* (July 31, 2003), 2, https://www.vatican.va/roman_curia/congregations/cfaith/documents/rc_con_cfaith_doc_20030731_homosexual-unions_en.html.

28. See Congregation for Catholic Education, *Male and Female He Created Them* (February 2, 2019), 22, http://www.educatio.va/content/dam/cec/Documenti/19_0997_INGLESE.pdf. This passage quotes Pope Francis, *Amoris laetitia*, 34. Cf. *Amoris Laetitia*, 56, 285.

29. See, e.g., G. J. McAleer, *Ecstatic Morality and Sexual Politics: A Catholic Antitotalitarian Theory of the Body* (New York: Fordham University Press, 2005).

30. Cf. Jacob M. Kohlhaas, *Beyond Biology: Rethinking Parenthood in the Catholic Tradition*

(Washington, DC: Georgetown University Press, 2021), 49, 57.

31. Pope, "Natural Law in Catholic Social Teachings," 47.

32. Oakley, *Natural Law*, 104–5. The pope and Ockham disagreed on the moral legitimacy of the poverty of the Franciscans (Ockham was a Franciscan) insofar as poverty excluded ownership of goods. Ockham maintained that in imitation of Christ, the Franciscans did not own goods but rather had the simple use (*usus facti*) of them. The pope maintained that there was no legal validity to distinguishing between *dominium* and *usus facti* with respect to goods consumed. Ockham's cleverness here lies in his insight that no one would deny either that (1) Adam and Eve consumed things in the Garden as food or that (2) God owned everything in the garden and that private property originated following the Fall.

33. Thomas Hobbes, *Leviathan*, ed. Richard Tuck (New York: Cambridge, 1996); and John Locke, *Two Treatises on Government* and *A Letter Concerning Toleration*, ed. Ian Shapiro (New Haven, CT: Yale University Press, 2003). See also Pope, "Natural Law in Catholic Social Teachings," 49; and Oakley, *Natural Law*, 89–94.

34. Immanuel Kant, *Groundwork of the Metaphysics of Morals*, trans. Mary Gregor and Jens Timmerman (New York: Cambridge University Press, 2012).

35. United Nations, "Universal Declaration of Human Rights" (1948), https://www.un.org/en/about-us/universal-declaration-of-human-rights.

36. John XXIII, *Pacem in terris* (April 11, 1963), 28, https://www.vatican.va/content/john-xxiii/en/encyclicals/documents/hf_j-xxiii_enc_11041963_pacem.html. It should be made clear, though, that an endorsement of human rights as a framework for making sense of the *imago dei* does not also mean an endorsement of all human rights as enumerated by non-Catholic entities. Notable exceptions are the refusal to consider access to contraception or abortion care as human rights. See Paul VI, "Allocation to Midwives on the Nature of Their Profession" (1951), https://www.papalencyclicals.net/pius12/p12midwives.htm. The World Health Organization understands human rights to include access to contraception as well as safe abortion care. See World

Health Organization, "Ensuring Human Rights in the Provision of Contraceptive Information and Services: Guidance and Recommendations" (2014), https://apps.who.int/iris/bitstream/handle/10665/102539/9789241506748_eng.pdf.

37. This would be a central theme of the Second Vatican Council. See Vatican II, *Gaudium et spes*, 44.

38. Lisa Sowle Cahill's works at the intersection of natural law, gender, and sexuality are incredibly significant. See *Between the Sexes: Foundations for a Christian Ethics of Sexuality* (Philadelphia: Fortress, 1985); *Sex, Gender, and Christian Ethics* (New York: Cambridge University Press, 1996); and *Global Justice, Christology, and Christian Ethics* (New York: Cambridge University Press, 2013). See also Cristina Traina, *Feminist Natural Law: The End of the Anathemas* (Washington, DC: Georgetown University Press, 1999).

39. Todd Salzman and Michael Lawler, *The Sexual Person: Toward a Renewed Catholic Anthropology* (Washington, DC: Georgetown University Press, 2008); and Margaret Farley, *Just Love: A Framework for Christian Sexual Ethics* (New York: Continuum, 2008).

40. See Kohlhaas, *Beyond Biology*; and Lisa Sowle Cahill, "Catholic Families: Theology, Reality, and the Gospel," in *Catholic Women Speak: Bringing Our Gifts to the Table*, ed. Catholic Women Speak Network, 57–59 (Mahwah, NJ: Paulist Press, 2015); and Cristina L. H. Traina, "How Gendered Is Marriage?," in *Sex, Love, and Families: Catholic Perspectives*, ed. Jason King and Julie Hanlon Rubio, 79–90 (Collegeville, MN: Liturgical Press, 2020).

41. Craig A. Ford Jr., "Transgender Bodies, Catholic Schools, and a Queer Natural Law Theology of Exploration," *Journal of Moral Theology* 7, no. 1 (2018): 70–98; and Craig A. Ford Jr., "Born That Way? The Challenge of Trans/Gender Identity for Catholic Theology," in *Sex, Love, and Families*, 91–101. For a similar perspective that mobilizes the concept of freedom, see Elizabeth Sweeny Block, "Christian Moral Freedom and the Transgender Person," *Journal of the Society of Christian Ethics* 41, no. 2 (Fall/Winter 2021): 331–47.

# CHAPTER

# 3

# The Ecclesiological Contexts of Catholic Family Teaching

ANNIE SELAK

This chapter explores the ecclesiological contexts of Catholic Family Teaching (CFT), first by looking to the ecclesiological foundations of CFT and how teaching ought to be grounded in an understanding of revelation as ongoing, with God continuing to reveal Godself to the world. The chapter then examines authority and the Catholic Church's teaching, gradations in authority and church teaching, and topics of reception, dissent, and the *sensus fidelium*, followed by a focus on implications for the life of the church.

This chapter engages Catholic magisterial teaching from the framework that such teachings come from and are to be received by the entire church, from the laity to the hierarchical leadership. CFT and other forms of church teaching are guided by and grounded in the understanding that God continues to be present in the church and the world, and the faithful respond to this presence through developing tradition, guided by the Holy Spirit.

## EXPLORING THE ECCLESIOLOGICAL FOUNDATIONS OF CHURCH TEACHING

To understand Catholic teaching, it is first necessary to understand the church and its role in revelation. Church teaching does not come to us directly from God, inscribed on parchment paper or uploaded to the Vatican website directly from heaven to the internet. Such statements are intentionally absurd, but they touch on an incorrect belief that many hold and never engage: that humans have no role in formulating teaching. To affirm that church teaching is created by humans does not undercut its authority. Rather, it invokes a bold theological claim that God is present in the church and continues to guide the church through revelation.

A robust view of church teaching moves away from a propositional model and instead looks to how the Holy Spirit is still present with the church today, guiding the church through new situations. Much of the content of CFT are efforts by the church to respond to ongoing, pressing situations, some of which could not have been imagined in social contexts centuries ago. As such, tradition and revelation guide the church in creating teaching to advance its mission and guide the faithful in living lives based on the gospel.

To speak of "the church" is to speak of the one holy, catholic, and apostolic church. Too often, "the church" is used to refer to only the formal hierarchical leadership of the Catholic Church. While the hierarchy is an important aspect of the church, so too is the laity. God is present throughout the entire church, and the entire church has a special role in receiving the revelation of God. We must also affirm that the church is not the fullness of the presence of God.[1] As such, the church continues to move in its pilgrim way to express and respond to the ongoing revelation of God. *Lumen gentium*, Vatican II's dogmatic constitution on the church,[2] affirms that the church lives in such a way that "it may reveal in the world, faithfully, although with shadows, the mystery of its Lord until, in the end, it shall be manifested in full light" (*LG* 8).

Revelation speaks to God's ongoing relationship with the world. Revelation is not confined to the past but continues in the present and future. As Gerald O'Collins explains, "Revelation is not primarily a matter of revealing truths (plural) about God or even the truth (singular) about God. It involves God disclosing the Truth or Reality that is God. Primarily, it reveals a person, or rather three divine Persons, rather than information about a person or about three divine Persons."[3] God continues to reveal God's self to us, and in such a process, God is present. Revelation is a relationship with God. This relationship continues to inform the church's encounters with new situations, as reflected in the ongoing development of church teaching.

The church's mission is ongoing; to make known the already-but-not-yet reign of God requires God's grace as well as ongoing prayer and action. Richard Lennan explains the ongoing nature of teaching: "Both the developments in perceptions of the church and the range of cultural influences that the ecclesial community must navigate suggest that the unity of the church's faith, the vitality of its worship, and the fruitfulness of its service in the world are themselves ongoing tasks, rather than 'one-and-done' activities."[4] To view these tasks as "one-and-done" is an impoverished view of revelation that risks placing limitations on what God can and cannot do. Theologically, ongoing revelation of God may appear to be in tension with the authoritative role of any particular teaching. Insistences where the church has authoritatively spoken on a topic such that it is considered "case closed" are common within CFT. However, if revelation is not contained strictly in the past but instead God continues to reveal Godself to us, it then follows that church teaching is always ongoing, continuing to be received (or not) by the community, and lived out within the church. This is not a conflict that is unable to be resolved but rather an approach that affirms that the Holy Spirit was present in guiding the magisterium and the church community in receiving a teaching in its own time and continues to be present in the church's reception of teaching today. The nuances of reception will be addressed later in the chapter.

In proclaiming its understanding of God's revelation to contemporary contexts, magisterial teaching includes many tasks and actions spanning much beyond promulgated documents. According to Ormond Rush, the teaching office of the church includes five activities and responsibilities: proclamation, promotion, formulation, explanation, and preservation. Moreover, this teaching office extends beyond ordained ministers and members of the hierarchy, as "not all of those tasks are the exclusive prerogative of the magisterium," or the hierarchical church.[5] Rather, "most fall to all members of the church, and the fulfillment of those tasks is a vital dimension of the mission of the church and the transitioning of the Gospel throughout history." While the clergy and bishops relate to the teaching office in a unique way, the full church holds responsibility for the totality of the teaching office. This far-reaching responsibility underscores that church teaching is predicated on reception and the laity's special role in the preservation of church teaching.

CFT, in its modern form, encompasses more than 140 years of church teaching and is shaped by diverse and evolving views of what the church is, how church teaching functions, the role of the laity, and the relationship between the church and the world. Leo XIII issued his encyclical *Arcanum* in 1880, just after the First Vatican Council. This volume also includes teaching documents issued by Pius XI and Pius XII before the Second Vatican Council. In these early documents, the universal call to holiness, which constitutes a fundamental shift in how church teaching is issued and received, had yet to be established. But the "Copernican shift" of Vatican II subsequently reoriented the self-understanding of the church from primarily a hierarchy or a "perfect society" to a broader, more relational understanding, as demonstrated particularly by the first two chapters of *Lumen gentium*. *Gaudium et spes* likewise underscores the relationship between the church and the world, proclaiming "the joys and the hopes, the griefs and the anxieties" of the world, "especially those who are poor or in any way afflicted, these are the joys and hopes, the griefs and anxieties of the followers of Christ."[6]

More recent papacies have espoused diverse visions of the church. Francis's emphasis on a synodal church that understands that "listening is more than simply hearing" undergirds his vision for the church in relation to the world.[7] These ecclesiological commitments invite deeper integration and emphasize the role of reception and the *sensus fidelium*. Given these diversities, we must approach contributions to CFT with an appreciation for the ecclesiological context of their own time, including their theology of revelation and of the church, as well as consider how the development of the theological tradition impacts our ongoing reception of these teachings.

## UNDERSTANDING AND RESPONDING TO TEACHING AUTHORITY

CFT contains many different types of documents and, as a result, varying degrees of authority. Authority is "what enables a community to be bound together in all its interactions."[8] It is not an external designation of what or how to believe; instead, authority allows communities to have shared understandings of roles, expectations, obligations, and functions. Not all articulations of CFT contained in this volume carry the same authority, and none require absolute, unquestioning obedience from the believer. Rather, all elements of CFT require an engaged reception on the part of the believer in dialogue with the wider ecclesial community.

Magisterial teaching is intended to bring the faithful closer to God, to help understand, express, and respond to God's self-gift to creation. Church teaching is not the only form of God's ongoing revelation, and Catholics understand it to be guided by the Holy Spirit and received by the community of believers.

### Gradations and Types of Church Teaching

It may be tempting for those who gravitate toward order and structure to create clear delineations of magisterial teaching corresponding to gradations of authority. In fact, for a large portion of church history, moral and dogmatic theology manuals included "theological notes" that conveyed the authority of the teaching. Richard Gaillardetz has critiqued these detailed taxonomies, explaining that they "relied on an overly propositional view of the divine revelation and tended to overlook the fact that the Christian's most profound response in faith was not to a particular dogma or doctrine but to the good news of Jesus Christ crucified and risen who in the Holy Spirit offers life to the world."[9] Church teaching is intended to be an invitation into a relationship with God and a guide in how to live a life shaped by the gospel, not an instruction manual delivered from on high, full of statements that demand obedience.

In a less rigid way, it still remains possible to understand magisterial teaching as fitting into four categories: dogma, definitive doctrine, authoritative (nondefinitive) doctrine, and prudential admonitions and church discipline.[10] Again, these categories are not intended to belittle some church teaching or exalt others but rather to express the diverse types of teaching and appropriate responses of the faithful.

Three factors in particular help assess the authority of any specific teaching: source, topic, and ability to change. The question of the source asks, "Who issued this teaching and how was it issued?" Ecumenical councils, such as Vatican II, carry the most authority. In this volume, *Sancrosanctum concilium* (see chapter 11) and *Gaudium et spes* (see chapter 12), as constitutions of Vatican II, are the most authoritative. Items promulgated by a pope also carry significant authority, yet not all papal statements carry the same authority. As part of the ordinary magisterium, popes can issue several types of ecclesiastical documents, including an encyclical, an apostolic letter, an apostolic exhortation, or a papal address. While it is tempting to get into the weeds on the differences between ecclesiastical documents, the general gradations in teaching authority owe simply to the instinctive difference between an officially promulgated document and an offhand comment.

The question of topics asks, "What topic does this teaching address and what is its significance?" If the topic is foundational to Christian beliefs, it is more likely to carry substantial authority. Dogma concerns universal teachings most central to the core of the Catholic faith. Dogmas "directly mediate divine revelation."[11] Consequently, teachings clarifying dogma are highly authoritative and rarely contain groundbreaking developments. Dogma includes "specific historical mediations of the one revelation of God" and can often be thought of as creedal statements.[12] For example, the assertion at the Council of Nicea that the Son is "one in being" with the Father is dogma. By contrast, if a teaching addresses contemporary issues and is intended to serve as guidance in how to navigate an ongoing situation, it is likely to carry less authority. For example, "Open Wide Our Hearts" is a pastoral letter issued by the United States Conference of Catholic Bishops surrounding racism. It is important and carries significant teaching authority, but it is not dogma. Authoritative doctrine is intended to guide the faithful in expressing faith, especially as applied to contemporary situations. Likewise, any teaching connected to church practice, such as who can and cannot serve as ministers in the church, is not dogma.

A final question is this: "Can this teaching change?" Dogma does not change. In the example above, our understanding of the relationship between the Father and the Son as *homousia* has remained consistent since the

Council of Nicaea in 325; it is in the creed proclaimed by the faithful in the liturgy. Authoritative teaching occupies a middle ground, for these teachings issued by the magisterium are important and should be followed yet are taught in such a way that they are not irrevocable. Gaillardetz explains that "practically speaking, this means that, however remote, there is a possibility of error with respect to these teachings."[13] In contrast to dogma or definitive doctrine, prudential admonitions can and have changed. Prudential admonitions remain important, and their ability to evolve does not discredit their authority. Rather, these can be thought of as guidelines for expressing the core of faith; expression can vary, but the core remains consistent. For example, recent changes allowing women to serve as lectors[14] and catechists[15] are indicative of changing practice, not changes in the core of the faith. These changes align expressions of the faith with changing understandings of gender and the baptismal ministry.

It is important to note that very few teachings are infallible or held to be absolutely true and intimately connected to revelation. Vatican I defined the power to declare a teaching's infallibility as belonging to the pope's office. Cardinal Walter Kasper describes papal infallibility as only "if the pope speaks expressly as *typus ecclesiae*, as the holder of the *Cathedra Petri* in questions of faith and morals in a way that is authoritative for the whole Church."[16] That is, the pope can speak infallibly only on matters of faith and morals, not ecclesial, political, historical, scientific, or other categories and topics. Further, the pope must speak *ex cathedra*, with the full authority of the office, specifically categorizing a statement as infallible.

Church teaching that is not infallible or intimately connected to dogma remains important. In fact, much of CFT falls into the areas of authoritative doctrine and moral principles. Gaillardetz advises that "Catholics must treat these teachings as more than mere opinions or pious exhortations; rather, they constitute normative church teaching that Catholics must strive to integrate into their religious outlook."[17] These categories are designated as such because it is possible that they will change over time. For example, marriage and divorce are conditioned by culture, government, politics, and evolving understandings of families, love, relationships, conflict, and contracts. Church teaching on marriage and divorce, by its very nature, is open to evolving over time. This is demonstrated by the fact that marriage was not instituted as a sacrament until the Council of Trent in the sixteenth century. This does not mean that church teaching on marriage and divorce is not authoritative but rather that it has evolved throughout history and could potentially evolve in the future.

Assessing the authoritative status of CFT can be complicated by the fact that there is a desire among many to elevate much of church teaching to the level of dogma in order to express its importance. Oftentimes popes and bishops will connect authoritative doctrine with dogma, such as grounding teaching on gender in a more fundamental anthropology. Again, church teaching resists a clear delineation of what particular teaching is sorted into which category. Church teaching invites the faithful to contemplate how each teaching participates in revealing God and how the full ecclesial community continues to receive or reject teaching in dialogue with tradition. As such, the church participates and becomes the living tradition, affirming that church teaching is ongoing and not contained strictly in the past.

All of church teaching must be considered in regard to the "hierarchy of truths." *Unitatis redintegratio*, the decree on ecumenism issued at the Second Vatican Council, addressed the hierarchy of truths in guiding ecumenical dialogue. Importantly, it states that "when comparing doctrines with one another, they [theologians] should remember that in Catholic doctrine there exists an order or 'hierarchy' of truths, since they vary in their relation to the foundation of the Christian faith."[18] The most foundational truths surround the economy of salvation, God the creator who sent Jesus Christ to the world, and continues to be with creation through the Holy Spirit. All church teaching participates in revealing this economy of salvation, and some church teaching is closer

to this foundation than others. The proximity to the foundation of the faith influences the authoritative status of the teaching.

### *Reception, the* Sensus Fidelium, *Conscience, and Pastoral Guidance*

Church teaching does not simply come from the pope on a balcony at St. Peter's Basilica and immediately effect change, and it does not float above the faithful, separate from the life of the church. Rather, reception on the part of the faithful is an essential action that implements church teaching. If church teaching is valid, it will be received into the life of the faithful through the work of the Holy Spirit. The reception of church teaching is akin to the reception of divine revelation. As O'Collins explains, "Revelation always involves disclosure to someone. The invisible action of the Holy Spirit and their own graced predisposition enable human beings to receive in faith the self-revelation of God."[19]

The *sensus fidelium*, or sense of the faithful, is how the church receives or rejects church teaching. Amanda Osheim explains that "the *sensus fidelium* is God's faithfulness to the church through the Holy Spirit and allows the church in turn to be faithful to God in its pilgrimage."[20] The *sensus fidelium* is not a scientific formula or sociological survey that assesses whether reception has occurred but instead is an ecclesiological assertion of "the indwelling of the Holy Spirit within the baptized."[21] Confidence in the Spirit's faithfulness leads to the affirmation that if teachings are true and valid, they will be received into the life of the church and embraced by the faithful. *Lumen gentium* explains the *sensus fidelium* as follows:

The entire body of the faithful, anointed as they are by the Holy One, cannot err in matters of belief. They manifest this special property by means of the whole peoples' supernatural discernment in matters of faith when "from the Bishops down to the last of the lay faithful" they show universal agreement in matters of faith and morals. That discernment in matters of faith is aroused and sustained by the Spirit of truth. It is exercised under the guidance of the sacred teaching authority, in faithful and respectful obedience to which the people of God accepts that which is not just the word of men but truly the word of God. Through it, the people of God adheres unwaveringly to the faith given once and for all to the saints, penetrates it more deeply with right thinking, and applies it more fully in its life. (*LG* 12)

While teachings are generally articulated by the magisterium, teaching achieves its authority through expression in the life of the church through the guidance of the Holy Spirit.

If a teaching is not embraced in the life of the church, the issue of dissent arises. According to Gaillardetz, there is a "real possibility that legitimate dissent itself may be a manifestation of the Spirit in bringing the whole Church to truth."[22] We must resist contemporary pressures to translate dissent to a quantitative method, reducing it to polls and percentages of people who agree or disagree with church teaching. Dissent occurs within the lives of the faithful as the church universal continues on its pilgrim journey.

Dissent is connected with conscience formation. *Dignitatis humanae*, the Declaration on Religious Freedom issued at the Second Vatican Council, underscores the importance of conscience (in a gendered translation): "In all his activity a man is bound to follow his conscience in order that he may come to God, the end and purpose of life. It follows that he is not to be forced to act in a manner contrary to his conscience. Nor, on the other hand, is he to be restrained from acting in accordance with his conscience, especially in matters religious."[23] Conscience is the indwelling of God within ourselves; it is the law of God written in our hearts. Conscience is not simply my desires or what I want to do; rather, it demands formation through prayer, attentive listening to the teachings of the magisterium, and engagement with the tradition, social sciences, and contemporary knowledge as well as scripture, experience, and reason. A well-formed conscience may lead a believer to affirm or dissent from church

teaching. Regardless, all individuals are obligated to both form and obey their conscience.

Recent statements from Pope Francis underscore the pastoral dimension of reception and church teaching. In *Amoris laetitia*, Francis proclaims that "a pastor cannot feel that it is enough simply to apply moral laws to those living in 'irregular' situations, as if they were stones to throw at people's lives." Church teaching is not a weapon but instead is a way of shedding light on how the challenge of the gospel speaks to our context today. Francis continues: "By thinking that everything is black and white, we sometimes close off the way of grace and growth, and discourage paths of sanctification which give glory to God."[24] Such a disposition must guide our examination of CFT, resisting absolutes and instead examining how CFT might encourage "paths of sanctification which give glory to God."

Far from devaluing the magisterium, reception recognizes that church teaching achieves its authority when integrated into the life of the church. Lennan connects reception to tradition, explaining that "reception is the pivotal aspect of the church's historical existence: it takes place in the present, but connects the past to the future. Unless the present-day community of faith received the tradition as lifegiving, what comes from the past does not have a future."[25] Reception is rooted in an ecclesiology that views God as present in the church throughout history, including the present and future, in its embrace of tradition.

### Ongoing Questions in Authority

With the rise of social media, new ecclesiological questions appear surrounding how to interpret papal tweets and offhand comments. Perhaps the most well-known statement by Pope Francis on sexuality came in a press conference aboard a papal flight when he said, "If someone is gay and he searches for the Lord and has good will, who am I to judge?"[26] While his comment may have little teaching authority, it certainly made an impact in the church and in society. Social media also affects how bishops exercise their authority, especially as bishops of varying political persuasions utilize social media to express opinions on political events. Bishops may disagree with one another, and while disagreement can be a sign of a healthy church, it can cause questions surrounding teaching authority and how the faithful are to interpret such statements. In general, statements on social media do not enjoy any significant teaching authority, yet they can still influence the church and the world on contemporary topics.

## IMPLICATIONS FOR THE LIFE OF THE CHURCH

CFT addresses some of the most universal and intimate aspects of life and as such has an important role to play in the life of the church universal as well as in the lives of individual believers. At the same time, CFT must critically engage its own limitations, specifically around understandings and expressions of culture, race, and gender, in order to express the fullness of the church.

CFT speaks to the church universal, united as one and expressed locally throughout the world. The church is indeed one, holy, catholic, and apostolic, but church teaching is nonetheless influenced by the context from which it is written. CFT reflects its Eurocentric context most notably by proposing a vision of the family shaped by cultural notions of Western white Europeans. While this Eurocentric view does not invalidate the teaching authority of the magisterium, it certainly raises questions about how CFT is developed and received. The potential of the worldwide synod to listen to the local church in conversation with the church universal, as reflected in the synods on the family (2014, 2015) and the Synod on Synodality (2021–2023), are encouraging steps toward actualizing CFT informed by a worldwide church.

Further, CFT is often shaped by views of gender and sexuality that have not kept up with evolving understandings of gender identity, gender expression, and sexual orientation, even as there is evolution in understanding of gender

and sexuality in CFT. Throughout its history, CFT has been shaped by a binary understanding of gender. Further, its development by a particular segment of celibate religious men led to questions by marginalized genders regarding how celibate men who identify as cisgender can speak to experiences of marginalized genders. This is particularly important concerning issues of marriage, divorce, raising children, sexual violence, and gender discrimination, where imbalanced power dynamics result in different experiences for marginalized genders. CFT on sexual orientation, including same-sex marriage, is not reflective of public opinion throughout the West in support of same-sex marriage, and people from all sexual orientations point to the harm caused by the church's insistence that "homosexual acts" are "intrinsically disordered" and that homosexual orientation is "an objective disorder."[27] Even the language around "homosexual acts" and "homosexual orientation" diverge from the language preferred by the LGBTQ community.

The impact of Eurocentrism, patriarchy, heteronormativity, and a strictly binary view of gender cannot be viewed as simply political issues or apart from the church. The impact of teaching that is Eurocentric, patriarchal, and heteronormative or dismisses gender diversity can result in real harm to individuals and communities. For example, LGBTQ youths in the United States are more than four times as likely to attempt suicide than their peers, and approximately 50 percent of transgender and nonbinary youths seriously consider attempting suicide.[28] The mission of the church is to spread the gospel, the Good News of Jesus Christ, and live in the already but not yet reign of God. Church teaching has the capacity to express the church's ability to speak prophetically and meaningfully on areas that CFT addresses, or the potential to call into question the church's credibility. Again, conscience formation and reception are radically important, guiding CFT's expression in the world. CFT addresses topics that have the potential to be inclusive or divisive, promoting unity or resulting in violence if misunderstood or applied incorrectly. Further, topics such as marriage, divorce, and family vary greatly in expressions throughout the world. The church must not serve as an "export firm" of European religion, as warned by Karl Rahner,[29] but instead should live into the vision of Vatican II to actualize a world church.

CFT will continue to develop long after this volume is published. Its reception will also continue to be ongoing, as the *sensus fidelium* continues to receive and integrate teachings into the lives of the faithful. The analysis of CFT, like that contained in this volume, will also continue to develop. This does not make the teachings outdated. Rather, a robust understanding of tradition, reception, and revelation lead the church to continue to receive God's self-gift and respond to the ongoing call of the gospel to make the already but not yet reign of God known on Earth.

## NOTES

1. This section is informed by Karl Rahner's ecclesiology of the church as sacrament and symbol. For a more in-depth analysis, see Karl Rahner, "The Theology of Symbol," in *Theological Investigations*, Vol. 5 (New York: Herder and Herder, 1970); Karl Rahner, "The Church as the Subject of the Sending of the Spirit," in *Theological Investigations*, Vol. 7 (New York: Herder and Herder, 1971); and Karl Rahner, *The Church and the Sacraments* (New York: Herder and Herder, 1963).

2. Vatican II, *Lumen gentium* (November 21, 1964), https://www.vatican.va/archive/hist_councils/ii_vatican_council/documents/vat-ii_const_19641121_lumen-gentium-en.html (hereafter cited as *LG*).

3. Gerald O'Collins, *Revelation: Towards a Christian Interpretation of God's Self-Revelation in Jesus Christ*, 1st ed (Oxford: University Press, 2016), 6–7.

4. Richard Lennan, *Tilling the Church: Theology for an Unfinished Project* (Collegeville, MN: Liturgical Press, 2022), 16–17.

5. Ormond Rush, *The Eyes of Faith the Sense of the Faithful and the Church's Reception of Revelation* (Washington, DC: Catholic University of America Press, 2009), 194.

6. *Gaudium et spes* (December 7, 1965), 1, https://www.vatican.va/archive/hist_councils/ii_vatican_council/documents/vat-ii_const_19651207_gaudium-et-spes_en.html.

7. Francis, *Evangelii gaudium* (November 24, 2013), 171, https://www.vatican.va/content/francesco/en/apost_exhortations/documents/papa-francesco_esortazione-ap_20131124_evangelii-gaudium.html.

8. David J. Stagaman, *Authority in the Church* (Collegeville, MN: Liturgical Press, 1999), 35.

9. Richard Gaillardetz, "The Ecclesiological Foundations of Modern Catholic Social Teaching," in *Modern Catholic Social Teaching: Commentaries and Interpretations*, ed. Kenneth R. Himes, 72–98 (Washington, DC: Georgetown University Press, 2004), 87.

10. These categories were developed from the ecclesial documents "Profession of Faith and Oath of Fidelity" Congregation for the Doctrine of the Faith, "The Ecclesial Vocation of the Theologian." For a thorough examination of gradations of church doctrine, see Richard Gaillardetz, *Teaching with Authority: A Theology of the Magisterium in the Church* (Collegeville, MN: Liturgical Press, 1997), chap. 4.

11. Gaillardetz, *Teaching with Authority*, 102.

12. Richard Gaillardetz, *By What Authority? A Primer on Scripture, the Magisterium, and the Sense of the Faithful* (Collegeville, MN: Liturgical Press, 2003), 91.

13. Gaillardetz, *By What Authority?*, 100.

14. Francis, *Spiritus domini* (January 10, 2021), https://www.vatican.va/content/francesco/en/motu_proprio/documents/papa-francesco-motu-proprio-20210110_spiritus-domini.html.

15. Francis, *Antiquum ministerium* (May 10, 2021), https://www.vatican.va/content/francesco/en/motu_proprio/documents/papa-francesco-motu-proprio-20210510_antiquum-ministerium.html.

16. Walter Kasper, *The Catholic Church: Nature, Reality and Mission* (New York: T&T Clark, 2015), 263.

17. Gaillardetz, "The Ecclesiological Foundations of Modern Catholic Social Teaching," 90.

18. Second Vatican Council, *Unitatis redintegratio* (November 21, 1964), 1, https://www.vatican.va/archive/hist_councils/ii_vatican_council/documents/vat-ii_decree_19641121_unitatis-redintegratio_en.html.

19. O'Collins, *Revelation*, 75.

20. Amanda Osheim, *A Ministry of Discernment: The Bishop and the Sense of the Faithful* (Collegeville, MN: Liturgical Press, 2016), xi.

21. Osheim, *A Ministry of Discernment*, xi.

22. Gaillardetz, *Teaching with Authority*, 270.

23. Vatican II, *Dignitatis humanae* (December 7, 1965b), 3, https://www.vatican.va/archive/hist_councils/ii_vatican_council/documents/vat-ii_decl_19651207_dignitatis-humanae_en.html.

24. Francis, *Amoris laetitia* (March 19, 2016), 305, https://www.vatican.va/content/dam/francesco/pdf/apost_exhortations/documents/papa-francesco_esortazione-ap_20160319_amoris-laetitia_en.pdf.

25. Lennan, *Tilling the Church*, 217–18.

26. Rachel Donadio, "On Gay Priests, Pope Francis Asks, 'Who Am I to Judge?'," *New York Times*, July 29, 2013, https://www.nytimes.com/2013/07/30/world/europe/pope-francis-gay-priests.html.

27. Congregation for the Doctrine of the Faith, "Letter to the Bishops of the Catholic Church on the Pastoral Care of Homosexual Persons" (October 1, 1986), 3–4, https://www.vatican.va/roman_curia/congregations/cfaith/documents/rc_con_cfaith_doc_19861001_homosexual-persons_en.html.

28. "Facts about LGBTQ Youth Suicide," The Trevor Project, December 15, 2021, https://www.thetrevorproject.org/resources/article/facts-about-lgbtq-youth-suicide/.

29. Karl Rahner, "Towards a Fundamental Theological Interpretation of Vatican II," *Theological Studies* 40, no. 4 (December 1979): 717.

# CHAPTER

# 4

## Catholic Family Teaching before 1880

MATTHEW SHERMAN

Michael J. Schuck in his essay "Modern Catholic Social Thought, 1740–1890" typologizes Catholic responses to modern social change across three categories: traditionalist, cosmopolitan, and transformationist. Traditionalist approaches, often seen at the outset of the modern period, favor long-standing social customs, are cautious about social reform, and prefer long-range thinking and planning. The writing and rhetoric of traditionalism tends to border on the ideal and the (neo)classical, what Schuck calls "arcadian imagery."[1] Cosmopolitanism is a middle-ground approach, expressing a cautious optimism about social reform and a middle-range hope for social change. Its writing and rhetoric demonstrate an appreciation of both global diversity and local history, language, and culture.[2] Transformationism is the most radical and visionary of the three approaches. It is concerned with immediate social change in a locality but also makes urgent pleas for just social structures more broadly. The writing and rhetoric of a transformationist tambor range from utopian to revolutionary.[3]

While Schuck is specifically addressing the modern period in the eighteenth and nineteenth centuries, his typology may in fact be instructive for the history of premodern Catholic family teaching from the fourth through

nineteenth centuries despite its significantly wider time frame. In the Catholic tradition, marriage is often seen as an essential and foundational institution of the church, ordered at creation and elevated by Christ to a sacrament, which redounds to a properly ordered and godly society. As such, the family teaching tradition rarely uses marriage as an opportunity for immediate, urgent, or radical social reform. At most, marriage is seen in the Roman and medieval eras as a kind of cosmopolitan institution linking the radicality of the gospel with the more quotidian aspects of civic life through the family's engagement in just economic endeavors and its care for the common good for its members and within its proximate community. Most often and especially as the Counter-Reformation confronted the ecclesiastical abuses of the medieval era, marriage became a kind of mascot for traditionalism, even a kind of protoclassicist motif, at once a symbol of what society should be and of the proper role of the church in ordering that society through the spiritual (not merely financial), primordial (not merely expedient), and sacramental (not merely political) institutions of family life. Throughout most of the Catholic social tradition, exigent and radical reform is rarely associated with marriage. Nonetheless, it is instructive to see how and to what extent the Catholic social tradition relies on marriage and family as a sacramental sign of the church's work in the world and a medium for bringing about that work.

## FOURTH-CENTURY FOUNDATIONS

Premodern Catholic family teaching took definitive form, along with many other issues of doctrine, in the fourth century. The Council of Ephesus, against the disunity of Byzantine court politics and episcopal rivalries, affirmed the unity within Christ, who is both "life" and "the life-giving one," and Mary's exalted role as the bearer of God.[4] For Ephesus, Christ's place in history was not merely as a kind of ethereal divine exemplar but rather as the Word made flesh and thus human in every way but sin.[5] Lesser known from the council and seen in Cyril's Third Letter to Nestorius is an important reference to Christ's import for marriage. Through Jesus's union of flesh and divinity, he destroyed the death of sin and restored the fullness of life in our bodies, which is why he was able to bless the marriage union at Cana.[6] This view of the potency and goodness of the body, fashioned through centuries of debates with Gnostics and Manicheans, is almost a foreshadowing of the theology of the Second Nicene Council in the eighth century.[7] Second Nicaea argued that Christ's union with creation is what allows for the graced potential of icons, which mediate the divine presence through created objects. While worship is reserved for God alone, those images that mediate God's saving life may receive reverence.[8] Likewise, for the Council of Ephesus, whose work was ratified and expanded at the Council of Chalcedon, Jesus's union of flesh and divinity allows for the bodily union of marriage to carry salvific meaning from Cana forward. By celebrating the dignity, needs, and holiness of bodies, married relationships, and familial communities, the early medieval church took an essential step in laying the foundations of both Catholic Social Teaching (CST) and Catholic Family Teaching (CFT). The radicality of transforming the body

from a site of death to one of life is, theologically, a kind of transformationist hope situated within the traditional and foundational social institutions of marriage and family. It is a mix of the arcadian, or Edenic, vision of the family and the early Christian awareness that the gospel must be enacted through the traditional familial structures of the Roman and Hellenistic world.

## TWELFTH-CENTURY REFORMS

By the time of the First, Second, and Third Lateran Councils in the twelfth century, Roman Catholicism (now separated from Eastern Orthodoxy) was conscientiously trying to reform the practices of its clergy, who were often immersed in feudal politics and the investiture of ecclesiastical offices by lay nobility. Clerical marriage and the installation of those married into politically beneficial ecclesiastical positions were tempting avenues for feudal control.[9] Insistence on celibacy was as much about the spiritual order of the church as it was a means to solidify the institutional church's temporal control over its own territories. A celibate clergy and hierarchy were less easily entangled in secular fealties, and mandatory celibacy allowed the church to claim status as a pure community untainted by both bodily and political lusts.[10]

Consequently, the tone of medieval teaching on marriage moved from a patristic emphasis on what marriage accomplishes because of Christ to what marriage does to impede the life of Christ. Church teaching clarified that celibacy was not only important for averting ecclesiastical corruption but also secured the bodily purity needed for clergy and religious to perform their duties. The marriage covenant was invalid for anyone at the rank of subdeacon, deacon, priest, or bishop because it was preceded by the earlier precept of celibacy.[11] This injunction was repeated at the Fourth Lateran Council in the early thirteenth century.[12]

By the same token, the Second Lateran Council specifically affirmed that the sacraments as administered through the institutions of the Catholic Church are valid and necessary avenues for salvation in light of certain rigorist and paraecclesial medieval cults, such as the Cathars.[13] This insistence on the necessity of the church in consecration includes both ecclesiastical orders and matrimony, which interestingly groups the two in ecumenical council history as sacraments of vocation and avenues to salvation.

The Third Lateran Council confirmed the church's commitment to the standards of both holy orders and marriage by reprimanding ecclesiastical officials including bishops and priests, who exacted tribute for the performance or ratification of marriages. These protections against corruption were issued in tandem with support for universities, theological study, and canon law; together, Lateran III's prohibitions and encouragements clarified the meaning of marriage and the marriage rite as avenues for covenant and communal belonging free of the fetters of payment or graft.[14] Moreover, Lateran IV issued the requirement that public notification must precede any licit marriage, which allows for greater knowledge and regulation on the part of both church and civil officials.[15] Marriage in this vision was to be a carefully vetted ecclesial opportunity for continued holiness, not a transactional moment for personal gain.

When the Lateran councils forbade marriage for clergy, they affirmed marriage as a part of the rites and sacraments of the church but, at the same time, almost revoked the Council of Ephesus's emphasis on marriage as a result of the purification of the incarnation and resurrection. Here, family teaching tended toward the traditionalist, seeing marriage as a barometer of a traditional Christian order and an institution for promoting both social stability and a more disciplined clergy.

Thus far, the church's family teaching revolved around the transformative and salvific realities of the human body due to Christ's incarnation and the importance of marriage as a covenanted site of God's blessing. Even though it ranked below holy orders or religious life in the spiritual hierarchy, marriage was recognized as a sacrament by the twelfth

century, and it was understood to bring salvific and social power because it is consecrated by a promise not unlike other religious vocations. The marriage promise is not, however, to supersede prior commitments to Christian celibacy.

## LATE MEDIEVAL REFORMS

The tendency to discuss marriage in negative terms, that is, who cannot be married, continued into the late medieval period alongside dogmatic assertions of marriage as a graced relationship. As with the Early and High Middle Ages, statements of dogma and prohibition from the late medieval era carry social consequences for family life. The Council of Basil-Ferrara-Florence-Rome in the early fifteenth century produced the rather painful-to-confront prohibition of marriage between Christians and Jews. The council began as an attempt to root out corruption in the Roman Curia, yet this desire for a purer moral community seems also to have taken on purist notions of ethnicity.[16] The council even prohibited socialization between recent converts from Judaism to Christianity lest they steer each other astray from their new religious values.[17] Such decisions manifested a widespread European cultural prejudice against the faith, culture, and ethnicity of the Jewish people, who were wrongly associated with putting Jesus to death. Unsurprisingly, these antisemitic beliefs accompanied a rise in European national rivalries especially among England, France, and the kingdoms of the Mediterranean.[18] Because of the prejudice embedded in their statements, Basel-Ferrara-Florence-Rome proffered an attenuated social message; yet they also, somewhat inadvertently, reaffirmed marriage as a sacramental commitment grounded in Christian baptism and oriented toward the Augustinian ends of offspring, faith, and holiness.[19]

The Council of Basil-Ferrara-Florence-Rome also sought a politically motivated and ineffectual reunion of Western and Eastern Christians as something of a panacea in the wake of the Western Schism, the political and human destruction of the crusades, and the Byzantine Empire's waning power in the East.[20] As a consequence, the council's exclusion of non-Christians may be read as a regrettable counterpart to its attempt to include both Catholic and Orthodox Christians under its understanding of the unity and universality of the sacraments as well as the importance of the apostolic hierarchy for both the East and the West. The council also reasserted the indissolubility of the sacrament of marriage.[21] Similar to the Lateran Councils' insistence on the priority of religious vows over marital vows, Basil-Ferrara-Florence-Rome insisted on the enduring and causal nature of the marriage promise. In doing so, the council promoted the sacramental and social stability of the family. This idea became an anchor for later Catholic social thought and provided a cosmopolitan linkage between Catholic interests in sacramental-marital life and the well-being of society.

Finally, Basil-Ferrara-Florence-Rome provided one of conciliar history's clearest statements of the seven sacraments, referring explicitly to marriage as "that seventh of which is marriage as a sacramental sign of Christ's union with the Church."[22] This scholastic reprisal served as a foundation for the council's claims of the importance of the apostolic faith uniting the sacraments of the East and West. Moreover, the reprisal reaffirmed the Council of Constance's insistence on the necessity of the hierarchy and sacraments over and against the rising influence of reformers such as John Wycliff and Jan Hus.[23]

## TRENT'S RESPONSE TO THE REFORMATION

A century later, the Protestant Reformation's spiritual, ecclesial, and political consequences reshaped both Western Christianity and European society. In response, the Catholic Church convened the Council of Trent to both solidify and reform clerical formation, catechesis, and sacramental practice.[24] The church and its ministers were now concerned with regulating and disseminating teaching and sacraments with

renewed organization apart from dependence on religiously feuding rulers. In its twenty-fourth session, Trent built upon the sacramental theology of Basil-Ferrara-Florence-Rome. Trent taught that marriage is "one of the seven sacraments of the evangelic law"; while not "above the state of virginity," marriage is both a sacred union and a public good.[25] Hence, marriage must be publicly announced ahead of time, adhere to ecclesial prohibitions regarding marriage impediments, and be witnessed by local parish clergy.[26] As a traditional unit of Christian society and under the care of the church, Tridentine marriage served as both a traditionalist anchor for championing Catholic law and morals and a cosmopolitan institution that combated dangerous, anticanonical, or reformist ideas.

## EARLY MODERN PAPAL TEACHING

Three hundred years later, the late medieval emphasis on the corporate nature of both the church and the Christian family remained important, especially as teaching on the family shifted to a new modality, the papal letter or encyclical.[27] Papal teaching in the eighteenth century faced rising skepticism about the rights of traditional rulers, both secular and religious, and rising doubts about any belief system that did not adhere to a rigorously rational worldview.[28] *Ubi primum*, Pope Benedict XIV's first encyclical, addressed the duties of bishops.[29] Benedict XIV drew upon the ancient motif of the church as the household of God (as seen in Ephesians, Timothy, Titus, and Colossians) and portrayed the bishop as paterfamilias of his local church. Just as "the head of the family himself frequently inspects all things," the local bishop acts as both a steward of local resources and clergy as well as a shepherd, tending all of the parts and persons of his diocese (*UP* 5–6). As a head of the local family of the church, the bishop may not always know of the pains and infractions of his family, but by "repeated visits" he will be able to provide "wholesome medicines for expelling the diseases of souls" (*UP* 5).

By use of the arcadian image of the father-shepherd, Benedict XIV incorporated a traditionalist model of family order to both rally the ecclesial hierarchy and guard against secular ideologies of the family and the state.

Just three years later *Nimiam licentiam*, Benedict XIV's encyclical addressed to the Catholic Church in Poland, returned to the now ancient concern about the connection between marriage, the church, and its clergy.[30] The pope was concerned that the bishops and priests of Poland were delegating celebrations of marriage in their parishes but were hesitant to perform these ceremonies themselves. Moreover, clerics were not exploring impediments and were not dutiful in implementing the requirement of a public marriage announcement. This laxity in practice augmented the possibility of scandal regarding the payments given to clergy who did not themselves perform the rite; it also compromised the integrity of the couple's intentions, the pastor's knowledge, and the communal fulfillment of consent in the marriage itself. Furthermore, these practices gave rise to dubious cases of nullity in the Polish church and threatened to confuse the faithful who frequently witnessed the impermanence of marriages with such loose ecclesial oversight (*NL* 5–6). The problems were so significant that some couples were supposedly making pacts of dissolution to end their marriages (*NL* 7). Benedict XIV therefore draws an important connection between the hierarchical structure of the church and its significance for the integrity of the marriage rite among the laity; he also shows the import of marriage as a unit of social stability because it is an enduring bond that manifests in the couple's long-standing commitment to one another and to ecclesial authority. For Benedict XIV, stable marriages and families witness to a stable society, and both marriage and wider social life are better protected when a bishop secures the stability of his diocesan family as its traditional head.

In his 1749 *Apostolica constitutio*, "On Preparation for the Holy Year," Benedict XIV returns to the motif he used in *Ubi primum*, that is, that the church is hierarchically modeled as a kind of spiritual household and that the bishop and his clergy should exemplify the importance of pilgrimage by their own example.[31] Yet, much like the medieval era's insistence on the nullity of marriage within holy orders, Benedict XIV insists that anyone wishing to embark on a pilgrimage must respect a spiritual hierarchy of goods and promises. If the health of the body or the health of a relationship such as marriage demands that one stay at home, this prior commitment is more important than the prospective spiritual benefits of pilgrimage. Thus, if a bishop is dealing with infirmity, he should seek spiritual rejuvenation by means other than pilgrimage for the sake of himself and those he serves. Likewise, if a wife does not consent to the pilgrimage of her husband or if the continence of a marriage relationship will suffer if either spouse departs on pilgrimage for a long duration, then pilgrimage must be forgone as a fitting sacrifice for the sake of marital virtue (*AC* 7).

Pope Benedict cautions that if a woman is on pilgrimage, she should be protected by her traveling companions so that her virtue will be safeguarded against the devices of the weaker souls she may meet along the way. In this sense, not only are a woman's prior commitments to be safeguarded by her fellow Christians, but wider Christian society also bears responsibility for protecting the virtues of marriage and the dignity of the bodies of the men and women who are on a sacred journey. Benedict XIV's letter urges brothers and other kin to act as guardians of women on pilgrimage if their husbands cannot attend also. In his words, "they should be entrusted to men whose kinship both frees them from suspicion and makes them concerned about the preservation of chastity" (*AC* 7). Christian pilgrimage brings to light, then, both the social importance of preserving the bond of marriage and, conversely, the social forces at work that might be a threat to the safety and stability of marriages and women. Thus, Benedict XIV highlights a kind of cosmopolitan responsibility that all Christians must bear in the act of pilgrimage. In this way, the traditional safeguards and consecrated commitments of marriage and family become the carriers of a social responsibility to preserve the God-given dignity of persons on pilgrimage who are, in truth, a kind of migrant. Using the traditional stability of Christian family life, the church can extend its care even to distant persons and places for the well-being of God's people.

For Pope Benedict XIV, his hope was for a spirit of pilgrimage to unite the church; no spiritual quest can accomplish its proper ends when it results in vice and disunion whether of the family or of a wider network of kinship (*AC* 7).[32] Thus, there is an important reprise here: early modern family teaching highlights the virtue and union that marks all Christian life as rightly anchored in the sacraments of vocation, and for the laity, marriage is an essential unit of social virtue and social unity. Family is a seedbed and guarantor of social charity; the love of God, needed in society, flows in a primary way through the Christian family and through the family of the church. The sacramental promises of marriage help to bring about the social virtue that is required of all the faithful.

## THE NINETEENTH CENTURY

Papal thought took an important turn as it faced the rise of the modern state. By the time of Gregory XVI in the 1830s, the papacy had come to view itself as oppositional to the oft-changing mores of the Enlightenment and its revolutions in both thought and power structures.[33] This instability and social change, manifested most clearly in the chaos and bloodshed of the French Revolution, gave rise to a centralized understanding of the institutional church, with papal authority acting as a safeguard of the sacraments and societal cohesion. Gregory XVI was particularly concerned that he and Catholics throughout Europe avoid inciting revolution for the sake of order and longevity. He was so wary of the threat of revolution that he ignored the Russian czar's despotic and violent repression of Poland.[34]

In his encyclical *Mirari vos*, Gregory XVI condemned any attempt to insist that dissolution or divorce is possible within marriage.[35] He was no doubt contending with the rise of modern states whose laws were beginning to challenge the Catholic Church's long-standing authority to grant, annul, and dissolve marriages. At the same time, he was defending the idea of sacrament over and against the rising Enlightenment-influenced understanding of marriage as a civil contract between persons that can be entered and exited at will (*MV* 12). Emblematic of this era, Gregory XVI's encyclical *Commissum divinitus* strongly criticized Switzerland for pressuring local Catholic clergy to follow Swiss laws allowing for marriage between Catholics and non-Catholics. Moreover, Gregory rejected the validity of Swiss law insomuch as it understood marriage powers to flow from the state without any reference to the authority of the church.[36]

Against this backdrop, Pope Pius IX's condemnation of modern errors emerged almost organically. In the wake of Italian revolution and secular unification, Pius IX objected that the modern state was deleterious to a Catholic understanding of society and rejected assertions that states can legislate without reference to the religious order.[37] In his encyclical *Qui pluribus*, he notes the modern infringement on the rightful authority that the church should have over daily life, including marriage. Likewise, Pius IX is concerned that traditional governments are being plundered and overturned by modern preferences for secularism and democracy.[38] As he explains in his 1849 encyclical *Nostis et nobiscum*, the church suffers when the state tries to infringe upon its spiritual authority; drawing explicitly on Augustine, Pius IX affirms that the state fulfills its divinely given function only when the church and the sacraments are given their rightful place. As such, God's institutions, including the hierarchal church and sacramental marriage, are the foundation of society, which stands in contrast to the looming modern consensus that consent and civil government are the foundation of human freedoms, including religion.[39] Again, the social and spiritual institution of marriage is employed to argue for a partly cosmopolitan vision that traditional family life can rectify the iniquities of the social order.

This vision of marriage is also visible in Pius IX's encyclical *Quanta cura* and its appended "Syllabus of Errors." Herein, Pope Pius explains that the church aids society because it preserves, blesses, and fosters the natural communions of marriage and family. Because the church is the divine institution from which marriage emanates, it is also the case that civil institutions should not and cannot rightly influence ecclesial practices regarding marriage law, rites, criteria for marriage and divorce, and the proper education of children.[40]

## CONCLUSION

One may wonder how this resistance to modernity gave way to what we now know as the corpus of modern CST and CFT. My conjecture is this: Near the end of the nineteenth century, Leo XIII's return to Thomism allowed him to think not about the limits of secular institutions or the problems of doing politics apart from religion but instead about the role of Catholic faith as the kiln in which modern society might be fired. Drawing upon the ideas of social thinkers such as John Locke in addition to Aquinas allowed Leo XIII to defend private property not in terms of the Enlightenment but rather by asserting a Thomistic understanding that all of creation is given by God for our common human flourishing. The state and market are tools for the secular and spiritual flourishing of their workers, who have a right to enjoy the fruits of their labor.[41] Likewise, as a unit of society ordered and consecrated by God, marriage and the family it produces became clearly understood as an opportunity to inculcate Christian principles throughout society. Perhaps there is little hope for progress apart from the social stability of the church, but the key for Leo XIII was to have hope for social change and justice in society using the subsidiary structures created by God and sustained by the sacraments. This hope is what Leo XIII gave to CFT as its founding commitment.[42]

Leo XIII ushered in a belief that papal teaching must respond in ways universal enough to address the world church but specific enough to speak to the peoples, cultures, and geopolitical actors they were meant to address. The move from Eurocentric modern thought to more tradition-centered theological anthropology thus accompanied a parallel shift from papal letters that address local European churches to those that address issues, the faithful, and clergy across the universal church. In all, Pope Leo XIII demonstrated a newfound understanding that marriage and family are guarantors of proper Christian faith and morals and are also mediators between sacred life and modern institutions. This understanding allowed for a shift from the stalemates of the mid-nineteenth century into the more immediately cosmopolitan and even transformationist family understandings that pervade CST and CFT as they moved into and through the twentieth century.

## NOTES

1. Michael Schuck, "Modern Catholic Social Thought, 1740-1890," in *Modern Catholic Social Teaching: Commentaries and Interpretations*, ed. Kenneth R. Himes, O.F.M. (Washington, DC: Georgetown University Press, 2005), 101.

2. Schuck, "Modern Catholic Social Thought," 101, 104.

3. Schuck, "Modern Catholic Social Thought," 101, 109, and 118.

4. Joseph F. Kelly, *The Ecumenical Councils of the Catholic Church: A History* (Collegeville, MN: Liturgical Press, 2009), 40–41; and Jaroslav Pelikan, *The Christian Tradition: A History of the Development of Doctrine*, 5 vols. (Chicago: University of Chicago Press, 1971), 1:261.

5. W. H. C. Frend, *The Rise of Christianity* (Philadelphia: Fortress, 1984), 757–78.

6. "Third Letter of Cyril to Nestorius" in "Council of Ephesus—431 A.D.," Papal Encyclicals Online, https://www.papalencyclicals.net/councils/ecum03.htm.

7. James Hitchcock, *History of the Catholic Church: From the Apostolic Age to the Third Millennium* (San Francisco: Ignatius, 2012), 88–89.

8. Norman P. Tanner, *The Councils of the Church: A Short History* (New York: Crossroad Publishing, 2001), 35–36.

9. Kelly, *The Ecumenical Councils*, 76–83.

10. Kevin Madigan, *Medieval Christianity: A New History* (New Haven, CT: Yale University Press, 2015), 127–28.

11. Gerald O'Collins and Mario Farrugia, *Catholicism: The Story of Catholic Christianity* (Oxford: Oxford University Press, 2003), 290; "Second Lateran Council—1139 A.D.," canons 6–7, Papal Encyclicals Online, https://www.papalencyclicals.net/councils/ecum10.htm.

12. Kelly, *The Ecumenical Councils,* 91.

13. "Second Lateran Council—1139 A.D.," canon 23.

14. Eamon Duffey, *Saints and Sinners: A History of the Popes*, 4th ed. (New Haven, CT: Yale University Press, 2014), 144.

15. O'Collins and Farrugia, *Catholicism,* 291; and Tanner, *The Councils of the Church*, 60.

16. Duffey, *Saints and Sinners,* 172–73.

17. "Council of Basil-Ferrara-Florence, 1431–9 A.D.," Session 19, Papal Encyclicals Online, https://www.papalencyclicals.net/councils/ecum17.htm.

18. Justo L. González, *The Story of Christianity: The Reformation to the Present Day*, 2 vols., revised and updated ed. (New York: HarperCollins, 2010), 2:294–98.

19. "Council of Basil-Ferrara-Florence, 1431–9 A.D.," Session 19.

20. Kelly, *The Ecumenical Councils,* 114–19; and Madigan, *Medieval Christianity*, 384–85.

21. "Council of Basil-Ferrara-Florence, 1431–9 A.D.," Session 19.

22. "Council of Basil-Ferrara-Florence, 1431–9 A.D.," Session 19.

23. Kelly, *The Ecumenical Councils,* 108–13. The Lollards, who followed Wycliff's teachings, questioned the necessity of some sacraments as well as the traditional impediments restricting marriage. Jan Hus, the Czech reformer, echoes some of Wycliffe's beliefs but generally those pertaining to the moral and catechetical reform of the church. Hus's condemnation was thus suspect for a reform-minded council. See Duffey, *Saints and Sinners*, 171–72.

24. Hubert Jedin, *Ecumenical Councils of the Catholic Church: An Historical Outline* (New York: Herder and Herder, 1960), 179–86; and Madigan, *Medieval Christianity,* 245.

25. "General Council of Trent: Twenty-Fourth Session," canons 1 and 10, Papal Encyclicals Online, https://www.papalencyclicals.net/councils/trent/twenty-fourth-session.htm. See also Jaroslav Pelikan, *The Christian Tradition: A History of the Development of Doctrine*, 5 vols. (Chicago: University of Chicago Press, 1984), 4:290–95.

26. "General Council of Trent, Twenty-Fourth Session," "Decree on the Reformation of Marriage," chapter 1, Papal Encyclicals Online, https://www.papalencyclicals.net/councils/trent/twenty-fourth-session.htm.

27. Duffey, *Saints and Sinners,* 243.

28. Kelly, *The Ecumenical Councils,* 151–52; and Hitchcock, *History of the Catholic Church*, 329.

29. Benedict XIV, *Ubi primum* (December 3, 1740), https://www.papalencyclicals.net/ben14/b14ubipr.htm (hereafter cited as *UP*). For the writings of Benedict XIV, see at "Benedict XIV," The Vatican, https://www.vatican.va/content/benedictus-xiv/en.html. There are two later encyclicals with the same title.

30. Benedict XIV, *Nimiam licentiam* (May 18, 1743), https://www.papalencyclicals.net/ben14/b14nimia.htm (hereafter cited as *NL*).

31. Benedict XIV, *Apostolica constitutio* (June 26, 1749), https://www.papalencyclicals.net/ben14/b14apost.htm (hereafter cited as *AC*).

32. Duffey, *Saints and Sinners,* 243–44.

33. Thomas D. McGonigle and James F. Quigley, *A History of the Christian Tradition: From the Reformation to the Present* (Mahwah, NJ: Paulist Press, 1996), 86–87.

34. O'Collins and Farrugia, *Catholicism,* 312; and Hitchcock, *History of the Catholic Church,* 347.

35. Gregory XVI, *Mirari vos* (August 15, 1832), https://www.papalencyclicals.net/greg16/g16mirar.htm (hereafter cited as *MV*). For the writings of Gregory XVI in Italian, see "Gregory XVI," The Vatican, https://www.vatican.va/content/gregorius-xvi/en.html.

36. Gregory XVI, *Commissum divinitus* (May 17, 1835), 8–9, https://www.papalencyclicals.net/greg16/g16commi.htm. See also Gregory XVI, *Summo jugitar studio* (May 27, 1832), https://www.papalencyclicals.net/greg16/g16summo.htm; and Gregory XVI, *Quas vestro* (April 30, 1841), https://www.papalencyclicals.net/greg16/g16quasv.htm, where Gregory XVI likewise chastises Bavaria and Hungary for allowing mixed marriages without proper dispensation from the church.

37. González, *The Story of Christianity,* 401–5; and McGonigle and Quigley, *A History of the Christian Tradition,* 113.

38. Pius IX, *Qui pluribus* (November 9, 1846), 18, https://www.papalencyclicals.net/pius09/p9nostis.htm. For the writings of Pius IX in Italian and

Latin, see "Pius IX," The Vatican, https://www.vatican.va/content/pius-ix/en.html.

39. Duffy, *Saints and Sinners,* 295; and Pius IX, *Nostis et nobiscum* (December 8, 1849), 32–33, https://www.papalencyclicals.net/pius09/p9nostis.htm.

40. Hitchcock, *History of the Catholic Church,* 349; and Pius IX, *Quanta cura* (December 8, 1864), 4, https://www.papalencyclicals.net/pius09/p9quanta.htm; *Syllabus of Errors,* 65–74, https://www.papalencyclicals.net/pius09/p9syll.htm.

41. Duffey, *Saints and Sinners,* 311–12; and McGonigle and Quigley, *A History of the Christian Tradition,* 125–26.

42. González, *The Story of Christianity,* 405–8.

# 5

# Racial Memory and Catholic Family Teaching

JACOB M. KOHLHAAS

This chapter explores the origins of Catholic Family Teaching (CFT) with specific attention to how the classist, Eurocentric orientation of CFT's content and concerns in the late nineteenth and early twentieth centuries shaped and continue to shape CFT's subsequent development and reception. The chapter concludes by considering what a responsible reception of this tradition, one that both recognizes the impacts of its limited perspective and attempts to understand, elaborate, and account for the challenges and ongoing effects of this legacy, might look like in the contemporary period.

CFT and its parallel tradition, Catholic Social Teaching (CST), are commonly presented as having originated, respectively, from landmark documents of Pope Leo XIII, *Arcanum divinae sapientiae* of 1880 and *Rerum novarum* of 1891. Rather than occasional documents aimed at localized issues in particular times and places, as is typical of earlier papal interventions, both encyclicals proceed with a new sense of universal authority in which timeless Catholic truths are presented by the pope as necessary to redirect a changing (and often hostile) world. As such, each of these encyclicals established new trajectories and possibilities for the ongoing development of what would become their corresponding bodies of moral teaching.

While there are good reasons for presenting these documentary traditions in such a way, this emphasis can neglect aspects of the texts that are not repeated or overtly reaffirmed by the later tradition but nonetheless continue to exert influence in its development. Such forgetfulness is further exacerbated by the early documents' own tendencies to present their judgments as floating free of historical context or, in the infamous words of Pius XI "as from a watchtower," as if separate from and overlooking earthly reality.[1] Contemporary theologians no longer share the critical naivete of Leo XIII and Pius XI, but their presumptions still influence our readings. CFT's origins overlap historically with religiously justified practices of colonization and slavery as well as expressions of overtly xenophobic reasoning, despite the documents themselves remaining virtually oblivious to these realities.[2] The documents do not speak to everyone from nowhere; they support specific social agendas and exclude known human experiences.[3] Nonetheless, they have been decisive in setting the trajectories and possibilities of moral traditions that have realized significant achievements, often in spite of the continued influence of these foundational limitations.

Developmental possibilities are more limited in CFT relative to CST, as CFT has been more overtly understood as aligned with specific and unchanging anthropological and moral norms (particularly related to gender, sexuality, and the sacrament of marriage). And while CST prefers principles and social outcomes over support for any particular social, political, or economic system, CFT asserts the nuclear family based in heterosexual marriage and generally realized through biological offspring as the foundational structure through which the moral ends of the family are realizable. If and to what extent any particular family structure necessarily underlies actual functioning as an "authentic community of persons" is far less certain than magisterial texts have admitted.[4] Early in the tradition, this purportedly necessary family structure required the natural hierarchal complementarity of husband over wife.[5] But after *Gaudium et spes* introduced a more egalitarian vision of marriage, John Paul II connected the necessity of the gendered coupling of husband and wife not to hierarchy but instead to the anthropological realities of gendered persons as equal and yet complementary.[6]

Despite such changes, investigations into how this particular conception of the family was influenced by social context have been rejected or shielded from earnest consideration within the documentary tradition. Consequently, limited attention has been given to the countless persons, past and present, who have been excluded from access to this family structure or have found value in other familial arrangements. With exceptions only in the most recent documents, CFT has not generally received deviations from the structural norm of the family as theologically significant. Instead, structural diversities in family systems are treated as results of unfortunate circumstances, misguided ideological or moral deviation, or simply as affronts to magisterial authority itself. Under such guarded sensitivities, self-critical evaluation of the contextuality of CFT's foundational documents and the tradition's capacity for self-critique have been unfortunately fraught and limited relative to CST.

## HISTORY AND RESPONSIBILITY

When *Arcanum* and *Rerum novarum* were written in the late nineteenth century, the Catholic magisterium had not recanted the many affirmations it had made of the "doctrine of discovery" that continued to shape the geopolitical world. And despite Gregory XVI's condemnation of the transatlantic slave trade and the unjust means through which many of its passengers (reduced to cargo) had been enslaved, uncontested Catholic doctrine still affirmed the possibility of "just" enslavement.[7] Leo XIII avoided overtly recognizing this standing doctrine in his 1888 encyclical *In plurimis* celebrating the abolition of slavery in Brazil. Instead, he constructed a revisionary history of Catholicism's consistently humanizing influence on the historical institution.[8] Thus, given that almost exactly three years later CST's founding document, *Rerum novarum*, failed to mention slavery even as it affirmed the inherent dignity and spiritual freedom of all persons, a serious interpretive challenge ought to arise regarding how to understand its selective appropriation of Catholic history.[9] The interpretive tension is heightened in CFT, as its founding document, *Arcanum*, was written before either *Rerum novarum* or *In plurimis* such that its universal vision of Christian marriage was articulated even while slavery still remained legal in Brazil and Cuba.

Catholic nations in Europe had tolerated slavery well into the nineteenth century, while abolition in the Americas continued beyond midcentury. By 1880, many Catholic countries remained less than two generations removed from legal slaveholding. It should be startling that *Arcanum* laments the decline of marriage and family at a time when many persons of African descent in the Americas were only newly able to freely contract marriages and form families without fear of arbitrary separation by predominantly white Christian masters (although economic marginalization and social violence remained defining experiences). In contrast, Leo XIII writes confidently of declines in social morality, which he measures primarily by European reforms to divorce law. To complicate matters further, these reforms were in no small part an outgrowth of the ascendency of women's rights movements that had appropriated and made free use of abolitionist ideas and metaphors.[10] By centering concern selectively on European traditions of patriarchal marriage rather than the newfound freedoms of formerly enslaved populations or the ascendency of women's social rights, Leo XIII constructs a narrative of moral decline in the institution of marriage that would be repeated ad nauseam in subsequent documents of CFT.[11]

To construct the moral pinnacle from which marriage had supposedly fallen, Leo XIII borrows freely and anachronistically from his own sociohistorical context as measured narrowly by the white upper-class European milieu. His standards also reflect a fondness for legal norms that protect permanent patriarchal marriage, some of which had only recently been established in European law codes following revolutions earlier in the century. Leo XIII pines for a time before the French Revolution when, as Stephanie Coontz describes, "subordination was the way of the world, with citizens subject to kings, wives to husbands and slaves to masters."[12] Meanwhile, Leo XIII's vision of how to reinstate this order freely mixes older notions with more recent developments as fits his ideological aims.

European industrialization had recently reshaped economies such that gendered divisions of labor more neatly mapped onto a distinction of public and private spheres than would have been possible only decades earlier when economic production had relied more on shops, homes, and farms than factories. With economic production more distanced, the new Catholic vision of domestic life drew readily from Victorian-Romantic ideals of feminine virtue and thus claimed the "private sphere" as a uniquely feminine space. Out of a hierarchically gendered vision of the social order, new economic realities facilitated clearer ideological lines separating male/public spaces from female/private spaces. These spheres came complete with gendered virtues and masculine and feminine natures fitting to men's and women's

socially and personally complementary realms. Of course, this gendered lens was only a possible and in some ways exaggerated interpretation of the personal and social order, as the Industrial Revolution did not actually divide labor so neatly for many. Lower-class women and children, foreigners, immigrants, and persons of color, some of whom were owned as slaves, were instead exploited in any number of industrial, extractive, and agricultural settings throughout Europe and the Americas. The new familial ideal simply did not include everyone. It was based in experiences of white persons of European descent and rising ideals among the upper class and was embraced largely for its ability to sustain old hierarchies within a new social context, even at the cost of excluding large segments of the population.

From this particular social location, *Arcanum* assumes a two-generational nuclear family based on freely contracted and state-sanctioned sacramental marriage in which male headship is tied to wage earning, while women's roles are tied to submission, childcare, and domestic life. Subsequent popes repeat this framing in what Philomena Cullen describes as "a non-contextual given rather than a relatively new historical construction."[13] Remarkably, the original statement of this certainty comes eight years before Leo XIII praised Brazil's final move to abolish slavery such that it de facto excludes enslaved populations of which the pope was incontestably well-aware. Imagine hearing as a slave or former slave, at a time when the church has refused to speak authoritatively against your subjugation, Leo XIII's unquestioned assertion that, as regards marriage, the church "is the best guardian and defender of the human race" such that "her wisdom has come forth victorious from the lapse of years, from the assaults of men, and from the countless changes of public events."[14]

The fact that the foundational document of CFT shows little concern for the lived realities of people beyond Europe or of non-European descent is concerning. The problem is significantly exacerbated by the subsequent tradition of CFT reaffirming *Arcanum*'s priorities as absolute and unchangeable while often assuming a confrontational stance toward social change and diversities in family life. A fuller appreciation of the possibilities for growth and development in CFT may remain unreachable so long as its social and historical limitations continue to be uncritically recapitulated. The brief review below of Catholic complicity in the entangled realities of colonialism and slavery is an insufficient but initial step in remembering more fully and accurately the context from which CFT first developed to begin to inform more expansive future possibilities.

## Colonialism

The Catholic Church played a pivotal role in establishing norms and justifications for European conquest, as Catholic powers were deeply invested in discovery and colonization. The "doctrine of discovery" was articulated in papal teaching prior to Columbus's voyage to the New World.[15] Driven significantly by the interests of papal political power, this framework initially gave the Portuguese monarchy rights over land, resources, and peoples in claimed territories.[16] As the framework guided centuries of European colonial expansion, countless indigenous families were killed, displaced, forcibly removed, separated, or otherwise impacted; many still suffer from the legacies of this history. This generational family trauma was fueled by European political and economic interests, with which the Catholic Church was often aligned, as well as a widely held and unshakable commitment to European cultural and religious superiority.

Willie Jennings argues that Europeans came to associate themselves with the chosen people of God through the displacement of Israel in their theological imagination. Through the expanding global awareness of the colonial era, this theological centrality eventually migrated from religion to race, leaving whiteness as its primary moniker.[17] Jennings writes that "people would henceforth (and forever) carry their identities on their bodies, without remainder. From the beginning of the colonialist moment, being white placed one at the center of the symbolic and real reordering of space.

In a real sense, whiteness comes into being as a form of landscape with all its facilitating realities."[18] Catholic teaching still largely fails to disentangle religious and cultural differences shaped by the Eurocentric imagination.[19]

Eurocentric Christian perspectives blinded many to the inherent dignity of persons encountered in colonized lands. By the sixteenth century, Catholics openly debated whether the inhabitants of the New World were fully human.[20] Beyond dehumanization, both active and theoretical, R. L. Green argues that European colonizers identified the demonic in indigenous populations and convinced themselves of their duty to condemn and destroy indigenous practices and institutions, including traditional family systems.[21] As Pope Francis recently acknowledged in an apology to the indigenous communities of Canada that had suffered injustices and indignities through the operations of Catholic missionary boarding schools, "It is chilling to think of determined efforts to instil a sense of inferiority, to rob people of their cultural identity, to sever their roots, and to consider all the personal and social effects that this continues to entail: unresolved traumas that have become intergenerational traumas."[22]

## Slavery

While the doctrine of discovery afforded near-absolute rights to expanding European empires, their brutality and abuse were also condemned by several popes from the sixteenth century onward. Similarly, Catholic doctrine both justified slavery and established norms for enslavement. Papal interventions prohibited "unjust" enslavement and abusive practices while permitting slavery itself. For example, in 1537 Paul III in *Sublimis Deus* argued against the enslavement of Native Americans, but nine years later he clarified that the lawfully enslaved would find no recourse through appeals to the Catholic Church.[23]

Although traditional justifications for slavery continued to be recognized as legitimate, the institution of slavery changed dramatically in the early modern period. Slavery increasingly centered on skin color and reduced enslaved persons to property. Diana Hayes writes that "despite claims to the contrary, the church was instrumental in the spread of a new and vastly more horrific form of slavery to the New World and in the establishment of a racial caste system that haunts us to this day."[24] As with colonization, Christian practices of slavery often sought religious conversions while simultaneously reinforcing a race-based social order defended as providential.[25] Modern slavery came to require denying the tension between simultaneously recognizing the enslaved as property and as persons. David Cochran explains that "slavery depended on lies for its legitimacy, lies that were deeply woven into its social justification and practice, so deeply that many people, particularly those not slaves themselves, reflexively believed them to be true."[26]

Like colonial expansion, the transatlantic slave trade was fueled by violence that destroyed African lives, families, and communities. This could take the form of sexual assaults, as slaveholding offered "the possibility of unrestrained sexual access and control"[27] or robbing persons of intimate familial relations, including, as John T. Noonan notes, "the full range of conjugal companionship and protection" and "the right to educate their children";[28] or by limiting rights to individual growth, as Jennings describes: "Basic human rights, such as literacy among slaves[,] both grasped at their dignity as persons and upset the paternal social order, and hence carried significant punishments, including the sale of family members."[29]

As W. E. B. Dubois argued, the lasting effects of these oppressive hierarchies include the development of "double-consciousness" in which the self is viewed "through the eyes of others."[30] Ultimately this leads to a fractured, split self that cannot integrate self-perception with negative social perception. James Cone adds that racism has so blinded American society to the dignity of Black persons that the theological tradition has been almost entirely unable to recognize the symbols of violent injustice against Blacks as invoking "the terrible beauty of the cross."[31]

Even as the Western Hemisphere moved toward emancipation, many Catholics remained active participants in slavery.[32] In mid-nineteenth-century America, only radical Catholic reformers were openly abolitionist. To correct their opinions, Bishop John England of Charleston composed a multivolume argument explaining the validity of slavery within the Catholic tradition.[33] His contemporary, Bishop Auguste Martin of Louisiana, professed Black enslavement to be "the manifest will of God."[34] In 1866 after the American Civil War, the Vatican's Holy Office once again declared that slavery was not an offense to natural or divine law, though slave ownership is bound by certain moral parameters, including protecting the "life, virtue, or Catholic faith of the slave."[35]

In stark contrast to this history, *Arcanum* tells a triumphalist tale of Christianity recognizing the dignity of persons, marriages, and families as it rose through a hostile pagan culture. The Catholic Church's advocacy for the fundamental equality of marital partners (within a hierarchically gendered social ideal) and the freedom of individuals to marry across social class are held up as examples of Christianity's tireless efforts on behalf of marriage.[36] Ancient practices of slavery are mentioned, but the recent and ongoing phenomenon of modern slavery is not. Similarly, *In plurimus* spins a tale of Christianity's long opposition to the abuses of slavery and unwavering commitments to humanize and ultimately see the end of the practice. This is buttressed through the selective citation of authoritative papal texts aimed at regulating slavery and the slave trade.[37] Moreover, Leo XIII echoed a growing antislavery movement in Europe in characterizing slavery in his day as essentially a Muslim issue, going so far as to degrade the humanity of "Mohammedans and Ethiopians" as "very little superior to brute beasts."[38]

By the early 1890s, the alignment of this Islamophobic antislavery rhetoric and German imperialist ambitions provided a convenient pretext for military action in East Africa under the guise of punishing slave traders.[39] Hence, celebrating the liberation of slaves in Christian nations closely coincided with the xenophobic condemnation of East Africans and Muslims even before Catholicism disavowed the institution of slavery itself. The ease with which dehumanization shifted from one target to another in alignment with the interests of European wealth and power is itself a devastating critique of Leo XIII's already contestable claim that the church has worked tirelessly on behalf of the marginalized.

It is within these experiences of colonialism and slavery that the modern concept of race was constructed. Racialized thinking continues to be a primary conduit through which historical patterns of violence and inequality are reinvented in the contemporary world, as is evidenced by racialized health and educational outcomes, poverty, incarceration, family separations, and many other factors. Unfortunately, CFT has done little to come to terms with the Catholic tradition's own complicity in the situations it often characterizes as consequences of sin, immorality, and misguided ideology.

## MOVING FORWARD

In *Amoris laetitia*, Francis writes that "the lack of historical memory is a serious shortcoming in our society. A mentality that can only say, 'Then was then, now is now,' is ultimately immature. Knowing and judging past events is the only way to build a meaningful future. Memory is necessary for growth."[40] This is true, but how far is the Catholic Church willing to follow this lament with demonstrable action? Would a response include critically interrogating the past and creating possibilities for Catholic reception of this complex history? Or is it merely another lament about the growing distance between current social standards and the ideological commitments of an ecclesial tradition informed by its own shallow and convenient reading of the past?

Contemporary Catholicism continues to experience profound difficulty in coming to terms with both the realities and consequences of its influence in patterns of European dominance that have shaped the contemporary world. As late as 1912, Pius X explained the horrors exacted on indigenous communities by European Christian colonizers in South

America as at least partially owing to the local climate.[41] For its part, CFT has preferred to accept and repeat the declension narrative of *Arcanum* that anachronistically places a historical high point of ideal marriage somewhere in the recent past rather than recognizing Catholicism's complicity in making its own ideal vision of the family impossible for many. Entrapped by a historically naive rhetorical tradition, CFT often says little "about the realities of family life beyond a characteristically sickly sweet eulogizing about Christian marriage."[42]

Informed Catholics have a responsibility to receive history as fully and accurately as possible and now have the historical and theological tools to do so constructively. Rather than being scandalized by the recognition that all ideas, no matter how hallowed, originate in distinctive times and places, trusting more fully in the mystery of the Incarnation can reorient our theological trajectory. In the Incarnation, the presence of God is manifest in physical time and place, in a single human life of modest origins. As Copeland writes, "the incarnation, the concrete, powerful, paradoxical, even scandalous engagement of God in history, changes forever our perception and reception of one another."[43] Similarly, CFT is limited and historical, being wrought with bias and vested interests in setting particular cultures and experiences above others, and yet it holds the promise of something greater as a practice of continued theological reflection on the central importance of intimate human relationships. It is time for CFT to set aside ideological commitments to become unapologetically rooted in the incarnational grace of lived realities and diversities in human family experiences, both past and present.

## NOTES

1. Pius XI, *Casti connubii* (December 31, 1930), 3, https://www.vatican.va/content/pius-xi/en/encyclicals/documents/hf_p-xi_enc_19301231_casti-connubii.html.

2. Arthur de Gobineau's 1853 book *An Essay on the Inequality among Human Races* influenced racial

thought in both Europe and the Americas. Gobineau, a French Catholic, made use of the biblical curse of Ham as a theological justification for Africa inferiority. Aurélien Mokoko Gampiot, "African Responses: The Birth of African Christianities," in *Kimbanguism*, trans. Cécile Coquet-Mokoko (University Park, PA: Penn State University Press, 2017), 37.

3. From Leo XIII's perspective, he was not in fact addressing "the world" but rather "civilization," an idea linked to uniquely European understandings of bringing improvement in the form of culture, religion, and commerce to the wider world. See Daniel Laqua, "The Tensions of Internationalism: Transnational Anti-Slavery in the 1880s and 1890s," *International History Review* 33, no. 4 (December 2011): 713–14.

4. John Paul II, *Familiaris consortio* (November 22, 1981), 19, https://www.vatican.va/content/john-paul-ii/en/apost_exhortations/documents/hf_jp-ii_exh_19811122_familiaris-consortio.html.

5. Pius XI, *Casti connubii* (December 31, 1930), 27–29, https://www.vatican.va/content/pius-xi/en/encyclicals/documents/hf_p-xi_enc_19301231_casti-connubii.html.

6. John Paul II, *Familiaris consortio*, 18.

7. Gregory XVI, *In Supremo Apostolatus* (1839), https://www.papalencyclicals.net/greg16/g16sup.htm.

8. Leo XIII, *In plurimis* (May 5, 1888), https://www.vatican.va/content/leo-xiii/en/encyclicals/documents/hf_l-xiii_enc_05051888_in-plurimis.html. Leo XIII's personal opposition to slavery was made public shortly before legal abolition in Brazil through a published account of his meeting with Brazilian abolitionist Joaquim Nabuco. Leslie Bethell, "The Decline and Fall of Slavery in Brazil (1850—88)," in *Brazil: Essays on History and Politics* (London: University of London Press, 2018), 142n55. If Catholic doctrine was opposed to the institution of slavery, it is a wonder that Leo XIII's view would need clarification or that he would wait a decade into his papacy to make it.

9. M. Shawn Copeland, *Knowing Christ Crucified: The Witness of African American Religious Experience* (Maryknoll, NY: Orbis, 2018), 83. Chief among these may be Leo XIII's own writing and those who initially constructed the revisionist history it presents. See John Francis Maxwell, "The Correction to the Common Catholic Teaching Concerning Slavery by Pope Leo XIII," in *Change in Official Catholic Moral Teachings,* ed. Charles Curran (New York: Paulist Press, 2003), 77. Joel S. Panzer's influential book actively reinterprets, in line with Leo XIII, the Catholic moral condemnation of slavery much deeper into the past through selective historical evidence. See Joel S. Panzer, *The Popes and Slavery* (Uxbridge, UK: Alba House, 1996).

10. See Ute Gerhard and Valentine Meunier, "Civil Law and Gender in Nineteenth-Century Europe," *CLIO. Women, Gender, History*, no. 43 (2016): 250–75.

11. Among other limitations, the approach does not acknowledge the different experiences across class in relation to motivations for marriage. People of lower economic class benefited less from property and inheritance laws relative to the upper classes and could and did abandon spouses and families more easily. See, e.g., Beverly Schwartzberg, "'Lots of Them Did That': Desertion, Bigamy, and Marital Fluidity in Late-Nineteenth-Century America," *Journal of Social History* 37, no. 1 (Spring 2004): 573–600.

12. Stephanie Coontz, "Op-Ed: American History Is a Parade of Horrors—and also Heroes," *Los Angeles Times*, August 14, 2022, https://www.latimes.com/opinion/story/2022-08-14/stephanie-coontz-slavery-shame-american-history-abolition.

13. Philomena Cullen, "Social Justice and the Open Family," in *Catholic Social Justice*, ed. Philomena Cullen, Bernard Hoose, and Gerard Mannion, 210–14 (London: T&T Clarke, 2007).

14. Leo XIII, *Arcanum divinae sapientiae* (February 10, 1880), https://www.vatican.va/content/leo-xiii/en/encyclicals/documents/hf_l-xiii_enc_10021880_arcanum.html.

15. First clarified in *Romanus Pontifex* (1436), it was reiterated by *Dum diversas* and *Romanus Pontifex* in 1452, confirmed in 1456, renewed in 1481, extended to include Africa and the New World in 1493, and renewed again in 1514. Diana Hayes, "Reflections on Slavery," in *Change in Official Catholic Moral Teachings*, ed. Charles Curran (New York: Paulist Press, 2003), 67.

16. For a detailed treatment of this history, see Pius Onyemechi Adielle, *The Popes, the Catholic Church and the Transatlantic Enslavement of Black Africans, 1418–1839* (Hildesheim, Germany: Georg Olms Verlag, 2017).

17. Willie James Jennings, *The Christian Imagination: Theology and the Origins of Race* (New Haven, CT: Yale University Press, 2010), 34.

18. Jennings, *The Christian Imagination,* 59.

19. See, e.g., Emma Anderson, "'White' Martyrs and 'Red' Saints: The Ongoing Distortions of Hagiography on Historiography," *American Catholic Studies* 127, no. 3 (Fall 2016): 9–13.

20. Diego von Vacano, "Las Casas and the Birth of Race," *History of Political Thought* 33, no. 3 (Autumn 2012): 401. Las Casas's adversary Juan Ginés Sepúlveda "argued that the natives were *homunculi,* or sub-human creatures, [but] Las Casas proposed they were in fact members of the human race, of *linaje humano,* as he put it." Neither doubted the supremacy of European empires or believed that the indigenous Americans were fully equal to their European colonizers.

21. See R. L. Green, *Tropical Idolatry: A Theological History of Catholic Colonialism in the Pacific World, 1568–1700* (Lanham, MD: Lexington Books, 2018).

22. Francis, "*Udienza alle Deleganzioni dei Popoli Indigeni del Canada*" (January 4, 2022), 6, https://press.vatican.va/content/salastampa/it/bollettino/pubblico/2022/04/01/0232/00500.html#en.

23. Paul III, "*Moto proprio,* 1546," in Hayes, "Reflections on Slavery," 68.

24. Hayes, "Reflections on Slavery," 74.

25. Copeland, *Knowing Christ Crucified,* 11.

26. David Carroll Cochran, *Catholic Realism and the Abolition of War* (Maryknoll, NY: Orbis, 2014), 134.

27. Dorothy Roberts, "The Paradox of Silence and Display: Sexual Violation of Enslaved Women and Contemporary Contradictions in Black Female Sexuality," in *Beyond Slavery: Overcoming Its Religious and Sexual Legacies,* ed. Bernadette J. Brooten (New York: Palgrave Macmillan, 2010), 43.

28. John T. Noonan Jr., *A Church That Can and Cannot Change: The Development of Catholic Moral Teaching* (Notre Dame, IN: Notre Dame University Press, 2005), 122.

29. Jennings, *The Christian Imagination,* 240.

30. W. E. B. Dubois, *The Souls of Black Folks* (New York: Fawcett Publications, 1961), 16–17.

31. James Cone, *The Cross and the Lynching Tree* (Maryknoll, NY: Orbis, 2011), 37–38.

32. Copeland, *Knowing Christ Crucified,* 89.

33. England's legacy is complex. Despite his effort to theologically justify slavery, he was personally opposed to the institution, ministered to persons of African descent, and operated schools for free Blacks and mixed-race children while simultaneously seeking to protect the institution of the Catholic Church in a strongly proslavery state. See John F. Quinn, "'Three Cheers for the Abolitionist Pope!': American Reaction to Gregory XVI's Condemnation of the Slave Trade, 1840–1860," *Catholic Historical Review* 90, no. 1 (January, 2004): 67–93.

34. Auguste Martin, quoted in Copeland, *Knowing Christ Crucified,* 90.

35. Hayes, "Reflections on Slavery," 69.

36. See Leo XIII, *Arcanum,* 7, 14, 21.

37. Leo XIII, *In plurimus,* 15–17.

38. Leo XIII, *In plurimus,* 18.

39. Laqua, "The Tensions of Internationalism," 717.

40. Francis, *Amoris laetitia* (March 19, 2016), 193, https://www.vatican.va/content/dam/francesco/pdf/apost_exhortations/documents/papa-francesco_esortazione-ap_20160319_amoris-laetitia_en.pdf.

41. "The lust of lucre has done much to make the minds of men so barbarous. But something also is due to the nature of the climate and the situation of these regions. For, as these places are subjected to burning southern sun, which casts a languor into the veins and as it were, destroys the vigor of virtue, and as they are far removed from the habits of religion and the vigilance of the State, and in a measure even from civil society, it easily comes to pass that those who have not already come there with evil morals soon begin to be corrupted, and then, when all bonds of right and duty are broken, they fall away into all hateful vices." Pius X, *Lacrimabili statu* (June 7, 1912), 2, https://www.vatican.va/content/pius-x/en/encyclicals/documents/hf_p-x_enc_07061912_lacrimabili-statu.html.

42. Cullen, "Social Justice and the Open Family," 219.

43. Copeland, *Knowing Christ Crucified,* xxiv.

PART

II

# Commentaries
# and Interpretations

*Leo XIII*

# CHAPTER

# 6

## *Arcanum Divinae Sapientiae*

MICHAEL G. LAWLER AND TODD A. SALZMAN

## CONTEXT

Vincenzo Gioachino Pecci was elected Pope Leo XIII in 1878 during a very troubled time in Europe and the world. The French Revolution and the French defeats in the subsequent Napoleonic Wars yielded unstable French governments. The reigning government of the Third Republic (1870–1940) detested the Catholic Church as a last remnant of the hated ancien régime and passed many anti-Catholic laws, including a law granting divorce. Religious instruction was banned in school, priests and nuns were banned from teaching, civil marriage was mandatory, and church marriage was prohibited. At the same time, Germany, unified and made a powerful world force under the "Iron Chancellor" Otto von Bismarck, also closed Catholic schools and mandated that all education be in state schools. In Great Britain Queen Victoria's long reign was in full flower, and in 1876 the government crowned her empress of India as a royal symbol of the hugely expanding British Empire. France, Germany, and America also had colonial aspirations, and in 1871 following the defeat of France in the Franco-Prussian War, Germany annexed the French territories of Alsace and Lorraine and embarked on the annexation of various territories in East and South Africa.

France and Belgium were also colonizing in Africa, and America, after its civil war of 1861–1865, pushed toward the Pacific with its vision of "manifest destiny." In Italy the Risorgimento movement, led by Giuseppe Garibaldi, established the Kingdom of Italy in 1861 under King Victor Emmanuel, greatly reducing the area and power of the Papal States and enclosed Pope Pius IX in what is now the Vatican City state.

Behind this political change, the Industrial Revolution had transitioned work from homes to factories. This led to more prosperity for many workers but also fueled social unrest, the rise of socialism, and, with the publication of *The Communist Manifesto* by Karl Marx and Friedrich Engels in 1847, incipient communism. Even with the vast changes in the European and global social-political landscape, the coming horror of a world war in which eight million young men were needlessly slaughtered was still on the horizon.

From the outset of his papacy, Leo XIII sought to tackle the situation with which he was faced. This included improving relations between the papacy and the European states, which had been seriously damaged by both the French Revolution and the defensive posturing of his predecessor, Pius IX. These efforts to calm deteriorating church-state relations had little success. Leo XIII's first encyclical, *Inscrutabili Dei consilio* (1878), dealt with what he judged to be the evils of society. His second, *Quod apostolici muneris* (1878), dealt with the specific evils and dangers of socialism. A year later in a third encyclical, *Aeterni patris* (1879), Leo XIII offered the restoration of Christian philosophy as a way to deal with society's evils. In 1880, he issued *Arcanum divinae sapientiae*, in which he sought to combat what he saw as the evils of civil marriage and tout the superior goods of Catholic sacramental marriage.[1] Again, his success, especially in France, was very limited.

## COMMENTARY

The new French Third Republic, empowered in 1870, introduced legislation distinguishing the civil marriage contract from the sacrament of marriage. The government claimed jurisdiction over the contract of marriage and left jurisdiction over the sacrament of marriage to the church. In *Arcanum*, Leo XIII strenuously opposes such legislation. He notes that civil lawyers have introduced a distinction "by virtue of which they sever the matrimonial contract from the sacrament, with intent to hand over the contract to the power and will of the rulers of the State, while reserving questions concerning the sacrament of the Church." This separation, he declares, "cannot be approved, for certain it is that in Christian marriage the contract is inseparable from the sacrament" and that "the contract cannot be true and legitimate without being a sacrament as well" (*AD* 21).

In this assertion, Leo resolved an unresolved debate from the Council of Trent in the sixteenth century. The connection between the contract and sacrament had been discussed at Trent, but the council could not reach a resolution. Instead, Trent taught that "if anyone says that marriage is not one of the seven sacraments . . . let him be anathema."[2] Confronted with the same French situation, the Sacred Penitentiary during the papacy of Leo XIII's predecessor, Pius IX, taught that "there can be no marriage between the *faithful* without it

being at the same time a sacrament."[3] It went on to describe the projected nonsacramental French civil marriage as "nothing other than dirty and destructive concubinage."

Leo XIII's assertion in *Arcanum* was no simple application of existing tradition but instead was a significant development of doctrine that continues to guide theological understanding of marriage today. Following Leo XIII, the inseparability of contract and sacrament in marriage was enshrined in the first *Code of Canon Law* in 1917, which stated unequivocally that "Christ the Lord raised the *marriage contract between baptized persons to the dignity of sacrament*. Therefore, there cannot be a *valid marriage contract between baptized persons* without it being, by that very fact, a sacrament."[4] The revised 1983 *Code* repeats this assertion.[5] The difference between Trent's doctrinal language and the *Code's* legal language is significant. The former teaches that marriage is a sacrament, while the latter legislates that the marriage contract between baptized persons is a sacrament. The two claims are vastly different.

Jesuit Aimé Duval points out that Trent deliberately taught that marriage, not something like marriage between baptized persons, was a sacrament, because the council wished to leave the ongoing debate among the theologians open. "Canon 1 of the Council," he writes, "wishes to affirm the existence in the New Law of *a* sacrament of marriage, but not that marriage in the New Law is always a sacrament."[6] The 1917 *Code's* switch from marriage to marriage contract between baptized persons attempts to close this debate and so constitutes a doctrinal development, not simply an interpretation of Trent's theological teaching.

Leo XIII's insistence on the rightful authority of the Catholic Church in governing marriage is based in his confidence in the church as a trustworthy and faithful guide to human society. Leo XIII insists that no right-thinking person can fail to see how the church "is the best guardian and defender of the human race and how, withal, her wisdom has come forth victorious from the lapse of years, from the assaults of men, and from the countless changes of public events" (*AD* 15). Despite his confidence, Leo XIII's claim was as hard to critically defend in his day as it is in our own.[7] Leo XIII further declares that "it is easy to see at a glance the greatness of the evil which unhallowed [that is, civil] marriages have brought, and ever will bring, on the whole of human society." The teaching of the naturalists, who argue that marriage is a purely civil reality, is full of "falsehood and injustice" and is "the fertile source of much detriment and calamity" (*AD* 24).

Continuing, Leo XIII considers the purpose of marriage and provides a traditional answer. "Not only, in strict truth, was marriage instituted for the propagation of the human race, but also that the lives of husbands and wives might be made better and happier" (*AD* 26). This formulation gradually evolved theologically into the "procreative" and "unitive" ends of marriage in the next century. The first step in this evolution was an influential book published in 1892 by Cardinal Pietro Gasparri, professor of Canon Law at the Institut Catholique in Paris. Three notions in that book controlled every discussion of marriage in the church until the Second Vatican Council in the 1960s: first, marriage is a contract; second, the formal object of the contract is the permanent and exclusive right of each spouse to the use of the other's body for sexual intercourse; and third, marriage has two ends, a procreative end that is primary and a unitive end that is secondary. As the primary author, Gasparri included all three of these notions in the 1917 *Code of Canon Law*. The opening canon on marriage firmly locates it as a contract and affirms the identity of the contract and the sacrament of marriage (canon 1012). The next canon establishes that the "primary end of marriage is the procreation and nurture of children; its secondary end is mutual help and remedying of concupiscence" (canon 1013, 1). Marriage is a permanent society (canon 1082) whose primary end is procreation (canon 1013); it is an indissoluble contract (canon 1012 and canon 1013, 2) whose substance is the spouses' exchanged rights to their sexual acts (canon 1081, 2). Gasparri's legalistic approach led to a very impersonal definition of marriage that made it difficult to

grasp that marriage was in fact a loving union of two persons. Unsurprisingly, this approach would later be challenged.

Fifty years after *Arcanum*, Pope Pius XI's encyclical *Casti connubii*, his rebuttal of the Anglican Communion's approval of artificial contraception, insisted on everything in Gasparri's definition but, unpredictably, did even more.[8] Pius XI retrieved and gave a prominent place to a long-ignored teaching from the *Catechism of the Council of Trent* that marriage is a union of spousal love and intimacy. This retrieval oriented the Catholic view of marriage toward a more personalist definition. Marital love, which is proved by deeds, Pius XI teaches, "must have as its primary purpose that man and wife help each other day by day in forming and perfecting themselves in the interior life, so that through their partnership in life they may advance more and more in virtue, and above all that they grow in true love toward God and their neighbor" (*CC* 23). So important is this mutual spousal love, he continues, that "it can, in a very real sense, as the *Roman Catechism* teaches, be said to be the chief reason and purpose of marriage, if marriage be looked at not in the restricted sense as instituted for the proper conception and education of the child, but more widely as the blending of life as a whole and the mutual interchange and sharing thereof."[9]

In both *Casti connubii* and *Arcanum*, divorce is identified as a preeminent threat to marriage that jeopardizes its very foundation. As Leo XIII argues, "Many and glorious fruits were ever the product of marriage" but only "so long as it retained those gifts of holiness, unity, and indissolubility from which proceeded all its fertile and saving power." Marriage would always have brought forth those fruits had it remained "under the power and guardianship of the Church, the trustworthy preserver and protector of these gifts" (*AD* 27). Now, however, following the French Revolution, "there is a spreading wish to supplant natural and divine law by human law; and hence has begun a gradual extinction of that most excellent ideal of marriage ... even [to Leo's horror] in Christian marriage" (*AD* 27). History shows, he continues, that "divorces were sanctioned by law in that upheaval or, rather, conflagration in France, when society was wholly degraded by abandoning God" (*AD* 28). He fears that "it must needs follow that the eagerness for divorce, daily spreading by devious ways, will seize upon the minds of many like a virulent contagious disease, or like a flood of water bursting through every barrier" (*AD* 30). Leo XIII further complains that the number of divorces has increased among Protestants and "to such an extent in Germany, America, and elsewhere [France and England] that all wise thinkers deplored the boundless corruption of morals and judged the recklessness of the laws to be simply intolerable" (*AD* 30).

For Leo XIII, the evils of divorce are so great as to be beyond adequate description. "Matrimonial contracts are by it made variable; mutual kindness is weakened; deplorable inducements to unfaithfulness are supplied; harm is done to the education and training of children; occasion is afforded for the breaking up of homes" (*AD* 29). Perhaps above all, "the dignity of womanhood is lessened and brought low, and women run the risk of being deserted after having ministered to the pleasures of men." Nothing has the power of divorce to lay waste to families and to be "hostile to the prosperity of families and States" (*AD* 30).

Leo's judgment about the evils of divorce was occasioned by the marital situation in 1880, but in 2023 his worst fears have been realized. Marriage rates have declined, marriage is being replaced by cohabitation, marriage and parenthood are often decoupled, single-parent families have increased and are headed mostly by women, and the dignity of many divorced women has been seriously lessened by their consignment to poverty. Though he was speaking of his own time, Leo XIII's judgments proved him a prophet on this issue.

Leo XIII argues that the church "has deserved exceedingly well of all nations by her ever watchful care in guarding the sanctity and indissolubility of marriage" (*AD* 33). He offers as examples Pope Paul III's opposition to the designs of King Henry VIII of England and Pope Pius VII's resistance to Napoleon "at the height of his prosperity and the fullness of his power" (*AD* 34). The church deserves praise "for having, during the last hundred years [of the French Third Republic], openly denounced the wicked laws which have grievously offended on this particular subject, as well as having branded with anathema the baneful heresy obtaining among Protestants touching divorce and separation; also, for having in many ways condemned the habitual dissolution of marriage among the Greeks" (*AD* 33). Strangely, however, Leo XIII never cites what the New Testament says about divorce.

The Gospels report four sayings of Jesus about divorce and remarriage: Matthew 5:32 and 19:9, Mark 10:11–12, and Luke 16:18. Paul, whose writing predates the gospels, reports in 1 Corinthians 7:10–11 a prohibition of divorce and remarriage and attributes it to the Lord: "To the married I give charge, not I but the Lord, that a wife is not to be separated from her husband. If she is separated, she is to remain unmarried or is to be reconciled to her husband. And a husband is not to dismiss his wife" (1 Cor. 7:10–11). He then moves on to a question that must have been common in the early Christian communities, as it is still common in mission countries today, when one spouse is a Christian and the other is not. Paul has two pieces of advice, each hinging on the choice of the non-Christian partner. In the first case, "if any brother has a wife who is an unbeliever and she consents to live with him, he should not dismiss her. If any woman has a husband who is an unbeliever and he consents to live with her, she should not dismiss him" (1 Cor. 7:12–13). In such instances, Jesus's instruction stands firm: "what God has joined together, let not man put asunder" (Matt. 19:6).

The second piece of advice is completely different. "If the unbelieving partner desires to separate, let it be so. In such a case, the brother or sister is not bound. For God has called us to peace" (1 Cor. 7:15). In this case, the nonbeliever separates herself or himself; she or he is not dismissed by the believing spouse. However, there is no suggestion that the marriage of the believer and nonbeliever is invalid and no suggestion that Jesus's instruction does not apply to it. There is only the suggestion that in this case Paul is making an exception: "*I* say, not the Lord" (7:12). The reason he gives for the exception is that "God has called us to peace." Peace, it would seem, is a greater value in first-century Corinth than the preservation of a disrupted but valid marriage. Given the personal pain and family disruption still caused by civil divorce procedures today, does peace remain a greater value? The Catholic Church sanctioned this approach to dissolving a valid marriage between a Christian believer and a nonbeliever in the twelfth century, still sanctions it today, and names the process the Pauline Privilege.[10]

## INTERPRETATION

*Arcanum* emphasized an important Catholic doctrine: a marriage between Christian believers is a sacrament, the classical definition of which is "an outward sign of inward grace." Since the thirteenth century, the Catholic Church has held consistently to this sacramental principle: every finite reality is capable of signifying and revealing the presence and action of God called grace. God (grace) reaches men and women through finite reality; men and women reach God through finite reality when they believe the sign and actively seek God. To say that a marriage between Christians, then, is a sacrament is to say that it is a two-tiered reality. On an obvious finite tier, it reveals and celebrates the intimate communion of life and love shared by two spouses. On a more profound tier and through its finite tier, it reveals and celebrates the intimate communion of life and love between God and God's created people and between Christ and Christ's saved people, the church.

Leo XIII's vision of marriage in 1880 was a rather materialistic and biological one, almost simply a baby-making institution. After the horrors of World War I, European theologians were poised to change that, most influentially two Germans, Dietrich von Hildebrand and Herbert Doms. Von Hildebrand argued that the modern age is guilty of "a progressive blindness toward the nature and dignity of the spiritual person."[11] This blindness expresses itself in a dangerous biological materialism that considers humans merely more highly developed animals. "Human life is considered exclusively from a biological point of view and biological principles are the measure by which all human activities are judged." The existing canonical approach, with its insistence on rights over bodies and their sexual functions, was wide open to the charge of biological materialism. Summoning Pius XI and *Casti connubii* in his support, von Hildebrand argues that the primary end of marriage is spousal love and the building up of communion between the spouses.[12] Doms agreed with von Hildebrand that humans are specifically spiritual animals and are not to be judged according to animal biology. Human sexuality drives people to make a gift of not simply their bodies but also their very selves. Marital sexual intercourse is a powerful interpersonal action in which a man gives himself to a woman and a woman gives herself to a man and in which each accepts the gift of the other to signify and create marital communion. This marital intercourse is both the sign and the cause, that is, the sacrament, of spousal union, which Doms calls "the conjugal two-in-oneness[,] . . . a living reality and the immediate object of the marriage ceremony and their legal union."[13]

As has so often been the case in Catholic theological history, the Catholic hierarchy's immediate reaction to these new theological ideas was a blanket condemnation that made no effort to sift truth from error. In 1944, the Holy Office (now the Dicastery for the Doctrine of the Faith) condemned "the opinions of some more recent authors, who either deny that the primary end of marriage is the generation and nurture of children, or teach that the secondary ends are not essentially subordinate to the primary end, but are equally primary and independent."[14] Catholic teaching could not have been made any clearer. But the Second Vatican Council was only fifteen years away.

Before the council opened, its bishops were sent a preparatory document titled "Marriage, Family, Chastity," and the fate of that document helps explain contemporary developments in Catholic theology of marriage. The document had been prepared by a commission under the presidency of Cardinal Ottaviani, who explained that the document laid out the "objective order ... which God Himself willed in instituting marriage and Christ the Lord willed in raising it to the dignity of a sacrament. Only in this way can the modern errors that have spread everywhere be vanquished."[15] Among those modern errors were specified "those theories which subvert the right order of values and make the primary end of marriage inferior to the biological and personal values of the spouses, and proclaim that conjugal love itself is in the objective order the primary end."[16] In the face of these demands to consign the mutual love of the spouses to a secondary place, the council declared love to be of the very essence of Christian marriage.[17] Marriage, it declared, is a "communion of love" (GS 47), an "intimate partnership of conjugal life and love" (GS 48). The council further reinforced its opinion on the place of interpersonal love in marriage by teaching that marriage is founded on a "conjugal covenant of irrevocable personal consent" (GS 48). This formulation abandoned the legal word "contract" and replaced it with the interpersonal word "covenant," thus establishing marriage as primarily an interpersonal rather than a legal reality. This was emphasized in the declaration that spouses "mutually gift and accept one another" (GS 48), abandoning the biological notion that they gift merely the right to the use of one another's bodies for sexual intercourse.

The Second Vatican Council teaches that marriage and the marital love of spouses "are ordained for the procreation and education of children" (GS 48), but the commission that edited Gaudium et spes explained that "this does not suggest [a hierarchy of ends] in any way."[18] Marriage "is not instituted solely for procreation" (GS 50). The intense debate that took place in the Second Vatican Council makes it impossible to claim that the absence of a hierarchy of ends was the result of an oversight. It was the result of a hotly debated and deliberated choice of the Catholic Church in council. Every doubt is removed by the 1983 Code of Canon Law's explanation that "the matrimonial covenant, by which a man and a woman establish between themselves a partnership of the whole of life, is by its nature ordered to the good of the spouses and the procreation and education of children" (canon 1055, 1). There is no suggestion that either end is primary or secondary. The revised Code added that "this covenant between baptized persons has been raised by Christ the Lord to the dignity of a sacrament" (canon 1055, 2).

The development of the teaching of the Catholic Church about the sacrament of marriage has been a theological development of Leo XIII's Arcanum from a material, biological approach to an interpersonal approach. That theological development was initiated by Arcanum. "Not only," Leo XIII teaches, "was marriage instituted for the propagation of the human race, but also that the lives of husbands and wives might be made better and happier." This comes about in many ways, he adds, "by their lightening each other's burdens through mutual help; by constant and faithful love; by having all their possessions in common; and by the heavenly grace which flows from the sacrament" (AD 26). Sacramental marriage "has the power to strengthen union of heart in the parents; to secure the holy education of children; to temper the authority of the father by the example of divine authority; to render children obedient to their parents" (AD 26). Leo XIII did not add to those benefits of sacramental marriage that the sexual intercourse by which the spouses express and strengthen their two-in-oneness and, perhaps, procreate children is a good and grace-filled gift of God. This could have banished the cloud of negativity that has hung over the church's approach to sexuality since Saint Augustine, but it was still too early in history for such a positive approach to sex and its expression. That reappraisal came later with the Second Vatican Council and, surprisingly to many, Pope Paul VI.

Spousal love, Vatican II teaches, "is uniquely expressed and perfected through the [sexual] marital act. The [sexual] actions within marriage by which the couple are united intimately and chastely are noble and worthy ones.

Expressed in a manner which is truly human, these actions signify and promote that mutual self-giving by which the spouses enrich each other with a joyful and thankful will" (*GS* 49). There can no longer be any doubt: sexual intercourse in marriage is not sinful but instead is "noble and worthy." Saint Augustine had taught, after his own sexual excesses, that "conjugal sexual intercourse for the sake of offspring is not sinful. But sexual intercourse, even with one's spouse, to satisfy concupiscence is a venial sin."[19] That judgment clouded the Catholic approach to sexuality for fifteen hundred years until Vatican II cleared it away. Pope Paul VI, who was intimately involved in shaping *Gaudium et spes*, continued this positive approach.

In his encyclical *Humanae vitae*, the understanding of which has been greatly skewed by the focus on its banning of artificial birth control, Paul VI had very positive words to say about married love.[20] The mutual love of spouses "is above all fully human, a compound of sense and spirit[,] . . . an act of the free will whose trust is such that it is meant not only to survive the joys and sorrows of daily life, but also to grow, so that husband and wife become in a way one heart and one soul, and together attain their human fulfillment." In addition, spousal love is a "very special form of personal friendship in which husband and wife share everything," and it "is also faithful and exclusive of all other, and this until death." Finally, it "is fecund. It is not confined wholly to the loving interchange of husband and wife; it also contrives to go beyond this to bring new life into being" (*HV* 9).

Beginning tentatively with *Arcanum* and developing in Catholic theology through to the Second Vatican Council, a couple entering a legal contract of marriage say to one another "I love you and I give myself to you." A couple who will their marriage to be sacramental say that too, but they also say "I love you and give myself to you as Christ loves his Church and gives himself to it." From its beginning, Christian marriage is more than just a civil institution for procreation; it is more than just a legal contract with its rights and obligations. It is also grace, the presence of God, and, in this sense, a

sacrament. None of this happens automatically or because of a ceremonial "I do." It happens only when spouses mutually and equally live the deeds they mutually promised with their "I do." In twenty-first-century Christian marriages, Jesus's first-century words still apply: "Not everyone who says to me, 'Lord, Lord,' shall enter the kingdom of heaven, but he [and she] who does the will of my Father who is in heaven" (Matt. 7:21). As Pope Leo XIII promised in *Arcanum*, only in loving deeds are the lives of husbands and wives "made better and happier" in and through their marriage (*AD* 26).

## NOTES

1. Leo XIII, *Arcanum divinae sapientiae* (February 10, 1880), https://www.vatican.va/content/leo-xiii/en/encyclicals/documents/hf_l-xiii_enc_10021880_arcanum.html (hereafter cited as *AD*).

2. Henricus Denzinger and Adolfus Schoenmetzer, *Enchiridion Symbolorum Definitioneu, et Declarationeum de Rebus Fidei et Morum* (Roma: Herder, 1964), 1801 (emphasis added).

3. Sacred Penitentiary, "*De matrimonio civili,*" in *Enchiridion Symbolorum et Declarationem de Rebus Fidei et Morum*, ed. Henricus Denzinger and Adolphus Schoenmetzer (Fribourg: Herder, 1964), 2991 (emphasis added).

4. *Code of Canon Law* (1917), canon 1012, 2 (emphasis added).

5. *Code of Canon Law* (1917), canon 1055, 2.

6. Aimé Duval, "*Contrat et sacrament de marriage au Concile de Trente,*" *Maison Dieu* 127 (1976): 50.

7. See chapters 5 and 19 in this volume, which address the racial contexts of Leo XIII's thought and the global sex abuse crisis, respectively.

8. Pius XI, *Casti connubii* (December 31, 1930), https://www.google.com/search?q=casti+connubii&rlz=1C1GCEU_enUS912US912&oq=casti&aqs=chrome.0.69i59j46i67j69i57j69i59l2j69i60l3.1264j0j4&sourceid=chrome&ie=UTF-8 (hereafter cited as *CC*). See also chapter 9 in this volume.

9. Pius XI, *Casti connubii*, 24.

10. For detail on the Catholic Church's approach to divorce and remarriage, see Michael G. Lawler, *Marriage and the Catholic Church: Disputed Questions* (Collegeville, MN: Liturgical Press, 2002), 92–117.

11. Dietrich von Hildebrand, *Marriage* (London: Longmans, 1939), v.

12. Von Hildebrand, *Marriage*, vi and 4.

13. Heribert Doms, *The Meaning of Marriage* (London: Sheed and Ward, 1939), 94–95.

14. *Acta Apostolicae Sedis* 36 (1944): 103.

15. *Acta et Documenta Concilio Vaticano II Apparando*, Series II (Praeparatoria), Vol. 2, para. 3 (Roma: Typis Polyglottis Vaticanis, 1968), 937.

16. *Acta et Documenta Concilio Vaticano II Apparando*, Series II, 910n16 and 917n50.

17. Vatican II, *Gaudium et spes* (December 7, 1965), https://www.vatican.va/archive/hist_councils/ii_vatican_council/documents/vat-ii_const_19651207_gaudium-et-spes_en.html (hereafter cited as *GS*). See also chapter 12 in this volume.

18. Bernard Häring, "Fostering the Nobility of Marriage and the Family," in *Commentary on the Documents of Vatican II*, Vol. 5, ed. Herbert Vorgrimler (New York: Herder, 1969), 234.

19. Augustine, *De Bono Coniugali*, para. 6; *Patrologia Latina* 40, 377–78; *Contra Julianum Pelagianum* 2, 7, 20; and *Patrologia Latina* 44, 687.

20. Paul VI, *Humanae vitae* (July 26, 1968), https://www.vatican.va/content/paul-vi/en/encyclicals/documents/hf_p-vi_enc_25071968_humanae-vitae.html (hereafter cited as *HV*). See also chapter 13 in this volume.

# CHAPTER

# 7

## *Rerum Novarum*

RICHARD N. RWIZA

## CONTEXT

Leo XIII was born Vincenzo Gioachimo Pecci in Carpineto Romano on March 2, 1810. He was the sixth of seven sons of the Italian family of Count Lodovico Pecci and his wife, Anna Prosperi Buzi. In 1841 Vincenzo Pecci was appointed delegate of Perugia, where he stood out as a social and municipal reformer. In February 1843, he was assigned as nuncio in Brussels and consecrated bishop. Three years later he was named archbishop of Perugia, where he served for over three decades. Throughout his ministry, he witnessed the social impact of the Industrial Revolution including urbanization and promotion of the power of the common person. According to Joe Holland, "Pecci was a moderate who stood between 'zealot' and 'liberal' candidates though more inclined toward the liberal side."[1]

The larger response of the Catholic Church to the Industrial Revolution can be understood in the context of modern secularization. This is the process by which religion loses some or all of its social authority, power, and dominance. Social, economic, and political changes of this era transformed the role of the state, as the new society required new forms of government records regarding birth, marriage, employment, and death. Such a central role for the state replaced the central role of the nuclear and extended family in community networks. Moreover, many families were so poor that their only type of ownership was their children. In Perugia, Pecci committed his life to pastoral and intellectual work and eventually "earned . . . the name, 'the Father of Perugia.'"[2] Archbishop Pecci published a series of pastoral letters while indicating a traditionalist and even triumphalist trait. He nevertheless appealed for reconciliation between the Catholic Church and modern civilization, a distinctively positive approach for his time.

In 1877, Pope Pius IX appointed Pecci to the office of camerlengo, the Vatican's chief administrative position in the event of a pope's death. Pecci was elected pope the following year and took the name Leo XIII. As pope, he continued his distinctive diplomatic and pastoral orientation. According to Holland, "Leo shifted external societal-diplomatic policy to the offensive but kept internal ecclesiastical policy defensive to the offensive to impose strict theological uniformity."[3] This commitment to reform included a call to return to the foundations of Christian marriage, which had increasingly come under civil control since the French Revolution.[4] As Leo XIII notes in *Arcanum*, the church is called "to set in order whatever might have become deranged in human society, and restore whatever might have fallen into ruin."[5] Leo's concern for marriage and the family stretched from his early papacy (1880) through *Rerum novarum* (1891) to his late papacy, where the encyclical letter *Dum multa* (1902) contained his final words on marriage legislation, noting that the sanctity of marriage had been impeded in various ways. Family lifestyles are also affected when the divine character of marriage is radically challenged.

This spirit of restoration also motivated Leo XIII to consider the condition of the working class in *Rerum novarum*, a landmark encyclical now widely considered the proximate historical origin of Catholic Social Teaching (CST). Holland notes, "Appearing one hundred and thirty-one years after the industrial revolution, forty-three years after *The Communist Manifesto*, and thirteen years after Leo's own election to the papacy, this, his thirty-eighth encyclical, was the first significant papal statement on industrial capitalism."[6] *Rerum novarum* functions as a *magna carta* of the working class, as it petitions for the rights of the worker in line with personalistic ethics and a relational anthropology that avoids the opposite extremes of individualism and collectivism in the conception of the human person and the family.[7] A worker, being human, deserves dignity. He or she is not a commodity to be manipulated. *Rerum novarum* critiques the inhuman conditions experienced by workers and appeals to employers and the wealthy to respect the family, which is the germ of society. The right of family is the right of all persons to have their established family life recognized and respected.

The Industrial Revolution came with radical changes to power-driven machinery, but the transformation was carried out alongside poor working and living conditions. Families often suffered terrible exploitation and poverty.[8] Out of such conditions, even children started working in wage-based factory labor. Children and women were valued assets on family farms but were financial liabilities in urban systems. Due to this low value in urban settings, factory owners could employ women and children as cheap labor, often in hazardous conditions.

Leo XIII was aware of various issues being raised within Catholic social movements, specifically those having to do with associations and corporations, wages, and the legislative administration of the state. He also drew upon the work of the Fribourg Union, a German Catholic social action movement, and was encouraged to write by the bishops of England, Ireland, and the United States.[9] *Rerum novarum* predictably emphasizes issues affecting continental Europe with some wider realities, such as the Anglo-Saxon influence, also taken into consideration.

The drafters of *Rerum novarum* include Tommaso Maria Zigliara, Giovanni Antonazzi, and Matteo Liberatore. The latter was a key figure in the Thomistic revival and a specialist in clarification of principles of political economic thought and moral theology, which shed light on the understanding of private property and just wages.[10] The revival of the scholastic philosophy of Thomas Aquinas was rooted in Leo XIII's encyclical *Aeterni patris*.[11] Beyond its theological inspiration, *Rerum novarum* is also oriented toward more practical concerns and the ethical norms of everyday family life. It is in ordinary life where the reality of deprivation is commonly experienced.

The concentration of wealth in the hands of a few meant that poverty was so extreme that many families lacked the basic means to provide for themselves. These inhuman conditions were the normal plight of working persons and were played out within a series of transformed relationships. Labor settings had shifted to the new urban industrial context, many crafts people were replaced by machines, low-skilled workers were demanded to fulfill the increasing demands of production, new employer-employee relations affected and displaced family networks, and even the physical environment was transformed due to the utilization of hydrocarbon fuels, especially oil, coal, and natural gas. Factories emptied pollutants into streams and rivers, while direct emissions polluted the air. This contamination affected public health and spread diseases such as cholera and typhoid.

## COMMENTARY

In defending the rights of the poor, *Rerum novarum* begins by recognizing the present conditions of workers and calls for radical change. Leo XIII states, "That the spirit of revolutionary change, which has long been disturbing the nations of the world, should have passed beyond the sphere of politics and made its influence felt in the cognate sphere of practical economics is not surprising" (*RN* 1). A few paragraphs later, Leo XIII points out that public authorities were not protecting the rights of the poor: "In any case we clearly see, and on this there is general agreement, that some opportune remedy must be found quickly for the misery and wretchedness pressing so unjustly on the majority of the working class" (*RN* 3). This concern for the plight of the poor would become a characteristic mark of CST, ultimately articulated as the "preferential option for the poor."[12] *Rerum novarum* considered poverty with a new urgency and an eye to its social consequences.

> Public institutions and the laws set aside the ancient religion. Hence, by degrees it has come to pass that working men have been surrendered, isolated and helpless, to the hardheartedness of employers and the greed of unchecked competition. The mischief has been increased by rapacious usury, which, although more than once condemned by the Church, is nevertheless, under a different guise, but with like injustice, still practiced by covetous and grasping men. To this must be added that the hiring of labor and the conduct of trade are concentrated in the hands of comparatively few; so that a small number of very rich men have been able to lay upon the teeming masses of the laboring poor a yoke little better than that of slavery itself. (*RN* 3)

In response to the enormous gap between the rich and poor, public authorities are called upon to defend the rights of the poor.

## Moral Foundations

In view of biblical interpretation, Leo XIII believed that by applying gospel principles, the Catholic Church can help reconcile and unify classes. *Rerum novarum* notes, "It is the Church that insists, on the authority of the Gospel, upon those teachings whereby the conflict can be brought to an end, or rendered, at least, far less bitter" (*RN* 16). Leo XIII's earlier encyclical, *Providentissimus Deus,* had offered the initial formal authorization for the use of critical approaches to the study of scripture among Catholics.[13] *Providentissimus Deus* reviews the history of the study of the Bible from the Patristic period and proposes guidelines for biblical scholarship. It was a response to attacks against Catholicism and an appeal for doctrinal restoration.[14] There is a challenge to cultivate families that are rooted and founded in Christ. The call for restoration is also a promotion of Catholic education, in the context of the study of scholastic philosophy as encouraged in *Aeterni Patris.* Leo XIII makes use of this approach in *Rerum novarum* to address social questions.

*Rerum novarum* is further centered on the two fundamental principles of respect for human dignity and for the common good. These two values have structured CST documents ever since. Human dignity is the inherent value of a human person from which no one may detract and is grounded in the nature of human persons.[15] Human beings are unique since they are made in the image and likeness of God. The distinction is found in the capacity to reason by which humans rule themselves (*RN* 6–7). Both self-love and love of neighbor are implied in the preeminent principle of human dignity.

The highest common good is God, the transcendent good of all human beings. The common good is also the end of civil society. As Pope Leo XIII clarifies, "Neither must it be supposed that the solicitude of the Church is so preoccupied with the spiritual concerns of her children as to neglect their temporal and earthly interests" (*RN* 28). All persons have the right to participate in society. According to Chika Onyejiuwa, "the common good is a vision of what will make for our flourishing as God's creation; the individuals as well as the community."[16] Each member in the family has a responsibility to contribute to the common good. Onyejiuwa further explains, "We are all connected because we all participate in God's love. We derive our being from God because it is in God that we live and move and have our being (Acts 19:27)."[17]

Living in society is a natural good. In the community of citizens, all have the right to participate in society. As Leo XIII notes, "Civil society exists for the common good, and hence is concerned with the interests of all in general, albeit with individual interests also in their due place and degree. It is therefore called a public society, because by its agency, as Saint Thomas of Aquinas says, 'Men establish relations in common with one another in the setting up of a commonwealth'" (RN 51).

Grounded in this commitment to human dignity and the common good, values widely shared by those living in civil society, Leo XIII asserts the right of the Catholic Church to speak out on matters of social concern. This is in fact an exercise of the church's essential prophetic role. Leo XIII explains his obligation regarding this role: "It is We who are the chief guardian of religion and the chief dispenser of what pertains to the Church; and by keeping silence we would seem to neglect the duty incumbent on us" (RN 16). The Catholic hierarchy cannot remain silent when the very foundation of the domestic church—that is, the family—is affected. This role also realizes the missionary nature of the church in proclaiming the kingdom of God as already present but not yet fully realized.

### Central Themes

Rerum novarum considers private property a key dimension in tackling basic social issues triggered by the Industrial Revolution.[18] What is implied is that property rights confer authority over property such that the right to ownership also includes a dimension of accountability in assuming responsibility for that property. Rerum novarum rejects the socialistic view of abolition of private property, as such a conception undermines the ability of workers and their families to have security and conditions for patient saving and modest investment. Private property helps ensure

the good and stability of the family as a social unity, while public authority and civil laws have an obligation to defend and foster the rights of families (RN 13–14).

This view of private property is informed by Thomas Aquinas (RN 22). He argues that a person should possess external things not as one's own alone but instead for the community so that one is ready to share them with others in case of necessity.[19] Because the goods of nature belong equally to all, private property must serve the common good. Thus, private property ought to be safeguarded by sovereign power of the state and through the bulwark of its laws (RN 38, 47).

Rerum novarum appeals for employers to provide convenient working conditions to uphold the dignity of workers and allow workers to attend to their religious obligations. "The following duties bind the wealthy owner and the employer: not to look upon their work people as their bondsmen, but to respect in every man his dignity as a person ennobled by Christian character ... and that he be not led away to neglect his home and family, or to squander his earnings. Furthermore, the employer must never tax his work people beyond their strength or employ them in work unsuited to their sex and age" (RN 20). Leo XIII further condemns child labor because it interferes with the education and development of children (RN 42). This condemnation responds to the abuse and exploitation of children, often in forced or illegal activities, who were employed in industrial factories due to the need for a larger labor force.

Workers also deserve fair wages that are justly and reasonably considered in relation to the value of the work done. A fair wage is conceived as enough to support an adult male worker, his wife, and his family, with a little savings left over for improving the family's condition over time. This wage should be suitable to raise a family but may also be relatively fragile to prompt financial responsibility. Leo XIII explains that "wages ought not to be insufficient to support a frugal and well-behaved wage-earner" (RN 45). This view also takes into consideration individual circumstances to determine what a fair wage and reasonable working conditions look like. By today's standards, Leo XIII's fair wage is above most minimum wages and is best compared to relatively frugal calculation of what is now commonly called a "living wage" in the sense that it meets basic needs with a little left for saving. In many places in Africa even this standard remains out of reach for many people, who are left behind with little hope of catching up. This situation results in heightened risks of social tensions that affect many families.

Beyond securing their financial stability, the rights of families must also be defended. Each family needs privacy: a state in which one is not excessively observed or disturbed by other people. Leo XIII writes, "The contention, then, that the civil government should at its option intrude into and exercise intimate control over the family and the household is a great and pernicious error" (*RN* 14). Privacy further implies being secure in their persons and houses against unreasonable search and seizures. Public authority and laws should protect citizens but often goes too far when it comes to security issues. However, there are cases in which interference is justifiable to prevent harm to individuals or the common good, such as preventing child abuse and neglect. In acting on the legitimate concerns of the state, the dignity of the family ought to be respected.

### The Family

The impact of the Industrial Revolution was also felt in family life. Edward Schillebeeckx observed the home and economic life had become separated from each other and this division contributed to isolation in various families.[20] Today, the challenges of balancing professional lives, parenting, and maintaining a household still exist.[21] Many working parents look to a network of extended family for help in striking a balance with the competing demands of work and parenting. In Africa, traditional dimensions of community have been very helpful. However, such extended communitarian networks cannot replace parental responsibilities. Not only do authentic family relations

protect children from poverty and economic insecurity, they also provide greater noneconomic investments of parental time, attention, and emotional support. Leo XIII presumes that the proper context for healthy child development is within the nuclear family. Recently, Robert J. Batule has expressed the same conviction, that "children do best when raised by their own married mother and father."[22]

Throughout his writings, Leo XIII understands marriage itself as a sacrament that indicates an image of the mystical union of Christ with the church. Leo XIII states in *Arcanum* that "Christ our Lord raised marriage to the dignity of a sacrament; that to husband and wife, guarded and strengthened by heavenly grace which its merits gained them, He gave power to attain holiness in the married state" (*AD* 9). The unity of the body of Christ needs unity in the family, hence the need to defend and foster the rights of families (*RN* 21). This implies that the building up of the community of believers on a firm foundation requires a similar structure for the family. It also calls for mutual love, obedience, and forgiveness in the household (Eph. 5:21–32).

For Leo XIII, defending the rights of the family included strong criticism of civil marriage. Pope Leo XIII was displeased with legislation, such as that regarding civil marriage in both Peru and Ecuador, that removed the church from the marriage contract. Seven years after *Rerum novarum*, Leo XIII, in describing civil marriage in Peru, noted that "under the appearance of regulating the marriage of non-Catholics, it introduced[,] in effect, what is called a civil marriage, even though that law does not affect people of all conditions."[23] In this move, ecclesial authority is put aside despite Leo XIII's insistence that the Catholic Church is an ideal guardian of humankind that is needed for preserving the dignity and sanctity of marriage. Four years later, *Dum multa* again addressed civil marriage legislation.[24] Here, Leo XIII observed that "the sanctity of Christian marriage has been impeded in various ways" (*DM* 1).

Years earlier in *Arcanum*, Pope Leo XIII had pointed out the evils that flow from divorce.

"Matrimonial contracts are by it made variable; mutual kindness is weakened; deplorable inducements to unfaithfulness are supplied; harm is done to the education and training of children; occasion is offered for the breaking up of homes" (*AD* 29). The law of permanence in the marriage of Christians when fully accomplished is holy, indivisible, and perfect. It cannot be dissolved for any reason other than the death of either spouse despite the increasing legality of civil divorce. Civil authority retains its right to regulate civil effects; however, marriage itself is subject to the church's authority. Intrusions by civil governments can lead to great and pernicious mistakes, as the family has rights and duties unique to itself that are quite independent of the state. The institution of marriage preserves morality, promotes love of the spouse for the other, and strengthens families with divine grace.

Marriage is an indissoluble covenant (Mal. 2:13–16), since the couple's union is brought about by God (Matt. 19:3–9). Yet, there are situations where it is not possible for couples to abide together any longer. In response, Leo XIII states, "When, indeed, matters have come to such a pitch that it seems impossible for them to live together any longer, then the Church allows them to live apart, and strive at the same time to soften the evils of this separation, and never despair of doing so" (*AD* 41). In separation, married couples live apart but are still sacramentally married. Mercy can take the turn of assisting a neighbor in need even though that person has no right or claim of justice in that assistance. "The deterioration and breakdown of a long standing, committed and previously loving relationship in marriage is invariably traumatic."[25] Such experience often results in a sense of personal isolation and social alienation. Today, each local church must devise its own pastoral strategies of hospitality toward the separated, civilly divorced, or civilly divorced and remarried.

## INTERPRETATION

*Rerum novarum* is an effort to bring the church out of the basically combative approach expressed by earlier denunciations of modern social and technological developments and into a more positive and even transformative relationship with the world.[26] In doing so, it fulfills the role of the church in scrutinizing the signs of time through evaluating the social questions triggered by the Industrial Revolution. In this interpretation and response to the challenges affecting the family of God, the teaching of Saint Thomas Aquinas and natural law theory were the central means of social analysis. The main context was the terrible exploitation and poverty of European and North American workers at the end of the nineteenth century. Even the domestic church—that is, the family—was affected by the impact of industrialization.

One wonders what developments might have been made if we were better able to realistically see and understand the voice of the voiceless of our time, if, for example, the women struggling for justice had found consistent support in the social teaching of the church.[27] Pope Leo XIII saw the condition of the workers as the critical issue of his time. However, the interpretation taken was apparently oblivious to the unique plight of women workers. As a consequence of industrialization, a considerable number of women joined the workforce, often in order to assist their families. However, they were low-paid and subject to very poor working conditions. Leo XIII's focus on men as workers is crucial. Despite some indications of awareness of female laborers as well as child laborers, *Rerum novarum* mentions women primarily as wives to be sustained by the wages of their husbands and in the context of rearing children (*RN* 42). The preferential struggle of women especially in the so-called Third World continues to appeal for just wages, fair treatment, decent working conditions, and access to convenient social services.

The context of *Rerum novarum* clearly indicates that its concern was to examine the situation of the poor people and workers in industrialized European countries. This context did not consider the greater part of the world, Africa included. Nonetheless, the key principles dealing with the social question of the workers are still valid for contemporary Africa.

Social institutions must be judged on how well they promote integral development. This is the state of well-being, the condition of prosperity. Viewed in terms of an African vitalogy, Martin Nkemnkia observes that "the African being is not a being-in-oneself but a being-with-everyone."[28] Vitalogy refers to thought that defines itself with life experienced in a unified vision of all.

In scrutinizing the signs of the time, *Rerum novarum* appeals for the rights of working persons to organize and to legitimate the role of the government in the economy. Rwelamira states that in East Africa, "the lowest paid workers in society often suffer from a lack of bargaining power and become easy targets for exploitation by the employers in both public and private sector."[29] The employee deserves a just wage to be able to have a dignified human life. According to *Rerum novarum*, an employer's "great and principal duty is to give everyone what is just.... To defraud any one of wages that are his due is a great crime which cries to the avenging anger of Heaven" (*RN* 20).

*Rerum novarum* warned that "great care should be taken not to place [children] in workshops and factories until their bodies and minds are sufficiently developed" (*RN* 42). Today, hundreds of young girls and boys flock to African urban centers in search of job opportunities. "Children, who live on the streets of urban areas either because they have been abandoned by their families or have run away from home, have become a tragic issue in modern Africa."[30] Child labor forces children to become adults before their time. This is a barrier to genuine development of children, depriving them of their childhood. It is a dilemma experienced by a considerable number of poor families in the modern world.

Pope Leo XIII's historical encyclical *Rerum novarum* indicates the inauguration of the modern tradition of CST. The encyclical still has contemporary relevance directly for the economic and social conditions within Africa, yet at the same time its vision needs to be expanded to include greater concern for working women and children exploited through labor. These were limitations of the document

even in its original context and probably an implication of Leo XIII wanting to uphold marriage and the nuclear family as norms, which led to him perhaps unwittingly missing the voices of the voiceless. Hence, contemporary readers need to receive the document with both appreciation and a critical awareness. We need to take that oversight as a challenge even in our own time.

## NOTES

1. Joe Holland, *Modern Catholic Social Teaching: The Popes Confronts the Industrial Age, 1740–1958* (New York: Paulist Press, 2003), 112.

2. P. C. Thomas, *A Compact History of the Popes* (Mumbai: St. Paul's, 2009), 170.

3. Holland, *Modern Catholic Social Teaching*, 114.

4. Edward Schillebeeckx, *Marriage: Human Reality and Saving Mystery*, trans. N. D. Smith (London: Sheed & Ward, 1965), 376–77.

5. Leo XIII, *Arcanum divinae sapientiae* (February 10, 1880), https://www.vatican.va/content/leo-xiii/en/encyclicals/documents/hf_l-xiii_enc_10021880_arcanum.html (hereafter cited as *AD*). See also chapter 6 in this volume.

6. Holland, *Modern Catholic Social Teaching*, 143.

7. Richard Rwiza, "On the Social Question of Workers: Analysis of *Rerum Novarum* and Its Application to the Contemporary Situation of Africa," *African Christian Studies* 30, no. 1 (March 2014): 22–44.

8. Leo XIII, *Rerum novarum* (May 15, 1891), https://www.vatican.va/content/leo-xiii/en/encyclicals/documents/hf_l-xiii_enc_15051891_rerum-novarum.html (hereafter cited as *RN*).

9. Peter J. Henriot, et al., *Catholic Social Teaching: Our Best Kept Secret* (Maryknoll, NY: Orbis, 1990), 28.

10. Diego Alonso-Lashers, "Matteo Liberatore y la Rerum Novarum: La propiedad Privada y el salario; Entre la economia y el magisterio social de la Iglesia," *Gregorianum* 19, no. 4 (2010): 824–41.

11. Leo XIII, *Aeterni patris* (August 4, 1879), https://www.vatican.va/content/leo-xiii/en/encyclicals/documents/hf_l-xiii_enc_04081879_aeterni-patris.html.

12. See John Paul II, *Centesimus annus* (May 1, 1991) 11, 57, https://www.vatican.va/content

/john-paul-ii/en/encyclicals/documents/hf_jp-ii
_enc_01051991_centesimus-annus.html.

13. Leo XIII, *Providentissimus Deus* (November 18, 1893), https://www.vatican.va/content
/leo-xiii/en/encyclicals/documents/hf_l-xiii_enc
_18111893_providentissimus-deus.html.

14. Richard T. Murphy, "The Teaching of the Encyclical *Providentissimus Deus*," *Catholic Biblical Quarterly* 5, no. 2 (April 1943): 125–40.

15. Robert J. Batule, "Defending Marriage: How Faith and Reason Are of the Same Mind," *The Priest* (July 2010): 39.

16. Chika Onyejiuwa, "Common Good Advocacy against Systematic Marginalization in Africa," in *Catholic Social Teaching and Common Good in Africa*, ed. Marco Moerschbacher and Elias Opongo (Nairobi: Paulines Publications, 2021), 137.

17. Onyejiuwa, "Common Good Advocacy," 137.

18. Thomas A. Shannon, "*Rerum Novarum*," in *Modern Catholic Social Teaching*, ed. Kenneth R. Himes (Washington, DC: Georgetown University Press), 141.

19. Thomas Aquinas, *Summa Theologica*, 2–2, q. 66, art. 2.

20. Schillebeeckx, *Marriage*, xvi–xvii.

21. Jacob Kohlhaas, "Family Matters: How Church Teaching Demands Tidy, Unrealistic Gender Roles," *US Catholic* 84, no. 4 (April 2019): 23–25.

22. Batule, "Defending Marriage," 42.

23. Leo XIII, *Quam religiosa* (August 16, 1898), 2, https://www.vatican.va/content/leo-xiii
/en/encyclicals/documents/hf_l-xiii_enc_16081898
_quam-religiosa.html.

24. Leo XIII, *Dum multa* (December 24, 1902), https://www.vatican.va/content/leo-xiii/en/encycli
cals/documents/hf_l-xiii_enc_24121902_dum
-multa.html (hereafter cited as *DM*).

25. Laurenti Magesa, "*Amoris Laetitia* on Pastoral Accompaniment of the Divorced," *New People*, July–August 2016, 10.

26. Stephen J. Pope, "Rerum Novarum," in *The New Dictionary of Catholic Social Thought*, ed. Judith Dwyer (Collegeville, MN: Liturgical Press, 1994), 842.

27. Amata Miller, "Catholic Social Teaching: What Might Have Been If Women Were Not Invisible in a Patriarchal Society," *Journal for Peace and Justice Studies* 3, no. 2 (1991): 52.

28. Martin Nkemnkia, *African Vitalogy: A Step Forward in African Thinking* (Nairobi: Paulines Publications, 1999).

29. Juvenalis Baitu Rwelamira, *Wages in East Africa: A Critique in the Light of Catholic Social Teaching* (Nairobi: CUEA Press, 2007), 19.

30. Richard N. Rwiza, *Formation of Christian Conscience in Modern Africa* (Nairobi: CUEA Press, 2001), 15.

*Pius XI*

# CHAPTER

# 8

## Divini Illius Magistri

### ELLEN VAN STICHEL

## CONTEXT

Pius XI's 1929 encyclical *Divini illius magistri* is the most substantial modern magisterial document on education, at nearly three times the length of Vatican II's *Gravissiumum sane* (1965) and fifteen times that of Leo XIII's *Spectata fides* (1885). Like *Arcanum* and *Rerum novarum*, *Divini illius magistri* departs from the occasional and particular style of earlier papal writings to address the topic of Christian education broadly in terms of church, state, and family obligations.[1] Beyond marking a transition in its teaching style, *Divini illius magistri* also occupies an intermediary position between Catholic Social Teaching (CST) and Catholic Family Teaching (CFT). On the one hand, responsibility for education is under the direct purview of parental authority and as such is placed within CFT. On the other hand, Catholicism's long history with education has brought the church's efforts into substantial interaction with public authorities. As such, formal education tends to fall under the concerns of CST even while *Divini illius magistri* is not usually considered a key text (textbooks and manuals hardly ever refer to the document). Within the document itself, this institutional emphasis tends to overshadow the primacy of parents and families in education, which received greater recognition in documents of and following Vatican II. Placing the encyclical into the context of CFT may help to bring its content into clearer focus for academic study.

### Social Context

In 1929 when *Divini illius magistri* was published, the year also saw the *Conciliazione* between Mussolini and the Vatican via the Lateran Treaty, which established Vatican City and specified the civil rights and duties of both the Italian state and the Catholic Church.[2] These agreements clarified the temporal powers of the church but did not end the struggle over its moral and political power. The interests of both church and state converged on control of educational systems. As Richard Wolff observes, "one of the chief instruments for the perpetuation of a religious or political ideology is naturally that of education."[3] From 1922 to 1928, both Pius XI and Mussolini attempted to reconcile their interests (e.g., by making instruction of Catholic dogma compulsory for all state schools), but tensions rose between 1928 and 1931. Pius XI warned against the increasing fascist control of educational systems "not only in physical, but also in moral and spiritual matters,"[4] while Mussolini outlawed all youth organizations.

*Divini illius magistri* can be seen as Pius XI's strategic response to these larger cultural threats through the disputed area of education. While it was certainly not the first time that the papacy resisted the "state sponsored secularization of the education of the youth,"[5] to retain control over the education became a central focus during Pius XI's papacy as he faced the challenges of totalitarianism in its different forms. For example, the encyclical refers to the education of children in socialist schools as renewing "in a real and more terrible manner the slaughter of the Innocents."[6] In response, Pius XI sought to "restore the peace of Christ and its roots in justice.... [T]his was possible only if the Church were restored to its public position of authority as moral and spiritual guide, over the individual, the family, and the society."[7] Hence, the aim of the encyclical was a part of a larger interest embodied by Pius XI of a "Catholic 'reconquering' of Italian society."[8] Viewed in this larger cultural context, *Divini illius magistri* was one among many of Pius XI's encyclicals that denounced "the great errors of his age: the materialist heresies of 'totalitarianism ('statolatry') in *Non Abbiamo Bisogno*, of 1931, communism in *Divini Redemptoris*, 1937, and biological racialism in both *Mit brennender Sorge* [1937] ... and the unpublished encyclical, *Humani Generis Unitas* of 1938, while always ascribing the root and ultimate cause of these great evils to liberalism."[9]

### Theological Context

Theologically, *Divini illius magistri* is influenced by Leo XIII's documents *Arcanum divinae saptientiae* and *Rerum novarum* and, in turn, influenced Pius XI's subsequent encyclical on marriage, *Casti connubii*, published exactly one year later. In contrast to Leo XIII's fondness for Thomism, Pius XI relied much more heavily on Augustine. *Divini illius magistri* contains ten direct citations of Augustine compared to only two of Aquinas.[10] This preference is reflected in the encyclical's anthropology. Against any dualistic understanding, human beings are considered in their "natural and supernatural faculties" as a unity between

body and soul (*DIM* 58). As such, the primary subject of education is the sinful human being, both body and soul. While Christians are redeemed by Christ and "restored to the condition of adopted [child] of God," the "effects" of original sin still remain, the "inborn weakness of human nature" (*DIM* 66), "the weakness of man's fallen nature" (*DIM* 75). In response,

> disorderly inclinations then must be corrected, good tendencies encouraged and regulated from tender childhood, and above all the mind must be enlightened and the will strengthened by supernatural truth and by the means of grace, without which it is impossible to control evil impulses, impossible to attain the full and complete perfection of education intended by the Church, which Christ as endowed so richly with divine doctrine and with the Sacraments, the efficacious means of grace. (*DIM* 59)

The encyclical thus rejects any form of "pedagogic naturalism," as it denies or forgets original sin and the need for grace, "relying on the sole powers of human nature" (*DIM* 60). Methods that take the self-determination and freedom of children as their starting point are rejected, especially as they seek independence from Christian revelation and divine law through a universal moral code of education (cf. *DIM* 62). While claiming to "emancipate" the youth, these tendencies "make him the slave of his own blind pride and his disorderly affections" (*DIM* 63).[11]

The encyclical's ecclesiology in relation to civil authority exemplifies what Charles Curran called the "classicist worldview," in which reality is conceived as an "eternal and unchanging order" determined by God, the "rational Creator" and "designer of the universe."[12] Through natural law, human reason can gain insight into the reasonableness and rationality of the created order. This classicism manifests in *Divini illius magistri*'s tendency to strictly distinguish between the supranatural and natural orders. While civil society and the state take care of the natural ends and needs of human beings, the church focuses on the higher and sublime end of the human person, but these spheres of concern are not isolated. The primacy of the supranatural end means that a purely "naturalistic" worldview or secular society is unacceptable, as it eliminates the legitimacy and relevance of supranatural goods.

Rather than strictly separating church and state, faith and reason, à la French *laïcité*, which reduces faith merely to the private sphere, Pius XI both distinguishes and connects the natural and supranatural orders (*DIM* 11). Equipped with both divine revelation and certainty of the intrinsic rationality of the natural order, the church has an important role in guiding culture and secular society. The result is a "hierarchical complementarity" in which church and state occupy distinct spheres, yet secular authorities have no right to interfere in the church's judgment of the supranatural order while the church has a legitimate authority to articulate proper standards of education, both religious and secular.[13]

Throughout *Divini illius magistri*, the primacy and extent of the church's authority is asserted so firmly that the difference between cooperation among family, state, and church and the subjugation of family and state to the church becomes vanishingly small. To understand the document in context, the modern reader must read it through the exclusivist point of view of its ecclesiological context as well as its Augustinian anthropology that places no confidence in human abilities apart from redemptive grace.

## COMMENTARY

### *The Church's Role in Education*

Following Jesus Christ's care for children and young people (*DIM* 1), the encyclical is addressed to both educators and parents, with concerns born from a "solicitude" for all people to instruct with "clear and sound principles" that it observes as lacking in the conditions of its day (*DIM* 2). Its solicitude for this particular group originates from the more general questions societies face as they grow

more materially wealthy but do not necessarily become more happy. In other words, created for true happiness in God, humans are "destined for Him Who is infinite perfection" (*DIM* 6). "Amid the most exuberant material progress," Christians must realize "the insufficiency of earthly goods to produce true happiness either for the individual or for the nations" (*DIM* 6).

The political and social context of the Western world was an important factor urging the church to speak up about education. The increasing influence of secularization threatened the Catholic educational system, and as these trends were understood by the magisterium to be based in an erroneous anthropology, their spread implied the decay of the whole society. While Catholicism and other forms of Christianity start from a heteronomous and relational view on human beings (as created and sustained by God), secularism and atheism's focus on self-determination and autonomy makes them "fall back upon themselves, becoming attached exclusively to passing things of earth" (*DIM* 6). For education, this implies the false belief that it is possible to "draw education out of human nature itself and evolve it by its own unaided powers" (*DIM* 6).

A conflict exists between these worldviews regarding their opposite and irreconcilable perspectives on the last end (God or earthly life). Thus, there is also a conflict in regard to education, as this is understood to be irrevocably connected with an understanding of the human person's ultimate end. As Pius XI clarifies, ultimately education is oriented to preparing human beings to become and do on Earth those characteristics and behaviors suitable to "attain the sublime end" (*DIM* 7). Catholic education thus cooperates "with divine grace in forming the true and perfect Christian" (*DIM* 94). Not surprisingly, the whole document is a plea for not only the importance and need for but also the superiority of Catholic education. According to *Divini illius magistri*, Christian education aims at "securing the Supreme Good, that is God, for the souls of those who are being educated, and the maximum of well-being possible here below for human society" (*DIM* 8). Hence, it has a twofold aim, both supernatural (serving and honoring God) and natural (the well-being of individuals and societies).

The mission to educate belongs to the family, civil society, and the church. The family is crucial but is also an "imperfect society," as it "in itself does not have all the means for its own complete development" (*DIM* 12). Civil society, by contrast, is a perfect society, as it does have all the means to accomplish its particular end, namely "the temporal well-being of the community" (*DIM* 12). Similarly, the church is a society of a supernatural order and universal nature and so is also a perfect society, as it is fully equipped to attain its purpose aimed at the "eternal salvation of man" (*DIM* 13). Education properly belongs to all three societies, as it aims at both individual and social well-being considered "in the order of nature and the order of grace" (*DIM* 14).

However, education belongs "preeminently to the Church, by reason of a double title in the supernatural order, conferred exclusively upon her by God himself" (*DIM* 15): the first title is based on its explicit mission and "supreme authority to teach," bestowed on her by Jesus himself (Matt. 28:18–20; *DIM* 16). This divine blessing has endowed the church with "infallibility," which, quoting from Pius IX, *Divini illius magistri* describes as the "'pillar and ground of truth,'" to secure the deposit of faith granted to the church and to orient people to "purity of morals and integrity of life." (*DIM* 16). Second, by its "universal motherhood," the church helps souls through sacraments and doctrine (*DIM* 17). God made the church "sharer of the divine magisterium" and "granted her immunity from error" so that it has "inherent in herself an inviolable right to freedom in teaching" (*DIM* 18). Hence, the church has "an independent right" to education grounded in its supernatural authority that it can use to both direct religious education and provide civil education with appropriate principles for its proper mission.

Directing everything to the supreme end, all actions of human beings belong to both the natural and the supernatural order and "fall under [the church's] judgment and jurisdiction" (*DIM* 19). The Catholic Church is understood to possess "the whole moral truth," both that which human persons can know by natural reason and that which is divinely revealed. As such, it is quite evidently the Catholic Church's right to safeguard the education of Catholic children regardless of the civil authority they are under. This prerogative includes not only religious education but also all learning that in some way concerns morality and religion (*DIM* 23).

If one fears that this position threatens to abandon the legitimate autonomy of science, one can be relieved. The supernatural "does not destroy" the natural order "but [instead] elevates and perfects it," an interesting Thomistic interpretation of the relationship between nature and grace; faith and science are understood as complementary, as both ultimately come from God (*DIM* 28; see also *DIM* 55–56). Hence, the church does not oppose the arts and sciences; it fosters and promotes them (*DIM* 56). The church recognizes their "just freedom" (*DIM* 57) while taking "every precaution to prevent them from falling into error by opposition to divine doctrine or by overstepping their proper limits and thus invading and disturbing the domain of faith" (*DIM* 56).

Though all branches of learning are emphasized, moral education is central both because it is understood as the proper purview of the church and because morality is pervasive in all human affairs. Consequently, the church's role as moral guide can be considered an important contribution to society, as it can protect "children from the grave danger of all kinds of doctrinal and moral evil" and keep them "far away from the moral poison" (*DIM* 24). It belongs to the Catholic Church's universal mission to exercise its responsibility for education in every nation (*DIM* 25) and to the whole of humanity (*DIM* 39), for all human beings are "called to enter the kingdom of God and reach eternal salvation" (*DIM* 26) and "to practice the one true religion" (*DIM* 39).

### The Christian Family's Role in Education

Paragraphs 30–40 of *Divini illuis magistri* focus more specifically on the role of the family in education. Here, Pius XI argues, God has communicated to the family the principle of life (fecundity), the principle of education to life, and the principle of order (authority) (*DIM* 30). To educate one's offspring is thus an "inalienable right" of parenthood (*DIM* 32–33). This parental duty extends to both the spiritual and moral education of children as well as to training them for their "temporal well-being," thus including "physical and civic education" (*DIM* 34, 36).

Paragraphs 70–73 return again to the unique role of families in education. Here, the encyclical clarifies that the family is one of the "circumstances" or "environmental conditions" for an "effective and lasting" education, especially when the family's role in education takes place in a "well-ordered and well-disciplined Christian family" and is supported by good examples (*DIM* 71). As worldly affairs such as work take more time, energy, and general preparation, the encyclical points to the lack or absence of preparation by parents for the education of their children (*DIM* 73). Here, the church should not only make parents aware of their obligations but also offer concrete methods to assist them with this task (*DIM* 74). Parents are moreover requested to take up their authoritative role, given by God, and not become relaxed of "parental discipline which fails to check the growth of evil passions in the hearts of the younger generation" (*DIM* 74). Respect for authority is needed to provide both family and society with "order, tranquility and prosperity" (*DIM* 74).

### The State's Role in Education

The state also has a legitimate right to educate its citizens, "in virtue of the authority which it possesses to promote the common temporal welfare" (*DIM* 42), so that people can exercise their rights freely in "peace and security" and live in "spiritual and temporal prosperity" (*DIM* 43). The state should cooperate with the church and the family and not overrule their legitimate responsibilities over education (*DIM* 43). Rather, these various entities with their own unique interests should form "a perfect moral union" (*DIM* 77). The state should protect the rights of both church and family to educate (*DIM* 44) and encourage and assist them in doing so (*DIM* 46). Hence, the state needs to take "distributive justice" into account and not have any educational "monopoly" that forces people to use mere public schools (*DIM* 48). If necessary, the state also has an obligation to protect children when the family is unable to fulfill this role. At times, the state's obligation may even require taking children away from their family (*DIM* 44) or supplementing the work of education (*DIM* 46) when familial conditions are particularly challenging. For the common good to thrive, the state should ensure that all citizens "have the necessary knowledge of their civic and political duties, and . . . physical, intellectual and moral culture" (*DIM* 47). Military schools (*DIM* 49) and initiatives to provide "civic education" (*DIM* 50) also belong to the proper tasks of the state as long as their methods and teachings are not opposed to the rights and doctrine of the church.

As with the family, Pius XI pleads for a division of labor between church and state that amounts to a "well-ordered harmony" between these two powers with respect to their proper ends (*DIM* 52). This view opposes any strict separation of power as if civil society and the state are not subjected to divine law (*DIM* 53) or that the church does not equally care for and have a proper authority to guide good Christians in being good citizens (*DIM* 54).

### The Balance of Authority in Education

As both the content and structure of *Divini illius magistri* make clear, appropriate education in the modern world depends on a shared and balanced exercise of family, state, and church authority. At the same time, the balance of power in the partnership among these institutions is not equal. The church is both a partner with the family and the state and the proper authority that dictates the appropriate roles of family and state. In other words, parents look to the church for reminders and guidance in their legitimate role as educators, and civil authorities ought to listen to and respect the church as it dictates the appropriate boundaries between civil and ecclesial authority. The church itself looks to no one aside from the will of God as known through both natural and supernatural revelation. Natural reason is itself incomplete without understanding humanity's ultimate destiny in God; hence, the church is the ultimate interpreter of and authority over universally available knowledge. Consequently, Pius XI's articulations of the church's proper role in education is considerably more expansive than those sections on the family and the state, and when addressing specific educational issues, the church consistently maintains a position of authority.

For example, the question of sex education is presented as a matter of "purity of morals" and thus within the proper authority of ecclesial judgment (*DIM* 65–67). The encyclical critiques those who from a naturalistic point of view promote "a so-called sex-education" based in the assumption that youth can be supported ("forearmed") "against the dangers of sensuality by means purely natural" (*DIM* 65). Such a view may result in a "foolhardy initiation and precautionary instruction" for all without distinction, even in public and at an early age (*DIM* 65). Grounded in an Augustinian anthropology, the document counters that the "evil practices" in this matter are not so much the consequence of "ignorance of intellect" but rather of a "weakness of the will exposed to dangerous occasions" that is due to the "inborn weakness of human nature" (*DIM* 66). The state's authority to teach a secular form of sexual education is therefore rejected as based in an erroneous naturalism that inadequately accounts for the weakness of the human will as known through Christian revelation. Nonetheless, the encyclical admits that "some private instruction" is "necessary and opportune" but immediately clarifies who is properly able to offer this instruction: "those who hold from God the commission to teach and who have the grace of state" (*DIM* 67). Referring to *Antoniano*, *Divini illius magistri* offers precautions that should be considered, namely that one should be "well on his guard" and not go into that which might stir the "heart of the child for sin, rather than extinguishing this fire" (*DIM* 67).

Likewise, coeducation is deemed unacceptable, and the naturalist plea for it is again deemed a "denial of original sin" (*DIM* 68). "The Creator has ordained and disposed perfect union of the sexes only in matrimony, and, with varying degrees of contact, in the family and society" (*DIM* 68). The document further argues that there is nothing "in nature itself" that suggests "there ought to be promiscuity and much less equality" between the sexes (*DIM* 68). The document then uses the naturalist argument against itself, claiming that as human nature shows, the natural difference in terms of "organism, temperament, abilities" between the sexes demonstrates that their educations should not be equal (*DIM* 68). As both sexes "are destined in keeping with the wonderful designs of the Creator to complement each other in the family and in society," it is only reasonable to have separate education so as to form them in a way that "maintains and encourages" these differences "with the necessary distinction and corresponding separation, according to age and circumstances" (*DIM* 68). Especially during adolescence, these principles should be applied in schools. Moreover, special care and prudence should be given to "Christian modesty in young women and girls in gymnastic exercises and deportment," which ought to be conducted away from public view (*DIM* 68).

Special attention should also be given to the education of adolescent youths, who—quoting Horatius—are "soft as wax to be moulded into vice" (*DIM* 89). Old and new means of communication can easily affect their moral purity. Thus, educators must be vigilant to the potential influence of "immoral books," cinema, radio, and theater (*DIM* 90). However, this is a plea not to remove Christian youths from society completely but instead to make them resilient toward the "errors of the world" (*DIM* 92). For example, reading proponents of "false doctrine" can be necessary in order to refute them, and young people need only have enough "antidote of sound doctrine" to grasp the falsity (*DIM* 86). The goal is to perfect and develop the natural faculties "by coordinating them with the supernatural" (*DIM* 97–98).

Divini Illius Magistri | 83

The encyclical also addresses "so-called 'neutral' or 'lay' schools, from which religion is excluded," which it judges "as contrary to the fundamental principles of education" (*DIM* 79). Catholic children are not allowed to attend non-Catholic schools open to Catholics and non-Catholics alike. Neither are mixed schools acceptable in which children follow the same courses but are provided with separate religious instruction (*DIM* 79). The reason for this is that "the mere fact that a school gives some religious instruction ... does not bring it into accord with the rights of the Church and the Christian family" (*DIM* 80). Suitable Catholic schools require that the whole organization, including the teachers and the textbooks in all subjects, be "regulated by the Christian spirit, under the direction and maternal supervision of the Church," so that instruction in every subject may be "permeated by Christian piety" (*DIM* 80).

The multiple religions and worldviews of a plural society do not create a sufficient excuse for excluding specifically Catholic education; rather, the state must "leave free scope to the initiative of the Church and the family" to facilitate distinctly Catholic education, even giving assistance to realize this necessity (*DIM* 81). For their part, Catholics have a responsibility to organize Catholic education wherever they are. This is truly an "important task of Catholic Action" (*DIM* 84) rather than a matter of "mixing in party politics," as it constitutes "a religious enterprise demanded by conscience" (*DIM* 85).

## INTERPRETATION

From a profoundly changed cultural context and with a renewed ecclesiological vision brought about by Vatican II and the diversity and complexity of contemporary theological anthropologies, the teachings of *Divini illius magistri* can easily be read as simply naive and hostile to social progress. However, the content of this encyclical is still instructive not only for those who want to understand the development of CFT but also for interpreting elements of contemporary Catholicism.

Although the passages on coeducation from *Divini illius magistri* may sound strange today, they are in line with social arguments of the time. Pius XI adopted elements of the rhetoric used within the public debate that had raged since the mid-nineteenth century.[14] This was spurred by the gradual introduction of coeducation in Europe but mainly in the United States. In the early nineteenth century coeducation, especially at the secondary level, remained a sensitive topic. The importance of secondary education and access to education for girls had become accepted as a general principle, but the next step was answering whether girls should be taught the same curriculum and in the same classrooms. From the 1870s–1880s, several secular European women's movements fought for this opportunity; however, the opposition proved more influential, especially regarding secondary schools. Opposition to coeducation was not particular to the Catholic Church and was more widely shared and often based on similar arguments. The only difference particular to Catholics was that the church offered no room for discussion or dissenting voices as was possible among the other interlocutors.

Quite apart from the political argument that coeducational proposals came from progressives, such as the freemasons and socialists,[15] the Catholic hierarchy feared moral decay in schools, as original sin would surely make young people unable to resist the temptations of human nature. Already at the beginning of the twentieth century, the clergy had argued that coeducation would lead to a feminization of the boys and a masculinization of the girls,[16] thus canceling natural differences to the detriment of both or, even worse, that "the stronger will corrupt the weaker,"[17] a fear that the Catholic hierarchy clearly still held at the time of Pius XI. Finally, there was an ongoing debate about the difference in intelligence between girls and boys. Some claimed—sometimes referring to Charles Darwin—that the sexes naturally have different mental powers, with those of girls being comparatively weaker.[18] The nurture-nature debate was also brought to the table by the observation that intellectual differences could be due to differences in education.

The question of suitable curricula also arose. Given their "natural" differences and complementarity, do not both sexes need curricula independently adapted to their intelligence, subsequent roles, or both in society (cf. *DIM* 68)? From this perspective, girls would be better prepared for their future (i.e., as mothers and housewives) by developing specific skills and knowledge and do not need the rational, abstract, and scientific knowledge offered to boys. As Pius XI firmly upheld the magisterium's conservative view on the public role of girls and women on the one hand and an Augustinian anthropology on the other, that he criticized coeducation in 1929 should come as no surprise.

The encyclical's claim that science and art should be under the direct moral and religious authority of the church is also striking from today's perspective. While the pope affirms the "just freedom" of the sciences, this "freedom" is rather limited, as scientific findings cannot be taught when they contradict the teachings of the church (*DIM* 56–57). Despite supporting "just liberty," this position actually denies the legitimate autonomy of secular knowledge from Catholic authority and was not corrected until *Gaudium et spes* (1965).

Reading the document retrospectively also reveals several blind spots. First, as the encyclical focuses on defending the legitimate role and right of the church in education, it missed out on the broader societal discussion of the need for schooling the masses (what socialism was indeed pleading for). Rather, Pius XI does not explicitly contradict and may have assumed the commonly held idea that education was and should remain something for the privileged. Second, the document is blind to global diversities (unsurprisingly, as only since Vatican II has CST gradually become more global). Exemplary of this Eurocentrism is the reference to the importance of learning Latin and the classics, which assumes European culture is the sum total of the culture that secularization risks to forget or ignore (*DIM* 87). Third, the document clearly starts from a patriarchal model of the family whereby children—following and quoting from Saint Thomas Aquinas (*DIM* 33)—are seen as an extension of the person of the father and under his authority, without mention of the mother.[19] Finally, the triumphalism embraced by this document fails to acknowledge the ongoing abuses of its time in the name of Catholic education. Certainly, Catholic education succeeded in serving many students well, but at the same time, many were also sacrificed to the educational system and were hurt or even broken through all kinds of abuses ranging from psychological to sexual. As the focus of the pope was more on the moral role and societal influence of the church through education, *Divini illius magistri* fails to recognize the systemic malfunctions of the church's own educational endeavors, thereby neglecting concern for the most vulnerable.

## NOTES

1. *Divini illius magistri* is also referred to as *Rappresentanti in terra*, the words from its opening line in Latin. See Joe Holland, *Modern Catholic Social Teaching: The Popes Confronts the Industrial Age, 1740–1958* (Mahwah, NJ: Paulist Press, 2003), 250.

2. See Jan Nelis, "The Clerical Response to a Totalitarian Political Religion: La Civiltà Cattolica and Italian Fascism," *Journal of Contemporary History* 46, no. 2 (2011): 245–70.

3. Richard J. Wolff, "Catholicism, Fascism and Italian Education from the *Riforma Gentile* to the *Carta Della Scuola*, 1922–1939," *History of Education Quarterly* 20, no. 1 (Spring 1980): 4.

4. Wolff, "Catholicism, Fascism and Italian Education," 4, quoting from Pius XI's speech before the Rome Diocesan Committee of Catholic Action in March of 1928.

5. Holland, *Modern Catholic Social Teaching*, 250.

6. Pius XI, *Divini illius magistri* (December 31, 1929), 73, https://www.vatican.va/content/pius-xi/en/encyclicals/documents/hf_p-xi_enc_31121929_divini-illius-magistri.html (hereafter cited as *DIM*).

7. Holland, *Modern Catholic Social Teaching*, 246.

8. Nelis, "The Clerical Response," 256.

9. John Pollard, *The Papacy in the Age of Totalitarianism, 1914–1948* (Oxford: Oxford University Press, 2014), 161–62.

10. See Jacob M. Kohlhaas, *Beyond Biology: Rethinking Parenthood in the Catholic Tradition* (Washington, DC: Georgetown University Press, 2021), 16.

11. Note the noninclusive language used when referring to the child (in 33, quoting from Thomas Aquinas, and 63), the teacher (in 57), and "man" as in "mankind" and so humankind (in 58). Considering the context and content of the documents, with a discussion on coeducation and female education, one might wonder whether this is deliberate. However, the male pronouns "him"/"his" are only mentioned a few times, and the document prefers "child" and "pupil" instead of using masculine language.

12. Charles E. Curran, *Catholic Social Teaching, 1891–Present: A Historical, Theological and Ethical Analysis* (Washington, DC: Georgetown University Press, 2002), 54.

13. Holland, *Modern Catholic Social Teaching*, 122.

14. Reality was often at odds with this rhetoric, as there were mixed schools in supposedly Catholic countries such as Belgium, France, Ireland, Italy, and Austria. Often these were public schools, but for demographic, geographical, or economic reasons they included some Catholic schools with a rural-urban discrepancy. For details and comprehensive analysis as well as the complete context analysis of the debate on coeducation, see James C. Albisetti, "Catholics and Coeducation: Rhetoric and Reality in Europe before *Divini Illius Magistri*," *Paedagogica Historica* 35, no. 3 (1999): 666–96.

15. See. James C. Albisetti, "Another 'Curious Incident of the Dog in the Night-Time'? Intelligence Testing and Coeducation," *History of Education Quarterly* 44, no. 2 (Summer 2004), 183–201; and James Bowen, "Towards an Assessment of Educational Theory: An Historical Perspective," *International Review of Education/Internationale Zeitschrift für Erziehungswissenschaft/Revue Internationale de l'Education* 25, nos. 2–3 (June 1979): 303–23.

16. See Albisetti, "Catholics and Coeducation," 676.

17. Francis Xavier Godts, *Erreurs et crimes en fait d'éducation: Le féminisme condamné par les principes de la théologie et de philosophie* (Roulers, 1903, 246), as quoted in Albisetti, "Catholics and Coeducation," 676.

18. For a very interesting overview of this debate, see Albisetti, "Another 'Curious Incident,'" 189–93. He also describes the paradigm shift, recognizing that female intelligence is not weaker, resulting in similar curricula but not coeducation.

19. Holland, *Modern Catholic Social Teaching*, 256.

# CHAPTER

# 9

## *Casti Connubii*

JASON KING

## CONTEXT

Reflections on *Casti connubii* often depict it as a response to the 1930 Lambeth Conference of the Anglican Communion that allowed the use of contraception for married couples despite the 1920 assembly's earlier resolution rejecting contraception.[1] While *Casti connubii* was promulgated on December 31, 1930, after the Lambeth Conference this framing of the encyclical's purpose is too narrow.[2]

Europe, the primary audience assumed by the Catholic Church at the time, was going through massive changes. World War I caused devastation across the continent, and the recovery in the 1920s was less a restoration and more an emergence of new realities. Driven by advances in mass production, jobs and consumer goods proliferated. More and more people moved from the countryside to the city for factory work. Movies and radio influenced large swaths of society. Automobiles and telephones became more ubiquitous. New art, fashion, and music emerged. In the United States, it was the age of the flapper and jazz, and the Harlem Renaissance spanned the decade.

Social norms were shifting too. Women took factory jobs in the city. They found a degree of freedom with their own income and gained strength in their push for social change. In the United States, women gained the right to vote. Homosexuality had a greater degree of tolerance in New York, and gay bars flourished in Germany before the rise of the Third Reich. These changes were not always welcomed. Nationalism was on the rise in Europe. Membership in the Ku Klux Klan peaked in the United States in the middle of the decade, and Prohibition was the law throughout the 1920s. In late 1929 the economy started to soften, and by the end of October the stock market had crashed. By 1930, the Great Depression had started.

When Pius XI wrote *Casti connubii*, he had more on his mind than the Anglican Communion's statement on contraception. He saw around him a society in trouble. Pius XI's concern was to address these forces and this situation, hoping to bring order to a world in chaos, an order that reflected God's designs. It should not be surprising, then, that his social encyclical *Quadragesimo anno*, issued in 1931 on the fortieth anniversary of *Rerum novarum*, was titled "On the Reconstruction of the Social Order." In it, he would discuss the problems of the modern economy and proposed new kinds of institutions for a better society, developing ideas of solidarity, subsidiarity, social justice, and private property. *Casti connubii* should be read within this broad concern of restoring society and as such part of the Catholic social tradition. Pius XI saw marriage as a social institution that contributed to the good of society and so argued that the state should support it politically and economically. He advocated for a living wage, housing, employment, and medical care for families. Without such support, marriage would weaken and so would the rest of society. The urgency, then, was to strengthen marriage, and the means for doing so was for countries to support God's design for marriage.

Despite these social concerns, Pius XI's understanding of marriage was moored in his social context. He claimed to preach the divine will on the proper ordering of society and marriage but often offered institutional and social configurations that reflected only his particular time and place. In attempting to preserve the primacy of the Catholic Church in Europe, for example, Pius XI negotiated several concordats with European countries, including ones with Nazi Germany and fascist Italy. While later he would come to see significant problems with these regimes, even drafting an encyclical condemning their racism,[3] he still held to the idea that the divine order required the state to be guided by the teachings of the Catholic Church. His vision of marriage and family suffered similar problems, such as when he claimed that women's equality was "not an emancipation but a crime" (*CC* 74) and that women's subordination was part of God's design (*CC* 28).[4]

Thus, *Casti connubii* is an encyclical in tension with itself. On the one hand, it is driven by the gospel imperative to love all people. It responds to the significant changes in social relationships, politics, and economics and wants to offer constructive ways forward that will build up the common good and a good order. On the other hand, it offers solutions that are more reflective of upper-class European values of the early twentieth century than God's wisdom. These two dynamics provide a better hermeneutics for understanding the encyclical than simply as an argument over contraception.

## COMMENTARY

*Casti connubii*'s focus on rebuilding the divine institution of marriage is part of Pius XI's overarching concern for rebuilding society. He addresses the encyclical to church leaders—patriarchs, bishops, local ordinaries—who have primary responsibility for restoring "the original purity of [marriage's] divine institution" (*CC* 1). He then emphasizes the importance of restoring marriage, as it is "the principle and foundation of domestic society and therefore of all human intercourse" (*CC* 1). To direct church leaders on what should be done, Pius XI organizes the encyclical into three sections. First, he sets out "the nature and dignity of Christian marriage." Next, he identifies the problems facing marriage at the time, the "vices opposed to conjugal union." Third and finally, he provides "remedies to be applied" to restore the institution of marriage within society according to the divine plan (*CC* 4).

Pius XI then sets out two principles to guide each of these sections. First, the Catholic Church preserves and preaches God's plan for the institution of marriage. This "constant tradition of the Universal Church" (*CC* 5) comes from scripture and tradition and was articulated in the early church by Augustine. Most recently for Pius XI, this unbroken line of divine inheritance had been reiterated by Leo XIII in *Arcanum* five decades earlier. Second, because marriage is a divinely ordained institution, the state has "the right and therefore the duty to restrict, to prevent, and to punish" those who do not conform to the divine laws governing marriage (*CC* 8). Together, these two principles provide Pius XI's logic for how the divine order concerning marriage needed to be clarified, established, and upheld to rebuild society.

### The Nature and Dignity of Christian Marriage

With these principles and his overall concern for society set out, Pius XI turns to the nature and dignity of Christian marriage in the first section of the encyclical. He organizes this first section (*CC* 10–43) around Augustine's three goods of marriage: "offspring, conjugal faith and the sacrament" (*CC* 10).

Pius XI begins by discussing procreation (*CC* 11–18), stating that "amongst the blessings of marriage, the child holds the first place" (*CC* 11). Quoting the 1917 *Code of Canon Law*, he writes that the "'primary end of marriage is the procreation and the education of children'" (*CC* 17). As demonstrated by the coupling of procreation and education, Pius understands this good not primarily in terms of conception but instead in terms of raising and caring for children. Parents do not just "propagate and preserve the human race on earth" but are to raise children who become "members of the Church of Christ," "fellow-citizens of the Saints," and "members of God's household" (*CC* 13). It is the responsibility of both parents to care for children—who are "as a talent committed to their charge by God" (*CC* 15)—and to bring them toward eternal union with God.

This broad understanding of the purpose of parenting leads Pius XI to put considerable emphasis on the importance of educating children (*CC* 16). Because of the procreative end of marriage, which includes children's upbringing, parents are bound in an indissoluble bond (*CC* 16). Part of Pius XI's concern for rebuilding institutions is this argument that marriage is the institution made for conceiving and caring for children, such that sex belongs only in marriage (*CC* 18). Yet, his argument is less about the nature of the sexual act than it is about the social functions of marriage. Thus, Pius XI emphasizes not an impersonal institution but rather genuine love as guiding these activities. In quoting Augustine, Pius XI states that children "'should be begotten lovingly and educated religiously'" (*CC* 17).

Pius XI next turns to fidelity, the second good of marriage. It is in this part (*CC* 19–30) that one finds some of Pius XI's most influential claims on love in marriage along with some of his most troubling claims about the subordination of women. While the gender hierarchy cannot pass without notice, contemporary readers should also appreciate the centrality of love in the pope's perspective. Pius XI writes

that marital love, far from being momentary excitement or passion, permeates all marital life. It "pervades all the duties of married life and holds pride of place in Christian marriage" (*CC* 23). This love is expressed outwardly, through mutual help and couples "forming and perfecting themselves" each and every day (*CC* 23). Pius XI even states that spouses' "mutual molding" and "determined effort to perfect each other" can be "the chief reason and purpose of matrimony" (*CC* 24). This affirmation and high valuation of couples' marital relationships is an important development in the teachings of the Catholic Church.

However, these positive statements on love as the heart of Christian marriage are found between strong condemnations. Before them are denunciations of polygamy, polyandry, and lustful thoughts (*CC* 21). The pope claims the teachings of Jesus for these positions, recognizing that while some of these were found in the Old Testament, Jesus "restored that original and perfect unity, and abrogated all dispensations" (*CC* 20).

Following the passages on love and marriage, Pius XI argues that the form of marital love "includes both the primacy of the husband with regard to the wife and children [and] the ready subjection of the wife and her willing obedience" (*CC* 26). Men are the head of the family, and women are the heart (*CC* 27). Thus, women are primarily about loving (*CC* 27), and men are primarily about ruling (*CC* 29). In these passages, Pius XI also claims that the subordination of women is a divinely ordained structure of marriage, a conviction he bases on the writings of Saint Paul (*CC* 26). This same pattern of male authority and female subjugation was affirmed in Leo XIII's *Arcanum*, from which Pius XI quotes (*CC* 29). Given his sense that this view is ensconced in the tradition, Pius XI presents the natural hierarchy of the spouses as a fundamental law and structure of family that is "established and confirmed by God" and "must always and everywhere be maintained intact" (*CC* 28).

In the third and final part (*CC* 31–43) of the first section on the blessings of marriage, Pius XI discusses the sacramental aspect of marriage. His focus is on the indissoluble bond between the couple as reestablished and elevated by Christ. Thus, a valid and consummated Christian marriage cannot "be destroyed by any human authority" (*CC* 34). For Pius XI, the indissoluble bond has many benefits. It provides stability in the relationship, especially over the years of marriage. It ensures mutual aid between the spouses. It secures the education of children. It is a source of virtue in family members and so serves society (*CC* 37). Most importantly, it is a source of grace for the couple (*CC* 39).

### Vices Opposed to Conjugal Union

Like the previous section, Pius XI divides this section (*CC* 44–93) into three parts. He discusses the vices opposed to procreation, then those opposed to fidelity, and then those opposed to sacramental unity. Before beginning, he provides an overview of how marriage is being "scorned and on every side degraded" (*CC* 44). He criticizes the entertainment industry, which includes movies, radio, and "amorous and frivolous novels," for promoting "divorce, adultery, [and] all the basest vices" (*CC* 45). Pius XI also rejects the position that "something should be conceded in our times as regards certain precepts of the divine and natural law" (*CC* 47).

For Pius XI, both the entertainment industry and those who seek accommodations advance a most dangerous principle, one that targets the heart of Catholic teaching: the belief that marriage is ultimately created by human beings (*CC* 49), not God, and can be changed by humans (*CC* 50). Examples of these changes come in "temporary," "experimental," or "companionate" marriages (*CC* 51). There is little nuance to be found here, as Pius XI believes himself the guardian of an uninterrupted tradition that sets out the divine plan for marriage in considerable detail. Such a path of questioning and eroding individual precepts of the larger plan will ultimately "reduce our truly cultured nations to the barbarous standards of savage peoples" (*CC* 52). Pius XI's Eurocentrism is a bit jolting here,

especially given that Europe was involved in World War I only a decade earlier.

Having set out this fundamental error behind the attacks on marriage, Pius XI turns to the attacks on specific goods of marriage. He begins with procreation (*CC* 53–71). Pius XI notes that some try to justify the "criminal abuse" of frustrating conception during sex with such inadequate reasons as couples wanting to gratify their desires without having children, mothers risking their health in having more children, or families living in difficult circumstances (*CC* 53). Pius XI does not believe that these reasons justify contraception: "But no reason, however grave, may be put forward by which anything intrinsically against nature may become conformable to nature and morally good" (*CC* 54). As such, Pius XI frames the issue as primarily about fidelity to divine law, such that no human circumstance, including health risks, can validate a direct violation. In so doing, Pius XI evokes the language of sin in condemning contraception, language that will later be avoided in *Humanae vitae*,[5] stating that contraception is a "sin against nature" and "shameful and intrinsically vicious" (*CC* 54). He claims that those who frustrate procreation are "branded with the guilt of a grave sin" (*CC* 56).

Following the same line of reasoning, Pius XI then condemns priests who excuse the use of contraception by the laity for pastoral reasons, claiming that these priests are leading people and themselves into "the pit" (*CC* 57). While Pius XI recognizes the agony of pregnancies that may put a mother's health or life at risk, he shifts attention to his admiration of and God's reward for mothers who risk their lives "with heroic fortitude" (*CC* 58). While there are times when children cannot be conceived, sexual expression under such conditions must still preserve the primary end of procreation in the "intrinsic nature of the act" (*CC* 59). As the pope is drawing on Augustine here, he is speaking more about old age and infertility than the rhythm method or natural family planning (both of which are later developments). The secondary ends of sexual expression remain worthy pursuits so long as couples' mutual aid and love remain subordinated to procreation in the structure of the sexual act (*CC* 59). While there are challenges in marriage, couples should have faith that nothing can arise that "justifies the putting aside of the law of God" because God's precepts are possible "for the just to observe" (*CC* 61).

An important caveat is that observation of God's precepts may well lead the just person to risk death. This implication becomes more pronounced in Pius XI's consideration of the last vice against procreation, abortion. He argues that medical reasons do not justify abortion (*CC* 63). Even when a mother's health and life are "gravely imperiled," this is not "a sufficient reason for excusing in any way the direct murder of the innocent" (*CC* 64). He condemns eugenics as a reason for abortion four times (*CC* 63, 66, 68, and 70), making it his strongest denunciation. He concludes this part by arguing that governments should protect innocent life (*CC* 67) and that people have "no other power over the members of their bodies than that which pertains to their natural ends" (*CC* 71).

Next, Pius XI turns to vices against couple's fidelity, described as "sin against conjugal faith" (*CC* 72). The primary vice explored in this part (*CC* 72–78) is the social equality of women. Pius XI is concerned with those who "do away with the honorable and trusting obedience which the woman owes to the man" (*CC* 74). Women having equal social rights so that they are free from domestic duties and able to be active in public affairs "is not emancipation but a crime" (*CC* 74). While equal rights between men and women are "much exaggerated and distorted" (*CC* 76), social adjustments might be needed to address the economic conditions of women. This is acceptable for public authorities to do as long as they adapt these rights to "the natural disposition and temperament of the female sex" (*CC* 77).

In the final part (*CC* 79–93) of this section, Pius XI turns to the attacks on marriage as a sacrament. Because sacramental marriage entails an indissoluble bond, Pius XI identifies threats as those actions that threaten indissolubility. Marriages between Catholics and non-Catholic Christians are forbidden (*CC* 82). What is not stated but implied is opposition to marriages between Catholics and any belief or religion that is not Catholicism. Legislation from the state that allows for divorce is also a threat to the sacrament of marriage (*CC* 85). Anyone who argues that marriage is just a private contract and so does not recognize God's design and law concerning marriage is a threat. God's will for basic structure and purpose of marriage applies to all marriages, not just Catholics, and must be universally upheld (*CC* 86–87). The challenges of living together, domestic abuse, and adultery are not grounds for divorce, and those saying otherwise contradict the church's clear teaching on the sacrament of marriage (*CC* 88). Pius XI concludes this section by quoting Leo XIII's claim in *Arcanum* that if the state does not uphold the indissolubility of marriage, it will "suffer absolute ruin" (*CC* 92).

### *Remedies to Be Applied*

In the third and final section of the encyclical, Pius XI offers "remedies" that might overcome the vices (*CC* 94). The basic approach is to restore the divinely ordained nature and purpose of marriage, and this will lead to rebuilding and strengthening society (*CC* 95–96). He highlights the remedies that the Catholic Church, married couples, and the state can provide.

For Pius XI, the main disrupter of the divine order is "the power of unbridled lust" (*CC* 97). This passion overpowers reason, displacing humanity's connection to God's will with sexual desire.[6] As humans cannot control their lust, they must avail themselves of the means of grace that God has provided for them to resist sexual desire. These means are attending mass, petitioning God, frequent participation in the sacraments, and persistent devotion (*CC* 101). The correct guidance on these means comes from the Catholic Church, so "it is necessary that a filial and humble obedience towards the Church should be combined with devotedness to God and the desire of submitting to Him" (*CC* 103). Moreover, the laity should be wary of trusting their own conscience on these matters. They should "guard against the overrated independence of private judgment" (*CC* 104), as their reason is attenuated by lust. Instead, laity should defer to the church in such matters. Because laity are to trust the church, the church must teach the truth about marriage clearly, in both writing and words, through argument but also through appeals to the heart (*CC* 105).

This obedience to the church should be paired with a couple's commitment to God's plan for marriage, the means God has provided to help people live the divine model of marriage, and the Catholic Church's teachings on marriage (*CC* 110–111). Married couples must enact their marital responsibilities, especially the education of children (*CC* 112). Teaching the divine message about marriage will help children understand it, be formed in it (*CC* 113), and resist the cultural pressures that are hostile to God's plan (*CC* 114).

The state also has a role in providing remedies for the problems facing marriage. Drawing upon Leo XIII's *Rerum novarum*, Pius XI insists that families need a living wage, stating that it is "a grave injustice" to pay the head of a family a wage insufficient to support a family (*CC* 117). Moreover, the state must ensure that children have suitable housing, husbands can acquire suitable employment, necessities are affordable, and mothers have "food, medicine, and the assistance of a skilled physician" (*CC* 120). If a state neglects these realities, it will damage itself and the common good (*CC* 121). It will also be beneficial if the state's laws regarding marriage align with the teaching of the Catholic Church and have penalties for offenders (*CC* 125). Having offered these remedies, Pius XI ends with a petition to God that God's vision of marriage "will flourish again" (*CC* 129).

## INTERPRETATION

At the heart of *Casti connubii* is the gospel's call to follow God's will. As Jesus prayed in the garden for God's will to be done, Pius XI calls for people to turn to God's will for marriage. The institutions of marriage, human happiness, and salvation depend on adhering to this divine

order. It is also why the state should be concerned about marriages and families. The state's responsibility for its citizens and the common good means that state actors should not only support families but must do so if their society is to flourish. For Pius XI, marriage is so fundamental to the good of humanity that it is a key institution for reconstructing society by helping Europe recover from World War I and by mitigating the effects of the coming global economic collapse of the 1930s. Marriage is so important to the social order that it deserves its own focus in an encyclical that preludes Pius XI's efforts to help rebuild society in *Quadragesimo anno*. This basic argument of *Casti connubii* is compelling, as it pushes toward articulating God's will as the basis for the ongoing good of humanity.

However, this overarching argument is weakened by the details of the encyclical. Even looking past the cavalier way that the pope pronounces judgments and condemnations of peoples and cultures, the pope presents the white upper-class nineteenth-century European model of marriage as the divine will. The result is that the encyclical looks less like a call to turn to the divine plan of love and more like a narrow parochial vision aimed at reestablishing an idealized past.

This problem can be seen at several points in the encyclical. Pius XI holds up children as the primary good of marriage, subordinating the relationship of the couple. There is a vociferous insistence on the subordination of women, making pushes for equality akin to a crime. He condemns romance novels and movies. He assumes that mothers should sacrifice their health and even their lives to give birth to children. He puts forward a vision of the laity as so corrupted by lust that they should just do what the church tells them rather than trust their own judgments. He hopes that the state will punish those who deviate from this vision of marriage.

The culture-bound nature of this vision can be seen even more clearly by looking forward and backward in Catholic teaching. Looking forward, the Catholic Church no longer holds many of these beliefs. Since at least *Humanae vitae*, the church has put the relationship of the married couple on the same level as the procreative good of marriage. While the church has upheld the importance of women's role in the home, it has insisted on the equality of women and their right to work in society.[7] Moreover, John Paul II and Francis have both spoken of the father's responsibility for parenting and home life.[8] Amid these teachings is the recognition that a model of the family where the mom stays home and the dad goes to work is neither the divine model nor the only model of a Christian marriage.[9] In many ways, the Catholic Church now teaches a companionate model of marriage that Pius XI saw as a sign of humanity's usurpation of God's plan for marriage. As early as *Humanae vitae*, official Catholic teaching has been more nuanced in its reflections on life-threatening pregnancies and, while not allowing for direct abortions, has grasped that the moral course of action does not always require that women sacrifice their lives. The universal call to holiness as found in documents of Vatican II recovers some of the dignity of the laity that cuts against assumptions about their weakness and the need for docility vis-à-vis church authorities. Also, with Vatican II's *Dignitatis humanae*, the church recognized the value of representative governments and distanced itself from a position that assumed that the state's role is to carry out the wishes of the Catholic Church.

If one looks backward, one can also see the time-conditioned nature of Pius XI's vision of marriage. Jesus's teaching on marriage focused more on how it was a threat to living out the gospel than on marriage's nature and form. Jesus worried that family obligations and their related responsibilities to the state would keep people from taking up their cross and following him.[10] He relativized family relationships, saying that whoever does the will of God is one's mothers, brothers, and sisters (Matt. 12: 46–50). Jesus's interactions with women speak to a dignity and respect that are at least in tension with Pius XI's characterization. Finally, one crucified by the state would probably be wary of Pius XI's call to employ the state for punitive measures.

Pius XI's presentation of a time-bound vision of marriage as the divine will for marriage weakens the encyclical in two key ways. First, it overshadows *Casti connubii*'s positive contributions to the Catholic Church's understanding of marriage. Pius XI's emphasis on love at the heart of marriage is significant. He says that love should guide all marital activity, directing actions and pushing spouses to seek what is truly good. It is a love that endures through all the vagaries of marital life and so is essential. It is this teaching that is echoed in Pope Francis's *Amoris laetitia* that, drawing on *Casti connubii*, emphasizes the way love should permeate married life (*AL* 120) and argues that the sacrament should be "a reality that permanently influences the whole of married life" (*AL* 215).[11]

In addition to the emphasis on love, Pius XI also argues for the important role of the state in supporting the family, including a living wage, shelter, and medical care. Thus, Pius XI links marriage and Catholic Social Teaching. It is a link taken up and reaffirmed in *Gaudium et spes* and *Familiaris consortio*.[12] It gives a new line of thinking to marriage and provides an enrichment to the church's social ethics. These contributions are overshadowed, though. Subsequent commentators have often focused on the arguments surrounding contraception. Contemporary eyes struggle to see these points amid the numerous condemnations and vilifications and, more troubling, the norming of European models of marriage and the dismissal of the equality of women.

Second, beyond eclipsing the positive contributions, Pius XI's substitution of time-bound understandings of marriage for the divine plan undermines confidence that the Catholic hierarchy intends to teach only God's truth about marriage. In insisting that women should be subjected to men and be willingly obedient, that women's equality with men is a distortion and criminal, and that this is established by God, the encyclical creates significant doubt that what is being proclaimed is God's wisdom. Even the attempt to explain these positions as not part of the church's authentic teaching raises the question of how one discerns what God's vision is. If claims about women's subordination in the document can be dismissed, why should other claims be allowed to stand? For example, why should the encyclical's position on contraception be taken as of continuing relevance when it too faces significant opposition? More than challenges to specific teachings, though, Pius XI's error on women's subordination exemplifies what he sees as a major threat to church teaching: substituting human perspectives about marriage for God's design.

In the end, the value of love in marriage and the social ethics needed to support it are the most important developments of *Casti connubii,* and their significance is affirmed by the way they have been incorporated into subsequent magisterial documents on marriage and family. Given Pius XI's hope for the rebuilding of society and the strengthening of marriages, these teachings are an important legacy for the Catholic Church and for married couples.

## NOTES

1. John Kippley, "*Casti Connubii*: 60 Years Later, More Relevant Than Ever," *Homiletic & Pastoral Review,* June 1991, 24–31; Michael Hull, "Marriage and the Family in *Casti Connubii* and *Humanae Vitae*," *Homiletic & Pastoral Review,* November 2004, 50–54; and Francesco Giordano, "From *Casti Connubii* to *Humanae Vitae*," *Angelicum* 95 (2018): 351–69.

2. Pius XI, *Casti connubii* (December 31, 1930), https://www.vatican.va/content/pius-xi/en/encyclicals/documents/hf_p-xi_enc_19301231_casti-connubii.html (hereafter cited as *CC*).

3. *New Catholic Encyclopedia,* 2nd ed. (Farmington Hills, MI: Gale, 2002), s.v. "Pius XI, Pope."

4. This problem of the subordination of women in *Casti connubii* is noted in Jacob Kohlhaas, "Constructing Parenthood: Catholic Teaching 1880 to the Present," *Theological Studies* 79, no. 3 (2018): 613–15.

5. See Gerard Coleman, "Discerning the Meaning of Humanae Vitae," *Theological Studies* 79, no. 4 (2018): 870.

6. Pius XI is drawing on Augustine's Neoplatonism for these anthropological assumptions. This is unsurprising given that Augustine's thought, developed by Aquinas, was the conceptual framework

for Catholic theology at the time. In this perspective, reason is the feature that distinguishes human beings from all other creatures, so all human activity was to be directed by reason, including the passions. While some passions were directed toward higher goods, lust was directed toward an almost exclusively this-worldly good, namely pleasure. The only way to tame it was to direct it toward the rational end of conceiving and raising children. This framework led to Augustine holding that even when sexual pleasure is in marriage and secondary to the intention of procreation, it is at best a venial sin because the experience of pleasure overwhelms reason. This framework led Aquinas to conclude that sexual desire would disappear in the resurrected body because it would have no purpose without the need of procreation. For a fuller and more nuanced account of Augustine's and Aquinas's takes on sexual desire, see John Cavadini, "Feeling Right: Augustine on the Passions and Sexual Desire," *Augustinian Studies* 36, no. 1 (2005): 195–217; and John Milhaven, "Thomas Aquinas on Sexual Pleasure," *Journal of Religious Ethics* 5, no. 2 (1977): 157–81.

7. See John Paul II, *Familiaris consortio* (November 22, 1981), 23, https://www.vatican.va/content/john-paul-ii/en/apost_exhortations/documents/hf_jp-ii_exh_19811122_familiaris-consortio.html.

8. See John Paul II, *Familiaris consortio,* 25; and Francis, *Amoris laetitia* (March 19, 2016), 176–77, https://www.vatican.va/content/francesco/en/apost_exhortations/documents/papa-francesco_esortazione-ap_20160319_amoris-laetitia.html (hereafter cited as *AL*).

9. See Cristina L. H. Traina, "How Gendered Is Marriage?," in *Sex, Love, and Families: Catholic Perspectives,* ed. Jason King and Julie Hanlon Rubio, 79–90 (Collegeville, MN: Liturgical Press, 2020).

10. See Julie Hanlon Rubio, "New Testament Vision," *A Christian Theology of Marriage and Family* (New York: Paulist Press, 2003).

11. Jacob Kohlhaas also notes how Francis picks up this theme. See Kohlhaas, "Constructing Parenthood," 630.

12. See John Paul II, *Familiaris consortio,* 42–48; and Second Vatican Council, *Gaudium et spes* (December 7, 1965), 47–52, https://www.vatican.va/archive/hist_councils/ii_vatican_council/documents/vat-ii_const_19651207_gaudium-et-spes_en.html.

*Pius XII*

# CHAPTER

# 10

## Addresses of Pius XII

JACOB M. KOHLHAAS

## CONTEXT

Like Benedict XV, Pius XII was a wartime pope whose legacy is colored by the decisions he made under fraught circumstances. Given the gravity of his context, Pius XII has rightfully attracted significant critical interest.[1] Although every modern pope has used the trope of moral and social decline for rhetorical purposes, few experienced anything near the social turmoil surrounding Pius XII's early papacy.[2] By the time his first encyclical was published in October 1939, several nations were embroiled in conflict, while many others had declared neutrality in the hopes of avoiding a second global war.

Unlike Leo XIII and Pius XI, Pius XII did not author an encyclical on marriage, the family, or education. Yet, he notably contributes to Catholic Family Teaching (CFT) through the seventy-nine addresses he delivered to newlyweds between 1939 and 1944. These cover numerous topics and reiterate key themes in early CFT, including the indissolubility of marriage and parents' responsibility for religious education. The addresses offer both basic catechetical instruction and ample advice on securing happiness in marriage and family life. In his wider teaching, Pius XII followed earlier popes in affirming the family as the basic unit of both church and society,[3] disdaining social acceptance of divorce, and criticizing the media's moral influence.[4] Along with the emerging social encyclical tradition, Pius XII also urged familial stability through secure housing, just wages, and rights to private property.[5]

Pius XII's engagement with questions arising in fields such as psychology and medicine foreshadowed the reforms that would follow his papacy.[6] For example, informed by the new field of genetics, Pius XII regarded the decision to refrain from biological parenthood due to the probability of hereditary disease as potentially licit.[7] Likewise, he is well known in moral theology for permitting the avoidance of pregnancy by intentional tracking of the fertility cycle (what became known as the rhythm method). Approval was still required from the parish priest, and the permission was narrow. It accommodated difficult circumstances while still maintaining procreation as the primary purpose of marriage and sexual intercourse but nonetheless marked a significant advance in moral theology.[8] Addressing the Roman Rota in 1941, he clarified that "ecclesiastical jurisprudence neither can nor must neglect the genuine progress of the sciences which treat of moral and juridical matters; neither can it be considered lawful and suitable to dismiss them merely because they are new."[9]

The extent to which order and hierarchy structure Pius XII's worldview, religious sensibilities, and understanding of marriage and family life will undoubtedly stand out to contemporary readers. For Pius XII, every person and institution occupies a specific location within a highly organized socioreligious superstructure. Every element therein also holds reciprocal and hierarchically dictated responsibilities. Parents raise and educate children, while children owe respect and honor to parents. Husbands lead and provide for the family, while wives owe husbands obedience and maintain their own proper responsibilities within the household. Priests provide parents with moral and spiritual guidance, who in turn raise faithful children to build the church.[10] Throughout, divine precedes natural, spiritual precedes material, male precedes female, virginity precedes marriage, and age precedes youth. Love and mutual respect are the ties that hold the system together, but these virtues are notably constrained by the structure itself. Every link in this chain is considered dignified, with its own suitable perfection, but each is still placed relatively closer or further from spiritual perfection.

Married couples have a natural responsibility to produce offspring and a supernatural responsibility to raise them in the faith. Though these tasks are fitting to their vocation, they also require great faith and courage, as personal and social conditions can tempt couples into limiting births for the sake of comfort. High standards are required for avoiding conception, as this contradicts the primary intention of marriage. Large families are the ideal, as they signify a willingly acceptance of spouses' role in the order of creation even despite risks and costs.[11]

Hierarchical thinking was nothing new to late modern Catholicism, but it increasingly gained legalistic clarity throughout this period. Under Pius XII, the procreation and education of children was clearly defined as the primary good of marriage.[12] This judgment followed the 1917 *Code of Canon Law* but stood in tension with then-recent papal teaching.[13] Pius XI had identified procreation as the primary end of sexual intercourse but affirmed this goal for marriage only from a certain restricted

perspective. From another perspective, the relationship of husband and wife could also be considered primary.[14] Similar to the view of Leo XIII, Pius XI held that while procreation and education are the primary end of marriage, the mutual aid of spouses may still be considered the "chief reason and purpose of matrimony."[15] This diversity in papal perspectives ultimately owes to long-standing differences between Augustine and Aquinas, but under Pius XII such historical tensions were flattened into a simple hierarchical ordering.[16]

Fitting this highly ordered worldview, grace often functions as a spiritual commodity that descends in discrete moments and quantities to enable specific spiritual tasks.[17] God's actions are consequently mechanistic in response to sacramental acts. Rather than raising theological questions about divine freedom, this divine predictability is presented as evidence of God's enduring faithfulness.[18]

Grace also functions to obscure limitations within the hierarchical ordering of reality. Those who find their present conditions untenable may simply lack the will to seek divine assistance. In its operations, grace always builds upon and never supplants nature.[19] This leads to a firm conviction that phenomena observed as natural manifest the will of God (though contemporary readers will note the absence of a critical interpretive framework). Consequently, perceived deviance is frequently interpreted as stemming from pride and distrust in God's will rather than as indicating flaws in the socioreligious framework itself. Similarly, tensions at the social level are commonly blamed on a widespread decline of faith and morals or are laid upon "the world" as a source of constant aggravation to the clarity and certainty of Catholic teaching and the natural social and moral order.[20]

## COMMENTARY

### The Sacrament of Marriage

Pius XII often spoke of the indissolubility of sacramental marriage as well as the importance of fidelity. In a 1940 address, he explained that in the union of husband and wife, like the union of Christ to the church, "the gift of self is total, exclusive and irrevocable."[21] The following year, he reminded newlyweds that just as they cooperated with God as ministers of the sacrament of marriage, they should cooperate with God in their married lives. This cooperation is predominately signaled by procreation. When a marriage becomes a family through procreation, spouses "summon in the flesh of your flesh the spiritual and immortal soul which God will create at your call, as He faithfully produced the grace at the call of the sacrament."[22]

Unsurprisingly, Pius XII also reserves harsh words for divorce, which he presents as a plague of modern society.[23] Speaking to newlyweds in April 1942, he explained that divorce both contradicts the indissolubility of marriage intended by God and is particularly harmful for women and children.[24] In October he reaffirmed that "however violated, repudiated, or torn, the pact never relinquishes its hold. It continues to bind with the same force as on the day when the consent of the contracting parties sealed it before God."[25] Six weeks later, Pius XII admitted that spousal separations may be permitted under narrow circumstances.[26]

In context, ecclesial permission for separations would have depended largely on the pastoral sensibilities of local priests. It is impossible to estimate how many people felt compelled (personally or by their priests, family, or community) to maintain common life with abusive partners out of loyalty to indissoluble marriage vows. To compound matters, while Pius XII waxes eloquent on the beauty and joys of marriage and shows true empathy and understanding for the difficulties of interpersonal relationships, he avoids the truly dark dimensions of marital experience. Throughout his allocutions, Pius XII only occasionally alludes to the reality of domestic violence and never raises the problem directly.[27] Given this lack of direct engagement and his overt confidence in male authority, it is difficult to discern what actions Pius XII would have considered abusive.

## Gender

In contemporary terms, Pius XII's understanding of gender is essentialist, hierarchical, and complementarian.[28] As such, his addresses frequently ascribe specific traits and capacities as inherent to genders that hold true down to the level of individuals. Speaking to newlyweds in 1941 on the beauty of Christian love, he describes men and women as

> two flowers of differing beauty, springing from such different roots as man and woman. In the man the root must be a fidelity, complete and inviolable, which does not permit the slightest blemish he would not tolerate in his own spouse, and which, befitting the head of the family, provides an open example of moral dignity and genuine courage in never swerving or retreating from the full performance of his duties. In the woman the root is a wise, prudent and watchful reserve which removes and cleanses the least shadow of anything that could obscure the splendor of a spotless reputation or endanger it in any way whatsoever.[29]

Still, the division between genders is not absolute, and not all human qualities are gendered.[30] It is, for example, very important to the permanence of marriage that man and woman stand equal in freedom and fundamental dignity as they enter the sacrament.[31] Speaking on the duties of husbands and wives in 1942, Pius XII explains that "in family life some duties are particularly the husband's, others devolve upon the wife and mother; but the mother cannot separate herself completely from the work of her husband nor the husband from the worries of his wife. Whatever is done in the family should be in some way the fruit of collaboration, and action in some way common to both husband and wife."[32] As for a male domestic role, men are to make use of their innate inclinations and physical endowments to assist their wives particularly in the area of household maintenance.[33] Despite the deep social divisions, Pius XII seems to view fathers and mothers as potentially equal collaborators in educating their children.[34] Moreover, he recognized that the preindustrial world had a different organization of labor in the home than his own time, but this seems to have had little influence on his confidence in essentially timeless gender roles.[35] Instead, the particular social ordering he espouses is supported with reference to divine will, natural law, and the innate weaknesses of women.

Pius XII explains in a 1941 address:

The authority of the head of the family comes from God, as there came from God to Adam the dignity and authority of the first head of the human race, endowed with all the gifts that were to be handed down to his progeny. For this reason Adam was formed first and then Eve; and Adam, St. Paul tells us, was not deceived, but the woman was deceived and was in sin. Oh, what harm was done by Eve to the first man, to herself, to all her children and to us, by her curiosity to look upon the beautiful fruit of earthly paradise and by her conversation with the serpent![36]

Pius XII goes on to assert that ordering the family under male authority is "one of the greatest achievements of Christianity."[37] As the head of the family, husbands are responsible for maintaining this hierarchical order, which preserves the "physical, intellectual, moral and religious sanctity of the family."[38]

While men are commonly admonished to assert greater control, warnings to women tend to emphasize immodesty and curiosity.[39] The troublesomeness of women is a recurring concern, as "women exert great power over men" and, like Eve, are prone to lead men to ruin.[40] Hence, Pius XII urged husbands and fiancés to restrain the impulses and behavior of their female counterparts.[41]

Given the preeminence of male authority, it is unsurprising that Pius XII took particular interest in instructing men both in his addresses to newlyweds and his wider writings. He asserted that the entire health and well-being of the family, not only physically but also intellectually and spiritually, rested on the virtue and hard work of the father.[42] He

likened fatherhood to God's original act of creation and added that fatherhood communicates "the superior life of intelligence and joy."[43] And he suggested that fathers fulfill not only the "priestly" role of parenting but also an "episcopal" role within the home.[44]

Functionally, the husband's role is professional and centered on economic provision despite vast diversities in the actual occupation this may take.[45] Even when a man's work does not remove him from the home, it is assumed that he will be distracted and unavailable throughout the working day.

The spiritual dimensions of fatherhood are modeled after the paternity of God the Father in their essential features and after Saint Joseph in their human characteristics.[46] Natural fatherhood is ordered below the clergy's spiritual fatherhood, but both are marked by the transmission of being.[47] The result, as explained in a 1941 address, is a hierarchical complementarity of manhood in which biological fatherhood and spiritual fatherhood constitute "two paternities" that "create and seal through the Priesthood and through Matrimony the fathers of the spirit and supernatural life, and the fathers of the flesh and natural life; two sacraments instituted by Christ for His Church to guarantee and perpetuate through the centuries the generation and regeneration of the children of God."[48] The spiritual fatherhood of the priesthood has a primacy over natural fatherhood through matrimony, but both are marked by leadership and authority.

If men can be understood as "top-down," from the qualities of God to priests to husbands and fathers, women, by contrast, are understood as "bottom-up," from their unique physical and emotional endowments to their role within the family.[49] Speaking on the role of the wife in 1942, Pius XII states, "Is it not a timeless truth—a truth rooted in the very physical conditions of a woman's life . . . that the woman makes the home and takes care of it and that the man can never replace her in this? This is the mission which nature and her union with man has imposed upon her for the good of society itself."[50] He also states that "God has endowed women more than men with a sense of grace and good taste, with the gift of making the simplest things pleasant and welcome precisely because, although she is formed like man to help him and to constitute the family with him, she was born to spread kindness and sweetness in her husband's home and to see to it that their life together is harmonious, fruitful and fully developed."[51]

At times a mother's role also takes on heroic proportions, with obligations extending over the emotional well-being and unity of the entire family. In August 1941, Pius XII declared that

> the woman, the wife, the mother is to be the source, the nourishment and special bulwark of family joy and peace. Is it not she who fosters, conjoins and binds the father in the love of his children? Is it not she who almost encompasses the family within herself through her love, who watches over it, guards it, protects and defends it? She is ... the first teacher who points their way to heaven, who places her sons and daughters on their knees before the sacred altars, who often inspires them with their most sublime thoughts and aspirations.[52]

The following month, Pius XII warned women against seeking beyond their allotted role by desiring to "usurp the scepter of the family." Instead, he encourages, "Let your scepter be the scepter of love given you by the Apostle to the Gentiles: attaining salvation through the procreation of children, provided you continue in faith and love and holiness and modesty."[53]

With such emphasis placed on women's role in the home, it is not surprising that Pius XII maintained a very cautious tolerance of women's growing social equality and participation in the public sphere.[54] In a September 1941 address on the authority of husbands, Pius XII worried that the order of the household and the marital relationship were being threatened by women whose professional status placed them near or equal to that of their husbands.[55] Later he warned states against replacing rather than supporting women's familial responsibilities and encouraged reducing women's time outside the home by locating employment opportunities nearby.[56]

## *Physical and Spiritual Procreation*

Despite Pius XII's emphasis on natural order, the superiority of spiritual goods held true for his conception of the family as well. He taught that the primary bond between children and parents is in passing on the faith, not biological procreation, and late in his papacy he affirmed that "the work of education exceeds by far, in its importance and its consequences, that of generation."[57]

In a July 1940 address, Pius XII reflected on "spiritual heredity," prompted by advancements in understanding hereditary disease. This new knowledge created a tension between the emphasis on biological procreation and the natural reality that loving parents will not want to be the source of sickness in their child. Pius XII responded by clarifying the greater value of spiritual parenthood over biological parenthood:

> In baptized people, when one speaks of transmitting inherited blood to descendants, who will live and die not as animals deprived of reason, but as men and as Christians, there is no need to limit the sense of these words to a purely biological and material element, but it may be extended to that which is, as it were, the nutritive liquid of the intellectual and spiritual life: the patrimony of faith, virtue, and honor transmitted by parents to their posterity is a thousand times more precious than the blood—be it ever so rich—infused into their veins.[58]

Nonetheless, justifications for limiting childbirth must meet a very high bar, as such actions are inherently fraught with moral and spiritual danger.[59] Elsewhere he urged infertile couples and those fearful of transmitting hereditary disease to consider adoption, which he described as "usually crowned with happy results" and free of moral objections.[60] Yet, adding ambiguity, Pius XII also surmised that "sterility is very often the punishment for the sinner."[61]

Elective contraception is overtly contrary to marriage, as it opposes rather than welcomes potential new lives. In a 1941 address, Pius XII claimed that contraception restrains God from calling new souls into existence from out of nothingness. Stepping into theological hyperbole, he asserted that such unrealized potential children would henceforward exist only as lights in the divine mind and "never be more than shimmering flickers quenched by the indifference of selfishness of men."[62] The rhetorical imagery utilized here to describe potential children coincides with a larger tendency to portray young children as both angelic and a serious responsibility for parents.[63]

## INTERPRETATION

Representative of a trend that originated before and continues after him, Pius XII's hierarchical vision and gendered ordering of the social sphere leads to centralizing the nuclear family to such an extent that it ultimately reduces the concept of the family to a small isolated unit. This narrow conception of the family neatly fit Western social ideals of gender and the emerging economic realities of industrialized society as well as the theological understanding of marriage as a contract between two autonomous individuals.

*Casti connubii* had asserted that by divine providence, the biological capacity to procreate ensures both the right and the capacity of parents to educate their children.[64] Pius XII continued in this confidence with his own emphasis on families supported nearly entirely by the gendered virtues of the parents, particularly those of mothers. By shifting familial responsibilities so firmly onto the shoulders of individual parents, the support offered by the community and the extended family becomes largely superfluous.[65]

This trend toward justifying narrow conceptions of the family by gendered ideals would reach a climax with John Paul II's embrace of gendered characteristics as anthropological foundations. However, the connection between John Paul II's sexual anthropology in the "Theology of the Body" and Pius XII's teaching on gendered differences in his "Addresses to Newlyweds" has not been widely appreciated. Parallels abound, from the format of using regular general audiences to promote a theological vision to central ideas, including bodily submission to the divine moral order, interpersonal mutuality and the gift of self, complementarity, openness to life, service to life,[66] and deep skepticism of currents in contemporary culture.[67] Even John Paul II's phenomenological methodology is anticipated by Pius XII's penchant for augmenting biblical narratives with imaginative details drawn from socioreligious ideals for a rhetorical purpose.[68] However, Pius XII's comfort with hierarchy and a largely ahistorical view of doctrine fits much less comfortably in theological discourse following Vatican II. Still, the words of Pius XII can help the contemporary reader appreciate both the sensibilities of those who find beauty in ordered and comprehensive theological visions and the limitations inherent to any such comprehensive socioreligious perspective, especially those bound by premises that redirect and refuse critical interrogation.

## NOTES

1. Pius XII's legacy related to World War II remains contested and an ongoing topic of historical research. Review of his archives, opened in 2020, has recently added greater complexity.

2. Pius XII, *Summi pontificatus* (October 20, 1939), 64, https://www.vatican.va/content/pius-xii/en/encyclicals/documents/hf_p-xii_enc_20101939_summi-pontificatus.html.

3. Pius XII, "The Gospel and Domestic Peace," in *Dear Newlyweds*, trans. James F. Murray Jr. and Bianca M. Murray (New York: Ferrar, Straus and Cudahy, 1961), 45. See also Pius XII, "The Priesthood and Matrimony," in *Dear Newlyweds*, 19; and Pius XII, "Allocution to Parish Priests and Lenten Preachers of Rome," February 17, 1945, in *Matrimony*, trans. Michael J. Byrnes (Boston: Saint Paul Editions, 1963), 360.

4. Pius XII, "Why Forever?," in *Dear Newlyweds*, 90.

5. Pius XII, "Radio Message to the World," in *Matrimony*, 330.

6. Pius XII, "The Laws of Conjugal Relations," in *Matrimony*, 417.

7. Pius XII, "Allocution to the International Congress of Catholic Doctors," in *Matrimony*, 383. Pius XII also condemned artificial insemination regardless of donor but with varying reasons. See Pius XII, "Allocution to the Members of the II World Congress of Fertility and Sterility," in *Matrimony*, 482; and Pius II "Allocution to the Members of the Seventh Congress on Hematology," in *Matrimony*, 513.

8. See Pius XII, "The Laws of Conjugal Relations," in *Matrimony*, 405–34.

9. Pius XII, "Matrimonial Cases," in *Matrimony*, 333.

10. Pius XII, "The Priesthood and Matrimony," in *Dear Newlyweds*, 19.

11. Pius XII, "Large Families," in *Matrimony*, 504. Cf. Pius XII, "Allocution to the Associations of the Large Families," in *Matrimony*, 440.

12. In 1944, the Roman Rota asserted that the primary end of marriage is the procreation and education of children, and the secondary is mutual aid and to remedy concupiscence. This ordering is said to be supported by numerous popes, theologians, and canonists. The Rota further argued that because the rights of mutual aid and common living are "intrinsically dependent" on the right to "acts of generation," this ordering is certain. Holy Roman Rota, "The Order of the Purposes of Matrimony," in *Matrimony*, 553.

13. The 1917 *Code of Canon Law* states that "the primary end of marriage is the procreation and nurture of children; its secondary end is mutual help and the remedying of concupiscence." *The 1917 or Pio-Benedictine Code of Canon Law* (San Francisco: Ignatius, 2001), canon 1013. Later Pius XII confirmed, "Now, the truth is that matrimony . . . has not as a primary and intimate end the personal perfection of the married couple but the procreation and upbringing of a new life. . . . This is true of every marriage, even if no offspring result." Pius XII, "Allocution to Midwives," in *Matrimony*, 424.

14. Pius XI, *Casti connubii* (December 31, 1930), 24, https://www.vatican.va/content/pius-xi/en/encyclicals/documents/hf_p-xi_enc_19301231_casti-connubii.html. In *Arcanum* Leo XIII states,

"Not only, in strict truth, was marriage instituted for the propagation of the human race, but also that the lives of husbands and wives might be made better and happier." Leo XIII, *Arcanum* (February 10, 1880), 26, https://www.vatican.va/content/leo-xiii/en/encyclicals/documents/hf_l-xiii_enc_10021880_arcanum.html. This nonhierarchical perspective follows from Aquinas, who argues that love is the form of marriage, while procreation is marriage's end. Thomas Aquinas, *Summa Theologiae*, 3, q. 29, a. 2.

15. Pius XI, *Casti connubii,* no. 24.

16. Much of the debate surrounds the use of terms and the significance of what is and is not made explicit. Suffice it to say that in the early to mid-twentieth century it was possible to describe the value of marriage in terms of a hierarchy of ends and in terms of goods with different orderings depending on how one was considering marriage's values and purposes. The movement to conformity was in part a reaction to perceived innovations in moral theology by authors such as Doms and Von Hildebrand. See Todd Salzman and Michael Lawler, *The Sexual Person: Toward a Renewed Catholic Anthropology* (Washington, DC: Georgetown University Press, 2008), 39–40.

17. Pius XII, "The Priesthood and Matrimony," in *Dear Newlyweds*, 18.

18. Pius XII, "Guarantee of Holiness," in *Dear Newlyweds*, 9.

19. Pius XII, "Why Forever?," in *Dear Newlyweds*, 90.

20. Pius XII, "The Gospel and Domestic Peace," in *Dear Newlyweds*, 45.

21. Pius XII, "The Canticle of Love," in *Dear Newlyweds*, 73.

22. Pius XII, "Husbands and Wives Ministers of the Sacrament," in *Dear Newlyweds*, 12.

23. Pius XII, "Matrimonial Processes," in *Matrimony*, 369.

24. Pius XII, "Why Forever?," in *Dear Newlyweds*, 92.

25. Pius XII, "The Beauty of Fidelity," in *Dear Newlyweds*, 113.

26. Pius XII, "Tests of Fidelity," in *Dear Newlyweds*, 128.

27. "In some cases the guilty spouse does not destroy the family home [through infidelity and abandonment], but his infidelity, especially if it is combined with harsh and rude conduct, makes life

together even more difficult and almost intolerable." Pius XII, "Tests of Fidelity," in *Dear Newlyweds*, 128.

28. Pius XII, "The Matrimonial State," in *Matrimony*, 363.

29. Pius XII, "The Beauty of Christian Love," in *Dear Newlyweds*, 77.

30. See Pius XII, "Parents and Children," in *Dear Newlyweds*, 184.

31. Pius XII, "Husbands and Wives Ministers of the Sacrament," in *Dear Newlyweds*, 12.

32. Pius XII, "Collaboration between Husband and Wife," in *Dear Newlyweds*, 62.

33. Pius XII, "The Husband's Duties in the Home," in *Dear Newlyweds*, 175.

34. "The principal end of marriage is not only to procreate children, but to educate them as well, and to raise them in the fear of the God and in the faith." Pius XII, "Collaboration between Husband and Wife," in *Dear Newlyweds*, 64. Cf. Pius XII, *Summi pontificatus*, no. 90.

35. Pius XII, "The Husband's Duties in the Home," in *Dear Newlyweds*, 177.

36. Pius XII, "Authority of Husband over Wife," in *Dear Newlyweds*, 161.

37. Pius XII, "Authority of Husband over Wife," in *Dear Newlyweds*, 163.

38. Pius XII, "Fathers," in *Matrimony*, 398.

39. See Pius XII, "Bad Reading," in *Dear Newlyweds*, 217; and Pius XII, "Papal Directives for the Woman of Today" (September 11, 1947), https://www.ewtn.com/catholicism/library/papal-directives-for-the-woman-of-today-8962.

40. Pius XII, "Authority of Husband over Wife," in *Dear Newlyweds*, 163.

41. Pius XII, "Secretly Unfaithful," in *Dear Newlyweds*, 119.

42. Pius XII, "Fathers," in *Matrimony*, 398.

43. Pius XII, "The Mystery of Fatherhood," in *Dear Newlyweds*, 171.

44. Pius XII, *Summi pontificatus*, no. 89.

45. Pius XII, "The Role of the Husband," in *Dear Newlyweds*, 157.

46. See, e.g., Pius XII, "The Husband's Duties in the Home," in *Dear Newlyweds*, 177–78.

47. Pius XII, "The Mystery of Fatherhood," in *Dear Newlyweds*, 171.

48. Pius XII, "The Priesthood and Matrimony," in *Dear Newlyweds*, 16.

49. Pius XII, "The Bright Sun of the Family," in *Dear Newlyweds*, 178.

50. Pius XII, "The Role of the Wife," in *Dear Newlyweds*, 153.

51. Pius XII, "The Role of the Wife," in *Dear Newlyweds*, 155.

52. Pius XII, "Heroism of Christian Husbands and Wives," in *Dear Newlyweds*, 54.

53. Pius XII, "Authority of Husband over Wife," in *Dear Newlyweds*, 161.

54. Pius XII, "Respect for Life," in *Matrimony*, 436.

55. Pius XII, "Authority of Husband over Wife," in *Dear Newlyweds*, 162.

56. Pius XII, "Family Problems," in *Matrimony*, 479.

57. Pius XII, "Artificial Insemination," in *Matrimony*, 491.

58. Pius XII, "Spiritual Heredity," in *Matrimony*, 312.

59. Pius XII, "Marriage Gifts," in *Dear Newlyweds*, 24.

60. Pius XII, "Allocution to the Members of the Seventh Congress on Hematology," in *Matrimony*, 520.

61. Pius XII, "Allocution to Midwives," in *Matrimony*, 408. This is likely an allusion to sexually transmitted disease.

62. Pius XII, "Husbands and Wives Ministers of the Sacrament," in *Dear Newlyweds*, 13.

63. Pius XII, "Fatherhood," in *Matrimony*, 328. See also Pius XII, "The Priesthood and Matrimony," in *Dear Newlyweds*, 19.

64. Pius XI, *Casti connubii*, 16.

65. The newfound autonomy of married couples from community and extended family oversight that came along with industrialization is a source of moral concern, but the fact of this autonomy itself seems given. Pius XII, "The Example of St. James the Great," in *Dear Newlyweds*, 235. In advising career choice, proximity to extended family is never mentioned. Pius XII, "Preparation for Marriage," March 19, 1953, in *Matrimony*, 447.

66. This term appears to have been originally used for members of various medical professions and then later applied to parents.

67. Pius XII, "Ruins of the Moral Order," in *Matrimony*, 392.

68. Pius XII is particularly fond of the Pauline Epistles and the Book of Tobit. Gendered virtues themselves are drawn somewhat unevenly from scripture. At times, silences in biblical testimony are freely filled in with imaginative ideals; this is particularly true for Joseph, who serves as a model for earthly fatherhood. Elsewhere, biblical judgments are taken as irreproachable; this is especially true for statements about women's roles in the epistles. See Pius XII, "The Model of Nazareth," in *Dear Newlyweds*, 140.

# *Vatican II*

# 11

# The Postconciliar Marriage Rite

PAUL TURNER

## CONTEXT

The bishops participating in the Second Vatican Council (1962–1965) approved a framework for changes to the traditional Catholic wedding in two succinct paragraphs of their Constitution on the Sacred Liturgy, *Sacrosanctum concilium*.[1] The changes were intended to make the ceremony more expressive of realities and more understandable to the participants.

Prior to this, all Catholic weddings took place apart from mass. The bride, the groom, and the witnesses usually gathered inside the church with the priest, who was vested in cassock, surplice, and stole, not the vestments associated with mass. The priest asked the groom and then the bride if they wished to marry according to the rite of the church. They expressed their willful consent. Then, the priest announced that he joined them together in matrimony. He sprinkled the couple with holy water and blessed a ring in the same way. The groom placed the ring on the finger of his bride. Prayers concluded the ceremony. Usually the priest then vested for mass, celebrated it in the presence of those who had gathered, and offered the nuptial blessing after the Lord's Prayer. In some cases, mass did not immediately follow the wedding. That deferred the nuptial blessing, which could not be given at certain times of the year, such as Lent.[2]

In the wake of this tradition, *Sacrosanctum concilium* provided a new vision: "The marriage rite now found in the Roman Ritual is to be revised and enriched in such a way that the grace of the sacrament is more clearly signified and the duties of the spouses are taught" (*SC* 77). The same paragraph permitted regional variations, citing a precedent from the Council of Trent and acknowledging the different marriage customs across the globe. However, Vatican II clarified that whatever the variations, the minister "assisting at the marriage must ask for and obtain the consent of the contracting parties" (*SC* 77). The couple themselves are the ministers of the sacrament, administering it to each other by their consent to marry. Nonetheless, they must formally exchange that consent in the presence of an official witness of the Catholic Church, usually a priest or deacon.

The constitution next requested that the wedding take place within the mass, not before it. This mirrored a practice developing in other rituals that situated the celebration of sacraments after the homily: baptism, confirmation, and ordination, for example.

Regarding the nuptial blessing, *Sacrosanctum concilium* called for its content to expand beyond the blessing of the bride and to add a blessing of the groom. It also permitted the use of the vernacular language so that both bride and groom would understand the prayer (*SC* 78).

The same paragraph permitted a wedding apart from the mass, but it now required the proclamation of scripture readings before the exchange of consent. Many Catholics familiar with contemporary weddings may find unimaginable a wedding without readings from the Bible, yet that was the Catholic custom for hundreds of years. Even when a mass followed the wedding, the only readings were those within the mass; the wedding itself included no proclamation from scripture.

This new framework helped the study group of liturgical experts, who then developed the postconciliar rite. Their work, completed in 1972, was revised in 1991, and the updated English translation became available in 2016.[3] The remainder of this chapter will explore the significant changes that made for a better expression of the duties of spouses and of the church's teaching about the Catholic family in the celebration of the sacramental rite of marriage.

## COMMENTARY

### *The Procession*

*The Order of Celebrating Matrimony* (OCM) gives more detail on the Catholic wedding procession than the previous ritual had offered.[4] In the absence of pertinent rubrics, traditions developed and solidified, especially those pertaining to the procession of the bride. Customarily, instrumental music accompanies the entire procession. The groom and the attendants take their places. Then, the music changes to a special march for the entrance of the bride. She processes, escorted by her father, who upon reaching the end of the aisle before the sanctuary entrusts her to the groom as if the wedding fulfills a now unacceptable convention that a woman's ownership passes from one male to another. The preconciliar Catholic ritual

neither described nor favored this procession, but the tradition solidified it nonetheless.

The revised OCM offers two forms of entrance depending on whether the priest greets the couple at the door of the church or in its sanctuary. In either case, the rubrics of the typical edition in Latin are egalitarian, calling for the entrance of the *couple* as if they walk together, not at opposite ends of a procession. The English translation changed the recommended first form of the entrance and now calls for a procession "in the customary manner" (OCM 46), which allows the greatest flexibility including the commonly practiced entrance of the bride with her father. Still, the postconciliar description of a Catholic wedding procession considers the bride and groom as equals who will each administer this sacrament to the other.

Every mass is to begin with an entrance chant. The missal supplies one, usually a sentence drawn from scripture. *The General Instruction of the Roman Missal* (GIRM) gives other options, including its replacement by a hymn, a practice quite common in parishes.[5] One option allows the priest to adapt the given antiphon "as an introductory explanation" (GIRM 48).

After the council, the missal replaced the single set of antiphons and prayers from the mass "For the Bride and Groom" with three new sets that a priest may use during the ritual mass now called, "For the Celebration of Marriage." The entrance antiphon of the first set comes from Psalm 20, verses 3 and 5. The revised ritual for weddings offers the priest two sample introductions that he may use after the sign of the cross and the greeting of the wedding mass. The second of these (OCM 53) alludes to that first entrance antiphon, thus adapting the words as an introductory explanation, as GIRM 48 permits. It is a prayer that presumes that the hearts of people have desires, and it asks God to fulfill their designs. For a couple finally reaching the sanctuary on their wedding day, this antiphon prays for the fulfillment of their best hopes.

As at any mass, a hymn may replace the entrance antiphon at a wedding. At some Catholic weddings, the congregation sings a hymn once the procession has reached the sanctuary. In others, the congregation sings their praise to God as the wedding party processes up the aisle, replacing the traditional instrumental music. The ritual then instructs the priest at a wedding mass to greet the couple "warmly" (OCM 45, 49), as if there's some fear that he may not. Those preparing the revised liturgy aimed to make the minister an exemplar of the hope-filled joy that permeates a wedding and anticipates the happiness of family life.

## The Collect

At any mass, to bring the introductory rites to a close, the priest invites the people to pray. After some silence he offers the collect, a prayer that "collects" the intentions of those gathered. In the previous missal, the mass "For the Bride and Groom" contained only one collect, which the revisers thought was too general in nature: "Hear us, almighty and merciful God, that what is administered by our office may be more greatly filled by your blessing." Furthermore, it seemed to emphasize the role of the priest, who is merely a witness to the sacrament that the couple administer. Seeking to fulfill the council's desire for enriched celebrations (*SC* 77), the revisers removed this collect and replaced it with others.[6]

The second edition offers a choice of six collects from a variety of sources ancient and new. These pray that the couple may live out their faith in deeds, that their love may be inseparable, that their love be confirmed, that they grow in faith and enrich the church with offspring, that God would keep their union safe, and that they be bound in affection, like-mindedness, and holiness (OCM 188–93). These collects all pertain to the celebration at hand. They help the gathered community formulate their prayers for this couple based on the purposes of marriage and family life.

## The Lectionary

The liturgical renewal also brought with it a revised *Lectionary for Mass*, greatly expanding the repertoire of scripture readings throughout the liturgical year. For weddings, the preconciliar mass "For the Bride and Groom" included an epistle that compared the love of Christ for the church with the love of a groom for his bride (Eph. 5:22–33), a gradual that praised the blessing of children (Ps. 128:3), a tract on the longevity of married life (Ps. 128:4–6), an alleluia verse about the protection that God gives (Pss. 20:3 and 134:3), and a gospel about God's plan to join husband and wife inseparably (Matt. 19:3–6). These readings could be used as long as no greater feast that day replaced them with its own readings for the mass. For example, if a wedding was to take place on a holy day such as the Assumption of Mary (August 15), the readings for that mass prevailed over those of the mass "For the Bride and Groom."

The lectionary now features a greatly expanded variety of options from the Bible. Those preparing the ceremony choose from nine Old Testament readings, fourteen New Testament readings, seven responsorial psalms, four verses for the gospel acclamation (replacing the gradual and tract), and ten gospels. The former readings remain as options among these. As before, these may be used as long as no greater feast falls on that day. The Catholic Church recognizes thirteen ranks within its Table of Liturgical Days. The wedding mass may not be used on any day within the first four levels, such as a Saturday evening wedding mass on Pentecost weekend or All Souls Day on November 2. A wedding may take place on those days but with the readings of the liturgical day.

The second edition adds a feature absent from any other liturgical book. The OCM affixes an asterisk to the citations of certain readings, requiring that one of them be used (OCM 144) so that the faithful hear at least one passage that refers explicitly to marriage. Therefore, Saint Paul's excursus on love (1 Cor. 12:31—13:8a), which does not carry an asterisk yet is arguably the most popular reading at weddings, may continue to be used but only if supported by another passage that explicitly speaks of marriage, such as the creation of man and woman (Gen. 1:26–28, 31a) or the account of Jesus's miracle at the wedding in Cana (John 2:1–11).

The readings that do not relate directly to marriage take up other important themes. Many of them, such as the popular passage from First Corinthians, have to do with conducting a loving, respectful life within the Christian community. These encouragements seem all the more pertinent to a newly married couple, who are embarking on a lifelong commitment that is open to forming a family in a home that may become a more intimate version of the church's own idealized community life.

### The Consent

The postconciliar marriage ritual has added several questions for the minister to ask the couple before they express their consent. These concern the freedom of their decision to marry, their resolve, and their openness to children (OCM 60). The revisers introduced these into the ceremony so that the couple could hear what the church expects of marriage and family life and be able to give their assent. Something similar happens in the ordination of priests and deacons, where the candidates hear and respond to a series of questions pertaining to their upcoming ministry. The new questions for the groom and bride are both catechetical and probing. They remind the couple of the moral duties of marriage and have them express their understanding of the church's expectations before they enter matrimony.[7]

Next follows the consent, which many people colloquially call "the vows." These are less vows made to God as consent given to the partner. In weddings before Vatican II, the priest asked first the groom and then the bride if each was willing to marry according to the rite of the church. This prompted the iconic reply "I do." The revised English translation still permits a question-and-answer format but prefers an assertion, fuller than two words, that by which the groom and the bride make a more complete declaration of their consent to each other. In this consent they promise faithfulness even in adversity, and they promise to love and honor each other all the days of their lives (OCM 62). Although they are permitted to respond to questions from the minister with a simple "I do" (OCM 63), the ritual prefers that they each say the complete form of consent so that their own lips profess the intentions of their heart.

In parishes, the groom and bride usually repeat the consent phrase by phrase after the minister cues them. Surprising to many, the Catholic marriage rite does not envision it that way. Rather, it presumes that each partner says the complete text to the other without the intervention of another voice. The minister's voice supplies a practical means for couples to recite the complete consent. However, there are other ways. Each could read the consent directly from the same ritual book that the minister is using, or they could each read it off cards prepared for them in advance. By removing the voice of the minister, the ceremony stresses the consent of the couple and reinforces the role of the minister as a witness.

Furthermore, in the past the priest declared in Latin "I join you in matrimony. In the name of the Father, and of the Son, and of the Holy Spirit. Amen." He made the sign of the cross over the couple while reciting the names of the Trinity, and he sprinkled the couple with blessed water.[8] However, this formula and sprinkling made it appear as though the priest conferred marriage on the couple, whereas the Catholic Church believes that the couple confer marriage on each other through their words of consent. The same anomaly arose in the preconciliar collect for the wedding mass, which asked God to fulfill what the priest had begun. The diminishment of the minister's voice and action highlights the significance of the words that the groom and bride declare to each other. They are administering the sacrament.

The minister receives the consent by vocalizing the hopes and belief of the assembly. He does not declare that he binds the couple but instead asks God to strengthen the consent that the couple has made. The minister reminds all present that no one may put asunder what God has joined, not what a *priest* has joined (OCM 64).

To conclude the ceremony of consent, the second edition of the OCM now includes an acclamation by the people. The minister invites all to bless the Lord, and all respond "Thanks be to God." They may use other words (OCM 65). This dialogue has not yet become so familiar that it elicits a spontaneous response from the congregation. However, the one who conducts the wedding rehearsal can prepare the wedding party and other guests for these words. Any printed or online participation aids may detail the order of service and alert the assembly to the words they are to say. The groom and bride join in this acclamation, which means that their first words as a married couple are "Thanks be to God." For many couples who have asked for a Catholic wedding, this faithfully declares what is in their hearts. Yes, they love their partner, but they are also profoundly grateful to God for this day and for the future it promises.

## The Rings

In the past, a Catholic wedding involved a single ring, the one that the groom obtained for the bride. The priest blessed the ring, sprinkling it with holy water. The groom placed it on the bride's finger while the priest made a sign of the cross over the ring and declared in Latin "In the name of the Father, and of the Son, and of the Holy Spirit. Amen."[9]

The postconciliar rite calls for two rings, and significant words have moved from the mouth of the minister to the mouths of the couple. The minister blesses the rings, making the sign of the cross with his hand. The sprinkling with blessed water is optional. Each partner then invites the other to receive the ring as a sign of love and fidelity in the name of the Trinity. In practice, the couple often repeat the words phrase by phrase after the minister, but the ritual imagines that the minister remains silent while they read the words.

Even so, this ceremony tolerates an important variation. In the case of a Catholic marrying a non-Christian, the couple need not mention the names of the Trinity out of respect for the non-Christian. Or the Catholic party alone may pronounce the names Father, Son, and Holy Spirit (OCM 132).

## The Arras

The English translation of the second edition in the United States includes an option that is especially prized in the Hispanic and Filipino traditions, the blessing and giving of the *arras*, thirteen coins in a small box. The Spanish translation of this ceremony in Mexico explains that the giving of the *arras* "serves to express unity of life and of possessions established between the couple."[10] The United States Conference of Catholic Bishops supports this manifestation of cultural diversity.

Some couples enlist the assistance of a sponsor couple, the *padrinos* of the *arras*, who present the box of coins to the minister. These *padrinos* may be relatives or close friends who accept this responsibility to indicate their emotional, spiritual, or even financial support for the couple. In the past and especially in Mexico, the groom alone poured the coins into the hands of the bride. The action indicated that he, the provider, would take care of her needs. Now, as with the exchange of rings, both the groom and the bride participate in the same action.

First, the *padrinos* may present the *arras* to the minister, who blesses the box of coins. Next, the ritual assigns words to the groom and the bride as they enact this ceremony. The words of the couple do not promise earthly provisions, as the groom's action formerly assured; rather, the groom and bride each express the sharing of blessings. They each pour the *arras* into the hands of the other, calling their partner by name and declaring "receive these *arras* as a pledge of God's blessing and a sign of the good gifts we will share" (OCM 67).

The ceremony is optional. It is not limited by ethnicity. Any couple in the United States may incorporate it into their wedding. The brief ceremony focuses on the material necessities of any family. It recognizes that possessions come as a blessing from God. The mutual actions express the equality of the bride and groom who aim to appreciate together the possessions that they hold as gifts from God.

After the exchange of the rings and the *arras*, if included, all may sing a canticle of praise. Although this is little practiced, such a hymn engages the assembly in a vocal act of worship that employs the art of music to express what simple words cannot. It may refocus the spiritual nature of the couple's consent, affirming the decision of the bride and groom to conduct their ceremony inside a church and in the presence of a minister.

Variations occur in other countries because of legal requirements or local traditions. For example, in England the couple must make the Civil Declaration of Freedom while using both their first names and surnames, and the question-and-answer form of consent is not allowed.[11] In India the groom may place upon the bride a necklace called a *thali* to symbolize their union.[12]

### The Universal Prayer

Also called the prayer of the faithful, the universal prayer gathers the intentions of the community to place them before God. The second edition of the ceremony provides examples in an appendix. Other samples have been published online or in books. As with the universal prayer at any mass, someone may compose them for the particular occasion at which they will be read.

In practice, many of those preparing weddings in Catholic parishes do not exert much effort in the composition of these prayers. Doing so would require considerable time and attention when previously published intentions are readily at hand. However, like the homily, someone could compose petitions that attune to the particular circumstances of each couple. Their concerns for the church, their hopes for society, the charities that they support, their friends who are ill, and their relatives who have died all may be incorporated into the petitions that all pray at the wedding. This requires more preparatory work, but the results better express the hopes for the commitment that this particular couple is making.

### The Liturgy of the Eucharist

At any mass, members of the faithful may carry the bread, wine, and offerings for the church and the needy in procession as the Liturgy of the Eucharist gets under way (GIRM 36). The rubrics of the wedding mass permit an extra detail. Usually those in procession present the gifts to the priest or deacon, who receives them at a convenient place. However, at a wedding "the bride and bridegroom may bring the bread and wine to the altar" (GIRM 70). In practice, family members or friends may bring the gifts from a table near the front door of the church up the aisle to the bride and groom, who remain in the sanctuary. The family members then turn toward the altar, step forward, and set the gifts there.[13]

The indication of the altar may be an oversight in the rubrics, or it may underscore the significant role that the bride and groom play as the ministers of the sacrament to each other. As ministers of the sacrament, they enter last in the entrance procession, a position usually held by the presiding priest. As ministers, they declare their consent to each other while the priest witnesses. As ministers, they may set the Liturgy of the Eucharist in motion as they set the gifts of the faithful onto the altar of sacrifice. This role as ministers of the sacrament anticipates the position they will hold as ministers of family life.

Rarely does a wedding mass include a collection. However, if the bride and groom are active in a certain charity or even at their parish, they could request a collection so that their guests could contribute to the needy. This could demonstrate the impact that this couple will have on their family and on society.

The eucharistic prayer of any mass opens with words of thanksgiving to God, includes the institution narrative and consecration, makes an offering, and concludes with intercessions. At a wedding mass, the priest may add a special insert to the eucharistic prayer that invites all to pray for the bride and groom. This commemoration of the couple asks God to gladden them with the gift of children, bring them to a desired length of days, let them abide in mutual love and peace, and keep them faithful to the covenant that they have sealed (OCM 202–4). It is rare for a priest to pronounce any names during the eucharistic prayer apart from the pope and the local bishop, but at a wedding the names of the groom and bride are inserted into this most sacred prayer of the church.

## The Nuptial Blessing

After the council, the biggest change to the nuptial blessing was the inclusion of prayers for the groom. In the past this was very much a blessing of the bride, and the ritual offered no other option. The revised liturgy includes two other options, both composed after the council. The second edition further enriched these three blessings with an epiclesis, a prayer for the coming of the Holy Spirit upon the couple. This feature is much prized in the Eastern Rites of the Catholic Church, and it has now been adopted into the Roman tradition (OCM 72, 207, 209).

The ritual in the United States also permits the placement of a *lazo* on the couple, another Hispanic and Filipino tradition. In the United States its use is not limited to these cultures. The *lazo* is a large double loop, a kind of wedding garland, placed over the couple. Often a sponsor couple, the *padrinos* of the *lazo*, hold it for the minister's blessing before placing it over the couple's shoulders. The ritual envisions that the couple wear the *lazo* for the nuptial blessing, a sign of its unitive purpose.

The nuptial blessing includes an intention that the couple be blessed with children. These words may be omitted if the bride and groom are advanced in years. They may still marry even with the improbability of bearing or raising children as permitted by canon law (1084 §3).

## The Final Blessing

The ceremony concludes with yet another blessing. At any mass, the priest may offer a threefold solemn blessing over the faithful who have gathered for worship. At a wedding, the threefold blessing primarily concerns the bride and groom alone. It lists intentions such as unity, peace, the blessing of children, the solace of friends, true peace, the determination to bear witness to God's charity, the gift of joy, the compassion of Christ, the love of the Holy Spirit, and the hope of eternal life (OCM 213–15). The minister concludes the blessing with another one over all who have gathered. These final words of the ceremony recall the church's emphasis on the dignity of marriage and family life.

## INTERPRETATION

The revised Catholic wedding ceremony responded to the Constitution on the Sacred Liturgy, which wanted the rite "to be revised and enriched in such a way that the grace of the sacrament is more clearly signified and the duties of the spouses are taught" (*SC* 77). The changes show respect for the role of the couple while receding the role of the minister. They stress the mutual responsibilities of both bride and groom, especially in the giving of consent and in the wearing of a ring that bears testimony to their commitment. The changes underscore the anticipation of children as well as the responsibility that the couple will share to bring them up according to the law of Christ and the church. The changes presume the faithfulness of the couple to each other as well as the permanence of their commitment. Indeed, mutual fidelity and lasting consent are exemplars of true love.

The Catholic Church has fashioned this ceremony as a vibrant expression of its faith in the duties and joys of marriage. The wedding aims to set the couple on a secure platform as they step forward into the welcome yet unpredictable demands of married life.

## NOTES

1. Vatican II, *Sacrosanctum concilium* (December 4, 1963), https://www.vatican.va/archive/hist _councils/ii_vatican_council/documents/vat-ii_const _19631204_sacrosanctum-concilium_en.html (hereafter cited as *SC*).

2. *The Roman Ritual in Latin and English with Rubrics and Plainchant Notation*, trans. and ed. Philip T. Weller, Vol. 1, *The Sacraments and Processions* (Boonville, NY: Preserving Christian Publications, 2007), 460–75.

3. Paul Turner, *Inseparable Love: A Commentary on The Order of Celebrating Matrimony in the Catholic Church* (Collegeville, MN: Liturgical Press, 2017), xv–xix.

4. *The Order of Celebrating Matrimony* (Collegeville, MN: Liturgical Press, 2016) (hereafter cited as OCM).

5. *The General Instruction of the Roman Missal* (Washington, DC: USCCB, 2011) (hereafter cited as GIRM).

6. Turner, *Inseparable Love,* 241–46.

7. Turner, *Inseparable Love,* 82.

8. *The Roman Ritual,* 462.

9. *The Roman Ritual,* 462 and 464.

10. Turner, *Inseparable Love,* 40.

11. See Liturgy Office England and Wales, "Preparing Your Wedding Liturgy," https://www.liturgyoffice.org.uk/Resources/Marriage/Preparation/Prep-Texts.shtml.

12. Neela Kale, "Are There Catholic Wedding Traditions in India That Are Particular to That Culture?," Busted Halo, January 6, 2011, https://bustedhalo.com/questionbox/are-there-catholic-wedding-traditions-in-india-that-are-particular-to-that-culture%E2%80%A8.

13. Turner, *Inseparable Love,* 120–21.

# CHAPTER

# 12

## Gaudium et Spes

CLAUDIA LEAL

## CONTEXT

This chapter examines the reception of the concept of the family in the pastoral constitution *Gaudium et spes* in order to highlight theological teachings that derive from the document and their repercussions for the Catholic Church in the modern world in both their theoretical and practical aspects.[1] This exercise requires great methodological flexibility, since *Gaudium et spes* does not have a unique thematic focus and is widely addressed to all men and women of goodwill. Similarly, our approach must also avoid an all-encompassing exegesis. As such, this chapter will highlight some aspects, accents, and intuitions that could be relevant for the contemporary reader and, at the same time, might provide new paths for further theological developments. It should be noted that this chapter will not inquire deeply into the semantics of the concept of the family, because this task far exceeds our purpose here as well as the available space. Indeed, how to interpret the word "family" is a topic widely debated in the social sciences, particularly in law.[2] Rather, our analysis of the topic will examine the inclusivity of various cultural and theological heritages that still allow the family to be framed in religious terms. We will do so without exhaustively interrogating the operative definition of the term "family" in *Gaudium et spes* or settling differences among various conceptions of the family in contemporary theology or social sciences.

*Gaudium et spes* understands history as a space of salvation and the family as the basis of society. These insights cannot be adequately appreciated without recalling the historical climate that preceded them: the polemic response of the post-Tridentine mentality to the excessive secularization of social situations, the techno-scientific impetus in the field of human reproduction, and the growing influence of other Christian churches.[3] *Gaudium et spes* seeks to overcome the abyss between reason and faith that had been constructed amid modernity. In so doing, the constitution aspires to build a path for the category of experience as a formal and material theological principle for the interpretation of the gospel (*GS* 46).

The significance of *Gaudium et spes* regarding the family transcends its declarations about marriage. This applies to its theological concept of the family as well as its treatment of the family in connection to social justice and other matters related to the *res publica*. Thus, one of the most important motivations in this chapter's presentation of *Gaudium et spes* will be to underline as one of the church's unfinished tasks the necessary development of a comprehensive reflection on family in its social dimension beyond the area of sexual relations.

## COMMENTARY

*Gaudium et spes* has been analyzed from many perspectives. The constitution's laborious editorial history highlights the inexperience of the Catholic Church in those restless years of the mid-twentieth century in addressing humanity from a place that does not assume *a priori* a simple mission to announce doctrinal truths. In contrast, this Vatican II document aimed to generate a mutual confidence through dialogue with "the world."[4] The preparatory process for *Gaudium et spes* was for many people a sign of weakness and internal conflict.[5] Important personalities in the conciliar environment considered the constitution to be inessential to the council's final set of documents. Nevertheless, its influence and significance have increased over the years. Perhaps the growing relevance of *Gaudium et spes* has to do precisely with the fact that both its history and its contents continue to reflect the world we live in today: that of a fluid culture that prefers contextual stories in which contradictions and cracks emerge from the real lives of men and women.

### The Global Human Family

Reflecting upon the influence and meaning of *Gaudium et spes* enables us to understand the most important traits of its teaching on the family. Here, the constitution represents a Copernican Revolution, as the dynamics already set out by Jesus and Saint Paul in the New Testament open the gates for Christian and Catholic identity to acknowledge humankind as a single family that is on its way to salvation by diverse ways and various means. The resulting ecclesiology, as has often been acknowledged, transcends previous interpretations of *extra ecclesia nulla salus* and, without formally canceling its magisterial validity, reformulates its meaning and creates a new hermeneutic horizon for its interpretation.[6] In the same way that Saint Paul persuaded early Christian communities that a person need not be Hebrew to be a Christian, Vatican II acknowledges that it is not necessary to be within the visible boundaries of Catholicism in order to belong to the Church of Christ. Such boundaries are not entirely useful, and there are other ways, mysterious but clear, in which a human being may be a witness to Christ.

Broadening the frontiers of Catholic identity is entirely consistent with the ecclesiological turning point of the dogmatic constitution *Lumen gentium*.[7] In the same way that *Lumen gentium* moves away from the idea of the Catholic Church as a perfect society, characterized by a strict hierarchy with clear degrees of belonging, *Gaudium et spes* moves away from the vision of two histories—one human and the other divine—that run on two parallel lines without real connection. In *Gaudium et spes*, all dualisms, almost mysteriously, are replaced by a message of salvation that can only be told "in the light of the Gospel and human experience" (*GS* 46).[8]

The understanding of humankind as a family also has a social and political dimension that cannot be ignored. Previous decades had seen the rise of authoritarian regimes capable of committing horrible atrocities and barbarities within Europe and beyond. Above all, for the first time in history the technological power of modernity put human beings in the position of being able to annihilate life as we know it. In this new situation, what metaphor could humanity find to think about its future or, in theological terms, to reflect on salvation? The family is probably not the only possibility, but it is a fruitful and compelling option, as it carries the conceptual and symbolic strength to signify in the lives of all human beings a claim of belonging and coresponsibility that moves us together to look ahead toward an uncertain future.[9] The metaphor of the family allows all human beings to recognize themselves as members of a plural body, intimately connected in its origin and destiny. It is universal enough to speak to every man and woman at any time and in any tradition and yet particular enough to acquire in the history of every human being its own unique traits. This tension between the individual and society must not be artificially resolved, nor should it eliminate room for multiple interpretations: the social order is primarily at the service of the person, not the other way around.

The Kantian liberal principle of each person as an end in him or herself is compatible with the affirmation of a universal family, since the concepts are linked in both origin and destiny. The theological expression of this anthropology appears in a particularly beautiful and accomplished way in paragraph 24, which establishes a mysterious resemblance between human love and divine love. The resolution of this tension is remarkably in favor of the dignity of the person who finds and expresses her or his dignity through self-giving love. This conclusion must also be considered as a basis for dialogue between the Christian tradition and feminism at any stage. In fact, while many authors focus on criticizing religious traditions in general for having considered women only as means to an end, the conciliar assembly exposed their adherence to the Kantian principle and their conviction for the promotion of women (*GS* 52).

*Gaudium et spes*'s insights regarding humankind as a family have ongoing relevance for our present times as events of war that once appeared remote rise with devastating and threatening power. Today as at the time of the council, the language of a narrow metaphysics is not enough to build the common basis of understanding and commitment necessary to preserve the continuity of life. If humanity is a family, it has the responsibility to manage with adequate resources its own internal diversity, dissent, and disagreement and eventually to face fair penalties when its members hurt one of their own. Looking at the global community not only as a collection of nation states but also as a global family that must manage its own destiny is a precious contribution of *Gaudium et spes* that could be further developed in our own time.[10]

## Toward a Rearrangement of the Purposes of Marriage

The magisterial teachings regarding marriage that immediately preceded *Gaudium et spes*

were naturally placed within a dualistic understanding that, as pointed out above, relied on the opposition of grace and nature. In that paradigm, the natural and the supernatural are part of marriage by way of the categories of contract and sacrament, meticulously guarded in both doctrine and in canon law. In the twentieth century, canon law exerted an oversized influence on the understanding of marriage in the Catholic Church.[11] This led to marriage being presented primarily as a contract without deeply recognizing the need to attend to the spiritual and pastoral dimensions of marital and family experience.[12] Importantly, *Gaudium et spes* does not cancel this contractual dimension of marriage but instead recovers a sapiential tone to integrate and recompose the order of the purposes of marriage.

Chapter 2 of *Gaudium et spes*, dedicated specifically to the dignity of marriage and the family, set the basis for the rearrangement of marriage's purposes in doctrinal and canonical terms (*GS* 23–32). The constitution's hesitation to explicitly establish a primary purpose of matrimony, as had the 1917 *Code of Canon Law*, was a necessary consequence of the famous notes of "renewal" and "pastoral care" that, in Alberigo's opinion, represent the principal novelty of the council's proposal as a whole.[13] Concerns for renewal and pastoral outreach moved the council to uphold the priority of evangelization on the basis of a serene and prolific dialogue with realities that until recently were seen as antagonistic and opposed to the ideals of Christianity.[14] This development, which had many of its own issues and difficulties, provided a renewed recognition of the mission entrusted to the church in the midst of temporal realities. *Gaudium et spes* recognized that the church's relationship with society and consequently with the family is one not only of service and charity but also, and perhaps especially, reciprocal understanding as a joint search for truth that aspires to achieve the greatest benefit in given circumstances (*GS* 44). Only in this scenario is it possible to correctly understand that *Gaudium et spes* supports the importance of mutual love between spouses as a good that reaches the level of esteem previously reserved only for procreation and the care of offspring to the point of making spousal love the precondition thereof.

The need for renewal in the field of the theology of marriage was already being felt before the council.[15] This was demonstrated in part by the genesis of pastoral marriage movements that, under the influence of *Casti connubii* and updated theologies, were starting to recover pastoral intuitions enunciated within the Christian tradition before the polarization between faith and culture moved the Catholic Church toward an almost exclusively juridical interpretation of marriage.[16] The rediscovery of subjectivity and the goodness of the conjugal union were the basis for new practices of spirituality and pastoral accompaniment.

Understanding this rearrangement of marriage's objectives has often gone hand in hand with a degree of caution, which was subsequently heightened by the ecclesial events linked to *Humanae vitae* as well as philosophical and cultural debates on the relationship between sexuality and procreation. Likewise, the emergence of feminist philosophies in the second half of the twentieth century generated a whole series of contextual theologies that are still developing and bearing fruit.[17] *Gaudium et spes*'s decision to turn to the world in a relationship of reciprocal understanding, beyond the institutions and doctrines of the Catholic Church, serves as a guide for how these continued developments might be incorporated into the life of the church.

### The Family as a "School of Humanism"

The social network of the family depends on the delicate balances of the relationships between spouses and with their children as well as the relationships between different generations. What's more, we must also consider the mutual empathy and support between families and the social institutions that ensure their harmonious development as well as the singular individuals who live within them. The first chapter of the constitution explains that the search for fair relations is only possible by developing an anthropology that contradicts the anthropological pessimism of modernity.[18] It does so by offering a reading of the social contract in which the communal vocation of the human being is a gift to be celebrated, not a problem to be tolerated.

In this way, interdependence as a hermeneutic key to the interpretation of reality is an important theological contribution for accurately understanding social questions. Efforts to measure quality of life worldwide indicate that people tend to find the most meaning in their lives within the private sphere and that their emotional family ties are the source of significant joy and a sense of belonging. The related implication of this finding is that in social institutions, people tend to experience a loss of prestige and credibility. While not all people find their greatest joy in the private sphere and while families are not always hospitable or safe relational spaces, for many the social world beyond the family is a source of oppression, uncertainty, and injustice.[19] In this context, we should not be surprised by phenomena such as the demographic crisis, worrisome reports about mental health, and losses of associative capacity.

Contemporary moral philosophy is emphatic in its own diagnosis. Institutions have not learned to adequately manage human vulnerability. They have not become spaces where individuals can display their capacities without paying the price—both real and symbolic—of a contractualist anthropology that, against all historical evidence, has described us as free, equal, and independent human beings.[20] In contrast, the family is a "school of humanity" that is capable of transmitting an ethical wisdom to institutions and concerns first and foremost how to manage human vulnerability. However, transmitting and strengthening this wisdom depends dialectically on the guarantees offered by social institutions to family praxis.

*Gaudium et spes* portrays marriage as a social issue rather than an institution that only regards individuals (*GS* 52). This is an authentically avant-garde reflection in the context of the social ethical theories of modernity, which unfortunately long considered marriage and the family as institutions relegated to the private sphere. This view removed marriage and family from public scrutiny and left unprotected their most fragile members: women and children. Following the council, magisterial teachings did not develop this aspect of the constitution incisively. Instead, when speaking of marriage and the family, the magisterium privileged a perspective that overemphasized the perfection of the marital bond as the basis of family. *Gaudium et spes* strongly affirms the duty of institutions to protect the family and to ensure that people without a family can understand the experiences that families offer. Institutions primarily serve the family, not the other way around.

## INTERPRETATION

Although some approaches to theologies on marriage have been established within the Catholic academic and pastoral tradition, a theology of the family in its deepest sense with all that this implies, especially in the public sphere, remains underdeveloped. Despite frequent references, personalism has not permeated certain aspects of moral theology, and its implications have yet to be fully realized. The relationships within the family that are not included within the sphere of the conjugal, sexual relationship are rarely the object of study in moral theology in and of themselves. Nor do these relationships generate significant interest when it comes to outlining a theological anthropology of the family.[21]

Language that emphasizes and embraces the vulnerability of family members and the healing of wounds within family histories is often an important part of the theological and pastoral task. But this alone does not fully encompass the task that *Gaudium et spes* entrusts to the Christian community of learning from the family and reflecting theologically on how familial relationships beyond the sexual union (such as maternity, paternity, filiation, and generation) give shape to family life. The Christian tradition has the necessary elements to offer not only a message of compassion toward those in need but also the

anthropological bases for understanding the experience of family in a positive and universal way. Thus, various elements of *Gaudium et spes* are still hidden pearls waiting to transform reality.

Likewise, the pastoral constitution's commitment to temporal realities should not be confused with a gesture of generosity, not even from a political perspective. On the contrary, an adequate understanding of creation necessarily leads to a vision of historicity as a way of being human. In this theologically informed perspective, everything is part of a loving, creative design that is sustained even within the trials of our daily tasks. This vision of historicity necessarily moves the church to set in motion a constant discernment aimed at understanding the mystery of salvation as it is revealed in history. This mystery certainly includes the extraordinary creativity with which families manage their resources—economic, affective, intellectual, and human—in order to respond to the multiple demands and contingencies they face. It is still necessary to chart the horizon of the future and to do so on the basis of *Gaudium et spes*, since the depth of what the constitution offers remains both pertinent and universal. Moreover, the various dialogues that *Gaudium et spes* proposed are far from being fully realized. When considering the family from a theological perspective, the disposition to dialogue can be realized in the exercise of contemplating and listening to human love, in all its beauty and vulnerability, in the light of the divine mystery.

### Understanding Human Love

The challenges of today's context—interculturality, mass media, and artificial intelligence, among others—indicate the urgency of developing a more robust anthropology that is capable of providing human love with a rich spectrum of conceptual and symbolic resources to describe its nuances. Such a theological anthropology would be able to read experiences of human love in terms of mystery and gift without abstracting or enclosing the vitality and profound historicity of their expressions within philosophical systems.

The need for less idealized presentations of family realities is a frequent complaint. This is not only because proclaiming the Gospel of the Family appears less credible if the problems of violence, abuse, and ambiguity (both as documented by the social sciences and experienced in countless individual lives) are simply ignored but also because everything indicates that in the experience of family, as in mystical experience, aridity and scarcity are indispensable realities. If in the mystical life we speak about "deserts" and "dark nights," it is necessary to also talk about these categories with respect to human love and to focus on ideas such as asymmetry, mourning, passion, failure, and conflict with greater clarity and complexity.[22]

The close relationship between human love and divine love mentioned above cannot be understood by a metaphysics that is unaffected by history. The similarity between love as a human experience and love as a constitutive feature of divine identity acquires its particular coherence within creation as it unfolds in filial, fraternal, conjugal, and erotic relationships. *Gaudium et spes* takes up the image of the covenant to speak of the sacred character of marriage and the family (*GS* 48) but does not theologically explore the collective dimension of this covenant. This absence has been prolonged by socially incomplete theologies of marriage ever since. But now, various voices are beginning to explore the fact that the weakening of family ties is intimately associated with the weakening of marital bonds. There is an interdependence between these two that demands attention from not only the social sciences but also theological anthropology.[23] So too in the field of ecclesiology, a more careful observation of family ties will help to recover a qualitative notion of catholicity that might correct the mistaken identity hierarchies that are sometimes imposed when speaking about the Christian family.

It is the language of *Gaudium et spes*, more than its actual content, that helps to open these horizons today. In the apostolic exhortation *Amoris laetitia*, the magisterium of the Catholic Church addresses itself specifically to pregnant women, parents-in-law, grandparents, and divorced fathers and mothers.[24] Putting actual faces on the ties generated by human love, beyond simple nuclear families, is a first step toward a theological anthropology that fosters reflection on lived human experiences in the light of faith. Through *Gaudium et spes*, the Catholic Church shows that God's saving action has no limits and is simultaneously at work in every human reality.[25] Salvation is both universal and, at the same time, relates to each human event.

## CONCLUSION

Many communities are experiencing a declining stability of the institution of marriage both juridically and symbolically. This situation often yields merely perplexed inaction in Catholic communities, which often do not appear to notice that the decreasing desire for marriage is often accompanied by a persistent or even increasing desire for family. If we do not inquire honestly about the reasons for this phenomenon in a spirit of empathy and good faith, it is likely that we will continue to ignore the experiences, both just and unjust, of the most vulnerable groups in society.

Family models change, mutate, and adapt, yet they nevertheless continue to be recognized in the image of that core where unique persons, just as they are, find acceptance, protection, refuge, and committed companions with whom to share their lives. Social sciences can provide us with empirical data, both quantitative and qualitative, that confirm the relevance of the family as a space for growth and meaning for human beings across cultures and societies. This data should stimulate the sciences in general and theology in particular to explore in detail the resources that families deploy, in diverse cultural and religious contexts, in their care for human life.

The salvific strength of *Gaudium et spes* was and still is its open horizon to dialogue with any interlocutor who is willing to undertake the search for what is good without closing any door *a priori*. In this sense, any discipline, religious tradition, culture, or philosophy is a suitable partner for gaining understanding and walking side by side toward horizons of justice and kindness.

## NOTES

1. Vatican II, Pastoral Constitution on the Church in the Modern World: *Gaudium et Spes* (December 7, 1965), https://www.vatican.va/archive /hist_councils/ii_vatican_council/documents/vat-ii _const_19651207_gaudium-et-spes_en.html (cited hereafter as *GS*).

2. See Yolanda López, "La Familia Como Campo de Saber de las Ciencias Sociales," *Trabajo Social* 5 (2005): 25–40; Roswitha Hipp, "Orígenes del Matrimonio y de la Familia Modernos," *Revista Austral de Ciencias Sociales* 11 (2006): 59–78; and Jorge del Picó Rubio, "Evolución y Actualidad de la Concepción de Familia: Una Apreciación de la Incidencia Positiva de las Tendencias Dominantes a Partir de la Reforma del Derecho Matrimonial Chileno," *Ius et praxis* 17, no. 1 (2011): 31–56.

3. See Gabriella Zarri, "Il Matrimonio Tridentino," in *Il Concilio di Trento e il Moderno,* ed. Paolo Prodi and Wolfgang Reinhard, 437–83 (Bologna: Il Mulino, 1996).

4. See Jesús Santiago Madrigal Terrazas, "Fundamentos Doctrinales de la Nueva Relación Iglesia-Mundo. Releyendo Gaudium et Spes (nn. 40–45)," in *Los Nuevos Escenarios de la Iglesia en la Sociedad Española: En el 40 Aniversario de la Constitución Gaudium et Spes*, 103–20 (Madrid: Instituto Social León XIII).

5. See, Carlos Schickendantz, "Un Género Literario y Teológico en Formación: Debates en la Historia de la Redacción de Gaudium et Spes," *Revista Teologia* 57, no. 133 (2020): 185–215.

6. See Antônio Lopes Ribeiro, "Do Exclusivismo ao Inclusivismo: A Virada da Igreja Católica Frente à Diversidade Religiosa," *Protestantismo em Revista* 44, no. 2 (2019): 156–75; and Gustavo Gutiérrez, "Iglesia y Mundo: Crisis de un Sistema Teológico," *Revista Mensaje* 20, no. 199 (June 1971): 203–9.

7. Vatican II, Dogmatic Constitution on the Church: *Lumen Gentium* (November 21, 1964), https://www.vatican.va/archive/hist_councils/ii _vatican_council/documents/vat-ii_const_19641121 _lumen-gentium_en.html.

8. See also Sandra Arenas, "Desdibujando las Fronteras Eclesiales: ¿Cuál Es y Dónde Está la Ecclesia Semper Reformanda?," *Teología y Vida* 59, no. 1 (March 2018): 33–58.

9. Gerardo Romo Morales, "La Familia Como Institución y Universal: Análisis de los Cambios Modernos," in *La Familia Como Institución. Cambios y Permanencias*, ed. Gerardo Romo Morales (Tonalá, Mexico: Universidad de Guadalajara, Centro Universitario de Tonalá, 2016), 103.

10. This is not a new idea. Indeed, some theologians have warned of the need and power of this idea within societies that claim to found their existence without reference to transcendent truths. However, it is still a task to be done. See Carlos Federico Schickendantz, "Una Elipse con Dos Focos: Hacia un Nuevo Método Teológico a Partir de Gaudium et Spes," *Teología* 110 (2013): 85–105; and Ildefonso Camacho Laraña, "La Huella de Juan XXIII en la Constitución Pastoral Gaudium et Spes," *Revista de Fomento Social* 70 (2015): 443–78.

11. This is a developing argument. For Western culture (which strongly believes in courtly and romantic love), it has not been easy to persuasively reformulate the contents of marriage as a contract. The issue becomes urgent when it comes to providing protection to the most fragile members of the family community, especially children, economically dependent spouses, etc. See Javier Hervada, "La Inseparabilidad entre Contrato y Sacramento en el Matrimonio," *II Simposio Internacional de Teología de la Universidad de Navarra* (Pamplona, Spain: EUNSA, 1980); and Teresa Cervera-Soto, "Piero Pellegrino, Il Consenso Matrimoniale nel Codice di Diritto Canonico Latino, G. Giappichelli, Collana di Studi di Diritto Canonico ed Ecclesiastico, Torino, 1998, 319 pp. [RECENSIÓN]," *Ius Canonicum* 39, no. 78 (1999): 801–4.

12. See chapter 6 in this volume.

13. Marco Vergottini, "Vaticano II: L'Evento Oltre il Testo?," *Teologia* 22, no. 1 (1997): 87. See also Gabriel Richi Alberti, "La Familia Como Emblema de la Pastoralidad de la Iglesia," *Revista Española de Teología* 76 (2016): 109–24; Luis Carlos Bernal, SJ, "El Amor Conyugal en la Constitución Gaudium et Spes," *Theologica Xaveriana* 35 (1975): 7–20; and Ardian Ndreca, "La Libertà come Destino dell'Uomo alla Luce della *Gaudium et Spes*," *Urbaniana University Journal* 67, no. 2 (2014): 216.

14. An informative reconstruction of the text's editorial history can be seen in G. Marengo, *Generare nell'Amore. La Missione della Famiglia Cristiana nell'Insegnamento Ecclesiale dal Vaticano II a Oggi* (Assisi: Citadella, 2014), esp. chapter 2.

15. See Marengo, *Generare nell'Amore*, 34–35.

16. See Enrique Berzal de la Rosa, "El Impacto del Concilio Vaticano II en los Movimientos Seglares de Acción Católica," *Gerónimo de Uztariz* 32 (2016): 89–108.

17. See Virginia Azcuy, "Teología e Inequidad de Género: Diálogo, Interpretación y Ética en el Cruce de las Disciplinas," in *Puntos de Encuentro: Foro Sobre Teología y Género*, 37–63 (Buenos Aires: Instituto Universitario ISEDET, 2006).

18. See Dries Bosschaert, "Understanding the Shift in Gaudium et Spes: From Theology of History to Christian Anthropology," *Theological Studies* 78, no. 3 (2017): 634–58.

19. See Bryan H. Massam, "Quality of Life: Public Planning and Private Living," *Progress in Planning* 58 no. 3 (2002): 141–227.

20. See Eva Feder Kittay, *Love's Labor: Essays on Women, Equality and Dependency* (New York: Routledge, 2013); and Martha C. Nussbaum, *Hiding from Humanity* (Princeton, NJ: Princeton University Press, 2009). These and other authors, such as Carol Gilligan, Nancy Fraser, and Amartya Sen, confirm the deficit that social and philosophical ethics have when it comes to recognizing care work within societies. Indeed, throughout history an invisible army of human beings–with women in the absolute majority—have assumed the care of children, the elderly, and the sick and have rarely received compensation or recognition for this work.

21. There is an incipient interest in giving motherhood a more robust and sophisticated theological matrix, but it is clear that the work remains to be done. See Alba Rocio Machuca Rueda, "Una Construcción de Teología Narrativa desde la Experiencia de Maternidad en las Niñas de la Calle," MA thesis (Universidad Pontificia Bolivariana, 2014); and Carolina Carriero, "La Gratitudine per la Nascita e la Cura della Vita nella 'Teologia del Corpo' di Giovanni Paolo II," *Studia Bioethica* 1, no. 1 (2008): 21–24.

22. A beautiful example of this wider concern is found in María Marcela Mazzini, "La Maternidad como Celda: Un Lugar para el Hijo, un Camino para la Madre (o la Solidaria Esperanza de Abrir un Espacio Espiritual)," *Cuadernos Monásticos* 139 (2001): 423.

23. See Pierangelo Sequeri, *La Fede e la Giustizia degli Affetti: Teologia Fondamentale della Forma Cristiana* (Siena: Cantagalli, 2020); and Aristide Fumagalli, *L'Amore Sessuale: Fondamenti e Criteri Teologico-Morali* (Brescia, Italy: Queriniana, 2017). See also Pierangelo Sequeri, "Affetti e Sessualita: L'Attualità del Significante Coniugale di Humanae Vitae," *Anthropotes* 34, no. 1 (2018): 211–34.

24. Francis, *Amoris laetitia* (March 19, 2016), 169, 192, 198, and 297, https://www.vatican.va/content/dam/francesco/pdf/apost_exhortations/documents/papa-francesco_esortazione-ap_20160319_amoris-laetitia_en.pdf.

25. In a certain sense, it is possible to affirm that the theoretical basis for developing this reflection already exists. Indeed, the so-called theology of the signs of the times is a good exercise in understanding temporal realities, an exercise that certainly requires discernment and that could serve as a starting point for our argument. See Ignaco Ellacuría, "Discernir 'el Signo' de los Tiempos," *Diakonía* 17 (1981): 57–59; Juan Noemi, "En la Búsqueda de una Teología de los 'Signos de los Tiempos,'" *Teología y Vida* 48, no. 4 (2007): 439–47; Virginia Raquel Azcuy, Carlos Schickendantz, and Eduardo Silva, eds., *Teología de los Signos de los Tiempos Latinoamericanos,* Vol. 11 (Santiago de Chile: Ediciones Universidad Alberto Hurtado, 2013).

*Paul VI*

# CHAPTER

# 13

## Humanae Vitae

ERIC MARCELO O. GENILO, SJ

## CONTEXT

*Humanae vitae*, published in 1968, describes four developments that prompted the Catholic Church to revisit its teaching on marriage and birth regulation.[1] These were rapid population growth, increased recognition of the dignity of women and their role in society, a shift in the church's understanding of conjugal love and its relationship to the marital act, and advancements in reproductive technology that made artificial means of birth control more effective and accessible (*HV* 2).

In response to these developments, John XXIII formed the Pontifical Commission for the Study of Population, Family, and Birth in 1963.[2] The body was tasked to study the various issues surrounding birth regulation and submit its recommendations to the pope. Paul VI continued papal support for the commission's work after the death of John XXIII. The commission held five meetings from 1963 to 1966. Apart from theologians, bishops, doctors, and social scientists, the commission also included the lay founders of the Christian Family Movement. These members gave voice to the experience of Catholic couples trying to follow the church's teaching on family planning.[3] Because the commission's work was ongoing, the Second Vatican Council refrained

from including definitive statements on birth regulation in *Gaudium et spes*.[4]

The commission submitted its final report in 1966. The report, "Schema for a Document on Responsible Parenthood," commonly referred to as the Majority Report, called for a change in the teaching on contraception. The report argued that the morality of marital sexual activity depends not on every conjugal act's openness to procreation but instead on a couples' practice of responsible parenthood throughout their marriage. The report recommended that the church give spouses the responsibility to decide the most prudent means to plan their families, excluding sterilization in general and abortion in all cases.[5] A small group of commission members submitted a separate report, "State of the Question: The Doctrine of the Church and Its Authority," commonly referred to as the Minority Report. The group argued that the prohibition on contraception is irreformable and that a change in the teaching of *Casti connubii* would undermine the magisterium's authority to bind consciences.[6]

In *Humanae vitae*, Paul VI decided to retain the prohibition against contraception, contrary to the recommendation of the Majority Report, but also chose not to use the authority-based arguments of the Minority Report. While the 1968 encyclical gave direction to marriage preparation and family planning programs in the church, it also caused divisions within the Catholic community. The document's reception by clergy and laity ranged from ready acceptance to public dissent. In the years after *Humanae vitae*, the church refined the application of its norms on contraception in response to new situations.

## COMMENTARY

### Conjugal Love

*Humanae vitae* describes several essential characteristics of conjugal love (*HV* 9). First, the love between spouses must be fully human and free, expressing a personal decision to share a permanent union with another. Second, conjugal love embraces the totality of each spouse. Husbands and wives are to accept, support, and accompany one another in their journey of growth and integration. Third, this love is faithful and exclusive. It calls for monogamy, lifelong fidelity, and a commitment to face the daily challenges of married life with patience and forgiveness. Fourth, conjugal love is fecund. Spouses should be open to raising children when possible and timely.

Nearly fifty years later in *Amoris laetitia*, Pope Francis warned against proposing "a far too abstract and almost artificial theological ideal of marriage, far removed from the concrete situations and practical possibilities of real families."[7] Thus, a fitting complement to the characteristics of conjugal love mentioned in *Humanae vitae* is Francis's reflections in *Amoris laetitia* on Saint Paul's words on love (1 Cor 13: 4–7) addressing the concrete difficulties couples face in their marital relationship (*AL* 90–118).

### Responsible Parenthood

*Humanae vitae* calls on married couples to practice responsible parenthood (*HV* 10). This entails an awareness of and respect for the biological processes of reproduction, the use of reason, and serious consideration of

physical, economic, psychological, and social conditions that can affect the family's welfare. *Humanae vitae* prescribes to couples a set of duties according to a "right order of priorities" (*HV* 10). The couple's first duty is to follow God's will in the natural order, followed by duties to themselves, their family, and society.

In practice, most couples give weightier consideration to factors such as their household's available resources and readiness to raise children, risks related to the mother's and child's health, and the state of the marital union. While *Humanae vitae* places great value on the good of procreation in God's plan for marriage, it fails to explicitly acknowledge that any duty of a married couple to God's will cannot be separated from or conflict with their commitment to protect and foster the good of the family and its members.

### Conscience

*Humanae vitae* presents following one's conscience mainly as faithful obedience to God's will as interpreted by the magisterium (*HV* 10). The encyclical reminds couples that their actions must correspond to God's will as inscribed "in the very nature of marriage and its use" that the "constant teaching of the Church spells it out" (*HV* 10). The encyclical emphasizes the "objective moral order which was established by God, and of which a right conscience is the true interpreter" (*HV* 10). The meaning of "right conscience" is implied in *Gaudium et spes*'s admonition to couples that they should "always be governed according to a conscience dutifully conformed to the divine law itself, and should be submissive toward the Church's teaching office, which authentically interprets that law in the light of the Gospel" (*GS* 50).

However, the activity of the conscience cannot be so easily reduced to unreflective submission to magisterial teaching. *Gaudium et spes* defines conscience as "the most secret core and sanctuary of a man" where one is "alone with God, Whose voice echoes in his depths" (*GS* 16). A key phrase here is "alone with God." The magisterium offers its wisdom and guidance to discerning individuals who make their final decision before God and take responsibility for it. More recently, Pope Francis has reminded the church that it is "called to form consciences, not to replace them" (*AL* 37).

Church leaders have recognized that individuals have the duty and capacity to make prudential moral choices, especially when extraordinary circumstances make it difficult or dangerous to follow the church's prohibition on contraception. For example, in 2001 the South African Bishops Conference addressed the case of a couple where one spouse is infected with HIV:

> The Church accepts that everyone has the right to defend one's life against mortal danger. This would include using the appropriate means and course of action. Similarly, where one spouse is infected with HIV/AIDS, they must listen to their consciences. They are the only ones who can choose the appropriate means in order to defend themselves against the infection.[8]

The bishops of Chad advised couples in a similar situation to use their conscience as "the ultimate moral rule."[9] They reminded spouses that "no one is bound to do the impossible."[10]

These examples demonstrate that every couple has the right to decide according to their consciences whether the church's teaching on contraception applies in a situation where serious factors hinder its safe and viable implementation.

## Interpreting Natural Law

According to *Humanae vitae*, couples must follow God's designs in nature as interpreted by the church's magisterium. From this basis, the encyclical teaches that any intervention intended to disrupt biological processes that lead to procreation is prohibited. However, the magisterium has utilized different approaches to interpreting natural law with different subject matter. In situations involving sexual activity and procreation, Catholic teaching favors a physicalist approach that views the structure of the human reproductive system as an unchanging blueprint of God's will for the use of reproductive faculties. Well beyond *Humanae vitae*, this physicalism can be seen in magisterial teachings on contraception, sterilization, same-sex activity, and assisted reproduction. In contrast, on matters involving social conditions and interactions, the church uses a personalist approach that gives importance to the whole person's totality and the full development of every member of society.[11] This personalism can be seen in the church's social teaching on just wages, human rights, the death penalty, and slavery. The magisterium also applies personalism in the realm of medical ethics to allow interventions in the human body to prevent disease, disability, or death. For example, Catholic teaching permits organ transplants, blood transfusions, vaccinations, and the implantation of medical devices such as pacemakers, stents, and metal pins. These interventions manipulate, replace, or enhance body parts and processes, enabling the body to function differently from what it can naturally do on its own.

The church's selective application of a physicalist interpretation of natural law to sex and procreation may not adequately consider situations where pregnancy can have severe consequences on a mother's health and the family's stability. In such cases, a personalist approach that values the integral good of individuals, the marital relationship, and the family may be more appropriate. Since the church regards the family as the primary unit of society, family planning must also be guided by the church's social teachings and its commitment to promoting the common good and human flourishing. A year before *Humanae vitae*, Paul VI in *Populorum progressio* had reminded that "endowed with intellect and free will, each man is responsible for his self-fulfillment even as he is for his salvation. He is helped, and sometimes hindered, by his teachers and those around him; yet whatever be the outside influences exerted on him, he is the chief architect of his own success or failure."[12]

## Inseparability of the Unitive and Procreative Aspects of the Marital Act

*Humanae vitae* acknowledges that human fertility has natural cycles and that "new life is not the result of each and every act of sexual intercourse" (*HV* 11). However, the encyclical still asserts that the church "teaches that each and every marital act must of necessity retain its intrinsic relationship to the procreation of human life" (*HV* 11). It further contends that this teaching is based on the "inseparable connection, established by God, which man on his own initiative may not break, between the unitive significance and the procreative significance which are both inherent to the marriage act" (*HV* 12). However, this principle of inseparability was not actually present in official Catholic teaching until *Humanae vitae* asserted it as a necessary teaching. Research on the origin of *Humanae vitae* gives strong evidence that the principle does not in fact come from the "constant teaching of the church" but instead owes its creation to the ideas and writings of Karol Wojtyła, the future Pope John Paul II, who had assisted Paul VI in the preparation of *Humanae vitae*.[13]

Despite this assertion of inseparability, it is clear that spouses still need to exercise conscientious discernment about whether maintaining the connection between the unitive and procreative aspects of the marital act is necessary in extraordinary situations. As seen from the bishops' statements on HIV, allowing such discernment is in keeping with the proper respect owed to the consciences of couples.

### Unlawful Birth Control Methods

*Humanae vitae* describes three methods of birth control that it considers illicit (*HV* 14). The first method is direct abortion, even for therapeutic reasons. Direct abortion is always objectively wrong because it terminates the life of an embryo or fetus and carries the canonical penalty of excommunication. However, a careful examination of every case of abortion is necessary to determine the subjective culpability of persons involved and whether the penalty of excommunication is applicable. Factors such as grave fear, coercion, ignorance, misinformation, and uncontrollable emotions can affect the level of culpability of those who commit or assist in a direct abortion. Without denying the objective gravity of abortion, in 2016 Pope Francis extended the faculty to lift the excommunication for direct abortion to all priests as a means of making the sacraments more accessible to penitents who incurred excommunication.[14]

The second method of birth control condemned by *Humanae vitae* is direct sterilization. Less grave than direct abortion, direct sterilization is still deemed objectively wrong because it involves mutilation of a part or parts of the reproductive system and termination, often permanently, of the capacity to bear children. This condemnation is in line with earlier Catholic teaching in both its clear judgment and its reductive understanding of the full complexity of such decisions. Church leaders who are celibate and have no children of their own sometimes have difficulty understanding the situations of married couples contemplating the option of sterilization. For example, in 1993 a question was raised to the Congregation for the Doctrine of the Faith (CDF) whether it was lawful for a woman with a damaged uterus to have it removed to avoid a future pregnancy that could endanger the woman's health. The CDF responded that removing the damaged uterus in such a case would be illicit sterilization because there was no immediate danger to the woman unless a pregnancy was present. Instead, the CDF advised such a woman to use approved methods to prevent pregnancy, such as total abstinence or periodic continence.[15] In 2018, the CDF allowed the removal of a damaged uterus in a case where the uterus could not bring a pregnancy to term.[16] The CDF explains that removing the uterus in this case is not direct sterilization, since the reproductive organs are "not capable of fulfilling their natural procreative function." In its later judgment, the CDF clarified that the previous response to the case given in 1993 was still valid because the latter case presented a relevant difference. According to the CDF, the difference between the two cases is the capacity of the damaged uterus to carry a child to term or not. Remarkably, the risk to a woman's health if she were to become pregnant was not considered a significant factor in deciding the liceity of removing a damaged uterus. Instead, the CDF response stresses that "the malice of sterilization consists in the refusal of children: it is an act against the *bonum prolis*."[17] This narrow view of the wrongness of sterilization is overly concerned with the physical structure of reproductive organs and lacking in pastoral sensitivity toward couples who have to deal with grave health risks during pregnancy and childbirth.

Five years before *Humanae vitae* and fully thirty years before the case of the damaged uterus was presented to the CDF, the moral theologian John Ford had given the probable opinion that removing a damaged uterus that could endanger a mother's life in a future pregnancy was not illicit direct sterilization. He questioned the suggestion that the woman should practice abstinence: "To say that she can avoid this danger by imposing perpetual abstinence on herself and her husband is to require a degree of heroism to which our moral principles do not oblige her."[18] Ford's insight remains valid to this day. When couples cannot risk or afford to have more children and the options of abstinence and natural family planning (NFP) are not possible, reliable, or safe because of health risks, dysfunctional marriages, addictions, and situations of abuse, sterilization may be the only humanly possible option to avoid grave harm to persons or to the family. Once again, discerning such a decision ought to be clearly appreciated as within the competence of the couple's consciences.

The third means of birth regulation prohibited by *Humanae vitae* is "any action which either before, at the moment of, or after sexual intercourse, is specifically intended to prevent procreation—whether as an end or as a means" (*HV* 14). The encyclical rejects the argument that contraceptive sex can be justified as a lesser evil compared to a greater evil one is trying to avoid. *Humanae vitae* also rejects the reasoning that the morality of an act of contraceptive sex can be subsumed into the goodness of past and future marital relations that faithfully observe

the church's teaching. Instead, it asserts that to directly intend to break the connection between the unitive and procreative significance of sexual relations is intrinsically wrong.

Church leaders, however, have shown sensitivity to some extraordinary situations where intention and circumstances can diminish the gravity of direct contraception or justify it as the more prudent choice. The bishops of South African and of Chad allowed HIV-discordant couples to discern the appropriate means to prevent the transfer of infection in sexual activity even if these include means that have contraceptive effects. Moreover, in cases of sexual assault, including marital rape, the bishops of the United States allow a victim to be treated in a Catholic medical facility with "medications that would prevent ovulation, sperm capacitation, or fertilization" as long as appropriate testing has shown that conception has not yet occurred and that the means used is not abortifacient.[19] In a 2016 interview, Pope Francis was asked about ways couples could avoid the Zika virus. The pope stated that "avoiding pregnancy is not an absolute evil" and referred to a historical case when Paul VI tacitly permitted contraceptive pills for nuns threatened with rape in a situation of war in Congo.[20] In all these examples, traditional moral principles and attentive consideration of intention and circumstances are crucial in evaluating the use of contraceptives in extraordinary situations. In the HIV and Zika cases, the principle of double effect allows the use of condoms to prevent infection with the unintended consequence of contraception. In the rape cases addressed by the US bishops and the case of threatened nuns in Congo, the principle of self-defense allows nonabortifacient contraception to prevent pregnancy from sexual assault. Thus, not every use of contraception is sinful or morally wrong.[21]

### Lawful Therapeutic Means

*Humanae vitae* allows therapeutic means to cure diseases even if these treatments have foreseen contraceptive or sterilizing effects as long as these effects are not directly intended (*HV* 15). This is an application of the principle of double effect, which morally permits an action with simultaneous good and harmful effects under the following conditions: the object of the act should not be intrinsically evil, the good effect is intended, and the harmful effect is not intended. In addition, the harmful effect must not cause the good effect, and the good effect must be proportionally more significant than the harmful effect.

As seen from the examples of episcopal and papal responses to HIV, the Zika virus, and sexual assault, the church is capable of refining its application of moral norms to address unique situations. These examples show us that creative use of the moral tradition, respect for the conscience, and attentiveness to the realities of persons and families can enable church leaders to form responsive pastoral solutions to protect the vulnerable and the threatened.

### Recourse to Infertile Periods

For couples planning the number and spacing of their children, *Humanae vitae* allows the use of the natural cycles of fertility and infertility. The encyclical clarifies that there is a difference between recourse to infertile periods and the use of contraception even if they have the same intention of regulating births. *Humanae vitae* considers the use of infertile periods as a legitimate exercise of "faculties provided by nature," while the use of contraceptives "obstruct the natural development of the generative process" (*HV* 16).

At present, a variety of modern and scientific methods of NFP have been developed and are effectively used by many couples, often with positive effects on their marriage. The success of these methods depends on accurately and consistently monitoring physical signs of ovulation. NFP also requires the cooperation of each spouse to abide by the method's regime and to refrain from sexual activity during fertile periods when necessary. While many couples practice NFP successfully, some cannot use NFP because of marital circumstances and the limitations of the methods. NFP does not prevent sexually transmitted diseases and thus is not recommended for couples where one is

infected with such a disease. Mutual agreement and cooperation between spouses are also necessary for NFP to be practiced effectively. Some spouses do not share the same level of assent to church teaching, and spouses might belong to different religious traditions with contrasting views on birth regulation. The presence of substance abuse, personality disorders, domestic violence, and situations that constrain the time couples spend together can make NFP very difficult or even impossible to practice. Therefore, pastors may propose and encourage the use of NFP but should not impose it as a solution to every family planning situation. The use of NFP is also a matter for the discerning consciences of couples according to their circumstances.

### Consequences of Artificial Methods

*Humanae vitae* warns that artificial birth control methods will encourage marital infidelity, lower moral standards, provide an incentive for young people to break the moral law, and reduce women's dignity and objectify them as instruments of desire. Acceptance of artificial birth control may also provide an impetus for governments to impose contraception and sterilization programs on their citizens. This warning about the improper use of reproductive technology by governments was important, as forced sterilization of persons deemed undesirable by society and coercive population control policies constitute significant violations of individual rights.

It is also true that contraception has aided acts of infidelity and premarital sex. However, a lack of access to contraceptives will not always deter a person already intent on engaging in adulterous or promiscuous behavior. The claim that contraceptives lower moral standards and induce young people to immorality presumes that contraception itself is a moral evil. As shown earlier, there are therapeutic and defensive uses of contraception that do not violate moral law. The assertion that the marital use of contraceptives can foster disrespect toward women and reduce them to sexual objects likewise presumes that contraceptive sex in marriage is always motivated by a selfish desire for pleasure or expresses an objectification and devaluation of one's spouse. This is not always the case, and once again the conclusion follows from a reductive perspective on complex situations. Artificial birth control can also be motivated by concerns for one's health and the well-being of one's spouse and family, particularly in situations where pregnancy, childbirth, and raising additional children can lead to harmful consequences or unbearable burdens. The encyclical's warning also narrowly focuses on male control of contraceptive use, disregarding the agency of women to choose contraception or sterilization according to their conscience and in mutual agreement with their husbands. It is not pastorally helpful to immediately impute ill motives in every use of artificial birth control without considering intention and circumstances.

## Concern of the Church

*Humanae vitae* anticipates that its teaching on birth regulation will elicit criticism and resistance (*HV* 18). This opposition is part of the reality of the church as "a sign of contradiction" in the world. The church sees it as her duty to proclaim this teaching as a contribution to promoting the good of spouses and fulfilling Christ's mandate to accompany humanity to the fullness of life.

The encyclical asserts that the church cannot change moral law because it did not create the law. Instead, the magisterium sees itself only as a guardian and interpreter of moral law and that it "could never be right for her to declare lawful what is in fact unlawful, since that, by its very nature, is always opposed to the true good of man" (*HV* 18). Nonetheless, the history of theological development has many examples where the church has changed long-held moral teachings, making lawful what was previously deemed unlawful (e.g., the charging of interest on loans, interfaith marriage,[22] and cremation) and making unlawful what was deemed lawful (e.g., capital punishment, slavery,[23] and the persecution of heretics).[24] Moral teachings can develop, and they legitimately move forward

according to changing times and circumstances. The church can repropose its interpretation and application of moral law when it opens itself to scientific evidence, social realities, and new insights into what it means to imitate Christ and promote human flourishing.

## Pastoral Directives

*Humanae vitae* recognizes that the church's norms for birth regulation can be difficult and even impossible to observe if one relies only on human effort. The encyclical assured families of God's grace that will sustain and strengthen them in their efforts to persevere in living out the church's teaching (*HV* 19–20).

The encyclical calls on couples to practice self-denial, draw grace from prayer and the sacraments, and be evangelizers to other married couples (*HV* 21, 25–26). Priests are instructed to show compassion, mercy, and encouragement toward penitents who confess their failings following the prescribed norms. Further pastoral guidance for confessors was provided by an instruction from the Pontifical Council for the Family in 1997. The instruction states that "sacramental absolution is not to be denied to those who, repentant after having gravely sinned against conjugal chastity, demonstrate the desire to strive to abstain from sinning again, notwithstanding relapses."[25] This is an application of the law of gradualness. Confessors are to "avoid demonstrating lack of trust either in the grace of God or in the dispositions of the penitent, by exacting humanly impossible absolute guarantees of an irreproachable future conduct."[26]

*Humanae vitae* recognizes that cooperation from different sectors of society is necessary to support couples planning their families according to the church's norms. The encyclical urges governments implementing population programs to respect moral laws and the freedom of couples to regulate births. Scientists are encouraged to develop and improve NFP methods, and doctors and nurses are to provide the appropriate advice to couples seeking guidance.

The encyclical also reminds priests and moral theologians of their duty to obey the magisterium. They are to communicate the teaching of the church entirely and faithfully, avoiding any dissension to preserve the peace and unity of the faithful. Their religious assent to the magisterium is based not on the arguments behind the teachings but instead on the belief that the Holy Spirit guides the church. Some in the church found this call to obedience both more restrictive than necessary and challenging to fulfill.

While many Catholics received the encyclical positively, critical voices within the church often prominently disagreed with *Humanae vitae*'s position on artificial forms of family planning. While most episcopal conferences came out with statements supporting *Humanae vitae*, the church had to contend with public dissent from clergy and laity.[27] In the years after its publication, *Humanae vitae* has been considered by its supporters as a prophetic document that shields marriages and families from the harmful effects of a "contraceptive mentality." At the same time, its critics viewed the document as a missed opportunity to respond adequately to the situation of families in difficult circumstances. Some see the encyclical as a timely and inspired gift of the church to humanity. In contrast, others see it as a flawed document that has discouraged Catholics and diminished the church's unity and moral credibility.

## INTERPRETATION

*Humanae vitae* is not a standalone document or the final word on contraception and the regulation of births. It is part of an evolving body of family teaching that continues to develop nuances and exceptions as new knowledge and situations present themselves. The encyclical's teachings must be understood in relation to other integral elements of the church's moral tradition, such as the primacy of conscience, care for the vulnerable, promotion of the common good, and the call to imitate Christ's mercy. The application of its teachings to concrete cases must always consider the circumstances and intentions of persons.

While authoritative, *Humanae vitae* is not infallible teaching, and Catholics are to render it religious assent as their sincere and formed conscience permits. The encyclical is intended for married couples who have the necessary capacity and freedom to fulfill its teaching. For couples in extraordinary situations where the teaching is extremely difficult or dangerous to carry out, they are to discern in their conscience what is the more prudent way forward for the good of the family. The couple can return to following the teaching when the extraordinary situation passes.

*Humanae vitae* can serve as a starting point to understanding what the church envisioned for the Catholic family shortly after Vatican II. Whatever is lacking or inapplicable in the document need not be a stumbling block to the faithful or a reason to dismiss church teaching. The encyclical's inadequacies can challenge theologians and pastoral leaders to draw creatively from the church's moral tradition to form timely and sensitive pastoral responses to the contemporary challenges faced by families seeking the fullness of life that God desires for them.

## NOTES

1. Paul VI, *Humanae vitae* (July 25, 1968), https://www.vatican.va/content/paul-vi/en/encyclicals/documents/hf_p-vi_enc_25071968_humanae-vitae.html (hereafter cited as *HV*).

2. Robert McClory, *Turning Point* (New York: Crossroad, 1995), 40.

3. McClory, *Turning Point*, 188–90.

4. Second Vatican Council, *Gaudium et spes* (December 7, 1965), Part II, chapter 1, footnote 14, https://www.vatican.va/archive/hist_councils/ii_vatican_council/documents/vat-ii_const_19651207_gaudium-et-spes_en.html (hereafter cited as *GS*).

5. Eric Marcelo Genilo, *John Cuthbert Ford, SJ* (Washington, DC: Georgetown University Press, 2007), 143.

6. Genilo, *John Cuthbert Ford*, 140.

7. Francis, *Amoris laetitia* (March 19, 2016), 36, https://www.vatican.va/content/dam/francesco/pdf/apost_exhortations/documents/papa-francesco

_esortazione-ap_20160319_amoris-laetitia_en.pdf (hereafter cited as *AL*).

8. South African Bishops Conference, "A Message of Hope," in Robert J. Vitillo, *Pastoral Training for Responding to HIV-AIDS* (Nairobi: Paulines Publication Africa, 2007), 73.

9. Michael Czerny, "The Second African Synod and AIDS in Africa," in *Reconciliation, Justice, and Peace: The Second African Synod*, ed. Agbonkhianmeghe Orobator (Maryknoll, NY: Orbis, 2011), 199.

10. Bishops of Chad, "Statement on AIDS," in *Pastoral Training for Responding to HIV-AIDS*, 74.

11. Charles Curran, "Catholic Social and Sexual Teaching: A Methodological Comparison," *Theology Today* 4, no. 4 (January 1988): 425–40.

12. Paul VI, *Populorum progressio* (March 26, 1967), 15, https://www.vatican.va/content/paul-vi /en/encyclicals/documents/hf_p-vi_enc_26031967 _populorum.html.

13. Michael J. Barberi and Joseph A. Selling, "The Origin of *Humanae Vitae* and the Impasse in Fundamental Theological Ethics," *Louvain Studies* 37 (2013): 364–89.

14. Francis, *Misericordia et miseria* (November 20, 2016), https://www.vatican.va/content/francesco/en /apost_letters/documents/papa-francesco-lettera-ap _20161120_misericordia-et-misera.html.

15. Congregation for the Doctrine of the Faith, "Responses to Questions Proposed Concerning Uterine Isolation and Related Matters" (July 31, 1993), https://www.vatican.va/roman_curia/congregations /cfaith/documents/rc_con_cfaith_doc_31071994 _uterine-isolation_en.html.

16. Congregation for the Doctrine of the Faith, "Response to a Question on the Liceity of a Hysterectomy in Certain Cases," *Vatican News,* December 10, 2018, https://www.vaticannews.va /en/pope/news/2019-01/congregation-doctrine -faith-question-liceity-hysterectomy.html.

17. Congregation for the Doctrine of the Faith, "The Liceity of a Hysterectomy."

18. John Ford and Gerald Kelly, *Contemporary Moral Theology*, Vol. 2, *Marriage Questions* (Baltimore: Newman, 1963), 335–36.

19. United States Conference of Catholic Bishops, *Ethical and Religious Directives for Catholic Health Care Services, Sixth Edition* (2018), 36, https://www.usccb .org/about/doctrine/ethical-and-religious-directives /upload/ethical-religious-directives-catholic-health -service-sixth-edition-2016-06.pdf.

20. James Keenan, "Pope Francis, Answering on Zika Risk, Says Use of Contraception Could Be Possibly Permitted," *America* (February 20, 2016).

21. Gerald Coleman, "Is Using Contraceptives Always Sinful?," *Health Progress* (January 1, 2017): 32–35.

22. See chapter 4 in this volume.

23. See chapter 5 in this volume.

24. See John T. Noonan Jr., "Development in Moral Doctrine," *Theological Studies* 54 (1993): 662–77.

25. Pontifical Council for the Family, "Vademecum for Confessors Concerning Some Aspects of the Morality of Conjugal Life" (February 12, 1997), https://www.vatican.va/roman_curia/pontifical _councils/family/documents/rc_pc_family_doc _12021997_vademecum_en.html.

26. Pontifical Council for the Family, "Vademecum for Confessors."

27. John Horgan, ed., Humanae Vitae *and the Bishops: The Encyclical and the Statements of the National Hierarchies* (Shannon, Ireland: Irish University Press, 1972), 4–32; and Charles Curran et al, *Dissent in and for the Church: Theologians and* Humanae Vitae (New York: Sheed and Ward, 1969), 3–26.

# John Paul II

# CHAPTER

# 14

## *Laborem Exercens*

KATE WARD

## CONTEXT

*Laborem exercens*, Pope John Paul II's 1981 treatise on work and human life commemorating the ninetieth anniversary of *Rerum novarum*, came into a world where the face of work was changing rapidly.[1] Perhaps the most significant change the document responded to was the twentieth-century irruption of women into professional workplaces and public life. While women had always worked to contribute to family livelihoods, the twentieth century saw them demand the right, previously reserved to men, to influence public life through work even while raising families. At the inception of modern Catholic Social Teaching (CST), Leo XIII and Pius XI taught that women's participation in the workplace was an evil born of economic necessity. But the women who were John Paul II's contemporaries insisted that their presence there was good, and he came to agree.[2]

Although not explicitly addressed in *Laborem exercens*, changing understandings of sexuality and family shaped the context of work that John Paul II addressed. Women's increasing presence in the workplace and public life were enabled, in many cases, by the ability to limit family size through birth control. Both the more generous welfare states that arose in the postwar period and advocacy for tolerance

of divorced, single, and same-sex parented families challenged the traditional view of the family's economic support flowing from a single male worker's wages. With wages and conditions improving for many workers, societies turned attention to work's more subtle influences on persons, which John Paul II would come to call work's subjective aspect.

## COMMENTARY

*Laborem exercens*'s most important contributions come from John Paul II's personalist standpoint: the human person is the standard for normative evaluation of human life. In the context of work, this demands attention to the worker as "subject" or doer of work and to working conditions reflecting their human dignity. The economistic focus on work's production has its priorities reversed: work is for humans and not humans for work (*LE* 6). Most types of creative, sustaining human activity can be considered work, not simply those activities done outside the home for wages.

### *The Personalist View of Human Work*

*Laborem exercens* explains that humanity's creation in the image of God is revealed in the first Genesis creation story partly through human work. Both caregiving and manual labor are highlighted as human work in the divine commands to "multiply" and to "subdue the earth" (*LE* 4). "The earth" that humans work to "subdue" means all the resources of the visible world on which people exercise work "in the transitive sense" as acting subjects shaping objects. Work is not limited to waged activity but instead is something every human does in carrying out God's divine plan and contributing to the good of the human family: "Each and every individual, to the proper extent and in an incalculable number of ways, takes part in the giant process whereby man 'subdues the earth' through his work" (*LE* 4).[3] Work changes in response to new problems but is consistently characterized by "personal effort and toil" as well as societal "tensions, conflicts and crises" (*LE* 2).

*Laborem exercens*'s discussion of work in its objective and subjective senses has been enormously influential in Catholic thought and has significant implications for family teaching. Work in its objective sense describes what is accomplished as humans dominate the earth. Fields plowed, goods produced, new technologies developed, and creative intellectual insights are all objective results of human work even if machines enable these tasks (*LE* 5–6). Nor is the divine call to dominate the earth limited to acting on the materials of creation. In a more important sense, control over creation is exerted through work as people shape themselves as free, responsible, and creative human beings. This is work in its subjective sense, which regards the fact that "the one who carries [work] out is a person, a conscious and free subject, that is to say a subject that decides about himself," (*LE* 6) and describes the way work shapes the worker. Through acts of work she recognizes herself as a creative, capable human being and grows in her abilities (*LE* 6). While different types of work may indeed contribute different values to society in their objective results, all work has dignity because the subject, the doer, of even the "most monotonous[,] . . . most alienating work" is a human being (*LE* 6).

Work shapes humans in positive ways even if the work undertaken is not particularly inspiring or fulfilling. John Paul II is careful to note that work after the Fall is difficult, but it remains a way of fulfilling the divine command to subdue the earth. Toil is an aspect of work known to all workers, including "women, who, sometimes without proper recognition on the part of society and even of their own families, bear the daily burden and responsibility for their homes and the upbringing of their children" (*LE* 9). However, "in spite of all this toil—perhaps, in a sense, because of it— work is a good thing for man. . . . [T]hrough work man *not only transforms nature*, adapting it to his own needs, but he also *achieves fulfillment* as a human being and indeed, in a sense, becomes 'more a human being'" (*LE* 9). By distinguishing between work's objective and subjective dimensions and giving priority to the latter, *Laborem exercens* profoundly challenges mainstream economic approaches to valuing human activity. While work's objective outcomes matter, they are not the most important aspect of work, which is instead the fact that a human being, through working, shapes herself and grows more into God's plans for her. As an analogy, preschoolers produce drawings that generate no economic benefit and will be thrown away. But this work is not useless; it forms the individual skills they will later use to communicate, create, and shape the common good. In the case of children, we readily judge a task's usefulness by how it shapes the working subject. John Paul II insists that this standard applies to adults as well.

When John Paul II refers to work that distances the worker from her human dignity as "alienating," he gives name to a phenomenon known in earlier CST.[4] His later encyclical, *Centesimus annus* (1991), explains that societies can distance or "alienate" persons from their human nature in many ways, such as by depriving human bodies of their basic needs or by fostering isolation or distance from spiritual life.[5] Similarly, since human nature is to be creative and solve problems, work may be alienating if it is monotonous or leaves no room for the worker's input. Humans are by nature dignified and exercise autonomy. Work alienates when it treats workers as cogs in a machine. There are many other ways work can be alienating, but work can also be bad or harmful without necessarily being alienating if, for example, it is creative, self-directed work performed under unjust conditions.[6]

Shortly after *Laborem exercens*, US sociologist Arlie Russell Hochschild described in *The Managed Heart: Commercialization of Human Feeling* (1983/2012) a significant way work can be alienating. Hochschild's enormously influential book coined the category "emotional labor" to discuss paid work that requires managing or manipulating one's emotions. For example, flight attendants must maintain positive demeanors even in the face of disrespectful treatment, and paid child caregivers must navigate emotional attachments in relationships that will end. Hochschild found that paid employment requiring intimate and profoundly human emotional capacities affected workers' experience of their jobs and, more concerningly, access to emotion in their personal lives.[7] In the atmosphere of abundance that characterized the twentieth century, "the worker question" broadened from finding adequate work for all who needed it to addressing aspects of well-being on and off the job.

John Paul II also attended to groups whose work is characterized by exploitation and exclusion. For example, although agricultural work is "the basis for a healthy economy," agricultural workers are often subjected to "objectively unjust conditions" (*LE* 21). "Disabled people," John Paul II writes, "are fully human subjects with corresponding innate, sacred and inviolable rights" who must be allowed to access their right to "professional training and work" "according to their capabilities" (*LE* 22).[8] Workers also have the right to migrate and to return, even though their migration may present challenges to families and their home communities (*LE* 23).[9]

A final and extremely important principle derives from this personalist approach to human work: the priority of labor. "Labor," that is, human workers, are more important than "capital" or the means of production, which are only instruments, while the worker "alone is a person" (*LE* 12). Both physical and intangible means of production, such as knowledge, are "*the result of the historical heritage of human labour*"; "*everything that is at the service of work . . . is the result of work*" (*LE* 12). The priority of labor has significant ramifications for work's social, political, and economic contexts.

### Work That Prioritizes Persons

John Paul II's personalist view of work recognizes that working conditions often fail to reflect the human dignity of workers. Consistent with the CST tradition, he reads this as a failure of systems, not the result of individual sins. "The liberal socio-political system" has defended the interests of capital at the expense of workers, whose past and current movements to defend their rights through solidarity are "justified from the point of view of social morality" (*LE* 8).[10]

Work is "the key to the social question," whose answers must lie "in the direction of making work more human" (*LE* 3). The Catholic Church staunchly supports worker solidarity in order to be "the Church of the poor," because

> in many cases [the poor] appear as a *result of the violation of the dignity of human work*: either because the opportunities for human work are limited . . . or because a low value is put on work and the rights that flow from it, especially the right to a just wage and to the personal security of the worker and his or her family. (*LE* 8)

The social conditions surrounding work can damage human bodily health, "dignity and subjectivity" and need to be addressed (*LE* 11).

John Paul II calls ascribing harmful working conditions to an inherent conflict between labor and the owners of capital an error of "economism" (viewing work only in terms of its economic purpose) or "materialism" (giving primacy to the material) (*LE* 13). In contrast, the church sees labor and capital as intertwined. So too, the church's view on property, including the means of production, differs from Marxist collectivism and absolutist capitalist views of private property (*LE* 14). *Laborem exercens* teaches that "*the right to private property is subordinated to the right to common use*, to the fact that goods are meant for everyone" (*LE* 14). Thus, the only legitimate reason for private ownership of the means of production is when it is the best way to meet human needs (*LE* 14). Socialization of the means of production and practices of joint ownership by workers are also legitimate ways to pursue the right to common use (*LE* 14). Private ownership may be justified as a way for the worker to feel he is working "for himself" (*LE* 15).[11]

Human rights also flow from work, even as work—meaning any activity through which humans develop themselves and shape creation—is "a duty" that imposes obligations (*LE* 16).[12] Workers' rights are the responsibility of both the direct employer—the party with whom the worker contracts—and the indirect employer (*LE* 16–17). The "indirect employer" refers to systems, institutions, and policies that shape work's conditions beyond the control of the direct employer. Indirect employers include the state, prevailing economic conditions, and international, national, and local organizations (*LE* 17).[13] Rather than "the criterion of maximum profit," "respect for the objective rights of the worker ... must constitute *the adequate and fundamental criterion* for shaping the whole economy" (*LE* 17).

States and international organizations, as indirect employers, are responsible for guaranteeing adequate work for all to exercise their talents and education to prepare them to do so by planning and coordinating the efforts of businesses and local communities rather than centralizing all initiative (*LE* 18). Unemployment is "an evil," and the church defends a right to "*suitable employment for all who are capable of it*" while urging grants to support unemployed workers and their families (*LE* 18).

Just wages reflect just relationships between the worker and direct and indirect employers and provide a mechanism for the distribution of necessary goods (*LE* 19). Other aspects of just compensation include "cheap or free" medical care, old-age and disability pensions, time off

for worship and longer periods of rest, and safe, dignified working environments (*LE* 19). Ultimately, the family is a reference point for justice in the social order that shapes work's conditions (*LE* 10). To safeguard this justice, workers have the right to form unions, which are "an indispensable element of social life" and "a mouthpiece for the struggle for social justice" (*LE* 20). Unions are not divisive contributors to the "class struggle" but instead are "a constructive factor of social order and of solidarity" (*LE* 20).

*Laborem exercens* concludes by discussing the spiritual value of work for persons (*LE* 24–27). Humans, created in God's image, imitate and "unfold" God's creative activity when they work and when they rest from labor (*LE* 25). Workers collaborate in Christ's redemptive activity when they endure the toil or "Cross" of work in union with Jesus (*LE* 27). Moreover, "it is through man's labour that not only 'the fruits of our activity' but also 'human dignity, brotherhood and freedom' must increase on earth" (*LE* 27).

### Work and the Family

Perhaps the most important contribution in *Laborem exercens* to Catholic Family Teaching is clearly and repeatedly identifying family care as work, equal in dignity and importance to paid work outside the home (e.g., *LE* 4, 9, 26). However, the document still contains ambiguities around care work and its dignity, including professional childcare and fathers' roles in families.

In addition to its subjective dimension, which develops individual persons, work touches on two more "spheres of values": the society and the family. The family is closely intertwined with work, including both waged and unwaged labor. "Work constitutes a foundation for the formation of *family life*, which is a natural right.... In a way, work is a condition for making it possible to found a family, since the family requires the means of subsistence which man normally gains through work" (*LE* 9).[14] Families "normally" gain their livelihood through waged work, but some still rely on subsistence agriculture, for example, and in nearly every case labor of caregivers remains important and unpaid. John Paul II acknowledges elsewhere that these "two aspects of work"—obtaining livelihood and giving care—both come into play in the process of raising children: "the one making family life and its upkeep possible, and the other making possible the achievement of the purposes of the family, especially education" (*LE* 10).

All of society shares a responsibility for families' well-being. Just wages can take the form of a "family wage" sufficient to support a family on one worker's earnings or "through *other social measures* such as family allowances or grants to mothers devoting themselves exclusively to their families" (*LE* 19). Furthermore, society as a whole is clearly the indirect employer for care work when "remuneration for work" includes grants to caregivers with little direct connection to paid employment.

Scholars continue to emphasize the importance of CST's commitment to government support for unpaid care work. Among others, Christine Firer Hinze writes that societies must "value and adequately provide for care" by implementing policies that "acknowledge the crucial economic and social contributions of care work and the complex and multilayered skills such work can require."[15] Sandra Sullivan-Dunbar argues that "nonmarket [that is, family] caring labor should be subsidized by governments," though government support for extrafamilial childcare also accords with *Laborem exercens*.[16] To use a framework from *Laborem exercens* itself, the care work that takes place in families has many "indirect employers" who contribute to setting the terms for that work's dignity, compensation, and chances of success. Care may take place in the family, but it is a whole society's responsibility.

Considering mothers working outside the home, John Paul II uses softer language than his predecessors, one of whom called the practice "an intolerable abuse."[17] However, he does not arrive at an egalitarian view of men and women in the world or of mothers and fathers in the home, as his view of distinct gendered natures prevents this.[18] In *Laborem exercens*, caring for children and helping them develop

into "responsible, morally and religiously mature and psychologically stable persons" is among the "primary goals of the mission of a mother" (*LE* 19). While "in many societies women work in nearly every sector of life" and should never face discrimination or diminished opportunities due to gender, it is "wrong from the point of view of the good of society and of the family" when mothers must pursue paid work instead of caring for and educating their children according to their needs (*LE* 19). "Labour should be structured in such a way that women do not have to pay for their advancement by abandoning what is specific to them and at the expense of the family, in which women as mothers have an irreplaceable role" (*LE* 19).

This careful attempt to blame labor structures rather than the choices of employed mothers threatens to backfire. So long as labor is not structured in the way John Paul II envisions, are these women "abandoning . . . their irreplaceable role" "at the expense of the family"? For mothers, caregiving is linked to "nature" and "mission," while work outside the home remains a bald "fact." Fathers appear relegated to the workplace, as no paternal role in childcare is mentioned. While focusing on the way social structures foster or inhibit workers' agency, *Laborem exercens* endorses restrictive gender roles in public life and in families, with implicit blame accruing to those who step outside those parameters.

*Laborem exercens*'s gloomy assessment of the downstream effects of working motherhood and its silence on professional paid care work grates against contexts where women's professional "advancement" was made possible by safe, accessible paid care for young children. Context is crucial. While quality professional care did exist in 1981, it was not accessible for the majority of workers. A 1978 United Nations study of childcare in five industrializing nations found that most women worked in the extended family unit or in agricultural or informal sectors where they could care for children amid other work tasks.[19] Nigerian researchers, typical of their counterparts in the study, saw nothing objectionable in mothers caring for children while doing agricultural

144 | Kate Ward

work or urban retail "hawking."[20] For mothers who are employed in formal sectors and are outside the home for long periods, childcare options were often "not sufficient and [were] poorly equipped for the developmental care of young children."[21] Postwar communist Poland tried to provide childcare centers to entice women into the workplace, but they were often overcrowded and never accommodated more than 5 percent of young children.[22]

Even if such conditions were (and are) common, we can see how distant they are from John Paul II's personalist aspirations for children and their caregivers. Recognizing family care as work reveals that the street hawker watching her children is balancing two jobs. When we consider the role of "indirect employers," we see that market conditions and the ways governments choose to intervene or not intervene in markets force too many workers to accept subpar childcare, with costs to children and surely moral injury to parents. In light of these realities, *Laborem exercens* and even earlier documents of CST should not be read as universally condemning mothers of young children who work outside the home.[23] Certainly it is now possible in many circumstances for mothers of young children to pursue careers while ensuring that children are "educat[ed] in accordance with their needs" (*LE* 19). But for many families, the educational infrastructure and societal support that would make this possible remain out of reach.

Hinze rightly observes that *Laborem exercens*'s assertions of women's important roles in public life and their preeminent place in the care of young children work at "cross purposes."[24] This raises the question of fathers' roles in raising and educating children, another area where *Laborem exercens* falls short, in this case by failing to describe men's full participation in relational personhood.[25] John Paul II's failure to mention men in the context of child-rearing reaffirms the trope that the public sphere is for men and troublingly erases men from their important roles within the family.[26] Catholics today can carry forward the affirmation of family care as work and support "the domestic and public vocations of all persons, and the

right and duty of all adults to participate in family and home work," as Hinze urges.[27]

## INTERPRETATION

*Laborem exercens*'s themes of work's objective and subjective aspects, worker's dignity, the indirect employer, and spirituality of work have been well received by interpreters of CST and are frequently discussed in communications aimed at the lay faithful. By contrast, the ideas that family care is work and that all of society has a responsibility to support this work are less widely known. Accepting family care as work not only demands societal provision and individual respect for this profoundly important activity but also carries implications for how we view work in general.

Societal support for family care remains controversial in the United States, where founding a family is often considered a private endeavor. Pervasive cultural ideas promote waged work as superior to family care and erode social policies designed to support family care. For example, though the US welfare system was originally designed to allow mothers to stay home with young children, after decades of so-called welfare reform nearly half of US states require caregivers to be working by the time a baby is three months old.[28] Reflecting the limited government support to those within the workforce, one in four US mothers returns to work within two weeks of giving birth.[29]

John Paul II's personalist view of work seems to miss an important truth about unpaid care work: it supports and undergirds the formal economy. As Hinze writes, "provisioning in modern market economies requires the combined labors of the unpaid, household sectors and the formal, waged sectors."[30] Unpaid family care "entails a systemic transfer of hidden subsidies to the rest of the economy that go unrecognized."[31] While John Paul II emphasized work's most important value as its subjective dimension, correcting misperceptions about family care's objective value is an important step in recognizing it as work and acknowledging society's role as indirect employer.

Care tasks often differ from what we traditionally envision as labor.[32] This is true for US culture and for Catholic teaching. Jacob Kohlhaas finds *Laborem exercens*'s insistence that parenting is work "conspicuously ill fit" for its formal definition of work. Kohlhaas distinguishes the "interpersonal relationship" of parenting from the "subject-object relationship" in *Laborem exercens*'s definition of work as shaping the materials of creation.[33]

Kohlhaas is right that this conception of work alone is not capacious enough to encompass all the activities *Laborem exercens* in fact recognizes as work. However, it seems clear that children (or anyone who receives care) are part of God's creation whom caregivers shape through work. The document says that human beings, "created as male and female in the image of God," respond to the divine call to have dominion over the earth even if our labor is intellectual or focused on the care of other human beings or even ourselves (*LE* 4–5). This is not to suggest that children are objects of labor in a different way than other human beings, somehow closer to the "matter" of creation like fields and rocks (*LE* 9). Rather, *Laborem exercens* makes clear that to "dominate the earth," in the biblical sense, includes shaping and forming humans (*LE* 6). The worker acts analogously as the Creator when she shapes material creation even as, through work's subjective aspect, she continues to be created herself as among the materials of creation shaped by her own labor.

The exercise of dominion over creation in accordance with God's plan takes place in outward activity, and "*at the same time* it is a process that takes place *within each human being*, in each conscious human subject" (*LE* 4). A straightforward reading of the Christian tradition would note that parents shape children and that children, like all human beings, are part of creation. Moreover, *Laborem exercens* says explicitly that when workers shape *themselves* through work, this is a way that they "dominate" creation. Consequently, it can be concluded that shaping other human beings, as in raising children or caring for others, is an aspect of shaping God's creation.

Kohlhaas rightly points out that *Laborem exercens* does not seem fully aware of the implications of its capacious subjective understanding of work when it comes to the care of families. A better understanding of family care as work might help more people understand work's subjective aspect as well if only because the subjective aspect of family care is so reliably attested. Care work can be boring, dirty, and disrespected by others, but it transforms workers' selves in ways that are felt from the inside out. "What I have found working in the home is a profoundly satisfying way to be of use," writes author Angela Garbes, reflecting on parenting during the COVID-19 pandemic. "Showing up every day and doing something real, however small, is the best thing you can do."[34]

Interpreters often cite John Paul II's experience with manual quarry labor in Nazi-occupied Poland to explain his sensitive articulation of workers' dignity.[35] The same lens reveals that as a celibate priest in his healthy middle years, left without family as a young man, he had relatively little experience giving or receiving family care.[36] It falls to his interpreters who know this work more intimately to elucidate the insights that his writing makes possible but does not fully articulate. If work's primary value is its subjective dimension, family care is a preeminently valuable form of work, as it profoundly and positively shapes our human capacities. Ensuring the ability to equitably and meaningfully undertake family care work requires material support, changes to the structure of paid work, and redefining gender roles, among changes incumbent on societies as indirect employers. These are not remote, utopian goals to tackle once paid work gains its due dignity but instead must accompany efforts for justice in the paid workplace. Family work and paid work flourish or fail together. Equal in dignity, they must be treated as equally important.

## NOTES

1. John Paul II, *Laborem exercens* (September 14, 1981), http://www.vatican.va/holy_father/john_paul

_ii/encyclicals/documents/hf_jp-ii_enc_14091981 _laborem-exercens_en.html (hereafter cited as *LE*).

2. Kate Ward, "Catholic Teaching Changes: Women in the Workplace," Women In Theology (blog), August 23, 2019, https://womenintheology .org/2019/08/23/catholic-teaching-changes-women -in-the-workplace/.

3. Throughout, I have sought to balance John Paul II's use of male as the default for humanity by using female as the default myself.

4. While not using the term "alienation," see Leo XIII, *Rerum novarum* (May 15, 1891), 42, http:// www.vatican.va/holy_father/leo_xiii/encyclicals /documents/hf_l-xiii_enc_15051891_rerum-novarum _en.html; and Vatican II, *Gaudium et spes* (December 7, 1965), 27, http://www.vatican.va/archive /hist_councils/ii_vatican_council/documents/vat-ii _const_19651207_gaudium-et-spes_en.html. Both are concerned with harm to the human person through monotonous or undignified work.

5. John Paul II, *Centesimus annus* (May 1, 1991), 39–42, https://www.vatican.va/content/john-paul-ii /en/encyclicals/documents/hf_jp-ii_enc_01051991 _centesimus-annus.html.

6. See my distinction between "bad" and alienating work in "Human and Alienating Work: What Sex Worker Advocates Can Teach Catholic Social Thought," *Journal of the Society of Christian Ethics* 41, no. 2 (2021): 261–78.

7. Arlie Russell Hochschild, *The Managed Heart: Commercialization of Human Feeling*, EBSCO Academic Collection Ebooks (Berkeley: University of California Press, 2012).

8. "Disabled people" is the phrase used in *LE*'s English translation. Some prefer it for focusing attention on the ways societal practices can disable. Others prefer "people with" disabilities or a particular disability.

9. For a discussion of CST on migration through a family lens, see Kristin E. Heyer, *Kinship across Borders: A Christian Ethic of Immigration* (Washington, DC: Georgetown University Press, 2012).

10. Much ink has been spilled trying to brand John Paul II as a partisan of various socioeconomic systems. He does not make this task easy (or, conversely, leaves himself open to it) by using terms such as "capitalism" and "socialism" in ways that do not always correspond to those used by economists and political scientists. For example, he writes that

regarding work as a product to be sold constitutes "the error of early capitalism," but this is also associated with a "materialistic" view, which seems to reference Karl Marx (*LE* 7).

11. The Latin translated as "for himself" is "*in re propria*," which is enclosed in quotation marks in the original document. In the legal context, "*ius in re propria*" refers to rights regarding one's own property, as opposed to another's, such as the right of enjoyment. In English, we should not hear *LE*'s assertion that the worker wants to feel she is working "for herself" as meaning self-employment. Better interpretations might be "on her own affairs" or a phrase *LE* uses elsewhere in this section, "on her own initiative." The context of the document points away from "for her own benefit," because this section discusses the subjective experience of self-directed action, not the ability to support oneself and one's family that flows from work.

12. Since "work" in the CST tradition means both waged and unwaged work, the tradition does not impose a duty to waged work, as some mistakenly claim. Rather, work is an anthropological reality that imposes itself on persons for the benefit of their own flourishing, whatever form it takes.

13. More recent interpreters focus on consumers as indirect employers whose choices shape market conditions. See, e.g., Kari-Shane Davis Zimmerman, "*Centesimus Annus* Twenty Years Later: Toward Christian Economic Practices That Reflect an Authentic Vision of Human Creativity," *Journal of Catholic Social Thought* 9, no. 1 (2012): 151–70; and David Cloutier, *The Vice of Luxury: Economic Excess in a Consumer Age* (Washington, DC: Georgetown University Press, 2015), 10.

14. That "normally" intrigues. If we take work to mean waged labor, the only families able to access subsistence without work would be the independently wealthy. While the second half of the twentieth century had more options available than ever for families to survive without wage earning in the context of postwar welfare states, I don't think John Paul II would see such families as subsiding "without work," as they would still be caring for themselves and their dependents. I have used this and other references to argue that Catholic social thought can support universal basic income. See Kate Ward, "Universal Basic Income and Work in Catholic Social Thought," *American Journal of*

*Economics & Sociology* 79, no. 4 (September 2020): 1271–1306.

15. Christine Firer Hinze, *Glass Ceilings and Dirt Floors: Women, Work, and the Global Economy*, 2014 Madeleva Lecture in Spirituality (Mahwah, NJ: Paulist Press, 2015), 107–8.

16. Sandra Sullivan-Dunbar, "Valuing Family Care: Love and Labor," in *Sex, Love & Families: Catholic Perspectives*, ed. Jason King and Julie Hanlon Rubio (Collegeville, MN: Liturgical Press, 2020), 152; and Kate Ward, "America's Child Care Crisis and Catholic Social Teaching," *America Magazine*, October 2021, https://www.americamagazine.org/politics-society/2021/09/16/childcare-work-catholic-social-teaching-241381.

17. Pius XI, *Quadrigesimo anno* (May 15, 1931), 71, http://www.vatican.va/holy_father/pius_xi/encyclicals/documents/hf_p-xi_enc_19310515_quadragesimo-anno_en.html. This view of adult men's and women's different spheres also led Pius XI to oppose coeducation for boys and girls. See chapter 8 in this volume.

18. Lisa Sowle Cahill, "Family and Catholic Social Teaching," in *Change in Official Catholic Moral Teachings*, ed. Charles E. Curran, 253–68 (New York: Paulist Press, 2003).

19. "Comparative Report on the Role of Working Mothers in Early Childhood Education in Five Countries," United Nations Educational, Scientific and Cultural Organization, 1978, ED.78/WS/71, UNESCO Digital Library, https://unesdoc.unesco.org/ark:/48223/pf0000030101?posInSet=2&queryId=aa7628f8-1af7-4268-b9c3-6209b8805454.

20. T. O. Fadayomi et al., "The Role of Working Mothers in Early Childhood Education: A Nigerian Case Study," 1978), 57, ED.78/WS/3, UNESCO Digital Library, https://unesdoc.unesco.org/ark:/48223/pf0000032599/PDF/032599engb.pdf.multi.

21. Fadayomi et al., "The Role of Working Mothers," 20. See also Richard Rwiza's observations of the consequences of CST's oversight of women and children as workers for contemporary Africa in chapter 7 of this volume.

22. Jacqueline Heinen and Monika Wator, "Child Care in Poland before, during, and after the Transition: Still a Women's Business," *Social Politics: International Studies in Gender, State & Society* 13, no. 2 (January 1, 2006): 194.

23. Safe childcare options were even fewer for those mothers who caused Leo XIII consternation by their waged work. Before sanitary, nutritious breastmilk alternatives, leaving a nursing infant with a nonfamily member was especially dangerous, as was the alternative of bringing a baby into industrial settings. See Melanie Reynolds, *Infant Mortality and Working-Class Child Care, 1850–1899* (New York: Palgrave Macmillan, 2016), 74–75, 129.

24. Christine Firer Hinze, "Women, Families, and the Legacy of *Laborem Exercens*: An Unfinished Agenda," *Journal of Catholic Social Thought* 6, no. 1 (2009): 63.

25. As a better example, see Hoon Choi, "Beyond 'Helping Out': Fathers as Caregivers," in *Sex, Love & Families: Catholic Perspectives*, ed. Jason King and Julie Hanlon Rubio, 69–78 (Collegeville: Liturgical Press, 2020).

26. Jacob M. Kohlhaas, *Beyond Biology: Rethinking Parenthood in the Catholic Tradition* (Washington, DC: Georgetown University Press, 2021), 206; and Hinze, "Women, Families, and the Legacy of *Laborem Exercens*," 64.

27. Hinze, "Women, Families, and the Legacy of *Laborem Exercens*," 64. It is worth noting that Catholic Family Teaching has finally begun moving in this direction. See Francis, *Amoris laetitia* (March 19, 2016), 286, https://www.vatican.va/content/dam/francesco/pdf/apost_exhortations/documents/papa-francesco_esortazione-ap_20160319_amoris-laetitia_en.pdf.

28. Thomas Massaro, *United States Welfare Policy: A Catholic Response* (Washington, DC: Georgetown University Press, 2007), 119–20; and Heather Hahn et al., "Work Requirements in Social Safety Net Programs: A Status Report of Work Requirements in TANF, SNAP, Housing Assistance, and Medicaid," The Urban Institute, December 2017, 7, https://www.urban.org/sites/default/files/publication/95566/work-requirements-in-social-safety-net-programs.pdf.

29. Sharon Lerner, "The Real War on Families: Why the U.S. Needs Paid Leave Now," *In These Times*, August 18, 2015, http://inthesetimes.com/article/18151/the-real-war-on-families.

30. Christine Firer Hinze, "Catholics and Feminists on Work, Family and Flourishing," in *Sex, Love & Families: Catholic Perspectives*, ed. Jason King and Julie Hanlon Rubio (Collegeville, MN: Liturgical Press, 2020), 249.

31. Hinze, *Glass Ceilings and Dirt Floors*, 90.

32. As Hinze notes, this is even true for paid care workers, who suffer from societal inability to understand what they do as skilled labor. Hinze, *Glass Ceilings and Dirt Floors*, 91–92.

33. Kohlhaas, *Beyond Biology*, 209, 197. Kohlhaas uses Francis's *Laudato si'* to articulate a vision of parenting as cocreation similar to the one I find in *Laborem exercens* as described above, where "dominion" over creation can be envisioned as "relational" (215).

34. Angela Garbes, *Essential Labor: Mothering as Social Change* (New York: Harper Wave, 2022), 13.

35. Edward Stourton, *John Paul II: Man of History* (London: Hodder & Stoughton, 2006), 56–59.

36. Stourton, *John Paul II*, 60.

# CHAPTER

# 15

## *Familiaris Consortio*

JULIE HANLON RUBIO

## CONTEXT

To reflect on Pope John Paul II's 1981 postsynodal apostolic exhortation, *Familiaris consortio*,[1] today is inevitably to see it through the lens of the more recent postsynodal apostolic exhortation, Pope Francis's *Amoris laetitia* of 2016.[2] Both popes chose to use the recently revived structure of a synod to call bishops from around the world to Rome to discuss issues affecting families in their contexts and to advise them on how to speak to the global church. It is well-known that *Amoris laetitia* has led to significant controversies regarding divorced and remarried Catholics, and most academic commentary has focused on these issues. Yet, at its core lies a profound appreciation of the "joy of love" in Catholic families and strong encouragement for the church to welcome and accompany families in good times and bad, which is often passed over. Similarly, many analyses of *Familiaris consortio* focus on its controversial reassertions of traditional Catholic teachings on sex, gender, and marriage while missing the document's major contributions: John Paul II's personalist reframing of marriage and his moving descriptions of four "tasks" identified as the work of families. These tasks (growing in love, serving life, embracing a social mission, and being the church in their home) firmly situate the family

between personal and social ethics, and they are entrusted equally to men and women, giving contemporary Catholic teaching on families an outward-facing egalitarianism that has yet to be fully realized.

Early in his pontificate (1978–2005), John Paul II convened a synod titled "The Role of the Family." Nearly 150 bishops and numerous experts from around the world gathered in Rome for four weeks in the fall of 1980.[3] They brought with them concerns from their distinct contexts:

> Bishops from developing nations, for example, complained that the pre-synodal documents reflected first-world problems, not theirs. Bishops from India wanted to talk about interreligious marriages. And while first-world Catholics might have problems with birth control, the Indian bishops were fighting a government that wanted to impose limits on family size. Latin American bishops spoke of poverty as the root of marriage problems in their countries. Bishops from Africa spoke about polygamy.[4]

At the end of the four weeks, the bishops found agreement on forty-three propositions to present to the pope.[5] These propositions were not supposed to be public but were leaked to the press and published by two Catholic news outlets in early 1981.[6] Substantial portions of the text of the propositions ended up in *Familiaris consortio*, and notably, one suggestion led to the publication of the Charter of the Rights of the Family in 1983. The pope declined to move forward on a number of more controversial suggestions, including consideration of a more flexible approach to divorce and remarriage.[7] In addition, while the bishops asked for more local control in difficult circumstances, the pope offered pastoral concern along with a reminder of universal moral laws. His closing homily at the synod, which leaned heavily on "the plan of God for marriage and family," was indicative of the limited flexibility that would mark his response to the synod, though *Familiaris consortio* also reflects developments that would continue in his thinking.[8]

## COMMENTARY

In *Familiaris consortio*, John Paul II gives families a mission that includes being a communion of love, giving and valuing life, being church together, and, most notably, serving society, that is, working to transform its unjust structures and soften its hard edges with works of charity, mercy, and hospitality. The whole corpus of the pope's teaching develops the social role of the family. Personalism leads him to highlight the social import of sacramental love and to stress the social mission of the family. Together, these two priorities signal a new role for families in the social order.[9]

### Light, Darkness, and Truth: Reading the Signs of the Times

Following the lead of Catholic Social Teaching, *Familiaris consortio* begins with a reading of the situation, pointing out "darkness" and "light." The pope draws upon what he heard during the synod from the world's bishops and chooses to stress two points of light and one overarching cloud of darkness. Light is apparent in increased attention to personal relationships, especially marriage and a related

awareness of the dignity of women. Darkness appears in denial of human dignity, manifested in the developing world in families' struggles to survive and in richer countries in consumerism accompanied by anxiety (*FC* 6).

It is worth noting some key differences between *Amoris laetitia* and *Familiaris consortio*. While Pope Francis devotes an entire chapter to considering the "experiences and challenges of families" (*AL* 31–57), John Paul II covers the situation in one paragraph (*FC* 6) within a brief introductory section (*FC* 4–10), the primary aim of which is to communicate the importance of truth and conversion. Unlike Francis, who writes especially to "Christian married couples," John Paul II names bishops, clergy, and the faithful as his audience. While Francis identifies an opportunity to speak "on love in the family," John Paul II addresses "the role of the Christian family in the modern world." Francis opens with the common experience of "the joy of love" before moving to where John Paul II begins, the family in crisis (*AL* 1 and *FC* 1). Francis makes it a point to remember the synod as a vibrant "process" involving debate and discussion, giving his official blessing to ongoing, lively ecclesial conversation, and chooses not to invoke his authority to settle controversies that arose during the synod. He also asserts his desire to share with married couples the wisdom of the tradition while accepting a certain level of diversity among Catholics (*AL* 3). In contrast, John Paul II thanks the synod for its work and recalls the trust and authority that belong to him, along with his intention to communicate the truth about the family. Though influenced by the reforms of Vatican II, *Familiaris consortio*, in keeping with the earlier documents of Catholic Family Teaching (CFT), is a document for a world confused about family from a pope ready to respond to uncertainty with timeless answers rooted in the Catholic tradition.

### A Personalist Theology of Marriage

John Paul II begins by offering serious attention to relationships between spouses. He draws upon his pastoral experience working with couples and his long-standing interest in marital love, evidenced in his plays, most notably *The Jeweler's Shop*.[10] The theology of the body, for which he is well known, is also a significant source of his thinking.[11] He begins with God, who is Love, calling human beings into being through love and for love. Thus, "the fundamental and innate vocation of every human being" is love (*FC* 11). This love involves the body and the soul ("the innermost being") of the person. The call to love is "inscribed" by God in the bodies of men and women. We are literally made for love. Marriage, in this personalist vision, is not externally imposed but instead is an "interior requirement" of love. If love involves the whole person, body and spirit, marriage is the only "place" giving one's whole self makes sense. Because sex expresses this gift, it fits best and exclusively within a lifelong committed bond.

Yet, John Paul II is not a traditional romantic. The spousal communion of which he speaks is total but not at all insular. "By virtue of the sacramentality of their marriage, spouses are bound to one another in the most profoundly indissoluble manner. Their belonging to each other is the very real representation, by means of the sacramental sign, of the very relationship of Christ with the Church," he writes (*FC* 13). Marriage is not just for the good of a couple. It is their participation in the cross and a sign to others of Christ's self-giving love. Children are the first and most tangible sign of their self-giving, "a living and inseparable synthesis of their being a father and a mother" (*FC* 14). John Paul II sees parents and children as one family, one sacrament. This image of husbands and wives poured out in children does not mean that the marital relationship is insignificant. Rather, "their deeply personal unity" points beyond itself (*FC* 13).

After speaking so highly of marriage, the pope articulates a vision of celibacy that fits within the broader framework of the human person made for love. The church holds that celibacy is a "superior charism" compared to marriage, because the vowed celibate is forgoing a true good while anticipating total union with God in the life to come. "In virginity or

celibacy, the human being is awaiting, also in a bodily way, the eschatological marriage of Christ with the Church, giving himself or herself completely to the Church in the hope that Christ may give Himself to the Church in the full truth of eternal life" (*FC* 16). The celibate person is also called to love, fidelity, and "spiritual fruitful[ness]." Esteem for celibacy thus underlines the value of marriage rather than detracting from it.

The vision of married love in *Familiaris consortio* is deeply personal, but it flows outward. The social dimension of the sacramental vision of marriage is something married persons are to embrace and actively live out as a vocation. Families then have the potential to become a transforming social force. Married love is discipleship, an "active choice of mutual giving and receiving."[12] It is defined by what it does.

### Four Tasks: The Work of Families

The core of *Familiaris consortio* is organized around tasks that are fundamental to who the family is (its "being") and central to how it is to act in the world (its "doing"). In a somewhat confusing phrase, the pope calls families to "become what they are," or to be more what they are called to be (*FC* 17). And the root of that call is self-gift (or being for others) in and outside of the home.[13] The family is not a private haven where one escapes from the world but instead is a community with a mission that goes beyond itself. John Paul II defines the family as "a community of life and love" that has four major tasks (*FC* 11). Each of these tasks has public dimensions.

The first is the most obviously familial and the least obviously social. The family must "live with fidelity the reality of communion in a constant effort to develop an authentic community of persons" (*FC* 18). John Paul II distinguishes himself from earlier popes by the inspired way in which he describes married love and demands that it rise to the heights for which it is destined, that it become what it is. He challenges those who marry to cultivate love, seeking "an ever deeper and more intense communion, which is the foundation and soul of the community of marriage and the family" (*FC* 18).

The communion between spouses is both a gift and a task, and by its nature it is, according to John Paul II, indivisible, indissoluble, and expansive. Without directly addressing the concerns raised by bishops at the synod about divorce and polygamy, the pope offers a definitive response. Spousal communion is rooted in the covenant of marriage and the "natural complementarity" between them, but it is their responsibility to "grow continually" and "to share their entire life-project, what they have and what they are" (*FC* 19).[14] Their imperfect efforts are taken up into the sacrament of marriage; the Spirit gifts them with a communion that is a reflection of the bond between God and God's people. Marital communion is inherently "unique and exclusive" and thus contradicted by polygamy and divorce. The total self-gift "rooted in the personal and total self-giving of the couple and being required by the good of children" is indissoluble by its nature; it cannot be broken apart (*FC* 20). In keeping with the central theme of the letter, love between spouses is linked to the "broader communion" of the family. Family members build up communion by "sacrifice," "care and love," and "sharing of goods, of joys, and of sorrows," and the Holy Spirit is "the living source" of their communion not only with each other but also with God (*FC* 21).

Throughout *Familiaris consortio*, the assumption is that marital communion exists only between a man and a woman, though gender is only addressed in three paragraphs that focus on the equal dignity of women and men (*FC* 22–25). Foundations for the dignity of women are found in creation; Mary, the Mother of God; Jesus's interactions with women; the women who were the first to proclaim the good news of the Resurrection; and Galatians 3:28, in which Paul writes that gender is transcended in Christ (*FC* 22). An attempt to balance women's right to work with the priority of their role as mothers and the value of work in the home follows, along with assertions of society's responsibility to ensure just wages and equal respect for different life paths so that mothers do not feel forced to work outside the home (*FC* 24). Offenses against women's dignity (including objectification, discrimination, slavery, prostitution, and pornography) are condemned (*FC* 24).[15] Men are given less attention, but here too respect for women is a key theme, though some broad distinctions in roles are maintained. Very little is said about the specific duties of men and women, though difference is insisted upon. A largely egalitarian call for commitment to communion is notable, and equal responsibility for the work of families continues throughout the document.

Second to love comes the task of "serving life." Parents have a responsibility to serve life by nurturing their own children and by bringing life to the world (*FC* 28). Serving life is not only having children but also educating them. This includes instilling "the essential values of human life," especially the idea that possessions do not make human beings what they are and that the faithful have a responsibility to adopt a simple lifestyle (*FC* 37). John Paul II also affirms that when parents teach their children about the gospel, "they become fully parents, in that they are begetters not only of bodily life but also of the life that through the Spirit's renewal flows from the cross and resurrection of Christ" (*FC* 39). This emphasis on spiritual forms of giving is extended when the pope uses the term "spiritual fecundity" to name the responsibility of families to share with others the self-giving love they nurture within (*FC* 41). This spiritual dimension of fertility is a development in Catholic theology that allows couples without children and those who adopt to see themselves in CFT.[16]

In this section, John Paul II also offers a personalist defense of Catholic teaching on contraception, which was reaffirmed with his blessing in *Humanae vitae* (1968). Contraception is not only a violation of the norm that persons must not block the inseparable procreative and unitive meanings of the sexual act but is also, for the pope, a violation of the dignity of persons. Couples who go against church teaching "'manipulate' and degrade human sexuality—and with it themselves and their married partner—by altering its value of 'total' self-giving." When they ought, in keeping with the "truth of conjugal love," to be giving themselves fully, they instead hold back their fertility, effectively lying with their bodies (*FC* 32, cf. 11). This unapologetic reaffirmation of the illicit nature of contraception ignored the pleas of bishops from the United States and Europe at the synod who asked for pastoral flexibility on this question.[17]

However, the overall thrust of the section is toward a broader notion of fecundity. The couple's commitment to be a "fundamental school of social living" flows out of their love for each other (*FC* 37). This commitment inspires their attention to education and formation of their children. "Service of life" is a duty, but it is also an essential part of the sacramental nature of marriage. God's grace is present through their love for each other and for children and in their efforts to make their home a place where people strive to become ever more open to others.

By the time we reach the third task, it is clear that families are not simply oriented toward their own good, for "far from being closed in on itself, the family is by its nature and vocation open to other families and to society and undertakes its social role" (*FC* 42). Families "cannot," John Paul II holds, "stop short at procreation and education"; they have distinct social and political duties (*FC* 44). Specifically, the pope asks families to do three things: practice hospitality, opening their table and their home to others; become politically involved, assisting in the transformation of society; and practice a preferential option for the poor, manifesting a "special concern for the hungry, the poor, the old, the sick, drug victims and those with no family" (*FC* 47). All of this is part of the social mission of the family.

Anticipating the criticism that such work is not at all what sacramental marriage is about, John Paul II insists that "by taking up the human reality of the love between husband and wife in all its implications, the sacrament gives Christian couples and parents a power and a commitment to live their vocation as lay people and therefore to seek the kingdom of God by engaging in temporal affairs and by ordering them according to the plan of God" (*FC* 47).

The sacramental nature of their relationship invests couples with the strength to be open to the needs of others and to participate in their own way in the transformation of the world; indeed, it obliges them to be and do so. Their marital covenant is not simply about fidelity to each other; it is also about keeping faith with all who need them. In reaching out to others, their love is strengthened, and their ability to serve as a sacramental sign of God's love is renewed.

Finally, in the fourth task John Paul II uses "domestic church" imagery to suggest that families have a responsibility to serve the church by being the church in their home (*FC* 21).[18] As a "church in miniature," a family "witnesses to the world," makes "its home as a sanctuary," and becomes, like the larger church, a "servant of humanity" (*FC* 49–64).[19] Here again, the emphasis is on both the social significance of practices in the home and the sending forth of the family into the world. The pope's emphasis on the social responsibilities of the family implies that an internal focus is insufficient. CFT refuses to limit families by calling them just to care for their own.[20]

## Pastoral Implications

The last section of *Familiaris consortio* is divided into four sections covering the stages, structures, agents, and situations of pastoral care for families. It begins with the church's commitment to accompany families, a concept that receives much more attention in the work of Pope Francis.[21] John Paul II considers the stages of preparation for marriage (remote, proximate, and immediate) and pledges the church's support along the way, briefly addressing a concern raised by bishops at the synod about the necessity of faith for Catholic marriage. While "hesitant to lay down strict criteria" and focusing more on the sincere desire for marriage, he insists that those who "have no intention to engage what the church expects to constitute a sacramental marriage . . . should not be allowed to participate in the ceremony" (*FC* 68).[22] Structures that assist families include the church, families themselves, and political associations working to support families (*FC* 72). The pope also comments on a range of difficulties families face, naming in particular migrants, refugees, the incarcerated, the unhoused, and those torn apart by ideological differences, and urges both prayer and advocacy (*FC* 77).

Most significant in this section is John Paul II's treatment of what he unfortunately calls "irregular situations": cohabitation, divorce, and remarriage. Taking care to make distinctions between those who "are unable to get married properly because of extreme poverty deriving from unjust or inadequate social and economic structures" and those who "scorn, rebel against or reject society, the institution of the family and the social and political order" (*FC* 81), the pope calls for charitable enlightenment and correction as well as prevention. Similarly, he takes pains to note that some divorced persons are "innocent" and says that when they refrain from entering into a second marriage, they offer an "example of fidelity and Christian consistency" to the whole church (*FC* 83). For those who do enter a new union without receiving an annulment, again there are distinctions. Some have been abandoned, remarry for the sake of children, or are certain their first marriage was invalid even though they have not sought an annulment. Still, the pope insists (rejecting the calls of bishops at the synod for greater pastoral flexibility) that no admission to the sacraments is possible; conversion and repentance is the only solution, including renunciation of the new union or, if this not possible, permanent discontinuation of sexual relations (*FC* 84).

The pope closes *Familiaris consortio* with a plea that the situation of the family be taken seriously, for "*the future of humanity passes by way of the family*" (*FC* 86). This strong claim is a final indication of the weight John Paul II assigns to families and the importance he attributes to their role in the world.[23]

## INTERPRETATION

Above, I have suggested that *Familiaris consortio* ought to be read from the center, with primary focus on the four tasks of the family that constitute its most significant contribution to CFT. However, John Paul II is remembered not for his vision of the social mission of the family but instead for his theology of the body, which focused Catholic teaching on gender complementarity in marriage and total self-giving in sex (to the exclusion of contraception) from the 1980s forward. For some Catholics, this vision is an inspiring, radical, and countercultural way of living in a world that has too little respect for sacrifice, fidelity, and sexuality.[24] For many others, the norms of sexual ethics that became central during the papacy of John Paul II were profoundly alienating and made it nearly impossible to hear the social justice message that is central to his family theology.[25]

However, especially when read in context, the social concerns of *Familiaris consortio* are clear. Lisa Sowle Cahill highlights the pope's global understanding of social justice and notes that his frequent comments about poverty that impedes family flourishing, the dignity of women, and the role of families as "interdependent agents within civil society" may be read more radically in that context.[26] Today, with greater awareness of the impact of social structures such as racism, colonialism, sexism, incarceration, migration, inequality, and oppression, it becomes even more necessary for theological reflection on families to include social analysis.[27]

The controversial parts of *Familiaris consortio* have only become more difficult with time. Catholic teaching has evolved since 1981, with an even greater appreciation of women's contributions to public life that began in 1995 with John Paul II's writings on women and continue with Pope Francis's slow, steady progress toward fulfilling John Paul II's assertion that "the church must in her own life promote as far as possible their equality of rights and dignity" (*FC* 23), but the church remains far behind most of the world on gender equity.[28] As same-sex marriage has become more broadly accepted and questions about gender identity are being raised, Vatican documents have placed greater stress on gender differences than Pope John Paul II did as they attempt to specify the differences gender makes.[29]

Despite these controversies, the enduring contribution of *Familiaris consortio* is the way it captures both the human desires for love and making a home while calling for a broadening of loyalties beyond blood family. Family is "the first and vital cell of society" (*FC* 42) where love and justice come together.[30] The most significant aspects of CFT are its insistence on the possibility of deep, enduring intimacy and its challenge to "love beyond" borders of all kinds.[31] From Leo XIII to Francis, CFT places families in their social contexts and gives them a crucial social role. Pope Francis follows John Paul II's lead in highlighting the openness that should be an essential mark of family life. Married couples are called to "go forth from their homes in a spirit of solidarity with others," to become "more than just two."[32] This is the social mission of the family that John Paul II articulated four decades earlier. While others may take up social justice apart from family or embrace family apart from social justice, CFT attends to families and calls them to love and justice. Especially from *Familiaris consortio* forward, the Catholic social vision cannot be separated from family life even as it continually presses its members beyond familial bonds.

## NOTES

1. John Paul II, *Familiaris consortio* (November 22, 1981), https://www.vatican.va/content/john-paul-ii/en/apost_exhortations/documents/hf_jp-ii_exh_19811122_familiaris-consortio.html (hereafter cited as *FC*).

2. Francis, *Amoris laetitia* (March 19, 2016), https://www.vatican.va/content/dam/francesco/pdf/apost_exhortations/documents/papa-francesco_esortazione-ap_20160319_amoris-laetitia_en.pdf (herafter cited as *AL*).

3. Joseph A. Selling, "Twenty-Five Years after *Familiaris Consortio*," *Intams Review* 12, no. 2 (2006): 157–66.

4. Thomas Reese, "Looking Back at the 1980 Synod on the Family," *National Catholic Reporter*, September 12, 2014, https://www.ncronline.org/blogs/faith-and-justice/looking-back-1980-synod-family.

5. Sean O'Riordan, "The Synod on the Family, 1980," *The Furrow* 31, no. 12 (1980): 759–77.

6. For a full version, annotated by Joseph P. Selling, see "The Propositions of the 1980 Synod," KU Leuven, https://theo.kuleuven.be/apps/christian-ethics/sex/history/h10b.html.

7. John Paul II, "Charter of the Rights of the Family" (October 22, 1983), https://www.vatican.va/roman_curia/pontifical_councils/family/documents/rc_pc_family_doc_19831022_family-rights_en.html.

8. Lisa Sowle Cahill, "Commentary on *Familiaris consortio*," in *Modern Catholic Social Teaching: Commentaries and Interpretations*, ed. Kenneth B. Himes (Washington, DC: Georgetown, 2005), 373–78.

9. For instance, in *Sollicitudo rei socialis*, John Paul II speaks of the option for the poor not simply as a priority for political decision-making but also as something that should shape the life choices of individuals. His prophetic statement that "private property is in fact under a social mortgage" begins to show how solidarity could function as a norm for families. John Paul II, *Sollicitudo rei socialis* (December 30, 1987), 42, https://www.vatican.va/content/john-paul-ii/en/encyclicals/documents/hf_jp-ii_enc_30121987_sollicitudo-rei-socialis.html. This theme is also developed by John Paul II in *Laborem exercens*, *Centesimus annus*, and *Ecclesia in America*. See Julie Hanlon Rubio, *Family Ethics: Practices for Christians* (Washington, DC: Georgetown, 2010), 37–65.

10. Karol Wojtyła, *The Jeweler's Shop* (1960; San Francisco: Ignatius, 1992).

11. See John Paul II, *Man and Woman, He Created Them: The Theology of the Body*, trans. Michael Waldenstein (Boston: Pauline Books and Media, 2006).

12. Thomas M. Kelly, "Sacramentality and Social Mission: A New Way to Imagine Marriage," in *Marriage in the Catholic Tradition: Scripture, Tradition, and Experience*, ed. Todd A. Salzman, Thomas M. Kelly, and John J. O'Keefe (New York: Crossroad, 2004), 149.

13. *Familiaris consortio* was published just three years after the social commentator Christopher Lasch's *Haven in a Heartless World: The Family Besieged* (New York: Norton, 1978), exemplar of a broader social movement pushing the family to focus inward.

14. This is the only place in the document that the word "complementarity" appears.

15. Violence is conspicuously absent.

16. Margaret A. Farley makes a similar point when she names "fruitfulness" as a necessary dimension of "just love" in *Just Love: A Framework for Christian Sexual Ethics* (New York: Continuum, 2006), 226–28.

17. Selling, "Twenty Five Years after *Familiaris Consortio*," 163–64.

18. The emphasis on domestic churches was influential in the US church in the 1980s and 1990s. See United States Conference of Catholic Bishops, *Follow the Way of Love* (1994), https://www.usccb.org /topics/marriage-and-family-life-ministries/follow -way-love; and Florence Caffrey Bourg, *Where Two or Three Are Gathered: Christian Families as Domestic Churches* (Notre Dame: Notre Dame Press, 2004).

19. Lisa Sowle Cahill also attests to this emphasis in recent Catholic teaching on the family. See her *Family: A Christian Social Perspective* (Minneapolis: Fortress, 2000), 89–91.

20. The social dimension of *Familiaris consortio* often goes unrecognized, and its transformative potential remains unrealized. See, e.g., Janet E. Smith, "The Family: A Communion of Persons," in *A Celebration of the Thought of John Paul II*, ed. Gregory R. Beabout (St. Louis: St. Louis University Press, 1998), 85–104; Christopher West, "A Basic Theology of Marriage," www.christopherwest.com; and the *Catechism of the Catholic Church* (New York: Doubleday, 1995), 446–62.

21. The concept of accompaniment appears only one time in *Familiaris consortio* (65) versus thirteen times in *Amoris laetitia*, where it provides the framework for chapter 8 ("Accompanying, Discerning, and Integrating Weakness").

22. Cf. Joseph A. Selling, "Twenty-Five Years after *Familiaris Consortio*," 160.

23. Thomas Knieps-Port Le Roi, "Innovation or Impasse? The Contribution of *Familiaris Consortio* to a Contemporary Theology of Marriage," *Bijdragen* 70, no. 1 (2013): 67–86.

24. See, e.g., Richard M. Hogan and John M. Levoir, *Covenant of Love: Pope John Paul II on Sexuality, Marriage and Family in the Modern World* (San Francisco: Ignatius, 2011); and Erika Bachiochi, ed., *Women, Sex, and the Church: A Case for Catholic Teaching* (Boston: Pauline Books and Media, 2010).

25. See, e.g., Charles E. Curran, *The Moral Theology of Pope John Paul II* (Washington, DC: Georgetown, 2005), esp. chap. 5, "Marriage, Sexuality, Gender, and the Family"; and Todd A. Salzman and Michael G. Lawler, *The Sexual Person: Toward a Renewal of Catholic Anthropology* (Washington, DC: Georgetown, 2008), which sets itself against the legacy of John Paul II on sexual ethics.

26. Cahill, *Family*, 89–95.

27. See, e.g., Julie Hanlon Rubio and Jason King, *Sex, Love, and Families: Catholic Perspectives* (Collegeville, MN: Liturgical, 2020).

28. Cindy Wooten, "Pope Francis to Give Women a Role in Choosing Bishops," *America*, July 6, 2022, https://www.americamagazine.org /faith/2022/07/06/pope-francis-women-bishops -243306.

29. See chapters 25 and 26 in this volume.

30. John Paul II frequently used this phrase, which he draws from *Apostolicam actuositatem* (1965).

31. Francis's most significant contribution on this point is *Fratelli tutti* (2020).

32. Francis, *Amoris laetitia*, 181.

# 16

## *Mulieris Dignitatem* and *Redemptoris Custos*

### EMILY REIMER-BARRY

## CONTEXT

*Mulieris dignitatem* was promulgated in the tenth year of the papacy of John Paul II,[1] and *Redemptoris custos* was promulgated the following year.[2] These each provide insight into John Paul II's theological anthropology, especially its gendered dimensions, but their stated purposes are to celebrate and honor Mary, the mother of Jesus, and her spouse, Joseph, for their witness and fidelity. *Mulieris dignitatem* is an apostolic letter, while *Redemptoris custos* is an apostolic exhortation. Neither document has the doctrinal weight of a conciliar dogmatic constitution or even a papal encyclical; instead, they are part of the ordinary papal magisterium that does not engage the charism of infallibility.[3] Both were issued on the Solemnity of the Assumption of the Blessed Virgin Mary, indicating their Marian themes and their complementary perspectives. *Mulieris dignitatem* is longer and more significant in terms of its impact; as such, it will receive greater attention in this chapter.

*Mulieris dignitatem* and *Redemptoris custos* were promulgated nearly a quarter century after the Second Vatican Council at a time when its reforms were still being implemented. John Paul II had already written on the role of the Christian family in the modern world[4] and on the dignity of work and the rights of workers.[5] John Paul II's general audiences, from 1979 to 1984, had outlined the major points of what would become known as his theology of the body.[6]

Already in 1988, John Paul II's leadership contained contradictions: he publicly condemned apartheid in South Africa but criticized liberation theologians and ecclesial base communities in Latin America. John Paul II traveled extensively throughout the world, frequently condemning human rights abuses—by this time in his papacy he had already visited the Dominican Republic, Haiti, the United States, Ireland, Poland, and England—but he was unwilling to advocate for change in women's roles in the church itself. John Paul II expressed love and concern for those affected by AIDS but did nothing to reevaluate church teachings on divorce, homosexuality, or birth control even though activists suggested that these teachings exacerbated the suffering of people living with AIDS.[7] The institutional Catholic Church of the 1980s remained dominated by a hierarchical ecclesiology even as John Paul II initiated new youth movements, including World Youth Day.[8]

The late 1980s was a time of sweeping changes for women in the workplace and family life. In the academy, third-wave feminism had begun to shape women's and gender studies curricula, with a greater focus on differences in women's experiences and attention to racism and classism as intersecting oppressions together with sexism.[9] Feminist hermeneutics appeared as a subject in the Society of Biblical Literature program for the first time in 1989.[10] Some prominent Catholic universities became coeducational in the 1970's;[11] female graduates continued to complain about "glass ceilings" they encountered in workplaces upon graduation. Female graduates of theology programs employed the phrase "stained glass ceiling" to reflect the difficulty women experienced in securing leadership positions at every level of the church. In 1979, Sister of Mercy Theresa Kane welcomed John Paul II during his visit to the United States and stated that the church must "respond by providing the possibility of women as persons being included in all ministries of our Church."[12] But the structures of the Catholic Church did not shift to engagement rooted in listening, respect, and mutual sharing of power between ordained and lay even as John Paul II declared himself "the feminist pope."[13]

## COMMENTARY

Ten key themes emerge when *Mulieris dignitatem* and *Redemptoris custos* are read together. These reveal the puzzling state of John Paul II's account of human nature as sexed, gendered, and sinful and the resulting implications for church teachings on marriage, gender roles, and holy orders.

### Unacknowledged Development of Tradition

*Mulieris dignitatem* begins by explaining that the "dignity and vocation of women" is not a new question for the church, having surfaced previously during the Second Vatican Council, the discourses of Paul VI, and the synod of bishops in 1987 (*MD* 1).[14] The introduction to *Redemptoris custos* also situates its reflection on Saint Joseph within a traditional framing. The pope states that his reflection is "inspired by the Gospel, the Fathers of the Church," Pope Leo XIII's

encyclical *Quamquam pluries*, and centuries of pastoral veneration of Saint Joseph (*RC* 1).[15] John Paul is emphasizing the continuity of his conclusions about the dignity of women and the role of husbands with previous teachings, but any recognition of previous papal teachings supporting women's natural inferiority to men is notably absent. This strategic lacuna overlooks *Casti connubii*'s admonishments that a wife's proper role is "willing obedience" to her husband, that a married woman pursuing a career sullies "womanly character and the dignity of motherhood," or that a marriage rooted in equality is "to the detriment of the woman herself."[16] These selective oversights enable John Paul II to appeal to the "eternal truth about the human being, man and woman—a truth which is immutably fixed in human experience" (*MD* 2), without addressing uncomfortable truths about the church's development of doctrine on the issue of women's dignity.[17]

### Biblical Interpretation

John Paul II's method for interpreting the Bible is not beholden to historical-critical scholarship, linguistic analysis, form criticism, or academic exegesis. Instead, he engages in what Gregory Baum describes as "transhistorical" reflection on divine revelation.[18] This allows John Paul II to depart from traditional interpretations in some cases without offering any reliable criteria for doing so other than his authority as pope. Some progressive claims come from this method, such as the "essential equality of man and woman" (*MD* 6), that patriarchy is a result of sin (*MD* 10), and that Saint Paul endorsed mutual subjection of husband and wife (*MD* 24).[19] These interpretations correct a tradition of patriarchal biblical interpretation in which women's roles were described as naturally inferior to men's but risk departing in key ways from the guidelines promoted by *Dei verbum*. Through this document, Vatican II promoted taking seriously the human authorship, original meaning, form, genre, and historical context of biblical texts as well as the possibility of development in understanding over time.[20] *Mulieris dignitatem* privileges an analysis of Genesis 1–3 and the gospels' portrayal of Jesus's encounters with women; *Redemptoris custos* focuses on the infancy narratives of Matthew and Luke. Given the paucity of references to Joseph in the Bible, much of the analysis is purely speculative, especially concerning Joseph's inner life.[21]

John Paul II acknowledges two creation stories (Gen. 1:1–2:3 and Gen. 2:4–3:24) but interprets these as noncontradictory despite available scholarship pointing to widely different dates and settings of composition (*MD* 6). From the first he highlights both male and female persons as being created in the "image and likeness of God" (Gen. 1:26–27), and from the second he highlights the woman's role as "helper" and "companion, with whom, as a wife, the man can unite himself" (*MD* 6). John Paul II underscores the inherent sociality of human life, arguing that the person "cannot exist alone" (*MD* 7), while seamlessly connecting the accounts of human nature found in Genesis 1 and 2 via the "spousal character" of interpersonal relationships.

### Human Nature as Sexed, Gendered, and Heterosexual

According to John Paul II, both scripture and natural law provide evidence of a gender binary, demonstrating "the Creator's decision that the human being should always and only exist as a woman or a man" (*MD* 1). In this, the pope supports sex (external genitalia) as determinative of gender (a woman's expression of femininity and a man's expression of masculinity). Neither *Mulieris dignitatem* nor *Redemptoris custos* use the term "heterosexual," but both assume that all licit sexual relationships reflect the male/female coupling cited in the creation stories and the infancy narratives of Matthew and Luke. Once again contrary evidence, this time in the form of living individuals who do not fit this gender binary or who do not conform to heterosexual desires, is ignored. The spectrum of human diversity envisioned by the documents is far narrower than a concerted engagement with individual experience, biological science, or the social sciences ought to reveal.[22]

### Gender Roles

Pope John Paul II explains that there are specific qualities or roles essential to being a man (masculinity) and specific qualities or roles essential to being a woman (femininity) and that it would be unnatural for a woman to adopt masculine qualities and roles.[23] This gender essentialism aligns more with some French feminists than with US-based feminists at the time, but there is no acknowledgment of feminist authors in the footnotes or text.[24]

John Paul II affirms that women are different but equal: "The personal resources of femininity are certainly no less than the resources of masculinity: they are merely different" (*MD* 10). To be a woman means to be an "Other" to man, to be man's "complement" and "helper" (*MD* 5, 7). This construction assumes man as the norm, while woman is described by her difference. She is the "bride," receptive of the bridegroom's love (*MD* 29). She is not active but instead is passive. She does not initiate but instead responds. She "can only hand herself by giving love to others" (*MD* 30). The pope describes the "perfect woman" as a source of spiritual support for others, without care for herself; her "genius" is reflected in her "sensitivity" (*MD* 30). She is a "mystery" to man (*MD* 31). Even women's rightful rejection of sinful domination "must not under any condition lead to the masculinization of women" (*MD* 10). Instead, women should be careful to remain "feminine" and retain men's "admiration and enchantment" (*MD* 10). "Women must not appropriate to themselves male characteristics contrary to their own feminine originality" (*MD* 10). Women were called into existence "at man's side as a helper fit for him" (*MD* 29); her mission is derivative from his.

There is no mystery to masculinity for John Paul II. To be masculine is to desire union with woman as "one flesh" (*MD* 6); to have authority, leadership, voice, and power in the family (*RC* 7); to be a protector and guardian of women and children (*RC* 20); and to engage in work outside the home to support one's family (*RC* 22). As Leo XIII explained, "Joseph was in his day the lawful and natural guardian, head and defender of the Holy Family" (*RC* 28). In the nuptial metaphor employed within *Mulieris dignitatem*, Christ is the bridegroom of the church. This analogy reveals God as the always faithful masculine partner and humanity as the often unfaithful feminine partner (*MD* 23). The symbol of the bridegroom is masculine; "Christ's divine love is the love of a bridegroom, it is the model and pattern of all human love, men's love in particular" (*MD* 25). The pope explains that "masculinity and femininity are distinct, yet at the same time they complete and explain each other" (*MD* 25). He then repeats earlier teachings forbidding women's ordination to the priesthood, since the priest acts "in *persona Christi*" (meaning in the person of Christ) (*MD* 26). The church's "hierarchical structure" that formulates and supports such teaching is, the pope states, "totally ordered to the holiness of Christ's members (*MD* 27). Here, John Paul II both departs from a patriarchal tradition in which women were considered naturally subservient to men, even while he creates a new symbol structure whereby women are understood as unable to fully resemble Christ because Christ is male.

### Eve-Mary Archetypes

Eve and Mary are drawn upon as biblical archetypes of true womanhood. It is a bit strange to put these two together, as Eve arises from a creation myth and Mary was a human person, but John Paul II is far from the first to do so.[25] Eve is "Mother of the Living" praised for being wife and mother while also being the first sinner. Her complex legacy leads to both praise and blame. Not so with Mary. Where Eve fails, Mary redeems. Mary is the "New Eve," the "new beginning" for women, for "in Mary, Eve discovers the nature of the true dignity of woman, of feminine humanity" (*MD* 11). *Redemptoris custos* presents Mary as a foil and corrective to Eve: "whereas Adam and Eve were the source of evil which was unleashed on the world, Joseph and Mary are the summit from which holiness spreads all over the earth" (*RC* 7). Mary is praised in a special way for her role in salvation history, as through gestation

and childbirth she made possible the "definitive point of God's self-revelation to humanity" (*MD* 3). Thus, "a woman is to be found at the center of this salvific event" (*MD* 3). Mary is unlike other women in that she "attains a union with God that exceeds all the expectations of the human spirit" (*MD* 3). Mary is so significant for John Paul II's vision of womanhood that she becomes the "essential horizon of reflection on the dignity and the vocation of women" (*MD* 5). Mary represents the "fullness of the perfection of what is characteristic of woman, of what is feminine" (*MD* 5). Mary is "full of grace," a "handmaid of the Lord" who shows what it means "to serve" (*MD* 5). In reading the pope's praises, one wonders if this version of Mary could ever have experienced any genuine human struggles. If not, how can women relate to her? As has often happened in modern Catholic Family Teaching, the depictions of Mary and Joseph are imaginatively constructed on the basis of contemporary ideals and with little regard for biblical or historical scholarship.[26] In *Mulieris dignitatem*, John Paul II exemplifies the reconstruction of womanhood through the male gaze. Mary is the perfect woman: obedient, submissive, compliant, and a helper to man.

### God-Talk and Gendered Language

John Paul II explains that in biblical revelation, "God speaks in human language, using human concepts and images" (*MD* 8). God is "like man" and man is "like God," but "the language of the Bible is sufficiently precise to indicate the limits of the 'likeness'" (*MD* 8). With regard to his theology of God, the pope highlights scriptural passages that attribute to God both masculine and feminine qualities (*MD* 8), for example, God as a mother who cannot forget her child (Isa. 49: 14, Pss. 131:2–3, Isa. 42:14). But the pope reminds that "God is spirit" (John 4:24) and asserts that the terminology "fatherhood of God" is an analogy meant to express the "completely divine" model of all "generation" (*MD* 8). The pope is clear that God is described as both father and mother and that God's generative power is neither masculine nor feminine

(*MD* 6). In so doing, John Paul II shifts away from earlier papal associations of generative power with masculinity and becomes an ally for efforts to reject toxic masculinity within the theology of God.[27]

### Sin-Talk and Gender

Pope John Paul II offers two interpretations of Genesis 3 and claims coherence between them. First, he says that the original sin of the "first parents" is the "sin of man, created by God as male and female," reflecting a break in the original unity they enjoyed, including breaks with God, in the self, in mutual relationship, and with the natural world (*MD* 6). At the same time, John Paul II references gender-specific roles in the first sin (1 Tim. 2:13–14) and gender-specific punishments (Gen. 3:16–19), which place blame on Eve in particular. The consequences of this transgression likewise shift between mutual and uniquely female. The "inclination to sin" will impact all future generations, yet sexual domination and the loss of the stability of gender-based equality are identified as "especially to the disadvantage of the woman" (*MD* 10).[28] John Paul II finds examples in marriage as well as other spheres of life: "the situations in which the woman remains disadvantaged or discriminated against by the fact of being a woman" (*MD* 10). Such is the backdrop for Joseph's vocation to "protect" Mary when she was pregnant (*RC* 2–3).

### Jesus and Women

Jesus, a "true man, a male" (*MD* 25), was nevertheless "a promoter of women's true dignity" (*MD* 12). The pope recounts Jesus's attention to women's needs in healing miracles, inclusion of women in parables, and recognition of the women who "accompanied him as he journeyed with the Apostles" (*MD* 13). John Paul II interprets Matthew 19 as evidence that Jesus was opposed to the domination of women in marriage (*MD* 12) and adds that Jesus's "words and works always express the respect and honor due to women" (*MD* 13). In the story of the woman caught in adultery, "Jesus enters into the concrete and historical situation of women, a situation which is weighed down by the inheritance of sin. One of the ways in which this inheritance is expressed is habitual discrimination against women in favor of men" (*MD* 14). John Paul II also interprets people's experiences of abortion in contemporary times through the lens of John 8:3–11, noting how behind "her sin" there lurks a man "equally responsible for it," thus complicating the narrative that abortion is only a personal choice (*MD* 14).

### Motherhood and Virginity

John Paul II explains that there are "two particular dimensions of the fulfillment of the female personality": motherhood and virginity (*MD* 17). Mary is the exemplar of both (*MD* 16).

When describing the maternal, the pope emphasizes self-giving love as natural to women during gestation, childbirth, and parenthood. Her whole focus becomes the needs of others. John Paul II claims (without evidence) that women "understand with unique intuition" what is happening inside them during gestation (*MD* 18) and asserts that "women are more capable than men of paying attention to another person, and motherhood develops this predisposition even more" (*MD* 18). Additionally, he claims (again without evidence) that the mother "often succeeds in resisting suffering better than a man" (*MD* 19). Misrepresenting the active role her body takes in gestation, John Paul II identifies motherhood as "passive" because new life "takes place" inside her (*MD* 19).

Mary is also venerated for her virginity (*MD* 20, *RC* 18). When describing the virgin, the pope emphasizes chastity, poverty, and obedience. A virgin's love is a "spousal love" for Christ the Redeemer; vowed celibates thus give themselves to the divine Spouse with a sincere gift of their whole lives (*MD* 20). In Mary's case, "her virginal desire to give herself exclusively and fully to God" was precisely fulfilled "by becoming the Mother of God's Son" (*MD* 18). Virginal love is described as a "gift of self for love in a total and undivided manner"

(*MD* 20). Virginal love can include "spiritual motherhood" (*MD* 21). Both mothers and virgins experience completion by union with the "Other" (either a man or God) through "marriage" (either natural or spiritual). A woman is "married" either through the sacrament of marriage or spiritually through marriage to Christ (*MD* 21). In this rendering, John Paul II explains that women find completeness only in relationship with another (physical or spiritual marriage); both mothers and virgins are defined by their receptivity to the Other.[29]

### Fatherhood

Despite the fact that "the gospels do not record any word ever spoken by Joseph," John Paul II claims biblical support for ascribing exceptional fatherhood to Joseph, the spouse of Mary and the guardian of Jesus (*RC* 17). Joseph's fatherhood "is not one that derives from begetting offspring; but neither is it an 'apparent' or merely 'substitute' fatherhood" (*RC* 21). Joseph's manual labor is celebrated by the pope, who explains that Joseph understood the importance of the "dignity of work" and the "sanctification of daily life" (*RC* 22, 24). The pope interprets the "silence" of Joseph's story in the gospels as evidence of a life of "deep contemplation." Joseph also shows contemporary men what it means to be a man by his example as "head and defender" of his family (*RC* 25, 8, 28). Because Joseph was both "humble" and "mature," he knew how to appropriately use his "legal authority" as father (*RC* 8).

Combining their claims about motherhood and fatherhood, *Mulieris dignitatem* and *Redemptoris custos* form an image of the nuclear family created by the marriage of a woman and a man who parent and nurture children. The woman and man are described as different and equal, having complementary responsibilities; she is the heart, while he is the head. Women are naturally fit for loving relationships and motherhood, while the family requires the strength and protection of the father who guards and defends the family. Whether these ideals actually come from scripture, as John Paul II claims, or from his own

particular understanding of gender is for the reader decide.

## INTERPRETATION

### Methodological Limitations

*Mulieris dignitatem* and *Redemptoris custos* are both missed opportunities for advancing Catholic teaching on theological anthropology that celebrate diverse gender identities and sexual orientations instead of rendering invisible people who do not fit a heterosexual norm and gender binary. The pope's method, including the lack of engagement with scientists and social scientists, did not position him well to respond to changing understandings of sexual desire and gender.[30] John Paul II argues that gender is ontological even as gender theorists of his day were beginning to claim that gender roles are socially constructed.[31] The pope's argument from authority is weakened by contradictory explanations for understanding human nature offered by scholarly authorities.

While John Paul II clearly supported the equal dignity of all persons, his understanding of gender relations did not focus on relational justice. Despite the pope's praise for women's feminine genius, the claim that women are different but equal to men continues to perpetuate unjust power relations including within ecclesial structures, because different roles ascribe different levels of power. Further, women are more than virgins and mothers despite John Paul II's limited moral imagination that fails to actively envision women as scientists, politicians, CEOs, soldiers, and priests. This could be seen as a methodological problem, since *Mulieris dignitatem* and *Redemptoris custos* together contain 113 notes without a single reference to a female author. John Paul II continued the papal tradition of citing conciliar documents; papal encyclicals, homilies, audiences, letters, and exhortations; synodal documents; the writings of male theologians and so-called fathers of the church; and liturgical texts. This perpetuates a methodology in which women are the *objects* of study, not *subjects* who speak for themselves. Thus, any claims about women's "nature" must be understood as a third-person account, not based in an experiential understanding of women's embodied experience.[32]

Furthermore, John Paul II's ahistorical meditations on the Eve-Mary typology and the "New Adam" theology of Christ reflect an alarming supersessionism (the idea that Christianity replaces Judaism in God's salvific plan).[33] Considering *Mulieris dignitatem*, Gregory Baum writes that "the unreflected ease with which the Letter contrasts the superior ethics of Jesus with the ethical ideals of the rabbis is problematic."[34] The same problematic method is found within *Redemptoris custos*, which describes salvation history as "God's predetermined plan" and emphasizes how reference to the Old Testament "serves to emphasize the unity and continuity of the plan which is fulfilled in Christ" (*RC* 8). John Paul II also characterizes the Hebrew Bible as patriarchal while failing to recognize similar aspects of the New Testament (*MD* 11).

## Queering the Texts for LGBTQ Communities Today

An unusual aspect of *Mulieris dignitatem* and *Redemptoris custos* is the degree to which Pope John Paul II's understanding of gender often betrays more fluidity than his binary assertions seem to permit. This creates opportunities for queer readings of these documents that creatively resist hegemonic discourse about gender and power in the Catholic Church. It appears that the pope wants to present gender roles as the result of fixed biological realities while also presenting moral exemplars whose virtues transcended gender-based expectations. For example, in describing Mary, the pope says that she "represents the humanity which belongs to all human beings, both men and women" (*MD* 4). Mary, a woman, can "represent" diverse expressions of sex and gender, demonstrating the possibility of gender fluidity.

John Paul II takes care to explain that the whole church—inclusive of both males and females—is bridal. The maleness of Christ

is reasserted as bridegroom; but men are also included in the feminine symbol of the bride (*MD* 23). While the nuptial metaphor of Christ and the church in general depicts a heterosexual union with Christ as male and the church as female, at the level of the particular the male faithful are described as in a nuptial relationship with Christ, rendering a homosexual spiritual nuptial union. The scriptural origins of the nuptial metaphor describe Israel as the bride and God as the bridegroom; in this metaphor, the bride includes both men and women (*MD* 23).[35] Men can be bridal in relation to the bridegroom; such an example of drag performance in nuptial spirituality seems to push back against the heteronormativity and gender essentialism that are more immediately obvious in the text.

In describing the meaning of Genesis 1:26–27, John Paul II explains that every individual is made in the image of God insofar as he or she is a rational and free creature capable of knowing God and loving God (*MD* 7). The foundational concept of human dignity presented here and tethered to reason and freedom provides a helpful and inclusive framework for queer love. Further, the pope emphasizes the importance of a "communion of love," "to mirror in the world the communion of love that is in God, through which the Three Persons love each other in the intimate mystery of the one divine life" (*MD* 7). This unity in relationship, or communion of love, is built not on gender difference and complementarity but instead on a rather queer invocation of the Trinity.

The vocation of the human person "willed for its own sake" can be achieved "only through a sincere gift of self," according to John Paul II. "This applies to every human being, whether a woman or a man" (*MD* 7). Thus, the "feminine" virtue of self-gift is also expected of men (*MD* 7). So too can the "masculine" virtues of Saint Joseph be lived by both men and women (*RC* 31). The gender fluidity in terms of virtuous role models contradicts earlier claims about what is considered natural and unnatural for men and women.

A further queer aspect of *Redemptoris custos* concerns the marriage of Mary and Joseph and their lack of sexual union, given the church's dogmatic commitment to Mary's perpetual virginity. The pope takes great care to emphasize that Joseph and Mary were really married even as contemporary canon law requires consummation of the marital union,[36] and the church's teachings describe marriage as free, faithful, and fruitful.[37] Since contemporary theology of sexuality celebrates the unitive and procreative aspects of married love, it seems odd that John Paul II is describing a real marriage that focuses on partnership, mutual love, companionship, a shared life, and shared parenting responsibilities without sexual encounter. These could also be positive resources for addressing a queer theology of marriage in which mutual flourishing and relational justice take center stage.

In short, while there are clear limitations to John Paul II's gendered theological anthropology, these are often undermined when the fuller implications of his writing are carefully considered. As such, contemporary readers may find in these texts resources for more expansive theological visions of personhood that promote life-giving relationships rooted in relational justice and in doing so express some of the freedom and creativity that John Paul II himself demonstrated in seeking fresh interpretations of scripture and tradition.

## NOTES

1. John Paul II, *Mulieris dignitatem* (August 15, 1988), https://www.vatican.va/content/john-paul -ii/en/apost_letters/1988/documents/hf_jp-ii _apl_19880815_mulieris-dignitatem.html (hereafter cited as *MD*).

2. John Paul II, *Redemptoris custos* (August 15, 1989), https://www.vatican.va/content/john-paul -ii/en/apost_exhortations/documents/hf_jp-ii _exh_15081989_redemptoris-custos.html (hereafter cited as *RC*).

3. Richard R. Gaillardetz, *By What Authority? A Primer on Scripture, the Magisterium, and the Sense of the Faithful* (Collegeville, MN: Liturgical Press, 2003), 81.

4. John Paul II, *Familiaris consortio* (November 22, 1981), https://www.vatican.va/content/john

-paul-ii/en/apost_exhortations/documents/hf_jp-ii _exh_19811122_familiaris-consortio.html. See also chapter 15 in this volume.

5. John Paul II, *Laborem exercens* (September 14, 1981), https://www.vatican.va/content/john-paul-ii /en/encyclicals/documents/hf_jp-ii_enc_14091981 _laborem-exercens.html. See also chapter 14 in this volume.

6. The general audiences can be found at "Audiences 1979," https://www.vatican.va/content/john -paul-ii/en/audiences/1979.index.html. An example of how this vision of theological anthropology has been elevated to prominence by the United States Conference of Catholic Bishops can be found at "Theology of the Body Overview," https://www.usccb .org/issues-and-action/marriage-and-family/natural -family-planning/catholic-teaching/theology-of-the -body.

7. Roberto Suro, "Vatican and the AIDS Fight: Amid Worry, Papal Reticence" *New York Times*, January 29, 1988, https://www.nytimes.com/1988/01 /29/world/vatican-and-the-aids-fight-amid-worry -papal-reticence.html.

8. The first World Youth Day was held in Rome in 1986. For more information, see "Past WYDS," World Youth Today, https://worldyouthday.com /past-wyds.

9. For example, Audre Lorde's open letter to Mary Daly examines the problem of white feminists claiming "herstory" without attention to difference across women's experiences. Audre Lorde, "An Open Letter to Mary Daly," *Sister Outsider: Essays and Speeches* (Trumansburg, NY: Crossing, 1984), 66. See also Traci West, "The Gift of Arguing with Mary Daly's White Feminism" *Journal of Feminist Studies in Religion* 28, no. 2 (Fall 2012): 112–17.

10. Ahida E. Pilarski, "The Past and Future of Feminist Biblical Hermeneutics" *Biblical Theology Bulletin* 41, no. 1 (2011): 20.

11. Boston College became coeducational in 1970, and the University of Notre Dame, the College of the Holy Cross, and the University of San Diego became coeducational in 1972. St. Mary's College was the first Catholic college in the United States to offer advanced degrees in theology to women.

12. Theresa Kane, RSM, "Welcome to John Paul II," Alexander Street, https://documents.alexanderstreet .com/d/1000690795.

13. Cathleen Kaveny, "Catholicism and Feminism," Contending Modernities (December 22, 2010), https://contendingmodernities.nd.edu/theorizing-modernities/catholicism-and-feminism/.

14. The synod in 1987 discussed women's roles in the church but did not take any substantive action. In public reporting during and after the 1987 synod, Cardinal Archbishop May revealed that there was strong support at the time for opening all nonordained ministries in the church to women (including acolytes, lectors, and altar servers). This was removed after the first drafting stage, and the final document had weaker language. See Stephen R. Wilson, "Synod Gives Women Backing but No Role" *Washington Post,* October 20, 1987, https://www.washingtonpost.com/archive/politics/1987/10/30/synod-gives-women-backing-but-no-role/9eb66577-48e6-4dd2-986a-2669252f8cb1/. In 2021, Pope Francis took this up again with the apostolic letter *Spiritus domini* (January 2021), https://www.vatican.va/content/francesco/en/motu_proprio/documents/papa-francesco-motu-proprio-20210110_spiritus-domini.html.

15. Cf. Leo XIII, *Quamquam pluries* (August 15, 1889), https://www.vatican.va/content/leo-xiii/en/encyclicals/documents/hf_l-xiii_enc_15081889_quamquam-pluries.html. Direct commentary on this document is not included in the present volume; however, the encyclical's ascription of uniquely masculine virtues to Saint Joseph and its ample allusions to scripture without any direct quotations or citations exemplify trends common to its era within Catholic Family Teaching.

16. Pius XI, *Casti connubii* (December 24, 1930), 26, 75, and 76, https://www.vatican.va/content/pius-xi/en/encyclicals/documents/hf_p-xi_enc_19301231_casti-connubii.html.

17. Cathleen Kaveny points out, for example, that the 1912 *Catholic Encyclopedia* draws on the Creator's design of gender difference and complementarity in order to claim that women should not have the right to vote. Cathleen Kaveny, "The 'New' Feminism?," *Commonweal* 135, no. 6 (March 28, 2008): 8.

18. Gregory Baum, "Bulletin: The Apostolic Letter *Mulieris Dignitatem,*" in *Concilium: Motherhood: Experience, Institution, Theology,* ed. Anne Carr and Elisabeth Schuessler Fiorenza (Edinburgh, UK: T&T Clark, 1989), 147.

19. Cf. chapter 1 in this volume, where Andrew Massena raises the question of whether it is exegetically sound to interpret Ephesians 5 as mutual subjection.

20. Vatican II, *Dei Verbum* (November 18, 1965), 11–13, https://www.vatican.va/archive/hist_councils/ii_vatican_council/documents/vat-ii_const_19651118_dei-verbum_en.html.

21. John Paul II stands in a long line of papal writings that imagine qualities of Saint Joseph without scriptural attestations. The pope acknowledges that an "aura of silence" envelops everything about Joseph. Nonetheless, the pope goes on to claim that Joseph proceeded by way of "deep contemplation" "in daily contact with the mystery hidden from ages past" and so forth. In doing so, John Paul II identifies Joseph as an exemplar who unites the contemplative and the active. To be clear, there are no scriptural foundations for these claims. See *Redemptoris custos,* 25–27.

22. Luke Timothy Johnson, "A Disembodied Theology of the Body," *Commonweal,* January 26, 2001, 12, 17.

23. No details are given. Is the pope referring to styles of dress and grooming, to conversation patterns, or to expressions of body language? There is significant ambiguity about what it would mean for a woman to unnaturally assume "masculine" roles or postures. Catholic hagiography could provide a range of examples of women who have challenged traditional stereotypes (Jeanne d'Arc, Catherine of Sienna, Hildegard of Bingen), but these remain unexplored in the documents.

24. Luce Irigaray, Simone de Beauvoir, Julia Kristeva, and Helene Cixous are some examples of French feminists who explored gender difference through their writings on feminism and language, psychoanalysis, social history, and relationships.

25. Well-known examples include Tertullian, Irenaeus, and Justin Martyr.

26. See chapters 1 and 10 in this volume.

27. For example, Pius XII's very clear association of fatherhood and generativity in his addresses to fathers and newlyweds. See chapter 10 in this volume.

28. The pope does not identify women's experiences within the structures of the Catholic Church as sinful in light of this analysis, however.

29. For further analysis, see Jacob M. Kohlhaas, *Beyond Biology: Rethinking Parenthood in the Catholic*

*Tradition* (Washington, DC: Georgetown University Press, 2021), 46–48.

30. This is also true of teaching on homosexuality and homosexual relationships, which was also significantly developed under John Paul II. See chapter 18 in this volume.

31. For example, the writings of Judith Butler. Catholic feminists who critiqued the gender essentialism of magisterial teachings include Lisa Sowle Cahill, "The Body-In Context," in *Sex, Gender, and Christian Ethics*, 73–107 (Cambridge: Cambridge University Press, 1996); Margaret A. Farley, "The Church and the Family: An Ethical Task," *Horizons* 10, no. 1 (1983): 50–71; Susan A. Ross, *Extravagant Affections* (New York: Continuum, 1998), 99; and Christine E. Gudorf, "Western Religion and the Patriarchal Family," in *Perspectives on Marriage: A Reader*, 2nd ed., ed. Kieran Scott and Michael Warren, 285–304 (New York: Oxford University Press, 2001).

32. One often reads the claim within Catholic magisterial documents that the church is "expert in humanity." It is a curious claim that is often asserted without evidence. See *Compendium of the Social Doctrine of the Church*, 61, https://www.vatican.va/roman _curia/pontifical_councils/justpeace/documents /rc_pc_justpeace_doc_20060526_compendio-dott -soc_en.html; and Paul VI, *Populorum progressio* (March 26, 1967), 13, https://www.vatican.va /content/paul-vi/en/encyclicals/documents/hf_p-vi _enc_26031967_populorum.html.

33. See Elena Procario-Foley, "Liberating Jesus: Christian Feminism and Anti-Judaism," in *Frontiers in Catholic Feminist Theology*, ed. Susan Abraham and Elena Procario Foley (Minneapolis: Fortress, 2009), 102.

34. Gregory Baum, "Bulletin," 147.

35. See also Tina Beattie, *New Catholic Feminism: Theology and Theory* (London: Routledge, 2006); Rosemary Radford Ruether, *Sexism and God-Talk: Toward a Feminist Theology* (Boston: Beacon, 1983); and Adrian Thatcher, *Gender and Christian Ethics* (Cambridge: Cambridge University Press, 2021), 37–120.

36. See *Code of Canon Law*, canons 1058 and 1084, https://www.vatican.va/archive/cod-iuris -canonici/cic_index_en.html.

37. Cf. Paul VI, *Humanae vitae* (July 25, 1968), https://www.vatican.va/content/paul-vi/en/encycli cals/documents/hf_p-vi_enc_25071968_humanae -vitae.html. See also chapter 14 in this volume.

# 17

## Letter to Families

MARIA ELISA A. BORJA

## CONTEXT

John Paul II was called the pope of the family. His personal experience of losing family members early in life (his mother when he was nine years old, only brother at twelve years old, and father when he was twenty-one) seems to have made him more reflective about and appreciative of the gift of family.[1] This led him to embark on one initiative after another to strengthen the family.

As pope, John Paul II wrote the postsynodal apostolic exhortation *Familiaris consortio* in 1981 after the 1980 Synod of Bishops on the task of the Christian family in the world today. This exhortation has been called his *summa* of the Catholic Church's teaching on the family. It also contains the "Charter of Family Rights," which was refined and presented to the world in 1983 by the Holy See as the "Charter of the Rights of the Family."[2] In 1992, John Paul II established the World Meeting of Families to provide the supreme pontiff with an opportunity to meet with families every three years to encourage them amid the struggles they face in order to dialogue, pray, work with, and strengthen families. The first World Meeting of Families gathered families in Rome in 1994.

Cardinal Trujillo, an outspoken proponent of Catholic teaching on sexuality, reproduction, and the family, was appointed president of the Pontifical Council for the Family by John Paul II in 1990 (an institution also established by John Paul II in 1981 to replace the Committee on the Family previously established by Paul VI). The cardinal relates how the declaration by the United Nations of 1994 as the Year of the Family was faced with opposition by certain nations and groups. When the Year of the Family was approved and preparations were under way, attempts were made to replace "family" with the plural form, "families," to allow for new and varying definitions of what a family could be. This made the pope more determined to reiterate the importance and truth about the family according to God's plan.[3]

John Paul II also expressed much concern prior to the International Conference on Population and Development (ICPD) held in Cairo in September 1994. While nothing was made official until a month after "Letter to Families" was published in February, he was aware that the Cairo Conference could introduce what the pontiff identified as dehumanizing concepts about the human person and the family. In March, the draft of the Programme of Action for the ICPD was released. Among its proposals were declaring abortion a human right justified in the name of reproductive health and supporting sexual and reproductive health services for adolescents.[4] John Paul II responded swiftly through a letter to the secretary-general of the ICPD and executive director of the United Nations Population Fund, Nafis Sadik. In this letter, the pope argued that to formulate responses to population issues on the basis of "individual 'sexual and reproductive rights,' or even in terms of 'women's rights,' is to change the focus which should be the proper concern of governments and international agencies."[5] He reminded Sadik of the international consensus that abortion should in no way be promoted as a form of birth control, as stated by the 1984 ICPD in Mexico. It appeared that this consensus was now being replaced with a right to abortion on demand, without consideration of the rights of the unborn.[6]

It was within this international landscape, a situation that John Paul II characterized as a war between a "civilization of love" and the destructive phenomenon of false "free love," that "Letter to Families" was written.[7] This document is the first of three letters written by John Paul II in less than eighteen months, also including "Letter to Children" of December 1994 and "Letter to Women" of June 1995.[8] These themes were based on initiatives in the preparations for the celebration of the Great Jubilee in 2000.

In the spirit of Saint Paul, John Paul the Great wrote these letters as a form of instruction to pastor and father the church community. In particular, "Letter to Families" aimed at promoting the dignity of marriage and the family. The year 1994 was meant to be one of greater awareness and discernment about the family as well as a discovery of Catholicism's great love for the family. The United Nations had declared this the International Year of the Family, and the Catholic Church followed suit with its own declaration of 1994 as the Year of the Family to highlight the fundamental importance of the family (LTF 3).

Writing as a father to his spiritual children or even like a doting grandfather to the faithful, John Paul II began the letter with "The celebration of the Year of the Family gives me a welcome opportunity to knock at the door of your home, eager to greet you with deep affection and to spend time with you" (LTF 1). The letter is divided into three main sections. The introduction contains the context, the aim of the Year of the Family, and the letter as a prayer. The first section focuses on the civilization of love, while the second focuses on the assurance that Christ, the bridegroom, is with families. The critical influence of John Paul II's previous writings are reflected in the letter, especially his first major book, *Love and Responsibility,* which discussed the human person and the true nature of human love. Equally noteworthy is his postsynodal apostolic exhortation *Familiaris consortio,* written more than a decade earlier.

## COMMENTARY

### *The Family as Way of the Church*

There are many paths each person walks, as individual and as a member of a parish, neighborhood, society, nation, etc. Yet, the family stands out as of singular importance. Just as "man is the primary route that the Church must travel in fulfilling her mission,"[9] because the family consists of human persons, it is also the way of the church. It is the church's mission to share in the human person's joys and sorrows along every path, including the first and most important path of family. On the one hand, this is a path common to all human persons, but on the other hand, it is a path that is "particular, unique and unrepeatable, just as every individual is unrepeatable" (LTF 2). It is common to all because everyone comes into the world naturally by way of a family, yet each family is unique.

The family is the first way of the church. This could be interpreted as the family being a form of church, because within the family one generally experiences trust, unconditional love, and support for the first time. It is in this way that the family forms persons. Another manner of expressing this is to equate the way of the church with the classic term popularized by Vatican II's *Lumen gentium,* the "domestic church."[10] This means that the family is a miniature version of the larger ecclesial community in the way it is called to be a community of love.

A second interpretation of the family as the way of the church is to return to previous teachings of John Paul II on the ways of the church. Family as the way of the church is rooted in humanity as the way of the church.[11] The human person is the basis of all the other ways that the church must walk. The human person must be the focus and attention of the church, for that is her mission. "The ultimate purpose of mission is none other than to make men share in the communion between the Father and the Son in their Spirit of love."[12] Christ wills that all be saved. As such, the church becomes responsible for the family as well. The church cares for the good of both the person and the family that each individual is a part of. Yet, as had been developed extensively in *Familiaris consortio*, the church is to care for the family, while the family is also to be a witness of God's love to the world. The family is a domestic church, the church in miniature, whose same mission is to shine its light of love and hope to a world that sorely needs to hear the gospel of love and life. This emphasis on the family's ecclesial mission is inferred in parts of "Letter to Families," including an early section on prayer where Christ is invoked to remain in every human family and the Holy Spirit is called upon to strengthen and unify families (LTF 4).

### From Communion to Community

In keeping with the Catholic tradition, the letter's instruction on the family begins with the sacrament of marriage as understood according to God's design. The Trinity itself is the primordial model of family, since this doctrine teaches that God is a "we." From an abundance of love, the Trinitarian God created humanity with the primal duality and equal dignity of male and female (Gen. 1:27), reflecting mutuality and complementarity in their corresponding fatherhood and motherhood. The irrevocable marital covenant set in the beginning (Matt. 19:8) is of a one-flesh communion of spouses. From a personal I-Thou relationship, the communion shifts to a "we," a community of persons. From

a communion of persons, it graduates to a communion of parents. Children born to the couple complete, enrich, deepen, and strengthen this covenantal communion (LTF 7, 11).

John Paul II's personalist philosophy and his Christian anthropology, which is focused on relationships, are reflected in the letter. Specifically, the pope recognizes how human persons are the only creatures capable of living in communion (LTF 7). The social nature of the human person calls each one out of self to connect and relate with others, for that is the very nature of the human being.

The letter reiterates the Catholic Church's teaching about the common good of marriage and family. The sacrament of marriage is a common good for the spouses because it unites man and woman to ensure the true good of each other through love, fidelity, honor, and the permanence of their union until death. This common good of spouses, fulfilled in a conjugal love that is capable of giving and receiving new life, leads to the common good of their children, which they have promised to welcome in God's sight during the wedding rite. Their promise to fulfill the two primary ends of family—acceptance and education of children—strengthens the conjugal union well beyond the bigenerational family and toward a communion of generations via the genealogy of persons. While the letter often focuses on the married couple and their children, there is also some mention of grandparents and grandchildren. This is a conscious effort on the part of John Paul II to bring in extended family and go beyond the bigenerational focus. The letter identifies a tendency of many to limit family simply to these two generations (LTF 10). Yet, the genealogy of the person precisely highlights the continuity of covenantal love across generations and the organic communion of each generation to the generations preceding it and succeeding it (LTF 9).

### The Civilization of Love

The letter presents two civilizations existing in the world: a civilization of love and a civilization of use. One is reminded of a similar contrast in *Evangelium vitae* between the culture of life and the culture of death.[13] These two sets of contrasts, civilizations of love or use and cultures of life or of death, appear to complement each other.

The letter acknowledges Paul VI for naming the family as a fundamental part of the civilization of love, and John Paul II builds on this truth. Such a civilization is also linked to the early Christian notion of the domestic church. This civilization of love embodies a culture of love that serves as a way of humanizing the world. It also has to do with the sincere gift of self for others in joy (LTF 14). The Vatican II phrase "sincere gift of self" is used in relation to persons being created in God's image and likeness and as "the only creature on earth which God willed for itself."[14] To fully find ourselves, we must sincerely give of ourselves. Hence, the pope criticizes the modern popular notion of self-sufficiency. A person cannot be fulfilled alone; instead, people must sincerely give themselves to others in love in order to find themselves.[15]

The family "is at the centre and the heart of the civilization of love" (LTF 13). The family both keeps this civilization alive and remains dependent on it to truly be a family. Without love, a "family" is simply a group of individuals brought together biologically but with no real relationships. Therefore, the family possesses the vocation to give love and receive love from its fellow members. To successfully be a civilization of love, the family must draw strength from God who is love (LTF 13).

The second civilization, a civilization of use, is a destructive type of anticivilization. Earlier, John Paul II's encyclical *Veritatis splendor* had discussed at length the crisis of truth that pervades modern society.[16] In "Letter to Families," this crisis is presented as corrupting the understanding of the person and the family, leading to confusion about what is authentic. Rather than considering the Other as an end in themselves, the Other becomes merely a means to an end. Such forms of interaction are egocentric and selfish. They cannot be sincere gifts of self because they focus on what is pleasing and useful to the individual. Relatedly, "free love" manifests a false sense of both freedom and love, as it leads the individual to become enslaved by instincts rather than yielding to the objective demands of the true good. By centering individual concern on immediate gratification, this civilization of use gets reality backward such that one "loves" objects and uses persons. Hence, women are objectified rather than loved, children are considered a bother rather than a treasure, and abortion becomes a right of choice (LTF 13). This concept of use springs from then Karol Wojtyła's *Love and Responsibility*, where the future pope explained that if love is not the telos, then eventually such "love" becomes utilitarianism and resorts to the use of the Other as a means to an end. "Love" is mere pretense, and pleasure becomes the sole and highest value.[17] This is an antipersonalist view of humanity that destroys relationships and reflects both a lack of love and a lack of responsibility for one's choices. It masquerades under a "'veneer' of respectability" to "'soothe' consciences by creating a 'moral alibi,'" ruining many families in the process (LTF 14).

### A Love That Is Demanding

In contrast to self-centeredness and self-indulgence, authentic freedom and authentic humanity are about a love that is demanding. The word "demanding" is often seen as negative, but the letter places it in a positive light when referring to authentic love. "Letter to Families" grounds its understanding of love in the love hymn in 1 Corinthians 13, the Magna Carta of the civilization of love. Love is not some soft and warm feeling like puppy love or a first date but instead is a love that is demanding. It is effortful, not effortless. It is a love that demands that one goes out of their comfort zone and suffers for the sake of the one that is loved; to forgo one's convenience and pleasure for the sake of the other. It calls us to go beyond ourselves even when it is uncomfortable, inconvenient, or difficult. The suffering and demands that accompany this love become beautiful because they are for the true good of the one from whom they are demanded. This is the fairest love (LTF 20). It is in giving oneself as a sincere gift despite the difficulties that one truly finds oneself. Such good likewise infects and influences others in positive ways (LTF 14).

This demanding love is most necessary in the daily interactions of family life. The letter uses the word "honor" in speaking about family relationships. Whereas the fourth commandment (Exod. 20:12) is traditionally about honor toward parents, the letter expands the meaning to include the entire family. Honor is defined as a deep bond of love that calls for the acknowledgment of persons, an attitude of unselfishness, and the sincere gift of persons to persons. Children are called to honor their parents, but parents must likewise honor their sons and daughters. This mutual respect is given not because of accomplishments or titles but rather by virtue of the dignity of the person; that one is a person is reason enough for a relationship of honor.

How is such a demanding love even possible, can it be sustained, and how is a civilization of love to succeed? It is certainly not a utopian kind of love. This effortful love that demands honor is only possible by grace. Grace is made available through the sacrament of marriage. At the same time, especially in terms of parenting and educating children, the letter encourages a solidarity among families so that they are able to draw strength and help from each other. Today there are several associations and communities that do just this, including the Catholic Family Movement, Couples for Christ, Catholics for Family and Life, and many local associations and communities focused on the family. These family associations commit to pray together and seek answers together, uniting parents to educate other parents and young people to educate other young people (LTF 16).

### The Great Mystery

Family love is grounded in spousal love confirmed and established through the sacrament of marriage. "Letter to Families" discusses the great mystery, referred to by Saint Paul in Ephesians 5:32, of what makes the husband and wife able to express the spousal love of Christ for the church. Such love is possible because of the sacramental gift of marriage. Since Christ, the bridegroom, loves the church, his bride until the end, authentic spousal love is made possible between the married couple. Whenever husband and wife and, by extension, other family members offer the mutual gift of self and express their love sincerely as a community of persons, they become a witness to the world that the bridegroom is alive in their love. And when they pray earnestly to the Holy Family, they too become a holy family.

The sense of mystery is essential to Catholics, for we hold a sacramental worldview. Mystery in this sense is indeed different from the common understanding, meaning something to be solved. A theological understanding of mystery views a reality as both knowable and exceeding knowledge due to its richness and depth. It cannot be fully contained in mere definitions or conceptual points of knowledge. Truths will always go far beyond what can be known about them. For John Paul II, what is physical points to the mystery of God. Each creature, especially the human person, points to God. Hence, the human body and the whole human person are a sacrament of God.

Bishop Laffitte, former secretary of the Pontifical Council for the Family, commented that the mystery of Christ's sacrifice on the cross is manifested in the sacramental union of husband and wife so that Christ's loving grace makes a faithful, fruitful, and enduring love between spouses possible. Their lifelong commitment of sacrificial love toward each other and the children engendered through their marriage become graced opportunities to practice their marital vocation, and thereby spouses become each other's pathway to salvation. Yet, the manifestation of the great mystery in the life of spouses remains imperfect due to human limitations.[18] Nevertheless, insofar as the spouses manifest the sincere, total, and free gift of self to each other and to their children, the great mystery of Christ's sacrifice bears fruit in them.

The great mystery of spousal love was never meant to remain inward; it was meant to proceed outward. Hence, families are to transform and renew the world and all humanity by their loving witness. From a communion of persons, they heed the call to become a communion of saints (LTF 14). This is, of course, a monumental task that is not achieved in a day or a year but requires constant effort and the ongoing assistance of the grace of God. The letter thus begins with a prayer for families on the Year of the Family and correspondingly ends with a prayer for each and every family.

### Interpretation

"Letter to Families" was an opportunity for John Paul II to instruct families on account of the 1994 International Year of the Family. At a time when families faced new and greater struggles a decade after *Familiaris consortio*, he desired to lovingly instruct and encourage them. Moreover, he perceived the critical need to return to basic teachings on the human person and the family, since precisely these were being challenged by forces in the United Nations and by the organizers of the Cairo International Conference on Population and Development. In response to this and to their move to redefine family, John Paul II warned against "various programmes backed by very powerful resources nowadays.... Concerted efforts are being made to present as 'normal' and attractive, even to glamourize, situations which are in fact 'irregular'" (LTF 5).

The strong foundation upon which John Paul II builds is that both the person and the family to which the person belongs are ways of the church. The civilization of love, while not a new concept, is articulated in a fresh way to counteract the culture of false love that dehumanizes and makes persons second-guess the truth about themselves and about the family. The presentation of love as demanding dispels a view of love that is soft, easy, and carefree and underscores the truth that love is a choice that suffers and sacrifices for the other. It requires everything from us (effort, time, free choice, etc.) and the assistance of God's grace. The celebration of the great mystery of Christ's love for the church serves as the basis for the love between spouses through the sacrament of marriage. While difficult to grasp by the

faithful, and even impossible to grasp by non-believers, this great mystery unites humanity with the divine and keeps the faithful at awe as God faithfully moves through individual marriages into family life. Indeed, these concepts remain relevant today because they return to the constancy of the personalist theological anthropology of the human person developed by John Paul II during and even before his papacy.

Postmodern liberal revisionists often reject the primordial mutuality and complementarity of men and women, questioning and deconstructing the male-female binary. Frederick Greene, for instance, explains that queer theorists challenge the heteronormative social framework that, he claims, is built on an oppositional gendered binary.[19] Greene goes on to explain the view of gender theorist Judith Butler, whose writings in the early 1990s challenged the binary system of gender as a mere product of cultural history rather than based on facts of human nature.[20] Furthermore, current mainstream thought would criticize the lack of openness to LGBTQ+ gender iterations and family forms, taking offense that these are included in a list of "irregular" unions. In addition, many cultures have celebrated families based on same-sex unions as an alternative family form.

This positive response is supported by the vast majority of gay parenting studies that have found that the no-difference hypothesis holds true: children raised by same-sex households were as well adjusted as children of different-sexed households. Consider the brief by family sociologists Manning, Fettro, and Lamidi. They analyzed studies, books, and reviews published between 2003 and 2013 and concluded that children from both households (same-sex and different-sex) were equal in terms of well-being, be it academic performance, social development, psychological development, etc. However, they also stated the need for further research, including requiring larger sample sizes.[21] Contrary to the nondifference hypothesis, family studies researcher Walter Schumm challenges the validity of conclusions made regarding gay parenting studies. He examined almost four hundred studies on same-sex parenting and discovered that the research was biased and incomplete and utilized incorrect statistical analyses.[22] The bias is evident, for example, in a 1984 news article that bloated the number of children in same-sex households to nearly fourteen million children, and these numbers were used in legal proceedings. Schumm said that later data revealed that the numbers were less than four hundred thousand.[23] Likewise, the American College of Pediatricians, a small conservative group of US pediatricians, issued a statement that whereas professional health groups, academics, and social policy makers and media have been asserting the no-difference hypothesis since 2009, there is no sound evidence supporting this. In fact, studies supporting same-sex parenting possessed critical design flaws: nonlongitudinal design, deficient sample size, biased sample selection, absence of proper controls, and inadequate consideration of confounding variables.[24]

John Paul II would have been aware of these contrasting worldviews that challenged the universal notions of humanity, sexuality, and family that the Catholic Church holds to and that societies for a greater part of history have held. In the 1990s, the LGBTQ+ community was beginning to gain greater acceptance and sympathy in many societies too. Still, even if Catholicism needed to address such issues, the letter was not the venue for it. In "Letter to Families," John Paul II's audience and message are clear: to declare with great love to the faithful God's divine plan for the person and the family. His clear intention was to encourage families to live out their vocation, albeit even in recognition of the difficulties this often faces. John Paul II did acknowledge irregular families but was wary of efforts to glamourize them.

It is evident that the letter holds an understanding of love and family from the context of God's plan. It is also understandable that the letter clearly takes a stand against irregular families as contrary to God's plan and not an equal option for what Catholic teaching considers the family to be, even while John Paul II expresses love and concern and offers prayers

for those in such family situations. However, to articulate these truths in the same manner today is likely to be alienating and polarizing to many. It is not that the truth must be changed, for the truth will always be the truth. It is that almost thirty years after "Letter to Families," there ought to be new ways to approach and articulate the truth. There ought to be new ways to bring together divergent groups and divergent thoughts into a dialogue of accompaniment and synodality as Pope Francis has been doing. At the same time, there must be a fidelity to the tradition of the church that values the beauty and truth about marriage and the family without compromise for fear of becoming unpopular. This is obviously not an easy task, but it is not an impossible task either.

There are new concerns that plague the family in this generation. One such concern is how to address growing mental health issues that torment family members, especially youths. For example, while all have been negatively impacted by the COVID-19 pandemic, creating fear about the spread of infection, isolation, and uncertainty about the future, youths are especially vulnerable due to their life stage. Thus, they have been more likely to suffer from depression, anxiety, and stress, possessing greater feelings of loneliness.[25] Another concern is the new forms of child and teen cyberbullying that make victims more vulnerable because they can be preyed upon constantly through the 24/7 nature of social media and more harshly and frequently due to the anonymity of these attacks.[26] Truly, globalization and social media have their benefits, but these developments have also threatened families, especially children, by isolating them from others when the human person is meant to relate and connect with others.

Given the current concerns that families face, there is wisdom in returning to the letter, thirty years old but still applicable and still very much relevant. The truths it communicates do not change. Among its most relevant truths are the most basic ones: that the human person is created for his or her own sake, that the person finds his or her identity as *Imago Dei* through sincere self-gift, and that this self-giving is first manifested in the conjugal union and family, humanity's "first and most important" path. It is these truths that every generation of family ought to hold on to, for we know in our hearts these truths never get old.

## NOTES

1. "St. Pope John Paul II," *Catholic Online*, https://www.catholic.org/saints/saint.php?saint_id= 6996 (accessed October 27, 2022).

2. See The Holy See, "Charter on the Rights of the Family" (October 22, 1993), https://www .vatican.va/roman_curia/pontifical_councils/family /documents/rc_pc_family_doc_19831022_family -rights_en.html.

3. Alfonso Lopez Trujillo, "Proclaiming the 'Splendid Truth of the Family,'" *L'Osservatore Romano Weekly Edition in English*, November 3, 2004, 8.

4. Curt Tarnoff, "Congressional Research Service Report for Congress," June 29, 1994, Library of Congress, 3–4.

5. John Paul II, "Letter of His Holiness John Paul II to the Secretary General of the International Conference on Population and Development" (March 18, 1994), 4, https://www.vatican.va/content /john-paul-ii/en/letters/1994/documents/hf_jp-ii _let_19940318_cairo-population-sadik.html.

6. John Paul II, "Letter of His Holiness," 10.

7. John Paul II, "Letter to Families" (February 2, 1994), 14, https://www.vatican.va/content/john -paul-ii/en/letters/1994/documents/hf_jp-ii_let _02021994_families.html (hereafter cited as LTF).

8. See, John Paul II, "Letter to Children" (December 19, 1994), https://www.vatican.va/content /john-paul-ii/en/letters/1994/documents/hf_jp-ii _let_13121994_children.html; and John Paul II, "Letter to Women" (June 29, 1995), https://www .vatican.va/content/john-paul-ii/en/letters/1995 /documents/hf_jp-ii_let_29061995_women.html.

9. John Paul II, *Centesimus annus* (May 1, 1991), 53, https://www.vatican.va/content/john-paul-ii /en/encyclicals/documents/hf_jp-ii_enc_01051991 _centesimus-annus.html.

10. Vatican II, *Lumen gentium* (November 21, 1964), 11, https://www.vatican.va/archive /hist_councils/ii_vatican_council/documents/vat-ii _const_19641121_lumen-gentium_en.html.

11. John Paul II, *Redemptor hominis* (March 4, 1979), 14, https://www.vatican.va/content/john-paul -ii/en/encyclicals/documents/hf_jp-ii_enc_04031979 _redemptor-hominis.html.

12. *Catechism of the Catholic Church* (Makati: Word & Life Publications, 1994), no. 850.

13. John Paul II, *Evangelium vitae* (March 25, 1995), 21, https://www.vatican.va/content/john-paul -ii/en/encyclicals/documents/hf_jp-ii_enc_25031995 _evangelium-vitae.html.

14. Vatican II, *Gaudium et spes* (December 7, 1965), 24, https://www.vatican.va/archive/hist_councils/ii _vatican_council/documents/vat-ii_const_19651207 _gaudium-et-spes_en.html.

15. Paul Scalia, "The Role of the Family in John Paul II's Program for Building the Civilization of Love," *Catholic Culture*, https://www.catholic culture.org/culture/library/view.cfm?recnum=2698 (accessed October 28, 2022).

16. See John Paul II, *Veritatis splendor* (August 6, 1993), https://www.vatican.va/content/john-paul-ii /en/encyclicals/documents/hf_jp-ii_enc_06081993 _veritatis-splendor.html.

17. Karol Wojtyła, *Love and Responsibility*, trans. H. T. Willetts (San Francisco: Ignatius, 1981).

18. Jean Laffitte, "The Sacramentality of Human Love According to Saint John Paul II," *Homiletic and Pastoral Review*, December 2, 2014, https:// www.hprweb.com/2014/12/the-sacramentality-of -human-love-according-to-st-john-paul-ii/#:~: text=For%20St.,and%20unfolds%20itself%20over %20time (accessed October 29, 2022).

19. Frederick L. Greene, "Introducing Queer Theory into the Undergraduate Classroom: Abstractions and Practical Applications," *English Education* 28, no. 4 (December 1996): 326.

20. Greene, "Introducing Queer Theory," 328.

21. Wendy D. Manning, Marshal Neal Fettro, and Esther Lamidi, "Child Well-Being in Same-Sex Parent Families: Review of Research Prepared for American Sociological Association Amicus Brief," *Population Research and Policy Review* 33 (2014): 499.

22. Walter R. Schumm, *Same-Sex Parenting Research: A Critical Assessment* (London: Wilberforce Publications, 2018), 47–60.

23. Schumm, *Same-Sex Parenting Research*, 65–74.

24. American College of Pediatricians, "Homosexual Parenting: A Scientific Analysis" (May 2019), https://acpeds.org/position-statements/homosexual -parenting-a-scientific-analysis. (Editor's note: The American College of Pediatricians was formed in response to a 2002 policy statement by the American Academy of Pediatrics favorable to same-sex parenthood. At present, membership in the American College of Pediatricians is roughly 1 percent that of the American Academy of Pediatrics. The American College of Pediatricians has been classified as an anti-LGBTQ hate group by the Southern Poverty Law Center).

25. Ma. Regina Hechanova, Alvin Patrick Valentin, and Karlos Pio Alampay, "Age, COVID-19, and Mental Health in the Philippines: A Multidimensional Perspective," *Asia-Pacific Social Science Review* 22, no. 1 (March 2022): 142.

26. Christopher P. Barlett, Douglas A. Gentile, and Chelsea Chew, "Predicting Cyberbullying from Anonymity," *Psychology of Popular Media Culture* 5, no. 2 (2016): 179.

# 18

# Documents on Homosexuality and Same-Sex Relationships

TODD A. SALZMAN AND MICHAEL G. LAWLER

## CONTEXT

In its 1975 declaration *Persona humana*, the Congregation for the Doctrine of the Faith (CDF) asserts a clear and unambiguous condemnation of same-sex sexual acts.[1] Such acts "are intrinsically disordered and can in no case be approved of" (*PH* VIII). *Persona humana* follows the revised reasoning in *Humanae vitae* that each and every sexual act, rather than the traditional ends of marriage, contains two intrinsic meanings, the unitive meaning and the procreative meaning. This is known as the inseparability principle and has become the foundational principle in magisterial moral evaluation of all sexual acts. According to this principle, all nonreproductive marital sexual acts and all reproductive or nonreproductive nonmarital sexual acts are intrinsically disordered. Same-sex, oral, and anal sex as well as masturbation, use of contraception and most reproductive technologies are prohibited based on this principle. This chapter focuses on the morality of homosexual sexual acts and considers three subsequent CDF documents on same-sex relationships, sexual acts, and parenting and critically analyzes those documents.

The first document, "Letter to the Bishops of the Catholic Church on the Pastoral Care of Homosexual Persons" (1986),[2] further

elucidates that although homosexual orientation is not in itself sinful, it "is a more or less strong tendency ordered toward an intrinsic moral evil; and thus the inclination itself must be seen as an objective disorder" (LTB 3). The Catholic Church's doctrine on homosexual sexual activity, the letter continues, is based "not on isolated phrases for facile theological argument, but on the solid foundation of a constant biblical testimony" (LTB 5).

The second document, "Some Considerations Concerning the Response to Legislative Proposals on the Non-Discrimination of Homosexual Persons" (1992),[3] came in reaction to "legislation . . . proposed in various places which would make discrimination on the basis of sexual orientation illegal" (SCC Foreword). The document declares that "it is deplorable that homosexual persons have been and are the object of violent malice in speech or in action" and reinforces the Catholic social doctrine that "the intrinsic dignity of each person must always be respected in word, in action, and in law" (SCC 7). Still, the document goes on to argue that "sexual orientation does not constitute a quality comparable to race, ethnic background, etc., in respect to non-discrimination," for "unlike these, homosexual orientation is an objective disorder and raises moral concern" (SCC 10). From its premise (asserted but not actually proven) that homosexuality constitutes a disorder, the CDF asserts that "there are areas in which it is not unjust [but just] discrimination to take sexual orientation into account, for example in the placement of children for adoption or foster care, in employment of teachers or athletic coaches, and in military recruitment" (SCC 11). Moreover, there is "no right to homosexuality which therefore should not form the basis for judicial claims" (SCC 14), and "the Church has the responsibility to protect family life and the public morality of the entire civil society on the basis of fundamental moral values" (SCC 16).

The third document, "Considerations Regarding Proposals to Give Legal Recognition to Unions between Homosexual Persons" (2003),[4] does "not contain new doctrinal elements" but reiterates "the essential points" on questions of homosexual actions and the dignity of marriage (CRP 1). It is a response to the growing legalization of gay and lesbian marriage throughout the Western world. Church teaching that "men and women with homosexual tendencies must be accepted with respect, compassion and sensitivity" and that "every sign of *unjust* discrimination in their regard should be avoided" (CRP 4, emphasis added) is reinforced, but "respect for homosexual persons cannot lead in any way to approval of homosexual behavior or to legal recognition of homosexual unions" (CRP 11). Marriage, the document insists, "exists solely between a man and a woman" (CRP 2), and in the plan of the Creator "sexual complementarity and fruitfulness belong to the very nature of marriage" (CRP 3). Since it judges homosexual intercourse as unable to realize these dimensions, the document concludes that "there are absolutely no grounds for considering homosexual unions to be in any way similar or even remotely analogous to God's plan for marriage and the family" (CRP 3). Moreover, the CDF explains, homosexual sex acts "close the sexual act to the gift of life; they do not proceed from a genuine affective or sexual complementarity. Under no circumstance can they be approved" (CRP 3). They are, it states, condemned in scripture as "a serious depravity" (CRP 4).[5]

"As experience has shown," the document later adds, "the absence of sexual complementarity in these unions creates obstacles to the normal development of children who would be placed in the care of such persons" and does "violence" to such children by impeding "their full human development" (CRP 7).

These documents, published between 1975 and 2003, address evolving ethical issues related to homosexuality and clearly condemn homosexual relationships, sexual acts, and parenting. Recently, however, several cardinals and bishops have been calling for changes in Catholic teaching on homosexuality, and Pope Francis has publicly defended same-sex civil unions.[6]

## COMMENTARY

### The "Solid Foundation" of Biblical Evidence

The CDF advances five texts for its claim of "clear consistency" in scripture that supports its judgment on the morality of homosexual behavior (LTB 5, 6).[7] However, when read as the Catholic Church requires these be read, that is, in the context and "literary forms" of the writer's "time and culture,"[8] the texts are far from solidly consistent. Rather, they are sociohistorically conditioned literary forms that demand careful historical analysis. A first question is obvious: Does the Bible say anything about homosexuality as we understand it today? This a question of definition, and its answer is embedded in what contemporary science and the Catholic magisterium today take for granted, namely the existence in some men and women of a definitive psychosexual condition named homosexual orientation.[9] By the mid-twentieth century, homosexual orientation had come to be understood as "a *condition* characterized by an emotional and psycho-sexual propensity towards others of the same sex,"[10] and a homosexual was understood as "a person who feels a most urgent sexual desire which *in the main* is directed towards gratification with the same sex."[11] In its contemporary, scientific connotation, homosexuality is a way of *being* before it is a way of *acting*. In contemporary scientific and theological-ethical literature, the noun "homosexuality" and the adjective "homosexual" are used to refer to a person's psychosexual condition, produced by a mix of genetic, psychological, and social "loading."

Neither the Bible nor the Christian tradition rooted in it prior to the nineteenth century ever considered homosexuality as a condition; heteronormativity was taken for granted. To look for any mention in the biblical texts of today's understanding of "homosexual orientation" is simply anachronistic. The biblical passages most frequently cited as condemning homosexuality actually condemn same-sex sexual acts specifically as a perversion of the heterosexual condition they assume as natural for every human being. The context in which both the Old and New Testaments condemn homosexual sexual acts includes a false assumption, shaped by the sociohistorical conditions of the times in which they were written, that all human beings are naturally heterosexual such that same-sex sexual actions are a perversion of nature and therefore immoral. Since that sociohistorical assumption is now scientifically shown to be incorrect, biblical passages that specifically address same-sex sexual acts have quite little to contribute to contemporary discussions of homosexuality. However, other biblical passages, such as the double love commandment (Matt. 22:37–39), remain highly relevant to all human relationships, including same-sex relationships.

The story of Sodom is probably the single most influential biblical text behind condemnations of homosexual sexual acts, yet its influence owes more to unnuanced interpretations than careful analysis of the text itself. Christian churches have consistently taught that the destruction of Sodom was brought on by unethical male homosexual behaviors, and many Christians have uncritically believed this interpretation. However, careful exegesis demonstrates that this interpretation is incomplete, inaccurate, and not supported by the text in its sociohistorical context.

The narrative context of the story begins with Abraham's hospitality to three men, one of whom is soon identified as "the Lord" (Gen. 18:2–22). These "men" pass by Abraham's house on their way to Sodom, and Abraham offers the strangers the hospitality required by the Levitical law. Two soon leave for Sodom (Gen. 18:22), where they meet Lot at "the gate of Sodom" (Gen. 19:1). Lot similarly offers them the required Jewish hospitality, bringing them to his house and feeding them. But before they retired for the night, the men of Sodom surround the house and call for Lot to bring the two men out "that we may know them (*yadha*)" (Gen. 19:5). The word *yadha* is critical for understanding what the men of Sodom were asking. *Yadha* is the ordinary Hebrew word for the English "know," but it is occasionally used as a euphemism for sexual intercourse. The context points to a clear insinuation of sexual intent against the two strangers at Sodom, although this does not necessarily mean that the sin of the men of Sodom was homosexual behavior.

In the Hebrew context, the clearer sin is inhospitality. Lot's concern for hospitality is made evident in the phrase "*do nothing to these men for they have come under the shelter of my roof*" (Gen. 19:8), that is, under the shelter of my hospitality, which now includes protecting them from the perverted sexual designs of the crowd. The men of Sodom demonstrate the extent of their inhospitality by seeking to violently rape the strangers. Although secondary and serving the primary emphasis on hospitality, the specific sexual action condemned in the text is the crime of rape carried out by perverted men. Condemning violent, same-sex rape is a long way from condemning loving sexual acts between persons of the same sex.

For Christians, the interpretation that inhospitality is the sin of Sodom is underscored by Jesus's mention of Sodom in the same breath as the inhospitality accorded his disciples. "Whenever you enter a town and they do not receive you ... I tell you it shall be more tolerable on that day for Sodom than for that town" (Luke 10:10–12). Jesus, exemplifying the Jewish tradition, also makes hospitality or inhospitality key to salvation or damnation in the great judgment scene in Matthew 25:34–46.

If the Sodom story is ultimately about inhospitable and not homosexual acts, no such reservation can be made about the prescriptions of the Holiness Code in Leviticus. "You shall not lie with a male as with a woman; it is an abomination" (Lev. 18:22). What the Holiness Code says could not be clearer: sexual acts between men, who are presumed to be heterosexual, is an abomination. Note that it is male acts that are prohibited; lesbian acts are not part of the prohibition. In English the word "you" in "you shall not lie" applies indiscriminately to both males and females; in Hebrew the word applies only to males. It is the homosexual actions of men that Leviticus says are an abomination, and that restriction yields insight into both the proscription's sociohistorical context and its implications.

The first thing to be noted about the Hebrew context of the time is bad biology. The ancient Hebrew, Greek, and Roman understanding was that the male provided seed that contained the whole of life; the female simply provided the "ground" or the "field" in which the seed developed into a fully fledged human.[12] To spill that seed anywhere it could not develop properly— in a male body, for instance—could be regarded as tantamount to murder and was held as an abomination. Those guilty of murder suffered the same penalty as Leviticus prescribes for men performing homosexual acts, namely death.[13]

Extended family was and is "the primary economic, religious, educational, and social network" in Mediterranean society.[14] Within the social network, family was the locus of honor, carried exclusively by males, particularly by the patriarch who headed the family and, for all intents and purposes, owned the females in it, whether they were wives, daughters, slaves, or servants. For a male to "lie with" another male, that is, to act passively and allow himself to be penetrated like a female, compromised male honor not only of the male being penetrated

but also of every male in the family. In such a sociohistorical context, male same-sex sexual acts were an abomination not because they are homosexual acts but instead because they are dishonorable acts that threatened the patriarchal arrangement that pervaded the Old Testament.

What about an utterly different social context, a context in which not every human being is presumed to be by nature heterosexual but some are known to be by nature homosexual, a context in which honor is not a dominant concern and in which male and female are understood to contribute equally to the procreation of new life? In such a context, male homosexual behavior need not be judged as dishonorable and ipso facto unethical; just and loving homosexual behavior, flowing from an innate homosexual orientation, cannot be regarded as a perversion of a universal heterosexual condition and therefore cannot be judged ipso facto unethical; and the spilling of male semen or seed would no longer be regarded as the spilling of life, murder, and an abomination. In short, when the interpreter considers the Old Testament's statements on homosexual behavior by men presumed to be heterosexual and the sociohistorical context in which these were made, they offer only limited resources for contemporary moral judgments.

Turning to the New Testament, many take Paul's letter to the Romans as the centerpiece of doctrine on homosexual behavior. It is important, again, to note the context of Paul's remarks, which is an attack not on homosexual acts in particular but instead on degenerate, especially idolatrous, Gentile society in general. Paul makes the standard Jewish accusations about Gentile idolatry: "What can be known about God is plain to them [Gentiles] because God has shown it to them" (Rom. 1:20). Gentiles, however, "did not honor God as God or give thanks to God." Rather, "they exchanged the glory of the immortal God for images resembling a mortal human being or birds or four-footed animals or reptiles" (Rom. 1:23). What is radically wrong with Gentiles is that they are idolaters, and he describes the actions of such idolaters. "God *gave them up* in the lusts of their heart to impurity, to the dishonoring of their bodies" (Rom. 1:24–28). Gentile idolatry is directly at stake in this text. Same-sex sexual acts by perverted heterosexuals are where this idolatry is presumed to lead.

Paul does not consider gay and lesbian sexual acts of those who by "nature" have a homosexual orientation or the just and loving homosexual acts in which this nature might issue.[15] He does not consider, because he has no concept of, relationships between modern homosexual couples who might justly love one another and be committed to one another as faithfully as any heterosexual couple. The condemnation of the homosexual actions of perverted heterosexuals does not easily translate to the condemnation of the just and loving actions of those who are definitively homosexual.[16] Thus, as Richard Sparks concludes, "on scriptural evidence alone we are left short of a clear and clean condemnation of what might be called committed or covenantal homosexual acts."[17]

### The Procreation and Complementarity Arguments

The CDF teaches that homosexual unions lack "the conjugal dimension which represents the human and ordered form of sexuality" and that "sexual relations are human when and insofar as they express and promote the mutual assistance of the sexes in marriage and are *open to the transmission of new life*" (CRP 7, emphasis added). This articulates the unitive-procreative principle that in the twentieth century became the foundational principle for all Catholic sexual teaching.

Procreation and the propagation of the human race is a good of marriage, but in the contemporary Catholic tradition it is not a necessary good of each and every individual marriage. In 1951, Pope Pius XII taught that for "grave reasons" of a "medical, eugenic, economic, or social kind," it is not unethical to avoid procreation for the lifetime of a marriage.[18] Pope Paul VI repeated this teaching in *Humanae vitae*, and Pope John Paul II repeated it again

in *Familiaris consortio*. The argument that same-sex unions cannot be called marriage because they cannot propagate is therefore an argument with no probative power in Catholic ethics. The mutual love and commitment of the spouses to one another and to their permanent union has been proven to be a necessary good of marriage for both the spouses and their children. Heterosexual marriages without biological children are not considered illegitimate on the basis of failure to fulfill the procreative meaning of the sexual act or end of marriage, even when these couples have not pursued nonbiological means of fulfilling this end such as adoption, foster care, mentorship, or other intimate intergenerational relationships. In the case of infertile and postmenopausal couples where biological procreation is an impossibility, the unitive meaning of the sexual act or end of marriage may, in fact, become the primary and sole meaning of the sexual act and good of marriage without compromising the marriage's integrity in any way. It is no more plausible to claim that such couples can, in some way, remain open to the transmission of life than it is to claim that same-sex couples can likewise be open to the transmission of life. In both cases, the mutual love of the spouses may become the primary meaning of the sexual act and the good of their marital relationship. Despite the CDF's reduction of homosexual relationships to nothing more than the moral value of illicit sexual acts, same-sex spouses have proved that both they and their unions can in fact possess this good. Pope Francis's statement that "same-sex unions may not simply be equated with marriage"[19] is a statement protecting marriage as a sacrament between one man and one woman. His other statements supporting same-sex civil unions, the baptism of children in same-sex relationships, and welcoming same-sex families in parishes all indicate a movement beyond the CDF's vision.[20]

A major change in the approach of Catholic theological ethicists to sexual sin parallels the change in this approach to marriage. The majority of Catholic ethicists are now agreed that decisions of morality or immorality in sexual ethics should be based on interpersonal relationship and circumstances, not on physical acts.[21] Lisa Sowle Cahill argues that "a truly humane interpretation of procreation, pleasure and intimacy will set their moral implications in the context of enduring personal relationships, not merely individual sexual acts. If human identity and virtue are established diachronically, then this will also be true of sexual flourishing."[22] Serious immorality or mortal sin is no longer decided on the basis of an individual sexual act against so-called nature, that is, against the natural, biological, physical processes common to all farmyard animals. It is decided on the basis of human goods and the human relationships built upon them. Cahill suggests such human goods as "equality, intimacy, and fulfillment as moral criteria."[23] To these could be added the virtues of love and justice. Sexuality has three bodily meanings: intimacy of bodily contact, pleasure, and procreation. All these meanings are realized and developed diachronically in the social institutions recognized in a society, whether they be civil unions, heterosexual marriages, or same-sex marriages. Immoral sexual behavior is defined not exclusively by any isolated sexual act but rather by any less than mutual, loving, just, and equal relationship.

Catholic teaching uses the term "complementarity" in relation to the unitive and procreative principle; this term indicates that two realities belong together and produce something that neither can produce alone. This classification is nearly always classified along masculine and feminine lines and is used both biologically and metaphorically. Sexual complementarity completes a heterosexual couple in marriage by bringing together their masculine and feminine elements to produce the biblical "one body" (Gen. 2:24) or person. The magisterium consistently condemns homosexual acts on the grounds that they violate heterosexual and reproductive complementarity, as they obviously do, but it fails to explain why they also violate personal complementarity other than to assert gratuitously that homosexual acts "do not proceed from a genuine affective and sexual complementarity."[24] This assertion implies that such acts can never be truly unitive on the level of sexual and personal

complementarity. Though the magisterium has not confronted this question either experientially or theologically, monogamous, loving, and committed homosexual couples have confronted it experientially and testify that they do experience unitive complementarity in and through their homosexual acts. Margaret Farley notes the testimony of these couples witnesses "to the role of such loves and relationships in sustaining human well-being and opening to human flourishing" and "extends to the contributions that individuals and partners make to families, the Church, and society as a whole."[25]

Psychologist Lawrence Kurdek has done extensive research on gay and lesbian couples and notes the following characteristics when comparing their relationships with heterosexual couples. Gay and lesbian couples tend to have a more equitable distribution of household labor, demonstrate greater conflict resolution skills, have less support from members of their families but greater support from friends, and, most significantly, experience similar levels of relational satisfaction compared to heterosexual couples.[26] Scientific evidence challenges magisterial claims not only that homosexual acts are detrimental to the human person and human relationships but also that homosexual parenting is detrimental to children.

### Same-Sex Parenting

There is abundant research data to indicate that gay and lesbian couples are as qualified to be adoptive and foster parents as heterosexual couples. Drawing from the CDF statement cited above that same-sex parents would "do violence" to children they parent, the United States Conference of Catholic Bishops (USCCB) opposes the Equality Act in the US Congress that would allow fostering and adoption by homosexual couples, arguing that "children raised by a married mother and father are statistically more likely to have positive social, economic, and health outcomes than those raised by same-sex couples."[27] Unlike the CDF statement, which offers no documented evidence to substantiate its claim, the USCCB offers three references in support of this position, two from priest sociologist Paul Sullins and one from sociologist Mark Regnerus.

Sullins claims that children of same-sex parents are more likely than children of heterosexual parents to suffer from depression, stigma, obesity, abuse, and parental distance.[28] He also advises, based on his limited evidence, that his findings should be "neither exaggerated nor dismissed out of hand on preconceived ideological grounds."[29] The USCCB ignores this caution and presents Sullins's evidence as if it were sound fact to substantiate its argument against the Equality Act.[30] The publisher of the journal in which Sullins's article appears posted an online "Expression of Concern," stating that Sullins's article "has been cited to support arguments about same-sex marriage that are hateful and wrong."[31] Regnerus surveyed fifteen thousand people ages eighteen to thirty-nine years to study the impact of LGBTQ+ parents on children. He concludes that people who had a parent in a same-sex relationship had a greater risk for negative outcomes such as being on public assistance, being unemployed, and having poorer education attainment.[32]

The scholarship of both authors on same-sex parenting has been severely and widely critiqued. Nathaniel Frank, director of Cornell University's What We Know project,[33] has collected and analyzed over seventy-five studies on same-sex parenting, including those by the American Psychological Association,[34] the American Academy of Pediatrics,[35] and the Child Welfare League of America.[36] He identifies deep methodological flaws in both Sullins's and Regnerus's studies. Drawing from that extensive research and considering Regnerus's method of collecting and analyzing his data, Simon Cheng and Brian Powell judge his conclusions "fragile." They conclude that "when equally plausible and, in our view, preferred methodological decisions are used, a different conclusion emerges: adult children who lived with same-sex parents show comparable outcome profiles to those from other family types, including intact biological families."[37]

Extensive research supports Cheng and Powell's conclusion. The American Psycholog-

ical Association conducted an extensive survey of more than thirty years of research on children of lesbian and gay parents and declared that since "lesbian and gay parents are as likely as heterosexual parents to provide supportive and healthy environments for their children . . . [and since] research has shown that the adjustment, development, and psychological well-being of children is unrelated to parental sexual orientation and that the children of lesbian and gay parents are as likely as those of heterosexual parents to flourish," it opposes any discrimination based on sexual orientation.[38] The American Association of Pediatrics concludes that "it is in the best interests of children that they be able to partake in the security of permanent nurturing and care that comes with the civil marriage of their parents, without regard to their parents' gender or sexual orientation."[39] The Child Welfare League of America is also convinced by the available research data that there are no significant differences between the parental attitudes and skills of heterosexual and homosexual parents.[40] The league's policy statement, approved in 1994, recommends that "gay/lesbian adoptive applicants should be assessed the same as any other adoptive applicant. It should be recognized that sexual orientation and the capacity to nurture a child are separate issues."[41] These data and recommendations fundamentally challenge a "presumption of harm" to children of sexually active gay and lesbian parents.

Some studies do detect mental stress on the children of homosexual couples, but they conclude that the stress is a result not of homosexual parenting but instead of social discrimination toward them generated by the kind of myths propagated by the CDF and the USCCB.[42] The conclusion of comparable outcomes has been substantiated by numerous authors and studies in several countries.[43] Therefore, the claim of the CDF that "as experience has shown the absence of sexual complementarity in [same-sex] unions creates obstacles in the normal development of children who would be placed in the care of [gay and lesbian parents]" ought to be acknowledged as disproven (CRP 7).

# INTERPRETATION

The CDF's claim of "a solid consistency" in the scriptures condemning homosexual acts is shown to be unfounded when the texts that provide this so-called solid consistency are read as the Catholic Church prescribes they be read. They provide a solid consistency only when read and interpreted through an unproven but accepted ideology. Human experience challenges ideology and is a long-accepted source of understanding human reality. John Courtney Murray correctly points out that practical human intelligence is preserved from ideology by having "a close relation to concrete experience."[44] Catholic claims about homosexual lives are far removed from concrete experience. The claims that homosexual acts "do not proceed from a genuine affective and sexual complementarity" and that same-sex parents "do violence" to children are contradicted by both concrete experience and serious scientific research. It is not surprising, then, that fueled with their concrete experience and practical intelligence of homosexual lives, many church leaders and Catholic faithful,[45] in the name of human dignity, the common good, justice, and the well-being of all human families, are demanding changes to Catholic teaching and language about homosexual relationships and actions. Given our analysis of that teaching and its bases, we here add our voices to that demand.

# NOTES

1. Congregation for the Doctrine of the Faith, *Persona humana* (December 29, 1975), https://www.vatican.va/roman_curia/congregations/cfaith/documents/rc_con_cfaith_doc_19751229_persona-humana_en.html (hereafter cited as *PH*).

2. Congregation for the Doctrine of the Faith, "Letter to the Bishops of the Catholic Church on the Pastoral Care of Homosexual Persons" (October 1, 1986), 3, https://www.vatican.va/roman_curia/congregations/cfaith/documents/rc_con_cfaith_doc_19861001_homosexual-persons_en.html (hereafter cited as LTB).

3. Congregation for the Doctrine of the Faith, "Some Considerations Concerning the Response to Legislative Proposals on the Non-Discrimination of Homosexual Persons" (July 24, 1992), https://www.vatican.va/roman_curia/congregations/cfaith/documents/rc_con_cfaith_doc_19920724_homosexual-persons_en.html (hereafter cited as SCC).

4. Congregation for the Doctrine of the Faith, "Considerations Regarding Proposals to Give Legal Recognition to Unions between Homosexual Persons" (June 3, 2003), https://www.vatican.va/roman_curia/congregations/cfaith/documents/rc_con_cfaith_doc_20030731_homosexual-unions_en.html (hereafter cited as CRP).

5. See also *Catechism of the Catholic Church*, 2nd ed. (Vatican City: Libreria Editrice Vaticana, 1994), 2357, https://www.usccb.org/sites/default/files/flipbooks/catechism/.

6. See Catholic News Service, "Cardinal Marx Calls for Change in Church Teaching on Homosexuality, Admits to Blessing Same-Sex Couples," *America*, March 31, 2022, https://www.americamagazine.org/politics-society/2022/03/31/cardinal-marx-germany-homosexuality-242735; and Joshua J. McElwee, "Not News: Pope Francis Has Supported Civil Unions for Years," *National Catholic Reporter*, October 21, 2020, https://www.ncronline.org/news/people/not-news-pope-francis-has-supported-civil-unions-years.

7. Genesis 19:1–11; Leviticus 18:22 and 20:13; Romans 1:26–7; 1 Corinthians 6:9; and 1 Timothy 1:10.

8. Vatican II, *Dei verbum* (November 18, 1965), 12, https://www.vatican.va/archive/hist_councils/ii_vatican_council/documents/vat-ii_const_19651118_dei-verbum_en.html.

9. See Richard C. Friedman and Jennifer I. Downey, *Sexual Orientation and Psychoanalysis: Sexual Science and Clinical Practice* (New York: Columbia University Press, 2002).

10. D. Sherwin Bailey, *Homosexuality and the Western Christian Tradition* (New York: Longman's, 1955), x (emphasis added).

11. Donald W. Cory, *The Homosexual in America* (New York: Julian Press, 1951), 8.

12. For Greek society, see Paige duBois, *Sowing the Body: Psychoanalysis and Ancient Representations of Women* (Chicago: University of Chicago Press,

1988), 39–85. For Jewish Society, see Sirach 26:19; and *Mishna*, Ketuboth, 1, 6.

13. Leviticus 24:17, 21; Numbers 35:30; and Exodus 20:13.

14. Bruce J. Malina and Richard L. Rohrbaugh, *Social Science Commentary on the Synoptic Gospels* (Minneapolis, MN: Fortress, 1992), 202.

15. See Dale B. Martin, "Heterosexism and the Interpretation of Romans 1:18–31," *Biblical Interpretation* 3 (1995): 332–55.

16. Space restrictions make it impossible to consider the two remaining texts cited by the CDF, 1 Corinthians 6:9–10, and 1 Timothy 1:10; however, they add nothing substantive to the supposed foundation for condemning same-sex sexual acts.

17. Richard Sparks, *Contemporary Christian Morality* (New York: Crossroad, 1996), 81.

18. *Acta Apostolicae Sedis*, 43 (1951): 835–54. See also chapter 10 in this volume.

19. Francis, *Amoris laetitia* (March 19, 2016), 52, https://www.vatican.va/content/dam/francesco /pdf/apost_exhortations/documents/papa-francesco _esortazione-ap_20160319_amoris-laetitia_en.pdf.

20. Francis DeBernardo, "Pope Congratulates, Blesses Gay Couple on the Baptism of Their Adopted Children," *New Ways Ministry*, August 9, 2017, https://www.newwaysministry.org/2017/08 /09/pope-congratulates-blesses-gay-couple-on-the -baptism-of-their-adopted-children/.

21. Christine E. Gudorf, *Body, Sex, and Pleasure* (Cleveland, OH: Pilgrim Press, 1994), 14–18.

22. Lisa Sowle Cahill, *Sex, Gender and Catholic Ethics* (Cambridge: Cambridge University Press: 1996), 112.

23. Cahill, *Sex, Gender and Catholic Ethics*, 11.

24. *Catechism of the Catholic Church*, 2357.

25. Margaret A. Farley, *Just Love: A Framework for Christian Sexual Ethics* (New York: Continuum, 2006), 287.

26. Lawrence A. Kurdek, "What Do We Know about Gay and Lesbian Couples?," *Current Directions in Psychological Science* 14 (2005): 251; Lawrence A. Kurdek, "Differences between Partners from Heterosexual, Gay, and Lesbian Cohabiting Couples," *Journal of Marriage and Family* 68 (May 2006): 509–28; and Lawrence A. Kurdek, "Are Gay and Lesbian Cohabiting Couples *Really* Different From Heterosexual Married Couples?" *Journal of Marriage and Family* 66 (2004): 880–900.

27. United States Conference of Catholic Bishops, "Equality Act Letter to Congress," March 20, 2019, http://www.usccb.org/issues-and -action/marriage-and-family/marriage/promotion -and-defense-of-marriage/upload/Equality-Act -Letter-to-Congress-House-1.pdf.

28. Paul Sullins, "Invisible Victims: Delayed Onset Depression among Adults with Same-Sex Parents," *Depression and Research Treatment* 2016 (May 29, 2016): 2410392, https://doi.org/10.1155 /2016/2410392. *Depression and Research* prefaced this article with an editorial "Expression of Concern." Paul Sullins, "Emotional Problems among Children with Same-Sex Parents: Difference by Definition," *British Journal of Education* 7, no. 2 (2015): 99–120.

29. Sullins, "Invisible Victims."

30. United States Conference of Catholic Bishops, "Equality Act Letter to Congress."

31. Hindawi Limited, "Expression of Concern on 'Invisible Victims: Delayed Onset Depression among Adults with Same-Sex Parents," National Library of Medicine, National Center for Biotechnology Information (August 22, 2017), https://www .ncbi.nlm.nih.gov/pmc/articles/PMC5567452/.

32. Mark Regnerus, "How Different Are the Adult Children of Parents Who Have Same-Sex Relationships? Findings from the New Family Structures Study," *Social Science Research* 41, no. 4 (2012): 752–70. Regnerus's study was "rebuked" for flawed methodologies in a letter signed by two hundred social scientists.

33. What We Know, "What Does the Scholarly Research Say about the Well-Being of Children with Gay or Lesbian Parents?," Cornell University, https://whatweknow.inequality.cornell.edu/topics /lgbt-equality/what-does-the-scholarly-research -say-about-the-wellbeing-of-children-with-gay-or -lesbian-parents.

34. American Psychological Association, "APA on Children Raised by Gay and Lesbian Parents: How Do These Children Fare?," June 11, 2012, https:// www.apa.org/news/press/response/gay-parents.

35. American Academy of Pediatrics, "Promoting the Well-Being of Children Whose Parents Are Gay or Lesbian: Technical Report," *Pediatrics* 131 (2013): 1381.

36. Ann Sullivan, ed., *Issues in Gay and Lesbian Adoption: Proceedings of the Fourth Annual*

*Peirce-Warwick Adoption Symposium* (Washington, DC: Child Welfare League of America, 1995), 41.

37. Simon Cheng and Brian Powell, "Measurement, Methods, and Divergent Patterns: Reassessing the Effects of Same-Sex Parents," *Social Science Research* 52 (July, 2015): 616–17.

38. American Psychological Association, "APA on Children Raised by Gay and Lesbian Parents."

39. American Association of Pediatrics, "Promoting the Well-Being of Children," 1381.

40. See "CWLA's Position on Same-Sex Parenting," The Child Welfare League of America, https://www.cwla.org/position-statement-on-parenting-of-children-by-lesbian-gay-and-bisexual-adults/.

41. Sullivan, *Issues in Gay and Lesbian Adoption*, 41.

42. Henny Bos and Nanette Gartrell, "Adolescents of the USA National Longitudinal Lesbian Family Study: Can Family Characteristics Counteract the Negative Effects of Stigmatization?," *Family Process* 49 (December 2010): 559–72.

43. See What We Know, "What Does the Scholarly Research Say about the Well-Being of Children with Gay or Lesbian Parents?"

44. See John Courtney Murray, *We Hold These Truths: Catholic Reflections on the American Experience* (New York: Sheed & Ward, 1960), 106.

45. The majority of Catholics in Western countries support same-sex marriage. See Jeff Diamant, "How Catholics around the World See Same-Sex Marriage, Homosexuality," Pew Research Center, November 2, 2020, https://www.pewresearch.org/short-reads/2020/11/02/how-catholics-around-the-world-see-same-sex-marriage-homosexuality/.

# 19

# The Global Sexual Abuse Crisis

ANGELA SENANDER

## INTRODUCTION

From the 1985 news coverage of clergy sexual abuse in Louisiana to the 2021 French report, voices of victim-survivors and their families reveal tragic effects of sexual abuse on their lives.[1] So often those who spoke out did so to prevent others from experiencing sexual abuse, and too often the abuse continued. This history of failing to respond effectively by creating a safe environment in the Catholic Church fashioned a crisis that the church has struggled with for decades even as its response in some countries during the twenty-first century has become one of leadership in safeguarding children.

The Vatican's response to the global sexual abuse crisis over nearly four decades has created its own documentary heritage that Catholic Family Teaching (CFT) would do well to engage. Pope Francis's 2018 "Letter to the People of God" underscores the need for solidarity with those abused and for a change in clerical culture.[2] These themes provide a structure for this brief consideration of the global sexual abuse crisis in the Catholic Church. Seven weeks after the "Letter to the People of God," Francis called for an investigation of the Vatican's knowledge and decision-making involving one of the most globally recognized

church leaders, Theodore McCarrick, who was removed from public ministry because of a credible allegation of sexual abuse of a minor and was forced to resign as cardinal.[3] By early 2019, "the *Congresso* of the Congregation for the Doctrine of the Faith issued a decree finding McCarrick guilty of solicitation during the sacrament of confession and sins against the sixth commandment with minors and adults, with the aggravating factor of the abuse of power."[4] This resulted in dismissal from the priesthood.[5] The report also revealed McCarrick's use of relationships with families and the language of familial relationships to violate boundaries and perpetrate abuse.[6] This report illustrates the need for solidarity with those abused and for a change in clerical culture.

## DEVELOPING GLOBAL SOLIDARITY

In his "Letter to the People of God," Francis witnesses to the pain of those who have been abused and calls on the church to listen and respond to rather than ignore or silence their outcry. Francis reminds the whole church that just as God hears the cry of those abused and stands with them, the people of God are to embody this solidarity.[7] This letter promotes global solidarity, which complements the Vatican's advocacy for national and diocesan subsidiarity in developing policies to respond to and prevent clergy sexual abuse, called for by the Congregation for the Doctrine of the Faith (CDF) in 2011 and reiterated by Francis in 2015.[8] In the latter document, Francis reinforces the importance of solidarity at the local level as he addresses presidents of episcopal conferences and superiors of religious communities about the Pontifical Commission for the Protection of Minors (PCPM). Describing his July 2014 encounter with those suffering from abuse by priests, Francis states, "I was deeply moved by their witness to the depth of their sufferings and the strength of their faith."[9] Francis reminds presidents of episcopal conferences and superiors of religious communities of the needs of families:

> Families need to know that the Church is making every effort to protect their children. They should also know that they have every right to turn to the Church with full confidence, for it is a safe and secure home. Consequently, priority must not be given to any other kind of concern, whatever its nature, such as the desire to avoid scandal, since there is absolutely no place in ministry for those who abuse minors.[10]

One rarely hears the voices of those who were abused or of their families in church documents about clergy sexual abuse. A notable exception is the *Report on the Holy See's Institutional Knowledge and Decision-Making Related to Former Cardinal Theodore Edgar McCarrick (1930–2017)*.[11] While the purpose of the report is to evaluate the Vatican's knowledge and decision-making regarding concerns and complaints about sexual misconduct by former cardinal Theodore McCarrick, the report includes quotes from interviews with individuals who experienced abuse as well as a mother who took steps to prevent abuse by McCarrick. Given testimonies that reveal travel as a context for McCarrick's abuse and records of his extensive international travel, the report invites global

solidarity responding to cases of sexual abuse by McCarrick as well as learning what changes are needed for the church to better respond to the global sexual abuse crisis.[12]

### Learning through Solidarity with Those Reporting Abuse by McCarrick

Just two months before Francis's 2018 "Letter to the People of God," the Archdiocese of New York announced McCarrick's removal from public ministry because its review board found credible the accusation of his sexual abuse of a minor in the early 1970s. The Vatican's report notes that the public announcement of McCarrick's removal from public ministry led other victim-survivors to share their experiences with law enforcement, the media, and church leaders.[13] The acceptance of and response to an accusation against McCarrick empowered more individuals to speak about their experiences of abuse, whether as minors or as young men in the seminary or the priesthood.

One might ask why it took nearly half a century for McCarrick to be held accountable for sexual abuse of a minor. First, listening to victim-survivors reveals that coping with the trauma of abuse as well as the fear of not being believed by family and church authorities and the fear of retaliation by the perpetrator often delays reporting.[14] In this case, the man reported his experience of abuse to the Archdiocese of New York's Independent Reconciliation and Compensation Program in 2017. Second, US society was not as aware of child sexual abuse in the early 1970s, and the Catholic Church had not begun to develop adequate policies or a culture of reporting sexual abuse of minors by clergy. In contrast, the Vatican's report describes the Archdiocese of New York in 2017 following its policies in responding to an allegation of clergy sexual abuse. The Archdiocese of New York did report the allegation to law enforcement based on policies reflecting the 2002 United States Conference of Catholic Bishop's Charter for the Protection of Children and Young People, but due to the statute of limitations, criminal charges could not be brought by the state in this case.[15] However, another man was able to bring criminal charges against McCarrick based on his experience of sexual abuse as a minor in the state of Massachusetts, where the statute of limitations for his case was paused when McCarrick left Massachusetts.[16] The Vatican report does not include the voices of these men abused as minors, since the first did not choose to make his interview with the Archdiocese of New York public or be interviewed for the Vatican's report, and the second brought criminal charges after 2017, the final year under consideration in the Vatican's report.[17]

The Vatican's report identifies McCarrick gaining access to minors through relationships with New York families who welcomed him into their homes. He developed relationships with family members and insisted on the children calling him "Uncle Ted."[18] For example, "Mother 1 stated that McCarrick would 'correct' the children if they did not call him 'Unk.'... Her son confirmed that it was '100% true that he basically forced you to call him 'Uncle Ted' or 'Unk'—and he would definitely correct you if you didn't.'"[19] Interviews with this family reveal a mother concerned with McCarrick's behavior, including inappropriate touching of two of her teenage sons and providing alcohol to her sons on a trip, lowering inhibitions.[20] While the sons did not identify their experience as sexual abuse, one son later described McCarrick's "behavior as 'creepy' and 'uncomfortable.'"[21] At the time, the family dismissed the mother's concerns, minimizing and excusing McCarrick's behavior because of the relationships McCarrick had developed with the family.[22] The report suggests that part of the reason the father did not share the mother's concerns was that he was an Irish immigrant who "revered priests" and had a close relative who was a priest in Ireland, preventing him from seeing the possibility of harm from McCarrick.[23]

Not only did McCarrick refer to teenage boys from certain New York families as "nephews," he also did so with certain seminarians and priests. The report quotes a 2008 open letter titled "Statement for Pope Benedict XVI

about the Pattern of the Sexual Abuse Crisis in the United States" from Richard Sipe, who had listened to seminarians' concerns about McCarrick's behavior when Sipe was a faculty member at St. Mary's Seminary in Baltimore. Sipe states, "It has been widely known for several decades that Bishop/Archbishop now Cardinal Theodore E. McCarrick took seminarians and young priests to a shore home in New Jersey, sites in New York, and other places and slept with some of them. He established a coterie of young seminarians and priests that he encouraged to call him 'Uncle Ted.'"[24] A priest who felt obligated to visit McCarrick's shore home as a seminarian describes his initial response to McCarrick's sexual advances as feeling "frozen and trapped."[25] He recalls that when he told McCarrick "I don't like this," McCarrick minimized his own actions, saying "'Oh, I am not doing anything'; 'Uncle Ted is under pressure.'"[26] This priest recalls McCarrick's anger when he removed himself from this situation: "And when I objected like that and let him know it would not be OK to continue like that, he got pissed.... I thought, 'I am finished in the diocese.'"[27] McCarrick also used familial language to normalize the presence of a seminarian or other young man at the bishop's residence for a dinner with wealthy donors, followed by the "nephew" staying the night in the bishop's bedroom.[28] During the Vatican's investigation of its response to McCarrick, "many of the victims stated that they had previously felt powerless to report McCarrick's misconduct because they feared that they would be disbelieved by their parents or by ecclesiastical superiors, or because they were convinced that they would be retaliated against if they came forward."[29] Their testimonies call for familial and ecclesial solidarity in responding to those sharing experiences of abuse.

### Recognizing Abuse of Sex, Power, and Conscience

Francis wisely identifies the complex nature of the experience of abuse. Rather than taking the frame of reference of an abusive priest who might view this behavior as an act-oriented sexual sin, Francis takes the perspective of a victim who has experienced sexual violation and betrayal of trust by a person in a position of power who is supposed to be a moral authority. Catholic teaching on family underscores the relational nature of sex for communicating love and life. In *Amoris laetitia*, Francis states, "Sexuality is not a means of gratification or entertainment; it is an interpersonal language wherein the other is taken seriously, in his or her sacred and inviolable dignity."[30] The testimony of another priest in the Vatican's report describes McCarrick using him for gratification and not taking seriously his dignity.[31] He "felt it was 'very strange' to be in a locked bedroom with the Archbishop. At McCarrick's urging, and despite Priest 3's reluctance, the massage led to explicit sexual activity."[32]

As this priest described, McCarrick not only used the priest for sexual gratification but also abused the power of his own office. This priest was an immigrant from Brazil who was working with a Portuguese-speaking population in the Archdiocese of Newark, where McCarrick was the archbishop.[33] Speaking of the sexual activity that McCarrick initiated, the Vatican's report states, "In light of the fact that McCarrick was his superior, Priest 3 felt 'conflicted, confused and afraid.'"[34] He also felt vulnerable because of his immigration status.[35] The report's identification of these vulnerabilities illuminates Francis's expansion of the definition of vulnerable person from minors and those "equivalent to a minor" (which is described as "a person who habitually has imperfect use of reason") to "any person in a state of infirmity, physical or mental deficiency, or deprivation of personal liberty which, in fact, even occasionally limits their ability to understand or to want or otherwise resist the offense."[36] McCarrick's continued pursuit of this priest led him to leave the Archdiocese of Newark for the Diocese of Metuchen "to be at a distance from McCarrick."[37]

Not only does this priest describe abuse of power, he also describes abuse of conscience. Speaking of his sexual activity with McCarrick, "Priest 3 stated that he 'knew these things were wrong and tried to object,' but that McCarrick

'tried to convince me that priests engaging in sexual activity with each other was normal and accepted in the United States, and particularly in that diocese.'"[38] This description illustrates a person's conscience knowing that something is wrong and the person communicating this but experiencing one in a position of moral authority challenging the person's conscience with the claim that this activity is acceptable.

## CHANGING A CULTURE OF CLERICALISM

Listening to victim-survivors reveals that abuse of power was not limited to those engaged in sexual abuse; too often, it also occurred when those who were abused and their families reported abuse to church leaders. In his "Letter to the People of God," Francis declares, "Clericalism, whether fostered by priests themselves or by lay persons, leads to an excision in the ecclesial body that supports and helps to perpetuate many of the evils that we are condemning today. To say 'no' to abuse is to say an emphatic 'no' to all forms of clericalism."[39] Clericalism has too often made it easier for a bishop to listen to and identify with a priest who abuses than with those who were abused.

Organizational cultures are in many ways shaped and reinforced by the "tone at the top," and at the same time, leaders' efforts to bring about change in a culture meet resistance.[40] Since Jason Berry's reporting on child sexual abuse by a priest in Louisiana, the leadership of three popes has set different tones regarding listening to victim-survivors and changing a clerical culture.[41] A comparison of three papal journeys to the United States and three papal responses to McCarrick reveal important differences in their words and actions.

### *Papal Listening in a Clerical Culture: John Paul II*

During the twenty-six-year pontificate of John Paul II, the "tone at the top" was one of virtual silence regarding sexual abuse in the Catholic Church. When John Paul II visited Louisiana in 1987, he said nothing about clergy sexual abuse in any of his addresses. However, the year before he had assigned Harry Flynn as coadjutor bishop of the Diocese of Lafayette after an editorial called for Bishop Gerard Frey to resign or be replaced because of his failure to protect children from Father Gilbert Gauthe, who was convicted of and imprisoned for sexual abuse of children in 1985. Regarding Frey, Berry notes, "After the first round of lawsuits settled, Frey visited the homes of families, willing to see them to apologize and listen.... Frey tried to make amends, something few other bishops did in the early decades of a building national scandal."[42] John Paul II did not follow this example of outreach to victim-survivors and their families in Louisiana.[43] The Vatican web page on the church's response to abuse of minors has only two links to John Paul II speaking about clergy sexual abuse over the course of two decades: one from his meeting with US cardinals in 2002 and the other with excerpts from meetings with three groups of US bishops in 2004.[44]

John Paul II's 2002 address reveals greater identification with the cardinals than with the victims and their families. Addressing the cardinals in familial terms as brothers, he says, "You have come to the house of the Successor of Peter, whose task it is to confirm his brother Bishops in faith and love, and to unite them around Christ in the service of God's People."[45] John Paul II identifies with the experience of the cardinals grieving the fact that priests and religious betrayed their vocations and caused the young to suffer. He takes on the perspective of cardinals he is encountering rather than the victim-survivors and their families, whom he is not encountering. Reflecting this lack of contact, he states in his address to the cardinals, "To the victims and their families, wherever they may be, I express my profound sense of solidarity and concern."[46] While John Paul II rightly speaks of solidarity, his actions do not express it like his successors' actions have. John Paul II's framework for interpreting the crisis as symptomatic of failures in sexual morality in society, which does not foster reflection on clerical culture.[47] As the US bishops developed their Charter for the Protection of Children

and Young People, which requires priests with a credible allegation of sexual abuse of a minor to be removed from ministry, John Paul II reminded the cardinals about the potential of abusive priests to experience conversion from their sin and change.[48] While expressing concern for the priest who abused, this also reflects and reinforces clerical culture, potentially at the expense of safeguarding the vulnerable and creating a culture of care for victim-survivors.

The *Report on the Holy See's Institutional Knowledge and Decision-Making Related to Former Cardinal Theodore Edgar McCarrick (1930 to 2017)* reveals the way in which clerical culture and canonical protection for the rights of priests prevented the voices of victim-survivors and families from being taken seriously during the pontificate of John Paul II. He appointed McCarrick to three dioceses of increasing prominence despite the efforts of people with knowledge of McCarrick's abusive behavior to draw attention to this problem.[49] For instance, a mother described sending letters to cardinals and the apostolic nuncio in the 1980s informing them of her concern about how McCarrick was relating to teenage boys. Fear of retaliation prevented her from identifying herself, and she noted that nothing seemed to happen as a result of the letters.[50] She would not have known that canon law would prevent her letters from being taken seriously. Had a culture of care rather than clericalism prevailed in this situation, McCarrick's abusive behavior and appointments to lead dioceses could have been stopped. As a result of other allegations in the 1990s, Cardinal John O'Connor of New York advised against appointing McCarrick as archbishop of New York, and then Apostolic Nuncio Gabriel Montalvo, after consulting with four other bishops, also advised John Paul II not to appoint McCarrick as archbishop of Washington, which John Paul II initially accepted to avoid potential scandal.[51] However, John Paul II's focus on the rights of a privileged prelate who denied the charges, complemented by bishops reluctant to speak during an investigation and by his own previous personal encounters with McCarrick, led him to appoint McCarrick archbishop of Washington.[52]

## Papal Listening in a Clerical Culture: Benedict XVI

During the eight-year pontificate of Benedict XVI, the "tone at the top" was more responsive to sexual abuse and abuse of power experienced by victim-survivors. Because of his prior responsibility leading the CDF, Benedict XVI brought a deep awareness of clergy sexual abuse to his ministry. He met with victim-survivors in the United States and Australia in 2008, in Malta and the United Kingdom in 2010, and in Germany in 2011.[53] These were not public events but rather personal encounters where victim-survivors shared their stories and prayed with the pope. In addition to these personal encounters, Benedict XVI also read the stories of victim-survivors in the Murphy Report, which documented sexual abuse in the Archdiocese of Dublin.[54] While he spoke about care both in relationship to victim-survivors and safeguarding minors from abuse, his theological interpretation of the origins of the sexual abuse crisis focused on secularism and theological formation in seminaries rather than clerical culture.[55]

When Benedict XVI visited the United States in 2008, he spoke about clergy sexual abuse during his meeting with the US bishops, his homily at the Washington Nationals' stadium, and his homily at St. Patrick's Cathedral.[56] Speaking to the bishops, Benedict stated, "Among the countersigns to the Gospel of life found in America and elsewhere is one that causes deep shame: the sexual abuse of minors. . . . As you strive to eliminate this evil wherever it occurs, you may be assured of the prayerful support of God's people throughout the world. Rightly, you attach priority to showing compassion and care to the victims."[57] Benedict XVI highlighted prayer for the bishops and an affirmation of their compassion and care for victim-survivors. He not only spoke with bishops about the abuse crisis but also chose to meet with victim-survivors in the United States. Benedict XVI met with a few victim-survivors whom Cardinal Seán O'Malley brought from Boston to the apostolic nunciature in Washington, D.C., where the pope prayed with them and listened to them

share their experiences.[58] This began Benedict XVI's practice of meeting with victim-survivors of clergy sexual abuse in different countries.

Despite his intentional encounters with victim-survivors and earlier leadership as prefect of the CDF, addressing clergy sexual abuse within the Legionaries of Christ, clerical culture made it difficult for Benedict XVI to hear the voices of those abused by McCarrick as seminarians. Rumors were hard to substantiate due to seminarians' and priests' fear of negative consequences for reporting McCarrick's abusive behavior.[59] Speaking of allegations that the Congregation for Bishops received, Cardinal Giovanni Battista Re "emphasized that the information 'did not relate to minors,' and that if 'there had been any involvement of minors, the approach to the question would have been completely different.'"[60] When two dioceses worked toward a settlement with a former priest who brought allegations of abuse and informed the apostolic nunciature in the United States, the Vatican's focus was on preventing scandal resulting from media reports of allegations regarding McCarrick rather than further investigating the allegations.[61] The lens of scandal led Benedict XVI to approve efforts to replace McCarrick as archbishop of Washington and to ask him to leave his seminary residence, stop traveling, and lead a quiet life of prayer in order to avoid scandal.[62] However, McCarrick's lifestyle remained in many ways unchanged by the request.[63] Had the Vatican not believed McCarrick's denial and instead believed a former priest whose allegations led to a settlement with two dioceses, canonical actions could have been taken by Benedict XVI to change the request into a requirement that would have protected potential victims.[64]

## Papal Listening in a Clerical Culture: Francis

With Francis as pope, the "tone at the top" now challenges clericalism; develops structures to promote child protection around the globe; promotes truth, transparency, and accountability in cases involving sexual abuse of minors and vulnerable adults; and advocates encounter with and accompaniment of those who have experienced sexual abuse, abuse of power, and abuse of conscience.[65] Not only has Francis continued to encounter victim-survivors on trips as had Benedict XVI, but he also meets regularly with them on Fridays, reflecting his powerful homily on encountering Christ crucified in victim-survivors.[66] In response, Francis has worked for structural change through instituting the PCPM and conversion of clerical culture through apology, transparency, and accountability.[67]

During Pope Francis's 2015 trip to Philadelphia for the eighth World Meeting of Families, he met with victim-survivors of sexual abuse including some abused within the family, where most sexual abuse of children occurs. Whether abused by family members or clergy, victim-survivors heard an expression of sorrow for the betrayal of trust and violation of human dignity they experienced. In his address Francis said, "Within our family of faith and our human families, the sins and crimes of sexual abuse of children must no longer be held in secret and in shame. . . . Your stories of survival, each unique and compelling, are powerful signs of the hope that comes from the Lord's promise to be with us always."[68] Francis affirmed the value of victim-survivors sharing their stories. Addressing those abused by clergy, Francis said, "I am deeply sorry for the times when you or your family spoke out, to report the abuse, but you were not heard or believed."[69] Francis makes an important commitment to victim-survivors that "we will follow the path of truth wherever it may lead. Clergy and bishops will be held accountable when they abuse or fail to protect children."[70]

Francis's January 2018 trip to Chile put these commitments to the test. A couple of days after he met with victim-survivors, he responded defensively to a journalist asking about a Chilean bishop accused of covering up child sexual abuse by asking for proof.[71] This initial failure to take the accusation of cover-up seriously did not reflect his commitment to victim-survivors being heard and believed. Cardinal Seán O'Malley gave voice to this publicly, reflecting his responsibilities to

victim-survivors as head of the PCPM.[72] Francis then took steps to seek the truth, sending Archbishop Charles Scicluna and Monsignor Jorge Bertomeu Farnos of the CDF to Chile and New York to listen to and receive the testimony of sixty-four victim-survivors. After Francis read this report, he apologized:

> With regard to myself, I recognize, and I would like you to convey this faithfully, that I have made serious errors in the assessment and perception of the situation, in particular through the lack of reliable and balanced information. I now beg the forgiveness of all those whom I have offended and I hope to be able to do so personally, in the coming weeks, in the meetings that I will have with representatives of the people interviewed.[73]

Francis also summoned the Chilean bishops to Rome, where they all offered their resignations during their meeting in May. In June, Francis accepted the resignation of the bishop he had initially defended, Bishop Juan Barros.[74] Barros had been accused of covering up sexual abuse of minors by Father Fernando Karadima. In September 2018, Francis changed Karadima's 2011 canonical penalty of a quiet life of prayer to removal from the priesthood.[75]

Following this, Francis further demonstrated his commitment to following the truth where it leads and holding bishops accountable with McCarrick's resignation as cardinal after a preliminary investigation of an allegation of sexual abuse of a minor resulted in McCarrick's removal from public ministry. This was followed in October 2018 by Francis's request for an investigation of the Holy See's knowledge and decision-making about McCarrick, which resulted in a thorough, comprehensive investigation followed by remarkable transparency in the publication of a 449-page report. By January 2019, the canonical penal process for McCarrick had resulted in his dismissal from the priesthood. Learning from the McCarrick experience, Francis made canonical changes, including the expansion of the definition of vulnerable, an obligation for clergy and religious to report sexual abuse and pornography, a new method for reporting abuse by bishops and religious superiors, protection for the one reporting, and criteria for a caring response for victim-survivors and their families in which they are treated with dignity and respect.[76]

## CONCLUSION

Francis has invited the church to reflect on how we are journeying together in communion through participation for mission, first in his "Letter to the People of God" in Chile in 2018 and then through a synodal process.[77] Synodal dialogue from local churches around the world reveals a growing solidarity in responding to the global clergy sexual abuse crisis. As the "Working Document for the Continental Stage" of the synodal process notes,

> An obstacle of particular relevance on the path of walking together is the scandal of abuse by members of the clergy and by people holding ecclesial office: first and foremost, abuse of minors and vulnerable persons, but also abuse of other kinds (spiritual, sexual, economic, of authority, of conscience). This is an open wound that continues to inflict pain on victims and survivors, on their families, and on their communities. . . . Careful and painful reflection on the legacy of abuse has led many synod groups to call for a cultural change in the Church with a view to greater transparency, accountability, and co-responsibility.[78]

In his "Letter to the People of God," Francis advocated these changes to convert a clerical culture. He also advocated developing a culture of care.[79]

In the spirit of synodality, CFT can both learn from and contribute to the Vatican's documentary heritage on the global sexual abuse crisis. Given the effects that sexual abuse by clergy, religious, and lay leaders has on families, CFT would do well to allow the experiences of victim-survivors to inform its development. As the Catholic Church works to develop a culture of care as described in Francis's "Letter to the

People of God," CFT has much to contribute to this conversation.

## NOTES

1. The *National Catholic Reporter*'s front-page story "Priest Child Abuse Cases Victimizing Families; Bishops Lack Policy Response" from June 7, 1985, can be seen in an article by Thomas Fox, who reflects on his experience of clergy sexual abuse and its effect on his family thirty years after the newspaper began drawing attention to clergy sexual abuse and its cover-up in the Catholic Church. See Thomas C. Fox, "Pages and Protection: A First Step in Bringing Clergy Sex Abuse Secrets to Light," *National Catholic Reporter*, July 7, 2015, https://www.ncronline.org/news/accountability /pages-and-protection-first-step-bringing-clergy -sex-abuse-secrets-light. Reflecting Francis's call to encounter in his "Letter to the People of God," the French report states, "It was necessary for the members of the Commission to listen personally to the men and women who had suffered sexual violence and to listen to them not as experts, but rather as human beings willing to expose themselves and confront, personally and together, a dark truth." French Independent Commission on Sexual Abuse in the Catholic Church, *Final Report: Sexual Violence in the Catholic Church, France 1950–2020*, 12, 2021, https:// www.ciase.fr/medias/Ciase-Final-Report-5-october -2021-english-version.pdf. For more on the role of media and external investigations, first in English-speaking common law countries and then more globally, see Angela Senander, *Scandal: The Catholic Church and Public Life* (Collegeville, MN: Liturgical Press, 2012), 2–4.

2. Francis, "Letter to the People of God" (August 20, 2018), https://www.vatican.va /content/francesco/en/letters/2018/documents/papa -francesco_20180820_lettera-popolo-didio.html.

3. Secretariat of State of the Holy See, *Report on the Holy See's Institutional Knowledge and Decision-Making Related to Former Cardinal Theodore Edgar McCarrick (1930–2017)* (November 10, 2020), https://www.vatican.va/resources /resources_rapporto-card-mccarrick_20201110_en .pdf. For an analysis of responses to other cardinals contributing to the crisis, see James F. Keenan,

SJ, "Hierarchicalism," *Theological Studies* 83, no. 1 (March 2022): 86–89.

4. Secretariat of State of the Holy See, *Report on ... Knowledge and Decision-Making Related to ... McCarrick*, 437.

5. Secretariat of State of the Holy See, *Report on ... Knowledge and Decision-Making Related to ... McCarrick*, 437–38.

6. Secretariat of State of the Holy See, *Report on ... Knowledge and Decision-Making Related to ... McCarrick*, 439–42.

7. Francis, "Letter to the People of God," 1–2.

8. Congregation for the Doctrine of the Faith, "Circular Letter to Assist Episcopal Conferences in Developing Guidelines for Dealing with Cases of Sexual Abuses of Minors Perpetrated by Clergy" (May 3, 2011), https://www.vatican.va/roman_curia /congregations/cfaith/documents/rc_con_cfaith _doc_20110503_abuso-minori_en.html; and Francis, "Letter to the Presidents of Episcopal Conferences and Superiors of Institutes of Consecrated Life and Societies of Apostolic Life Concerning the Pontifical Commission for the Protection of Minors" (February 2, 2015), https://www.vatican .va/content/francesco/en/letters/2015/documents /papa-francesco_20150202_lettera-pontificia -commissione-tutela-minori.html.

9. Francis, "Letter to the Presidents of Episcopal Conferences."

10. Francis, "Letter to the Presidents of Episcopal Conferences."

11. See, e.g., Secretariat of State of the Holy See, *Report on ... Knowledge and Decision-Making Related to ... McCarrick*, 250–258, 269. This is an example of Priest 1's voice being heard through written statements for legal proceedings and statements by legal representation. Interviews for this Vatican report provide additional examples of victim-survivors being heard.

12. Regarding travel, see Secretariat of State of the Holy See, *Report on ... Knowledge and Decision-Making Related to ... McCarrick*, 99, 138, 440–41, 31–32, 52–58, 202–7, 271–73, 341–42, 345–52, 362–63, 370–72, 376, 394, 412, 415, 418–19, 422.

13. Secretariat of State of the Holy See, *Report on ... Knowledge and Decision-Making Related to ... McCarrick*, 437.

14. Secretariat of State of the Holy See, *Report on ... Knowledge and Decision-Making Related*

to ... *McCarrick*, 440. For more on barriers to disclosing, see Australian Royal Commission into the Holy See's Institutional Responses into Child Sexual Abuse, *Final Report: Identifying and Disclosing Child Sexual Abuse*, Vol. 4, 2017, https://www.child abuseroyalcommission.gov.au/sites/default/files/final _report_-_volume_4_identifying_and_disclosing _child_sexual_abuse.pdf.

15. Secretariat of State of the Holy See, *Report on ... Knowledge and Decision-Making Related to ... McCarrick*, 433–34.

16. John Lavenburg, "Ex-Cardinal McCarrick Arraigned in Massachusetts on Sex Abuse Charges," *The Tablet*, September 2, 2021, https://thetablet.org /ex-cardinal-mccarrick-arraigned-in-massachusetts -on-sex-abuse-charges/.

17. Secretariat of State of the Holy See, *Report on ... Knowledge and Decision-Making Related to ... McCarrick*, 434, 437, 1–3.

18. Secretariat of State of the Holy See, *Report on ... Knowledge and Decision-Making Related to ... McCarrick*, 440.

19. Secretariat of State of the Holy See, *Report on ... Knowledge and Decision-Making Related to ... McCarrick*, 38n138.

20. Secretariat of State of the Holy See, *Report on ... Knowledge and Decision-Making Related to ... McCarrick*, 39–42.

21. Secretariat of State of the Holy See, *Report on ... Knowledge and Decision-Making Related to ... McCarrick*, 47.

22. Secretariat of State of the Holy See, *Report on ... Knowledge and Decision-Making Related to ... McCarrick*, 39–42.

23. Secretariat of State of the Holy See, *Report on ... Knowledge and Decision-Making Related to ... McCarrick*, 37, 40.

24. Secretariat of State of the Holy See, *Report on ... Knowledge and Decision-Making Related to ... McCarrick*, 280.

25. Secretariat of State of the Holy See, *Report on ... Knowledge and Decision-Making Related to ... McCarrick*, 72.

26. Secretariat of State of the Holy See, *Report on ... Knowledge and Decision-Making Related to ... McCarrick*, 72.

27. Secretariat of State of the Holy See, *Report on ... Knowledge and Decision-Making Related to ... McCarrick*, 72–73.

28. Secretariat of State of the Holy See, *Report on . . . Knowledge and Decision-Making Related to . . . McCarrick*, 35.

29. Secretariat of State of the Holy See, *Report on . . . Knowledge and Decision-Making Related to . . . McCarrick*, 440.

30. Francis, *Amoris laetitia* (March 19, 2016), no. 151, https://www.vatican.va/content/dam/francesco/pdf/apost_exhortations/documents/papa-francesco_esortazione-ap_20160319_amoris-laetitia_en.pdf.

31. Secretariat of State of the Holy See, *Report on . . . Knowledge and Decision-Making Related to . . . McCarrick*, 83–85.

32. Secretariat of State of the Holy See, *Report on . . . Knowledge and Decision-Making Related to . . . McCarrick*, 84.

33. Secretariat of State of the Holy See, *Report on . . . Knowledge and Decision-Making Related to . . . McCarrick*, 82–83.

34. Secretariat of State of the Holy See, *Report on . . . Knowledge and Decision-Making Related to . . . McCarrick*, 85.

35. Secretariat of State of the Holy See, *Report on . . . Knowledge and Decision-Making Related to . . . McCarrick*, 85.

36. Dicastery for the Doctrine of the Faith, "*Vademecum*: On Certain Points of Procedure in Treating Cases of Sexual Abuse of Minors Committed by Clerics, Ver. 2.0" (June 5, 2022), I.5, https://www.vatican.va/roman_curia/congregations/cfaith/ddf/rc_ddf_doc_20220605_vademecum-casi-abuso-2.0_en.html. Francis articulated this understanding of vulnerable person in *Vos estis lux mundi* in 2019. Francis, *Vos estis lux mundi* (May 7, 2019), I.2.b, https://www.vatican.va/content/Francesco/en/motu_proprio/documents/papa-francesco-motu-proprio-20190507_vos-estis-lux-mundi.html.

37. Secretariat of State of the Holy See, *Report on . . . Knowledge and Decision-Making Related to . . . McCarrick*, 85.

38. Secretariat of State of the Holy See, *Report on . . . Knowledge and Decision-Making Related to . . . McCarrick*, 84–85.

39. Francis, "Letter to the People of God," 2.

40. Sally Ganz and Linda Thorne, "Introduction to the Special Issue on Tone at the Top," *Journal of Business Ethics* 126, no. 1 (January 2015): 1–2, 167. Regarding resistance to changing a culture of clericalism to a culture of care, see Gerald O'Connell, "Abuse Survivor Marie Collins: 'Resistance' from CDF Led to My Resignation from Papal Commission," *America*, March 2, 2017, https://www.americamagazine.org/faith/2017/03/02/abuse-survivor-marie-collins-resistance-cdf-led-my-resignation-papal-commission.

41. For Jason Berry's reflection on his groundbreaking reporting from the Diocese of Lafayette, Louisiana, thirty years later, see Jason Berry, "A Strong Press Is the Lafayette Lesson," *National Catholic Reporter*, July 9, 2015, https://www.ncronline.org/news/accountability/strong-press-lafayette-lesson. For examples of writing that shed light on changing organizational culture in the Catholic Church, see Donald Cozzens, *Sacred Silence: Denial and the Crisis in the Church* (Collegeville, MN: Liturgical Press, 2004); and Joseph P. Chinnici, OFM, *When Values Collide: The Catholic Church, Sexual Abuse, and the Challenges of Leadership* (Maryknoll, NY: Orbis Books, 2010).

42. Berry, "A Strong Press Is the Lafayette Lesson."

43. John Paul II, "Apostolic Journey to the United States and Canada," September 10–20, 1987, https://www.vatican.va/content/john-paul-ii/en/travels/1987/travels/documents/trav_stati-uniti-canada.html .

44. John Paul II, "Address to the Cardinals of the United States," April 23, 2002, https://www.vatican.va/resources/resources_american-cardinals-2002_en.html. The "Speech to the American Bishops on Their *ad Limina* Visit, 2004" link on the church's "Abuse of Minors" web page (https://www.vatican.va/resources/index_en.htm) provides access to John Paul II, Extract from the "Address to the Bishops of the Ecclesiastical Provinces of Atlanta and Miami (U.S.A.) on Their '*ad Limina*' Visit," April 2, 2004; John Paul II, Extract from the "Address to the Bishops of the Ecclesiastical Region of Pennsylvania and New Jersey (U.S.A.) on their '*ad Limina*' Visit," September 11, 2004; and John Paul II, Extracts from the "Address to the Bishops of the Ecclesiastical Provinces of Boston and Hartford (U.S.A.) on their '*ad Limina*' Visit," September 2, 2004, https://www.vatican.va/resources/resources_adlimina-american-bishops-2004_en.html .

45. John Paul II, "Address to the Cardinals of the United States," no. 1.

46. John Paul II, "Address to the Cardinals of the United States," no. 1.

47. John Paul II, "Address to the Cardinals of the United States," no. 3.

48. The Dallas Charter states, "Diocesan/eparchial policy will provide that for even a single act of sexual abuse of a minor—past, present, or future—the offending priest or deacon will be permanently removed from ministry. In keeping with stated purpose of this charter, an offending priest or deacon will be offered professional assistance for his own healing and wellbeing, as well as for the purpose of prevention." United States Conference of Catholic Bishop, "Charter for the Protection of Children and Young People," *Origins* 32, no. 7 (June 27, 2002): 104. See also John Paul II, "Address to the Cardinals of the United States," no. 2.

49. Secretariat of State of the Holy See, *Report on . . . Knowledge and Decision-Making Related to . . . McCarrick*, 5–9, 21–191.

50. Secretariat of State of the Holy See, *Report on . . . Knowledge and Decision-Making Related to . . . McCarrick*, 37–47.

51. Secretariat of State of the Holy See, *Report on . . . Knowledge and Decision-Making Related to . . . McCarrick*, 131–68.

52. Secretariat of State of the Holy See, *Report on . . . Knowledge and Decision-Making Related to . . . McCarrick*, 6–9, 169–84.

53. John L. Allen Jr., "Pope Meets Abuse Victims in Germany," *National Catholic Reporter,* September 23, 2011, https://www.ncronline.org/blogs/ncr-today/pope-meets-abuse-victims-germany.

54. Holy See Press Office, "On the Meeting of the Holy Father, Benedict XVI, with Representatives of the Irish Episcopal Conference and Senior Officials of the Roman Curia" (December 11, 2009), https://www.vatican.va/resources/resources_irish-bishops-dec2009_en.html.

55. For an example of him speaking about a duty of care, see Benedict XVI, "Address to the Bishops of England, Scotland and Wales," September 19, 2010, https://www.vatican.va/content/benedict-xvi/en/speeches/2010/september/documents/hf_ben-xvi_spe_20100919_vescovi-inghilterra.html.

56. Benedict XVI, "Address for the Celebration of Vespers and Meeting with the Bishops of the United States of America" (April 16, 2008), https://www.vatican.va/content/benedict-xvi/en/speeches/2008/april/documents/hf_ben-xvi_spe_20080416_bishops-usa.html; and Benedict XVI, "Homily at Washington Nationals Stadium" (April 17, 2008), https://www.vatican.va/content/benedict-xvi/en/homilies/2008/documents/hf_ben-xvi_hom_20080417_washington-stadium.html; Benedict XVI, "Homily at St. Patrick's Cathedral" (April 19, 2008), https://www.vatican.va/content/benedict-xvi/en/homilies/2008/documents/hf_ben-xvi_hom_20080419_st-patrick-ny.html.

57. Benedict XVI, "Address to the Bishops of England, Scotland and Wales."

58. Holy See Press Office, "Meeting of the Holy Father, Benedict XVI, with a Group of Victims of Sexual Abuse by Members of the Clergy" (April 17, 2008), https://www.vatican.va/resources/resources_visit-usa-apr2008_en.html.

59. Secretariat of State of the Holy See, *Report on . . . Knowledge and Decision-Making Related to . . . McCarrick*, 439–40.

60. Secretariat of State of the Holy See, *Report on . . . Knowledge and Decision-Making Related to . . . McCarrick*, 235n805.

61. Secretariat of State of the Holy See, *Report on . . . Knowledge and Decision-Making Related to . . . McCarrick*, 249–59.

62. Secretariat of State of the Holy See, *Report on . . . Knowledge and Decision-Making Related to . . . McCarrick*, 259, 295–99.

63. Secretariat of State of the Holy See, *Report on . . . Knowledge and Decision-Making Related to . . . McCarrick*, 271–78, 345–77, 408–31.

64. Secretariat of State of the Holy See, *Report on . . . Knowledge and Decision-Making Related to . . . McCarrick*, 10–11. In addition to this summary of Benedict's decision-making, see 238–43 for McCarrick's denial.

65. See, e.g., Francis, "Letter to the People of God;" and Francis, "Letter to the Presidents of Episcopal Conferences."

66. Joshua J. McElwee, "Pope Francis Says He Meets Almost Weekly with Abuse Victims," *National Catholic Reporter,* February 15, 2018, https://www.ncronline.org/news/pope-francis-says-he-meets-almost-weekly-abuse-victims; and Francis, "Homily at Mass in the Chapel of *Domus Sanctae Marthae* with a Group of Clergy Sex Abuse Victims" (July 7, 2014), https://www.vatican.va/content/francesco/en/cotidie/2014/documents

/papa-francesco-cotidie_20140707_vittime-abusi
.html.

67. For an example of this transparency and accountability, see Secretariat of State of the Holy See, *Report on . . . Knowledge and Decision-Making Related to . . . McCarrick.*"

68. Francis, "Meeting with Victims of Sexual Abuse" (September 27, 2015), https://www.vatican .va/content/francesco/en/speeches/2015/september /documents/papa-francesco_20150927_usa-vittime -abusi.html.

69. Francis, "Meeting with Victims of Sexual Abuse."

70. Francis, "Meeting with Victims of Sexual Abuse."

71. Joshua J. McElwee, "Francis Defends Chilean Bishop Accused of Abuse Cover-up," *National Catholic Reporter*, January 18, 2018, https://www .ncronline.org/news/francis-defends-chilean-bishop -accused-abuse-cover.

72. Archdiocese of Boston, "January 20, 2018 Cardinal Sean P. O'Malley Statement" (January 20, 2018), https://www.bostoncatholic.org/press-release /2018/01/january-20-2018-cardinal-sean-p-omalley -statement.

73. Francis, "Letter to the Bishops of Chile Following the Report of Archbishop Charles J. Scicluna" (April 8, 2018), https://www.vatican.va

/content/francesco/en/letters/2018/documents/papa -francesco_20180408_lettera-vescovi-cile.html.

74. Holy See Press Office, "Summary of Bulletin: Resignations and Appointments, June 11, 2018," June 11, 2018, https://press.vatican.va/content /salastampa/en/bollettino/pubblico/2018/06/11 /180611c.html.

75. Holy See Press Office, "Summary of Bulletin: Holy See Press Office Communique, September 28, 2018" (September 18, 2018), https://press.vatican.va /content/salastampa/en/bollettino/pubblico/2018 /09/28/180928f.html.

76. Francis, *Vos estis lux mundi.*

77. Francisco, "Carta al Pueblo de Dios que Peregrina en Chile" (May 31, 2018), https://www.vatican .va/content/francesco/es/letters/2018/documents /papa-francesco_20180531_lettera-popolodidio -cile.html. (As of November 1, 2022, the Vatican only shares this letter in Spanish.) For more on the synodal process and its themes, see "Synod 2021– 2024, About" https://www.synod.va/en/what-is-the -synod-21-24/about.html.

78. General Secretariat of the Synod, "Working Document for the Continental Stage" (October 27, 2022), 20, https://www.synod.va/content /dam/synod/common/phases/continental-stage/dcs /Documento-Tappa-Continentale-EN.pdf.

79. Francis, "Letter to the People of God," 2.

*Benedict XVI*

# CHAPTER

# 20

## *Caritas in Veritate* and Cultural Development

### WILHELMINA UHAI TUNU, LSOSF

## CONTEXT

As is characteristic of the papal magisterium on the occasion of an epochal or commemorative event, Benedict XVI issued the encyclical *Caritas in veritate* to celebrate the recently passed fortieth anniversary of Paul VI's 1967 encyclical *Populorum progressio*.[1] Benedict XVI sought to commemorate *Populorum progressio* as an unforgettable document, calling it "the *Rerum novarum* of the present age."[2] Cognizant of both the positive and negative impacts that post–World War II development had wrought on humanity in general, Pope Paul VI had wanted to put these developments into social and theological context. His central thesis was that development has to have a human touch and human values; it cannot be just advancement in technology and material goods. After forty-two years of implementing *Populorum progressio*, Benedict XVI pursued the need to look at new issues that had emerged concerning human development (the publication delay owing initially to translation difficulties, then to seeking a fuller understanding of the 2008 economic crisis). Like other modern papal encyclicals, *Caritas in veritate* applies an anthropological understanding and explanation of the resultant development issues affecting the human race

from the view of the global human community as a single family.

In *Caritas in veritate*, Benedict XVI insists that development has to be holistic (*CV* 11–16). Focusing on love and truth, which are the points of departure in this encyclical, he indicates that these two values should form the foundations of all development efforts if they are to remain authentic for every individual and for all humanity (*CV* 1). Whatever can be achieved and categorized as authentically human must rely on the principles of love and truth. These principles are inborn in the human person because they are instilled by God. Every person, regardless of his or her cultural basis, has and feels these values from within "and should strive to prevent any form of untruth from poisoning relationships."[3] According to Benedict XVI, the human family can realize and feel love and speak the truth. He clarifies that charity is a virtue involving microrelationships of friends, family members, or small groups but also macrorelationships that are social, economic, and political. In both cases, people must be attentive not to separate charity from authentic truth and ethical living. Following this background, this chapter dwells on the impacts culture has had on development and the consequent effects on the family, which is at the center of human society.

## COMMENTARY

### Benedict XVI on the Human and Catholic Family

While quoting canon 1055 about the matrimonial covenant, Benedict XVI in his letter on family life states that "today, if they are to give a true face to society, no people can ignore the precious good of the family founded on marriage."[4] For him, the matrimonial covenant where a man and a woman establish a bond of the whole of life is the base of the family and the endowment and common good of humanity. In the Catholic teaching, the family is a divinely ordained institution. It has its origin in God, who created humans both male and female and commanded them to go and multiply (Gen. 1:26–28). God fashioned out of the two "one flesh" (Gen. 2:24–25)[5] to spread humanity.[6] In this light, the marriage union as a permanent bond between two persons and a fundamental necessity in the structuring of interpersonal relationships for humanity is clearly expounded (Gen. 2:18).

In the Catholic perspective, the church community therefore also plays a vital role in accompanying the couple to sustain their marriage and family. Catholics commonly make use of three models to help explain the Christian family: the Holy Trinity, the Holy family (Jesus, Mary, and Joseph), and the church. Christian marriage and family thus draw life from this tripartite font, a network of relations that implies that Christian marriage is among the institutions of God's kingdom. It is a stable union that can only be disbanded by God. In Matthew 19:4–6 Jesus endorses the indissolubility of marriage, which is understood in Catholic doctrine as a revelation of the first form of communion of persons.[7] This revelation makes both man and woman complete beings who become a prophetic sign of the union between Christ and the church through the sacrament of marriage. The Vatican II document *Gaudium et spes* teaches that "Christ makes himself present to the Christian spouses in the sacrament of marriage and remains with them."[8] This Christ-centered vision of the family provides a unique understanding of development for man and woman. Benedict XVI rightly says that "called to live a Christ-like love each day, the Christian family is a privileged expression of the church's presence and mission in the world."[9] The fifth chapter of *Caritas in veritate* in particular demonstrates the dynamic interplay of Benedict XVI's visions of development, the human family, and particular families.

### Benedict XVI on Culture and Development

Placing the family based in the marriage of man and woman at the center of authentic development puts in a clear light the concept of integral human development, which includes love and truth, religion and traditions, religious and cultural attitudes, and emancipation and inclusivity, to mention a few pairs of central values. This conceptualization of development allows for unrestricted explanations of authentic and integral human development as pivoting around education and enterprise.

Equally, integral human development, which is "the development of each man and of the whole man" (*PP* 14), is centered on charity, which manifests God's love in human relationships. It is "an authentic expression of humanity and element of fundamental importance in human relations" (*CV* 3). Hence, the human relationship is key to understanding human integrity, taking into account the dignity of the human person which is promoted by bonds of friendship and brotherly love."[10] Benedict XVI maintains that as a spiritual being, the human creature is defined through interpersonal relations (*CV* 53), which bring "a development in solidarity with all humanity" (*PP* 98). For him, the relation between the individual and the community is a relation between one totality and another. The unity of the human family makes each more transparent to each other and links them together more closely to their legitimate destiny (*CV* 53). Furthermore, authentic development is founded on solidarity guided by the values of justice and peace. In giving lessons on family, culture, and development, Benedict XVI insists on the inclusive relations of all individuals within the one community of the human family, built in solidarity on the basis of the fundamental values of justice and peace (*CV* 54).

Brotherhood and peace are also values we learn from Benedict XVI's teachings on culture, development, and family. Such values are underlying forces contributing to integral human development (a development that is authentic, holistic, and person-centered). For development to be authentic and complete, it must embrace every person and the whole human family. Such factors entail adequate discernment from diverse cultures and religions (*CV* 55) that embrace the principles of love and truth. As a result, denying the right to profess one's religion impedes authentic human development in public, and to bring the truths of faith to bear on public life has negative consequences for true development (*CV* 56).

Benedict XVI considers reciprocity as the heart of what it is to be a human being, because human relationships and development become authentic when linked to divine love and communion. In this context, the principle of subsidiarity is particularly well suited to managing globalization and directing it toward authentic development (*CV* 57). The principle of subsidiarity is a strong pillar against the danger of universal and tyrannical power. Subsidiarity is also a potential panacea for the shortfalls of globalization. Similarly, the principles of subsidiarity and solidarity are closely linked in that the most valuable resources in countries receiving development aid ought to be the human resource (*CV* 58). Benedict XVI asserts that authentic development calls for an uncritical and indiscriminate openness to cultures in order to enable trustworthy cooperation for development (*CV* 59). He argues that development aid for poor countries must be considered as a valid means of creating wealth for all (*CV* 60). The movement of international resources, particularly international development aid, must be understood through solidarity as an obligation of wealthier nations to the world community. Moreover, the principle of subsidiarity can assist in developing more effective systems of distribution (*CV* 60).

Education is another important aspect of authentic human development. This falls essentially within the scope of the family but also stretches to a public duty. Access to education is essential for development. Education involves both classroom teaching and vocational training, which are important factors in development, but also ought to focus on the complete formation of the person (*CV* 61). Its form and delivery call for scrutiny as to its relevance, accessibility, and affordability among other factors.

Benedict XVI identifies three additional areas of concern with direct consequences for the well-being of families. Families are increasingly subjugated to international dynamics resulting from multinational businesses. This affects the cultural fabric of particular societies and of families, which are custodians of their respective cultures. Families bear the burden of this cultural onslaught and in most cases suffer from it.

Benedict XVI focuses on international tourism and migration as additional factors in the problem of authentic human development. These involve physical movements of people and can be disruptive to mutual respect and cultural development. International tourism is often undertaken in exploitative ways without due respect for local cultures. This pattern of self-serving exploitation inhibits authentic human encounters (*CV* 61). Migration often takes place across uncoordinated state policies without adequate international norms (*CV* 62). For authentic human development to take place in the family, proper policies at the international and national levels need to be developed to address the problems associated with these issues.

Some of the problems associated with tourism and migration, including costs that local communities are not able to meet, directly link to poverty and unemployment. Poverty itself is another identified area of concern, with its ravages directly affecting the family. It is manifested at the individual family level, and its effects are often visible in a series of violations of human dignity (*CV* 63). Benedict XVI suggests the use of financial mechanisms and systems to address poverty, especially through wealth creation (*CV* 65).

Standing firmly with the tradition of Catholic Social Teaching, Benedict XVI asserts that in the business milieu, especially in the workplace and the employment sector, authentic development can also be achieved through appropriate initiatives aimed at protecting workers. This includes enabling trade unions to demonstrate the authentic ethical and cultural motivations that make it possible for them to play a decisive role in development (*CV* 64). Central to such a prescription is his insistence on the establishment and maintenance of a decent work environment.

Referring to labor and trade unions, Benedict XVI warns that they tend to defend the interest of their members rather than those of their customers or consumers (*CV* 64). In the developing world where the public sector is strong, the employers' roles are limited, curtailed, and politicized such that they end up being a satellite of the ruling elite. This breeds corruption on the part of labor and trade union leaders.

Regarding finances, the terms by which opportunities for international financial support are availed to the developing world are found to be unjust due to their inadequacy, high interest rates, restrictions to favored projects, etc. Benedict XVI insists that finance must be an instrument directed toward improved wealth creation and development through renewed and redesigned structures and operating methods in various sectors. The economy and financial resources must be used in ethical ways so as to create suitable conditions for human development and the development of peoples (*CV* 65). Regulations should ensure that weaker parties are safeguarded and that new forms of finance are encouraged, and there should be an effective regulatory framework that is ethically employed and safeguarded by legislation.

Benedict XVI also proposes a new financial regulation. For him, the proper functioning of the economy requires a people-centered ethic, and he condemns the attitude of the globalized economy that focuses on profit at all costs,

as this greed intensifies injustice and poverty. In any situation, profit is not to be earned by immoral means such as overcharging interest. Instead, profit has to promote the common good as its ultimate end; otherwise, it compromises wealth and creates poverty. The church and society must adapt to this inclusive new way of understanding the business enterprise. Individuals are to seek social support in transforming their social ministries into sustainable social enterprises for the common good.

By contrast, many available goods are overpriced, counterfeit, or not productive (fit only for consumption). This drains the limited liquidity of consumers, diverting it from productive ventures. Benedict teaches that purchasing is a moral act and not simply economic. Consumers therefore ought to practice social responsibility, and producers ought to find new strategies of marketing their products in order to build economic democracy and development of the human family (*CV* 66).

Benedict XVI proposes that true integral development of peoples and international cooperation require establishing a greater degree of international order for managing globalization. He is emphatic about subsidiarity as a key to bringing this about. Authentic development also requires the construction of a social order that at last conforms to the moral order, to the interconnection between moral and social spheres, and to the link between politics and the economic and civil spheres as envisioned by the United Nations Charter (*CV* 67).

## Integrating the Family, Culture, and Development

In his encyclical letter *Evangelii nuntiandi* on evangelization in the modern world, Pope Paul VI explains two major concepts: the grace and holiness of matrimony, by which Christian marriage and family become the center of evangelization.[11] The family is the first school of evangelization to individual members and "ought to be a place where the Gospel is transmitted and from which the Gospel radiates" (*EN* 71). It is in the family that individuals learn to assume a personal responsibility toward a humane society. In other words, integral human development begins in the family. Within the family, individuals improve their livelihood. Living in solidarity and fraternity is a remedy to isolation, which is the cause of poverty in the family as a social body. Isolation cannot allow one to progress outside the community. From the Christian perspective, poverty is a social sin that restrains the dignity and development of people. We need justice to enable the family to function well. The global society must work out a balanced dialogue for this type of human development.

In *Familiaris consortio,* his apostolic exhortation on the Christian family, Pope John Paul II similarly lays special emphasis on marriage and the family as central pillars in both the church and society. "Christian marriage and Christian family build up the Church: . . . by means of the rebirth of baptism and education in the faith the child is also introduced into God's family, which is the Church."[12] The third part of the document emphasizes that the essence and role of the family is to guard, reveal, and communicate love. However, these tasks need to be reviewed by the community to ensure that love is reciprocal.

For Benedict XVI, the development of the family is sustained through the lens of charity and truth and depends on the recognition that all people belong to the same single family working together in communion (*CV* 53). For him, "the Church considers that her most important mission in today's culture is to keep alive the search for truth, and consequently for God; to bring people to look beyond penultimate realities and to seek those that are ultimate."[13] In order to seek such realities, people are to live in communion with God and with each other to build a family of love, truth, and fidelity. It is a family united, committed to life, and celebrating faith who walk the path of promoting justice, peace, reconciliation, and fraternity in word and deed.[14] The core values of the Christian family include wisdom, relatedness, solidarity, generosity, responsibility, hard work, justice, reconciliation, restoration, reciprocity and charity. Charity for its own sake is sentimental. It must be genuine, rooted in truth, to

support the true development of every person and of all people (*CV* 11).

Benedict XVI insists that for proper development to happen, people ought to enhance the ability of each person, not taking individuals as needy and underdeveloped. Everyone in the human family must discern and differentiate between obstacles in various cultures. In this discernment, dialogue is essential to avoid excluding diverse cultures from Christian moral values. The gospel is not restricted to a certain culture. The message of Christ is universal and fits all positive cultural values within the human family. Thus, Benedict XVI advocates that the church appreciate and safeguard positive cultural values.[15]

## INTERPRETATION

Greater access to education is a precondition for effective international cooperation. Classroom teaching and vocational training are important factors in development and ought to focus on the complete formation of the person. However, there is the problem of a relativistic definition and understanding of the human person, which has an implication for education, especially moral education, in its universal extension. The realization of full human potential is also negatively impacted when people who are deprived of such holistic education lack economic and technical means, educational methods, and resources for human progress. Hence, it is important to impart the right education, that is, an education that flows from an understanding that each individual person has abilities to provide for the growth of themselves and for the common good.[16] Embracing fundamental and transcultural human and moral values will allow all people to treat each individual with dignity through communion and participation in both personal and communal development. However, development should not be centered merely on the process of change. It must also focus on the person who is the facilitator of change.

The United Nations Development Programme recognizes human development as a process of building an environment in which persons can make use of their abilities to be more productive, centering on their desires and interests in life.[17] We are to put into consideration the very understanding of human persons and their nature as moral and social beings.[18] To promote the family, culture, and development, there is a need to rekindle consciences and to call for a transformed responsiveness to persons, who cannot be reduced to mere pawns of the market, means of production, or consumers. Such responsiveness would lead to a reconsideration of the basics of a plausible economic model. It would also appreciate the proper relationship between human development and human dignity as promoted by Benedict XVI (CV 54, 4, 6, 7, 38).[19] Economics should not be disconnected from the vision of men and women who bear the image of God and, through redemption in Jesus Christ, the incarnate Word, are called to flourish as God's children.

Benedict XVI is also right to call attention to international tourism as a factor in economic development and cultural growth that often causes the emergence of local enterprises (CV 61). However, tourism can also be a factor in exploitation and moral degradation, since it can lead to negative educational impacts on development and cultural growth. There are many immoral and perverted forms of conduct as well as consumerist and hedonistic patterns and a resultant escapism that are not conducive to authentic encounter between persons and cultures that flourish in the shortcomings of present practices in international tourism.

Besides, some negative religious and cultural attitudes do not fully embrace the principle of love and truth, all of which impede authentic human development. Cultural orientations devoid of truth and love foster excessive individualism and, consequently, alienation and selfishness aimed at individual well-being and personal satisfaction. Authentic development needs different religions and cultures to point out the pivotal role they play in development. However, adequate discernment is needed based on the criterion of charity and truth for those holding and exercising political power.

Secularism and fundamentalism hamper a myriad of activities and initiatives, including those for human development. They can also inhibit fruitful dialogue between religious faith and reason. Faith and reason (political or otherwise) need to purify each other to show an authentically human face; otherwise, devoid of this dialogue, human development is jeopardized. Dialogue promotes the exercise of "freedom and participation through assumption of responsibilities" (CV 57).

In response to these challenges, the principle of subsidiarity is relevant for managing globalization and directing it toward authentic human development. At present, globalization has a myriad of problems. Despite its supposed litany of benefits, it also stands accused of the havoc it has wrought on the traditions and cultures of many peoples. The principles of subsidiarity and solidarity can serve to promote respect and regard toward those who are more vulnerable. For example, international development aid has been used as an ideological weapon by imposing inconvenient conditionals on the recipients. Such misuse of international mechanisms of support and cooperation has been perceived as an instrument of neocolonialism by many developing nations.

The principles of subsidiarity and solidarity are avenues for the church and governments to work together for the promotion of the common good. The common good is the safety of all members of society and calls for an interior enthusiasm of all persons. This is a promising possibility for upholding inclusive community values and concerns for the integral development of all people.[20] As the *Compendium of the Social Doctrine of the Church* clarifies,

> The common good does not consist in the simple sum of the particular goods of each subject or social entity. Belonging to everyone and to each person, it is and remains "common," because it is indivisible and because only together is it possible to attain it, increase it and safeguard its effectiveness, with regard also to the future.[21]

To sustain the common good, there is a need to promote the dignity of human work and make use of all opportunities for enhancing development, which will in turn alleviate poverty.

Poverty and unemployment have a connection to violations of the dignity of human work, limited opportunities (unemployment or underemployment), low value input and deprived rights, unjust wages, and personal security. In a certain sense, the formal economy is limited in a way such that only the formally employed are sure of their stable income. Since formal employment is considered the surest way of securing an income and a possibility of getting out of poverty, most graduates yearn for public or government employment. Without the availability of stable jobs, people are left in the grip of poverty and low standards of living. Thus, the *Universal Declaration of Human Rights* states that

> Everyone has the right to a standard of living adequate for the health and well-being of oneself and of one's family, including food, clothing, and housing and medical care and necessary social services and the right to security in the event of unemployment, sickness, disability, widowhood, old age or other lack of livelihood in circumstance beyond one's control.[22]

The right to an appropriate standard of living has its root in the dignity and social nature of all people. The human family is thus obliged to ensure that all people get provisions essential to leading a truly human life. All of humanity ought to have responsible freedom in search of a better standard of living.

Development is more than progress, as it involves the broader human environment. Even the very technologically advanced must use resources wisely and humanely. Economic and technological progress does not necessarily facilitate human values and contribute to human flourishing; these alone do not amount to integral human development. The more we misuse the natural and social environment, the more we harm people who should be at the center of all development. Pope Francis, in his encyclical letter *Laudato si'*, confirms the bond between the human and natural environment, as he states that the human environment and the natural environment are interrelated such that they flourish or deteriorate together. To

adequately establish a suitable standard of living, to promote integral human development and combat environmental degradation, there is need to pay attention to the issues related to human, social, and environmental degradation. The deterioration of the environment and of society affects the most vulnerable people on the planet: "both everyday experience and scientific research show that the gravest effects of all attacks on the environment are suffered by the poorest."[23]

Focusing on the care of Mother Earth, we should always bear in mind that we are custodians of nature. To uphold authentic and integral human development, we are to value nature and see the glory of God in it. Sean McDonagh writes that we are one with nature in which we recognize its creator: "It cannot be emphasized enough how everything is interconnected."[24]

Through interconnectedness, we are able to work in solidarity. Decent work expresses the essential dignity of every man and woman in their particular society, freely chosen, effectively associating workers with development of their community. However, foreign direct investment's incentives normally seek regions with a cheap source of labor, which in turn leads to indecent work.

The unrelenting advance of global interdependence causes uniformity and homogeneity that does not give countries their "freedom" to chart their own path for development. People ought to be set free to exercise their freedom to employ their individual talents and participate in the mutual strength and development of the body of Christ (*AM* 47). This aspect of the communion of human reality points to the good of each person, which is destined to the good of the community. Thus, there is a need to reform economic institutions and international finance systems if governments are to play a protective role to ensure that all people find their path for development. Provision of the common good, in accordance with the ethical principles of subsidiarity and responsibility, must be ensured by governments in line with the values of charity in truth.

In conclusion, to build an authentic human and Catholic family, there is need to uphold Christian values and family values. Observing social protection measures and being guided by the values of charity in truth leads to attaining true holistic development. For this development in the human family to be real, all people need to be led on the complex paths of mission by the Holy Spirit in order to participate in the construction and transformation of the human family by focusing on Christ, "the way, the truth, and the life" (John 14:6).

## NOTES

1. Paul VI, *Populorum* progressio (March 26, 1967), https://www.vatican.va/content/paul-vi /en/encyclicals/documents/hf_p-vi_enc_26031967 _populorum.html (hereafter cited as *PP*).

2. Benedict XVI, *Caritas in veritate* (June 29, 2009), 8, https://www.vatican.va/content/benedict -xvi/en/encyclicals/documents/hf_ben-xvi_enc _20090629_caritas-in-veritate.html (hereafter cited as *CV*).

3. Benedict XVI, "In Truth, Peace: Message of His Holiness Benedict XVI for the Celebration of the 39th World Day of Peace" (January 1, 2006), 6, https://www.vatican.va/content/benedict-xvi /en/messages/peace/documents/hf_ben-xvi_mes _20051213_xxxix-world-day-peace.html.

4. Benedict XVI, "Letter on Family Life," *Crossroads Initiative* (May 17, 2005), https://www .crossroadsinitiative.com/media/articles/letteron familylife/.

5. Marriage and family are uniquely valued in African societies and involves both families of the spouses.

6. Raymond Brown et al., eds., *The New Jerome Biblical Commentary* (Avon, UK: Bath, 1992), 155.

7. Pontifical Council for Justice and Peace, *Compendium of the Social Doctrine of the Church* (Rome: Libreria Editrice Vaticana, 2004), no. 209.

8. Vatican II, *Gaudium et spes* (December 7, 1965), 48, https://www.vatican.va/archive/hist_councils/ii _vatican_council/documents/vat-ii_const_19651207 _gaudium-et-spes_en.html.

9. Benedict XVI, *Ecclesia in Medio Oriente* (September 14, 2012), 58, https://www.vatican .va/content/benedict-xvi/en/apost_exhortations /documents/hf_ben-xvi_exh_20120914_ecclesia-in -medio-oriente.html.

10. Leo XIII, *Rerum novarum* (May 15, 1891), 25, https://www.vatican.va/content/leo-xiii /en/encyclicals/documents/hf_l-xiii_enc_15051891 _rerum-novarum.html.

11. Paul VI, *Evangelii nuntiandi* (December 8, 1975), https://www.vatican.va/content/paul-vi /en/apost_exhortations/documents/hf_p-vi_exh _19751208_evangelii-nuntiandi.html (hereafter cited as *EN*).

12. John Paul II, *Familiaris consortio* (November 22, 1981), 15, https://www.vatican.va/content /john-paul-ii/en/apost_exhortations/documents/hf _jp-ii_exh_19811122_familiaris-consortio.html.

13. Benedict XVI, "Address of His Holiness Benedict XVI: Meeting with the World of Culture" (May 12, 2010), https://www.vatican.va/content /benedict-xvi/en/speeches/2010/may/documents/hf _ben-xvi_spe_20100512_incontro-cultura.html.

14. Symposium of Episcopal Conferences of Africa and Madagascar, *Pastoral Exhortation of the Symposium of Episcopal Conferences of Africa and Madagascar: Kampala Document* (Acrra, Ghana: SECAM, 2019), no. 18, https://drive.google.com/file /d/1mzojsnefg_Xk9U-Eu1c1UEZIATwLaaVi/view ?usp=sharing.

15. Benedict XVI, *Africae munus* (November 19, 2021), 36–38, https://www.vatican.va/content /benedict-xvi/en/apost_exhortations/documents/hf _ben-xvi_exh_20111119_africae-munus.html (hereafter cited as *AM*).

16. Pontifical Council for Justice and Peace, *Compendium of the Social Doctrine of the Church*, nos. 164–170, 93–96. According to the *Compendium*, the principle of the common good sprouts from "the dignity, unity and equality of all people." In quoting *Gaudium et spes*, it defines the common good as "the sum total of social conditions which allow people, either as groups or as individuals, to reach their fulfilment more fully and more easily."

17. United Nations Development Programme, *Human Development Report* (New York: United Nations, 2001), 9.

18. John Paul II, *Centesimus annus* (May 1, 1991), 53–61, https://www.vatican.va/content/john-paul-ii /en/encyclicals/documents/hf_jp-ii_enc_01051991 _centesimus-annus.html.

19. Francis, *Evangelii Gaudium* (November 24, 2013), 184, 209, https://www.vatican.va /content/francesco/en/apost_exhortations/documents

/papa-francesco_esortazione-ap_20131124_evangelii-gaudium.html.

20. Samuel Bedijo, *The Moral Problems Posed by Individualism in the Church in Africa: A Case Study in Nebbi Catholic Diocese in North-Western Uganda* (Verlag: EOS, 2015), 239.

21. Pontifical Council for Justice and Peace, *Compendium of the Social Doctrine of the Church*, no. 164.

22. United Nations, *Universal Declaration of Human Rights* (December 10, 1948), article 25, https://www.un.org/en/about-us/universal-declaration-of-human-rights.

23. Francis, *Laudato si'* (May 25, 2015), 48, https://www.vatican.va/content/francesco/en/encyclicals/documents/papa-francesco_20150524_enciclica-laudato-si.html.

24. Sean MacDonagh, *On Care for Our Common Home* Laudato Si': *The Encyclical of Pope Francis on the Environment with Commentary* (New York: Orbis Books, 2016), 213.

# 21

*Caritas in Veritate*
and *Africae Munus*

LÉOCADIE LUSHOMBO, i.t.

## CONTEXT

While Benedict XVI did not produce an encyclical on the family, his influence on Catholic Family Teaching (CFT) during his distinguished academic career, tenure in the Congregation for the Doctrine of the Faith, and papacy cannot be overlooked. Joseph Ratzinger served for twenty-four years as prefect of the Congregation for the Doctrine of the Faith under John Paul II prior to his own election to the papacy in 2005. This chapter will put Benedict XVI's contributions to CFT in the fifth chapter of *Caritas in veritate*,[1] "The Cooperation of the Human Family," as well as his later exhortation, *Africae munus*,[2] in dialogue with his wider reflections on the family, guided by specific concern for the representation of African experiences, especially those of women.

According to his biographers John F. Thornton and Susanne B. Varenne, Benedict XVI's theological perspective is framed by the guiding principles of "obedience and fruitfulness."[3] These principles convey the virtues he wished to embody for his ministry and were inspired by scripture: "You are my friends if you do what I command you" (John 15:14) and "Father, if you are willing, take this cup away from me; still, not my will but yours be done" (Luke 22:42). Each affirms submission to God as the mark

of authentic human freedom.[4] Ratzinger's writing reflects "the courage to face any question or objection because of the confidence he has in the Truth revealed in Jesus Christ and handed on by the church's apostolic tradition."[5]

According to Benedict XVI, "human beings always need something more than technically proper care. They need humanity. They need heartfelt concern."[6] This conviction shaped his teaching on the family. We make the world human by acting humanely, and family is the place where human beings learn most basically what it means to be human. A second feature of his teaching on family is reinforcing the Christian foundations of Europe against the cultural changes of the twentieth century, particularly the rising influence of "cultural relativism" (*CV* 26). While his teaching on development in *Caritas in veritate* seems not to have "anything in mind other than European Catholicism,"[7] as noted by Orobator, Benedict XVI's teaching on family in Africa retrieves both ancient Egyptian foundations and salient macrodimensional features of the African culture known as *ubuntu*. Ancient Egypt's "continental memory and cultural products" are similar to those found throughout the African continent.[8] As Molefi Asante argues, Egypt cannot be divorced from the rest of the African continent.[9] According to the Congolese Egyptologist, linguist, and historian Théophile Obenga, significant features of the pharaonic kinship system are striking in their similarity to most modern African kinship systems. Likewise, the principle of *ubuntu* has widespread relevance throughout Africa. Some features of *ubuntu* noted by Benedict XVI include "hospitality, refuge and care" for the weakest (*DCE* 40). For him, such values are learned in families but oriented to the larger community and potentially preserve and strengthen Christian values. However, the unique challenges facing actual families in Africa must also be considered.

## COMMENTARY

### *Family as the Future of Humanity*

Benedict XVI's insight on the family as the place to learn how to be human is affirmed by *Apostolicam actuositatem*'s description of the family as "the first and vital cell of society."[10] It is the place par excellence where a human person learns about the meaning of life, love, identity, and vocation in society. In family, the bonds of communion and virtues are formed. It is also in the family where the concepts of right and wrong are shaped within relational societal paradigms. In this sense, a family is the "sanctuary of life."[11] As Benedict XVI argues, in the family, members learn to love and to recognize God's face among them, for the first revelation of God is conveyed through the attention of mothers and fathers toward their children. These learnings are fundamental; whenever they are lacking, "society as a whole suffers violence and becomes, in turn, the progenitor of more violence" (*AM* 42).

Benedict XVI's Christian anthropology further affirms the person as inhabited by God's charity, with reason broadened by faith in God. Considering the Christian duty to transform daily and social realities, the church counts the family among the places where human and Christian responsibility is to be exercised.[12] For this reason, Christian foundations are needed for family and society to advance toward their goals.[13] If family values are jeopardized, society

is in peril. Consequently, families are to be protected for the good of society. Benedict XVI reiterated John Paul II's claim that a threat to the family is a threat to society because the future of humanity can only be ensured through the family.[14] Healthy families make healthy societies, and Christian foundations are the cornerstone that protects the family from its most prominent contemporary threat: "cultural relativism."

### *Protecting against "Cultural Relativism"*

To assess Benedict XVI's understanding of cultural relativism, it is necessary to assess what he believes makes a family. Through marriage, a man and woman embrace the divine law that is "offered to everyone in order to be able to live in freedom and to be respected in their own dignity."[15] Jesus clearly and concisely affirms this universal truth in saying "What therefore God has joined together, let not man put asunder" (Mark 10:9). This union is also directed to procreation, which "is not primarily moral: it concerns being, the order inscribed in creation, before duty."[16] As such, indissoluble monogamous marriages are the basis of "the only authentic form of family."[17]

The love between spouses can only be fully understood by considering the True Author of Life who gifts families with life and the love of Christ Crucified (*DCE* 2). Marriage becomes the sacred symbol of the loving relationship of God with God's peoples and vice versa. God's love becomes the model for human love (*DCE* 11). Benedict XVI also emphasized the importance of love as the principle of life (*DCE* 44). Our way of loving, including married love, is to be grounded in God's love. Love of God is the rationale for the Pauline claim that "husbands should love their wives as their bodies. He who loves his wife loves himself. For no man ever hates his flesh, but nourishes and cherishes it, as Christ does the Church" (Eph. 5:28–29) (*AM* 52). Love of God is thus the cornerstone of marriage, which is foundational to Benedicts XVI's vision of the family (*AM* 115).

In *Africae munus*, Benedict XVI strongly asserts the need to defend the family against "distortion of the very notion of marriage and family, devaluation of maternity and trivialization of abortion, easy divorce and the relativism of a 'new ethics'" (*AM* 43). He invites parents to welcome and protect their children "from the moment of conception" (*AM* 52). In his Christmas address to the Roman Curia of 2008, he warned that gender theory accepts a new model of marriage and family in the name of progress, tolerance, and equal rights, including the right to adopt children. For him, this is a path to personal and societal self-destruction that seeks to change governing mentalities, beginning with those most vulnerable to indoctrination: children and adolescents.[18] In a 2009 homily during his visit to Cameroon and Angola, Benedict XVI warned against "the tyranny of materialism," reminding Africa not to embrace the path that does "not recognize the True Author of Life!"[19]

In his homily on the opening of the 2009 Second African Synod, Bendict XVI made an unusual metaphor, describing Africa as,

> an immense spiritual "lung" for a humanity that appears to be in a crisis of faith and hope. But this "lung" can also become ill. And at this moment at least two dangerous pathologies are infecting it: in the first place, a disease that is already widespread in the Western world, in other words practical materialism, combined with relativist and nihilistic thought.[20]

As in the West, Benedict XVI identifies materialistic, relativist, and nihilistic views as the main factors threatening the family in Africa but trusts that African cultures are resourceful enough to preserve the family because they tend to integrate authority and tradition (Christian and African) in their moral values.

## The Family in Africa

In 2009, the Synod on Reconciliation and Peace affirmed several perspectives on the family in Africa and established "the African family as the first place of evangelization and the place from which the challenges to evangelization in the Third Millennium will be confronted."[21] Family as the first place of evangelization is grounded in the idea of the church-family of God. A family of God implies that all members of the community, including domestic families, are to spread the good news of God in their social and political contexts.[22] It also implies that in Jesus Christ, all peoples become one family and share the hope of resurrection. The world, believers, and nonbelievers are to live as a family under the Creator's watchful eye.[23]

The African Church wants to be primarily a family.[24] The bishops considered how might the "Church-Family of God contribute to the reconstruction of an Africa" that fosters reconciliation, justice, and peace in small families, "the first and vital cell of society,"[25] who are increasingly dehumanized in Africa. How can a family confronting many economic and sociocultural challenges become a vital cell of God's family? As the bishops affirm, "family is always the basic place where" Christians learn to work in friendship with others, where the process of becoming God's family is engaged.[26]

As a family of God does not accept exclusion, families must be welcoming and be agents of reconciliation and peace. Excluding members contradicts the idea of the church as a family of God (*CV* 56), which implies mutual aid. As Teresa Okure suggests, "To be the Church-Family of God in service to reconciliation, justice, and peace impels us to be God's building and tilling (1 Cor. 3:9; Eph. 2:10), the visible, tangible witnesses of this divine reconciliation, by relating to one another as divine siblings."[27]

Regarding the church-family of God's members as divine siblings, Benedict XVI calls everyone to practice the principles of solidarity and subsidiarity that help families become more human and humanizing (*CV* 58). Benedict XVI affirms that "the Church is God's family in the world. In this family, no one ought to go without the necessities of life" (*DCE* 25b). The dignity of its members is affirmed through "education, health, aid to the needy, development projects, defense of human rights, and the commitment to bring about democracy and legally constituted States."[28] The church-family of God is the place where life is received and given, where those in need are cared for,[29] where talents and gifts are shared and put in service to others.

Benedict XVI welcomes diversity of cultures in families but always within the framework of the universal moral law. He states, "In all cultures there are examples of ethical convergence, some isolated, some interrelated, as an expression of the one human nature, willed by the Creator; the tradition of ethical wisdom knows this as the natural law" (*CV* 59). This universal law constitutes the foundation for "the multifaceted pluralism of cultural diversity" and is the hinge that keeps cultural diversity bound to and directed toward "the common quest for truth, goodness, and God" (*CV* 59). Relativism is a threat to this quest for truth that can "seek to banish God from our lives" (*AM* 7). Benedict XVI thus stands against what he identifies as relativist family cultures, hence his persistent calls "Family, become what you are!" and "*Family: live and transmit the faith!*"[30]

Benedict XVI also calls on Africa not to copy the Western model of family that tends to reduce the family to the nuclear family and instead to preserve the African concept of extended family. A family is a community within a community, bound by love and mutual services. As the bishops' synod puts it, "The family is a community of life in which there is a diversity of talents, charisms, ministries, functions, duties and services all of which contribute, each in its own way, to fulfilling the shared tasks."[31] Benedict XVI resists an individualistic vision of family, as each family is a member within the broader family of the world church. The second chapter of *Africae munus* assesses the theological significance of these tasks for fathers and mothers as well as the elderly and extended family members.

## Gender Roles in African Families

*Africae munus* affords men particular authority and a "noble responsibility of giving society the values it needs" (*AM* 51). Men represent God's fatherhood on Earth (Eph. 3:15); their task is to ensure that all family members play different roles for the well-being and development of the whole. Family is "the cradle and most effective means for humanizing society, and the place of encounter for different generations" (*AM* 53). Benedict XVI warns of men's place in the family being lost through cultural relativism and calls on Africa to preserve the roles of husbands as differentiated from those of wives. The father's role in protection seems a particularly vital component of Benedict XIV's theology of the family. During his apostolic journey to Cameroon and Angola he urged, "We are asking the Lord to protect the Church always—and he does!—just as Joseph protected his family and kept watch over the child Jesus during his early years."[32]

At the same time, Benedict XVI also recognizes the need for more respect for the dignity of women and wives in African models of family. He acknowledges women's talents and gifts that significantly contribute to their families and the church and affirms church and society's responsibility to promote women in taking their full place in the world (*AM* 55). He also recognizes that the rights and dignity of women are often abused in African societies (*AM* 56). Benedict XVI notes the progress made in educating women but acknowledges that many traditional and ancestral practices in Africa deny women's full dignity, such as cultures where educating girls is neglected in favor of boys (*AM* 56).

Pope Benedict XVI encourages women's activism as agents of peace in Africa (*AM* 58). The African bishops reinforce this recognition of women's talents and the hope women convey in church, family, and society both for peace and reconciliation. But they lament the unjust treatment of women, such as their exclusion from inheritance intended solely for men, widowhood rites, forced marriage, etc. and the many types of violence women suffer in the name of tradition.[33] Besides these problems, Benedict XVI emphasizes respect for the marriage of man and woman in African cultures as a unifying feature that turns to God as "the absolute" creator and source of life.[34]

## The Role of the Elderly

Benedict XVI extols African families' veneration of the elderly and recognition of the virtues of being elderly as a cultural custom for many African traditions.[35] The elderly are included in the African family model as a source of knowledge. Their wisdom is to be included in the search for the good and in the vision of society. In ancient Egyptian and several African languages such as Kikongo, being elderly suggests having the capacity to look and profoundly assess issues, to carefully recognize things that might be hidden to younger people, to have deeper memory, to discern more wisely, etc.[36] The elderly are considered a library for the clan because they embody the knowledge of history,[37] especially where oral tradition is prominent. As Asante says, "The elders can always find the crab's heart."[38] This means that due to their life experience and meticulous scrutiny, they are capable of locating and solving problems. In addition, the elderly remind society of the African customs that benefit the community beyond individuals and enrich all other family members (*AM* 48).

For Benedict XVI, African appreciation of the elderly as the "pinnacle" of African families should inform and inspire the Western world to recover the dignity due to the elderly. Scripture affirms the elderly as "rich in experience" and fearful of the Lord (Sir. 25:6) (*AM* 47) while the church "regards the elderly with great esteem" (*AM* 50).

## INTERPRETATION

The structures and social realities of families differ across cultures. Nevertheless, bonds of relationship are instituted or recognized among people either biologically or by forms of association. Benedict XVI rightly called on Africa's commitment, urging the church in Africa to conduct in-depth discernment to identify aspects of African culture that conflict with Christianity and aspects that uphold fraternal bonds and gospel values, beyond consanguinity (*AM* 36).

Benedict XVI reinforces Orobator's claim that "in Africa, religion is real, and the Church is alive."[39] Both African synods have affirmed the African church-family as alive and increasing in number. However, it is a family affected by "deep crises, contradictions, and strife."[40] These crises of the church as a family of God are similar to those of domestic African families. Families are challenged with finding balance between respecting each member's autonomy and diversity while building up the communion that is needed by the whole continent. Charles Curran describes the tension as making sure that "the relationships involved in a family do not submerge the identities of the individual members of the family."[41] Africa is interested in keeping the early Christian imagery of the communities, as *ekklēsia of God*, alive; hence, the pope's call to not copy the Western world is partially justified.

The extended notion of family in Africa dates from ancient Egypt, called Kemet, where the word "family" refers to a village section, not a nuclear cell.[42] The African family, rooted in Egyptian civilization, is a familial unit that is simultaneously nuclear and extended and subsequentially "a part of the small and the big clan."[43] Asante repeats an Akan saying to explain this complexity: "A family is like a forest. When you are outside, it is dense; when you are inside, you see that each tree has its place."[44] In certain African traditions such as those of the Bamana people (found primarily in Mali but also in Guinea, Burkina Faso, and Senegal), a family unit can reach "anywhere between 100 and 1,000 individuals."[45]

Obenga also speaks of the diachronic dimension of parenthood in ancient Africa. Parenthood is a system of relationships in which individuals are connected by a very complex network of links, with many ramifications beyond the nuclear family.[46] Ancient Egyptians did not possess concepts to designate nieces, nephews, cousins, uncles, and aunts. In ancient Africa, such extended family members were identified as brothers and sisters. Nonetheless, consanguinity and filiation were valued.[47] Today it remains common to hear African wives address their husband not by name but instead as the father of her son or daughter. There are diverse bonds to consider in African anthropology: maternal bonds (between mother and child), conjugal bonds (between spouses), and consanguineous and uterine bonds (between children, brothers and sisters, sons and daughters born from the same parents).[48]

Benedict XVI's approval of African family values is informed by his highly theological understanding of the foundation of the family. However, his perspectives on African families are colored by the European contexts in which those theological truths were articulated. Consequently, for an African context, they are too patriarchal and lack the maternal cultural bonds that are widespread on the continent. Moreover, Benedict XVI's references to African values actually reinforces traditional Western patriarchal family values, which do not fully resonate among African families.[49] For example, he suggests that the father's role as protector is based in the patriarchal notion of fathers as "head of the family." This obscures the increasing number of women who alone assume the family's expenses and education of children. Benedict XVI's affirmation of African values as models is based on a gender-biased patriarchal duality with predetermined roles for men as protectors and providers. This "discovery" of African values by way of importing Western gender ideals fails to recognize the changing dynamics of gender relations that have accelerated across Africa with increasing development.

Benedict's penchant for the father as protector also leaves behind the traditional African matriarchal models of family whereby mothers and their lineage assume responsibility for protection. For Obenga, considering the preponderance of matriarchy in ancient Egypt, mother-child bonds, not father-son bonds, constituted the fundamental unity. As Asante reinforces,

> Among many African people, the descent is through the mother—that is, matrilineal [inheritance is on the mother's side]. In that case, many of the ancestors to be revered would come from the matrilineal side of the family. The husband would be a part of the family by virtue of his marriage to the direct descendant.[50]

Only later did Africa replace the reign of the mother with patriarchy, and Christianity had much to do with this move. Thus, to speak of the African model of family and ignore the central protector role of the mother in African anthropology is to amputate from African families a predominant traditional feature. Asante reminds that "it is through the woman's womb that God continues God's creative work, thus making motherhood sacred."[51] Besides, "God's motherhood is widely expressed in proverbs, songs, and names given to God in various ethnic groups."[52]

### Preserving Africa from Western Vices

Benedict XVI uses African ecclesiology to counter the relativism that he perceives as threatening Western families. However, African families are infected by different types of internal pathologies that push them into what Benedict XVI mistakes for "Western" features despite not necessarily being the fruit of Western influence.

In 2010, no African country was listed as "very high" on the human development index. Tunisia and Algeria in the north and the island nation Mauritius (east of Madagascar) ranked among "high" human development countries at a distant 81st, 84th, and 72nd, respectively. Several other African nations ranked "medium," while most ranked low on the index.[53] Over the last decade, Mauritius moved up to 66th place, last among the "very high" countries in the 2020 human development index. Seven African countries now rank "high": Algeria, 91st; Tunisia, 95th; Botswana, 100th; Lybia, 105th; South Africa, 114th; Egypt, 116th; and Gabon, 119th.[54]

Continuing development has influenced changing gender relations, but these do not change only as a result of economic progress. Changes in gender norms also result from the failures of social policies and legal systems as well as the shortcomings of husbands or companions who often find themselves with less power and responsibility over households and children. Thus, utilizing the model of Saint Joseph as protector of the family leaves behind the women who are protectors of families as married or single parents across developing portions of the globe.

Belief in the centrality of procreation and hence marriage between man and woman seems natural to Africans. But here again, Benedict XVI's model of family overlooks single parents who trust in the Lord while leading their families. Female-headed families result from family breakdown, husbands' irresponsibility, unfaithfulness, or death due to wars and regional violence, gender inequalities, and other factors, which push women to divorce, separate, of otherwise assume sole responsibility for their family. Among African families, Mary is the model to whom the family is entrusted; she wakes, acts, and sometimes takes on heavy loads to feed the entire family. She cannot count on an absent Joseph.[55]

> In Africa, widows make up the largest segment of female heads (about 45%). Divorced women are about 20% and the never married are about 10%. And close to a quarter of the women who are female heads in the region are actually married with a non-resident husband. The husband has either migrated or is non-resident in a polygamous marriage.[56]

Women are heads and protectors of their single-parent families in all ways. In some African traditions such as of the Azande people (Sudan), a woman had the option to reject marriage "if she finds it unsuitable."[57] Separation and divorce are not simply the result of relativist Western influences.

Other socioeconomic contributions to single-parent families include restricted access to education, training, and skilled jobs for both husbands and wives. These deficits often lead to the marginalization of women and the feminization of poverty. What seemed to be immovable pillars of the family are collapsing due to economic crises, wars with their procession of refugees, violence, and other structural causes. Far more than gender theories, Africa's contemporary challenges put women on the front line protecting both children and husbands. Reassurances of conventional male power are cracking, crumbling, and laying bare increasingly unbearable contradictions and injustices.

The traditional belief that being a complete woman requires having children has led to women's deaths in African contexts without sufficient access to quality health care. The high birth rate often leaves women without sufficient resources to care for all of their children and increases female mortality, leaving children without care. The birth rate in sub-Saharan Africa has declined from 6.8 live births per woman aged 15–49 in 1970 to 4.7 today, with 4.1 expected in 2030.[58] However, pregnancy remains a significant threat to women's and children's lives and health, especially in areas without adequate health care. Women who are affected face many challenges and strive to act as responsive beings. They respond by taking initiatives to change the patriarchal gender norms and behavior to some degree. Thus, the increase of women heads and protectors of families goes hand in hand with their commitment to the family's well-being. It is not merely a result of globalized Western relativism, as Benedict XVI suggests. Instead, it affirms the family as a universal value that takes different forms in particular circumstances.

The model of the male breadwinner is ending in the West and never had firm footing in Africa. No society can claim that men alone can ensure the development of all members of the family. Several factors have brought women into paid work: education, declining fertility, changes in female aspirations, the transformation of cultural norms, etc.[59] Unfortunately, Pope Benedict XVI's teaching is not adapted to these changing roles. Instead, it relies on an increasingly irrelevant model of male protectors and breadwinners and female homemakers who take responsibility for non-paid care work. Gender norms in several parts of the world still make use of this model, but it is increasingly unsuited to the good of many families.[60]

Asserting the symbol of God's fatherhood can also be problematic in contexts where families are places of violence and abuse. As a report from UN Women put it, "The shocking pervasiveness of intimate partner violence means that statistically, home is one of the most dangerous places to be for a woman."[61] Benedict XVI's teaching failed to consider that not all families founded on male-female marriage are healthy and safe communities of life.

The many ways African families are torn between modernity and African patriarchal traditions are not even approximated in Benedict XVI's teaching on the family. Family structures are undeniably changing in Africa because of the increase in the number of families headed by women (sometimes grandmothers), single parents, and even children. Catholic teaching cannot content itself with providing patriarchal rules and models, because no single model can address all the challenges facing families throughout the world. Nonetheless, Christianity has much to offer in guiding the consciences of persons toward choosing what genuinely humanizes and divinizes family members so that each family can fully contribute to human flourishing and education in humanity. As Benedict XVI argues, "We have come to believe in God's love: in these words, the Christian can express the fundamental decision of his life. Being Christian is not the result of an ethical choice or a lofty idea, but the encounter with an event, a person, which gives life a new horizon and a decisive direction" (*DCE* 1). Guiding the people of God to believe in God's love, regardless of particular context, is a foundational commitment fitting to family ethics.

## NOTES

1. Benedict XVI, *Caritas in veritate* (June 29, 2009), https://www.vatican.va/content/benedict-xvi/en/encyclicals/documents/hf_ben-xvi_enc_20090629_caritas-in-veritate.html (hereafter cited as *CV*).

2. Benedict XVI, *Africae munus* (November 19, 2011), https://www.vatican.va/content/benedict-xvi/en/apost_exhortations/documents/hf_ben-xvi_exh_20111119_africae-munus.html (hereafter cited as *AM*).

3. John F. Thornton and Susan B. Varenne, *The Essential Pope Benedict XVI: His Central Writings and Speeches* (Pymble, New South Wales: HarperCollins e-books, 2008), ix.

4. Thornton and Varenne, *The Essential Pope Benedict XVI*, ix.

5. Thornton and Varenne, *The Essential Pope Benedict XVI*, xv.

6. Benedict XVI, *Deus caritas est* (December 25, 2005), 31a, https://www.vatican.va/content/benedict-xvi/en/encyclicals/documents/hf_ben-xvi_enc_20051225_deus-caritas-est.html (hereafter cited as *DCE*).

7. A. E. Orobator, "Caritas in Veritate and Africa's Burden of (Under)Development," *Theological Studies* 71, no. 2 (May 1, 2010): 320.

8. Molefi Kete Asante and Ama Mazama, eds., *Encyclopedia of African Religion* (Thousand Oaks, CA: Sage, 2009), xxiv.

9. Molefi Kete Asante and Clyde Ledbetter, eds., *Contemporary Critical Thought in Africology and Africana Studies*, Critical Africana Studies: African, African American, and Caribbean Interdisciplinary and Intersectional Studies (Lanham, MD: Lexington Books, 2016), 42.

10. Vatican II, *Apostolicam actuositatem* (November 18, 1966), 11, https://www.vatican.va/archive/hist_councils/ii_vatican_council/documents/vat-ii_decree_19651118_apostolicam-actuositatem_en.html.

11. John Paul II, *Centesimus annus* (May 1, 1991), 39, https://www.vatican.va/content/john-paul-ii/en/encyclicals/documents/hf_jp-ii_enc_01051991_centesimus-annus.html.

12. John Paul II, "Homily at the Beatification of Adolph Kolping (1813–1865)," October 27, 1991.

13. "The Film 'Bells of Europe: A Journey into the Faith in Europe': Interview with the Holy Father Benedict XVI," 1–3, https://www.vatican.va/content/benedict-xvi/en/speeches/2012/october/documents/hf_ben-xvi_spe_20121015_bells-of-europe.html.

14. John Paul II, *Familiaris consortio* (November 22, 1981), 85, https://www.vatican.va/content/john-paul-ii/en/apost_exhortations/documents/hf_jp-ii_exh_19811122_familiaris-consortio.html.

15. Benedict XVI, "Address of His Holiness Benedict XVI to the Participants in the International

Congress on the Natural Moral Law" (February 12, 2007), https://www.vatican.va/content/benedict-xvi/en/speeches/2007/february/documents/hf_ben-xvi_spe_20070212_pul.html.

16. Benedict XVI, "Homily of His Holiness Benedict XVI: Eucharist Celebration for the Opening of the Second Special Assembly for Africa of the Synod of Bishops" (October 4, 2009), 2, https://www.vatican.va/content/benedict-xvi/en/homilies/2009/documents/hf_ben-xvi_hom_20091004_sinodo-africa.pdf.

17. Pontifical Council for Justice and Peace, *Compendium of the Social Doctrine of the Church* (May 26, 2006), no. 229, https://www.vatican.va/roman_curia/pontifical_councils/justpeace/documents/rc_pc_justpeace_doc_20060526_compendio-dott-soc_en.html. The *Compendium* is a collection of church teachings but is not a teaching document in itself. In this paragraph it conflates marriage and family without reference to a primary source. Both John Paul II and Benedict XVI were clear that marriage is the foundation of family, but a marriage in itself is not a family until the end of procreation is realized. The text above reflects this understanding, which is not evident in the *Compendium*'s summary.

18. Martin Schlag, ed., *Handbook of Catholic Social Teaching: A Guide for Christians in the World Today* (Washington, DC: Catholic University of America Press, 2017), 63.

19. Benedict XVI, "Apostolic Journey of the Holy Father Benedict XVI to Cameroon and Angola: Homily of Pope Benedict on Saint Joseph" (March 17, 2009), https://catholicinsight.com/homily-of-pope-benedict-on-saint-joseph/.

20. Benedict XVI, "Homily of His Holiness Benedict XVI," 2.

21. Synod of Bishops, II Special Assembly for Africa, "The Church in Africa in Service to Reconciliation, Justice, and Peace" (March 19, 2009), sec. 2, https://www.vatican.va/roman_curia/synod/documents/rc_synod_doc_20090319_instrlabor-africa_en.html.

22. Benedict XVI, "Homily of His Holiness Benedict XVI," 4.

23. Charles E. Curran, *Catholic Social Teaching and Pope Benedict XVI* (Washington, DC: Georgetown University Press, 2014), 49.

24. Synod of Bishops, "The Church in Africa," 72.

25. Synod of Bishops, "The Church in Africa," 36.

26. Synod of Bishops, "The Church in Africa," 90.

27. Teresa Okure, "Church-Family of God: The Place of God's Reconciliation, Justice, and Peace," in *Reconciliation, Justice, and Peace: The Second African Synod*, ed. A. E. Orobator (Maryknoll, NY: Orbis Books, 2011), 13.

28. Synod of Bishops, "The Church in Africa," 41.

29. Synod of Bishops, "The Church in Africa," 61.

30. Benedict XVI, "Angelus" (July 2, 2006), https://www.vatican.va/content/benedict-xvi/en/angelus/2006/documents/hf_ben-xvi_ang_20060702.html.

31. Synod of Bishops, "The Church in Africa," 61.

32. Benedict XVI, "Apostolic Journey of the Holy Father."

33. Synod of Bishops, "The Church in Africa," 47.

34. Benedict XVI, "Homily of His Holiness Benedict XVI," 2.

35. Benedict XVI, "Homily of His Holiness Benedict XVI," 278.

36. Luka Lusala lu ne Nkuka, *De l'origine Égyptienne des Bakongo: Étude syntaxique et lexicologique comparative des langues r n Kmt et kikongo* (Centre-ville, Québec: Éditions de l'Érablière, 2020), 704–5.

37. Asante and Mazama, *Encyclopedia of African Religion*, 250.

38. Asante and Mazama, *Encyclopedia of African Religion*, 109.

39. A. E. Orobator, "No Lid Put on This Bubbling Pot: The Papal Audit the World Church; Africa," *The Tablet* 8–9 (2013): 2, https://epublications.marquette.edu/cgi/viewcontent.cgi?article=1491&context=theo_fac.

40. A. E. Orobator, ed., *Reconciliation, Justice, and Peace: The Second African Synod* (Maryknoll, NY: Orbis Books, 2011).

41. Curran, *Catholic Social Teaching and Pope Benedict XVI*, 33.

42. Lusala lu ne Nkuka, *De l'origine Égyptienne des Bakongo*, 61.

43. Asante and Mazama, *Encyclopedia of African Religion*, 23.

44. Asante and Mazama, *Encyclopedia of African Religion*, 24.

45. Asante and Mazama, *Encyclopedia of African Religion*, 100.

46. Théophile Obenga, "La Parenté Égyptienne : Considérations Sociologiques," *ANKH* 4, no. 5 (1995–1996): 147.

47. Obenga, "La Parenté Égyptienne," 141.

48. Obenga, "La Parenté Égyptienne," 141.

49. UN Women, "Progress of the World's Women 2019–2020," 2019, 16, https://www.unwomen.org/sites/default/files/Headquarters/Attachments/Sections/Library/Publications/2019/Progress-of-the-worlds-women-2019-2020-en.pdf.

50. Asante and Mazama, *Encyclopedia of African Religion*, 47.

51. Asante and Mazama, *Encyclopedia of African Religion*, 101.

52. Asante and Mazama, *Encyclopedia of African Religion*, 288.

53. *The Real Wealth of Nations: Pathways to Human Development*, twentieth anniversary ed., Human Development Report 2010 (New York: United Nations Development Programme, 2010), 169–71.

54. United Nations Development Programme, ed., *The Next Frontier: Human Development and the Anthropocene*, Human Development Report 2020 (New York: United Nations Development Programme, 2020), 344.

55. The World Bank, "Female Headed Households (% of Households with a Female Head)," Metadata Glossary, n.d., https://datacatalog.world bank.org/public-licenses#cc-by.

56. Kathleen Beegle and Dominique Van de Walle, "What Can Female Headship Tell Us about Women's Wellbeing? Probably Not Much," World Bank Blogs, June 6, 2019, https://blogs.worldbank.org/impactevaluations/what-can-female-headship-tell-us-about-womens-well-being-probably-not-much.

57. Asante and Mazama, *Encyclopedia of African Religion*, 84.

58. UN Women, "Progress of the World's Women 2019–2020," 57.

59. UN Women, "Progress of the World's Women 2019–2020," 36.

60. UN Women, "Progress of the World's Women 2019–2020," 117.

61. UN Women, "Progress of the World's Women 2019–2020," 2.

*Francis*

# CHAPTER

# 22

## The Synods on the Family

MARY BETH YOUNT

## CONTEXT

Pope Francis has brought many changes since his election in 2013. Among the most significant of these is uplifting input from lived experiences. His focus on contextual development—allowing teaching and pastoral practice to develop through grassroots movements and the experiences of those "on the ground"—remains an ongoing process. This approach was clearly conveyed through the processes of the 2014 and 2015 synods on the family, which tested many of the pontificate's approaches and priorities.

Francis clearly strives to prioritize and uplift the voices of those who are often marginalized and whose contributions are often overlooked. He described the role of synodality in a 2015 address commemorating the fiftieth anniversary of the Synod of Bishops as follows:

For Blessed Paul VI, the Synod of Bishops was meant to reproduce the image of the Ecumenical Council and reflect its spirit and method. Pope Paul foresaw that the organization of the Synod could "be improved upon with the passing of time." Twenty years later, Saint John Paul II echoed that thought when he stated that "this instrument might be further improved. Perhaps collegial pastoral

responsibility could be more fully expressed in the Synod." In 2006, Benedict XVI approved several changes to the *Ordo Synodi Episcoporum*. . . . We must continue along this path. The world in which we live, and which we are called to love and serve, even with its contradictions, demands that the Church strengthen cooperation in all areas of her mission. It is precisely this path of *synodality* which God expects of the Church of the third millennium.[1]

Francis's practice of visiting representative places to occupy spaces with people, sharing experiences while listening as possible, and soliciting broad input via synods (even including laypeople in the ecclesial synodal process itself) enables the Catholic Church to be in solidarity with and inclusive of those on the margins in a radical way and allows praxis to inform reflections, conversations, and ways of teaching.

The 2014 and 2015 synods on the family contributed to Catholic Family Teaching through a variety of documents and demonstrated both the developmental possibilities and the limitations of synod processes that draw upon tradition while informing ecclesial reflection with a plurality of voices describing current experiences that impact understanding and contextualization of that tradition.

223

## COMMENTARY

The structures of these synods, officially the III Extraordinary General Assembly of the Synod of Bishops on the Family of October 2014 and the XIV Ordinary General Assembly of the Synod of Bishops on the Family of October 2015, were intended to include many voices. Additionally, Francis's "step-by-step" approach built fuller participation through events including the World Meeting of Families (WMOF) held in Philadelphia in September 2015 and, to a lesser degree, the Humanum colloquium, hosted at the Vatican in November 2014.[2]

### The 2014 Extraordinary Synod

The 2014 synod built on the theme "The Pastoral Challenges of the Family in the Context of Evangelization." This was an "extraordinary" synod, outside of the regular cycle, called to address particular pressing issues, in this case, several intertwined topics related to the family in preparation for the larger ordinary synod. The purpose of the 2014 synod and its relation to the 2015 synod are described in its preparatory document of November 2013:

> Never before has proclaiming the Gospel on the Family in this context been more urgent and necessary. The importance of the subject is reflected in the fact that the Holy Father has decided to call for a Synod of Bishops, which is to have a two-staged itinerary: firstly, an Extraordinary General Assembly in 2014, intended to define the "status quaestionis" [current state of investigation] and to collect the bishops' experiences and proposals in proclaiming and living the Gospel of the Family in a credible manner; and secondly, an Ordinary General Assembly in 2015 to seek working guidelines in the pastoral care of the person and the family.[3]

The preparatory document further outlined the purposes of each synod, provided a basic catechesis on the "Gospel of the Family," and requested input on eight groups of questions about the current state of pastoral care

for marriages and families. This questionnaire was to be "distributed worldwide" and by the following year resulted in "a great number of detailed responses . . . submitted by the synods of the Eastern Catholic Churches *sui iuris*, the episcopal conferences, the departments of the Roman Curia and the Union of Superiors General."[4] Other responses, "categorized as observations," were also submitted by people and groups "interested in sharing their reflections."[5] The *Instrumentum laboris* of June 2014, conveyed the results of the preparatory document's questionnaire, outlined topics to be discussed at the 2014 synod, and invited bishops to prepare for that assembly.[6]

Francis's address in Saint Peter's Square on the eve of the 2014 synod set out his hopes for the work of the gathering and conveyed his awareness that the process would include considerable controversy among the bishops. Speaking to families and emphasizing the goals for the synod's accomplishments, he stated,

> The *convenire in unum* around the Bishop of Rome is indeed an event of grace, in which episcopal collegiality is made manifest in a path of spiritual and pastoral discernment. To find what the Lord asks of his Church today, we must lend an ear to the debates of our time and perceive the "fragrance" of the men of this age, so as to be permeated with their joys and hopes, with their griefs and anxieties (cf. *Gaudium et Spes*, n. 1). At that moment we will know how to propose the good news on the family with credibility.[7]

In order for this manifestation of collegiality and wisdom to come about, the pope petitioned:

> For the Synod Fathers we ask the Holy Spirit first of all for the gift of listening: to listen to God, that with him we may hear the cry of the people; to listen to the people until breathing in the will to which God calls us. Along with listening, we invoke openness toward a sincere, open and fraternal discussion, which leads us to carry with pastoral responsibility the questions that this epochal

change brings with it. Let us allow it to flow back into our hearts, never losing peace, but with serene trust which in his own time the Lord will not fail to lead us back into unity. Does Church history not perhaps—we know it does—recount many similar situations, which our Fathers were able to overcome with persistent patience and creativity?[8]

In his homily the following morning, Francis cautioned that "synod Assemblies are not meant to discuss beautiful and clever ideas, or to see who is more intelligent.... [T]he Lord is asking us to care for the family.... We are all sinners and can also be tempted to 'take over' the vineyard, because of that greed which is always present in us human beings." He then warned that "God's dream always clashes with the hypocrisy of some of his servants" and closed with an exhortation to allow the Holy Spirit to work.[9]

Throughout the 2014 synod, working groups engaged in conversation and gave brief presentations, while couples gave testimonies. Francis's address to the bishops on its conclusion rejoiced, cautioned, and commissioned them to prepare spiritually for the following synod.[10] Sending them forth, the pope pointed his audience to the next stage: a "year to mature, with true spiritual discernment, the proposed ideas and to find concrete solutions to so many difficulties and innumerable challenges that families must confront."[11] The following day, Francis led a mass both closing the synod and beatifying Paul VI. The *Relatio synodi* was also released,[12] which Francis described as "the faithful and clear summary of everything that has been said and discussed in this hall and in the small groups."[13]

### The 2014 Humanum Colloquium

In alignment with typical Vatican processes, congregations (now called dicasteries) hosted special events in and among the synods in relation to their work. Significant among these was the Humanum colloquium, which was opened by Francis in Vatican City on November 17, 2014, and gathered 180 representatives from

fourteen religious traditions and twenty-three countries.[14] The colloquium, held in Synod Hall, set out to examine human experience as it relates to male and female complementarity across religions. Francis's opening remarks set the stage for the conversations more broadly than is often the case. "When we speak of complementarity between man and woman in this context, we must not confuse the term with the simplistic idea that all the roles and relationships of both sexes are confined to a single and static model. Complementarity assumes many forms."[15] He further urged participants to "emphasize yet another truth about marriage: that the permanent commitment to solidarity, fidelity and fruitful love responds to the deepest longings of the human heart," then cautioned that "we must not fall into the trap of being limited by ideological concepts. The family is an anthropological fact, and consequently a social, cultural fact, etc. We cannot qualify it with ideological concepts which are compelling at only one moment in history, and then decline."[16] In closing, the pope expressed his wishes for the colloquium and announced his intention to attend the WMOF, to which the crowd responded with cheers and applause.

### The 2015 World Meeting of Families

Although the WMOF was a regularly scheduled event, it was imbued with special significance given the timing of its occurrence. On December 19, 2014, Pope Francis sent a letter to Archbishop Vincenzo Paglia ostensibly written to officially confirm, again, his attendance. As much more than official confirmation, the letter conveyed the theme of the WMOF, detailed various emphases of the event, and situated it within the extraordinary and ordinary synods on the family:

> The indications of the Final Report of the recent Synod, and the guidelines of the upcoming Ordinary Assembly of October 2015, invite people to fulfil in their commitment to proclaim the Gospel of marriage and of the family and to experience the pastoral proposals in the social and cultural

context in which we live. The challenges of this context should stimulate us to enlarge the space afforded to faithful love open to life, to communion, to mercy, to sharing and to solidarity.[17]

In its emphasis on the continuity of the WMOF with the synods, the letter lays stepping stones, from the work of the 2014 synod to the Humanum colloquium's emphasis on the expansion of complementarity and the family beyond ideological constraints to the WMOF. The latest of these, organized on the theme "Love Is Our Mission. The Family Fully Alive," sought to advance the Christian family's mission of "proclaiming to the world, by the power of the Sacrament of Marriage, the love of God" in preparation for the 2015 synod.[18]

### *The 2015 Ordinary Synod*

The 2015 synod also marked the fiftieth anniversary of the institution of the Synod of Bishops in the postconciliar church. Building from the 2014 synod, the 2015 synod's purpose was to "reflect further on the points discussed so as to formulate appropriate pastoral guidelines."[19] In what Cardinal Lorenzo Baldisseri, Secretary-General of the synod, described as demonstrating "the continuity between the two Assemblies," the first part of *Instrumentum laboris*, "Considering the Challenges of the Family," drew heavily on the 2014 synod. The second and third parts, "The Discernment of the Vocation of the Family" and "The Mission of the Family Today," Baldisserie explained, "introduce the topic of the second phase with the intention of offering to the Church and the contemporary world pastoral incentives to spur renewed efforts in evangelization."[20]

Some elements of *Instrumentum laboris* were controversial, as was the newly public nature of the synods' structures. During the synod, Archbishop Charles Chaput of Philadelphia, a delegate to the 2015 synod, voiced representative apprehensions of those with more traditionalist views in the *Wall Street Journal*. Chaput expressed concerns with the public nature of synod conversations and possible adaptations

to church teaching. To illustrate, he offered a story of a husband whose repeated insistence that he had never been unfaithful caused his wife to question. Chaput concludes that "even when done innocently, emphasizing one's fidelity a little too often and earnestly can yield unwelcome results. Such may be the case in Rome, where more than 250 Catholic bishops from around the world have gathered in a three-week synod, ending Oct. 25, to discuss 'the vocation and mission of the family in the contemporary world.'" Chaput then details his concerns with the synodal new process. "Pope Francis has encouraged candor at this meeting. Bishops can freely speak with the media. They can publish their synod interventions, which are three-minute speeches to the assembly, and many do. . . . Much of this differs from the past."[21] Finally, he notes his specific concerns with the *Instrumentum laboris*:

> Veterans of these gatherings note that every synod working document is a "martyr text." It exists to be pulled apart and improved. But precisely because the process this time is so new, the issues so neuralgic, the text so flawed and the working time frame so compressed, anxiety about the final product runs high. . . . What is at issue is the application of church teaching. In the case of divorced and civilly remarried Catholics, that means whether they should be admitted to Communion, under what conditions, and who should decide those conditions—the local bishop, bishops' conferences or Rome? Many bishops feel that the last thing the church needs is fragmentation of practice on a matter of substance. And that brings us back to the lesson of my married friend. The more some synod fathers claim that no doctrinal change is sought on matters of divorce and remarriage—only a change in "discipline"—the more other synod fathers worry. And for good reason. Practice inevitably shapes belief.[22]

In contrast to those who worried over potential doctrinal development, other bishops and laypeople advocated for change. One such initiative was the Catholic Women Speak Network, which launched a book in Rome just before the 2015 synod began, providing copies to the bishops in attendance. Nontando Hadebe explains that this "concrete intervention" was an important way to make the voices of people heard. She writes that "ideals cannot be realised without justice and equality that translates into the full inclusion and participation of groups experiencing the 'unequal equality' phenomenon."[23]

In his early remarks at the 2015 synod, including words from prayer vigil on the eve of the conference, a homily for the opening of the synod, and introductory remarks to the assembly, Francis repeated sentiments from the year prior. Notably, he also clarified that "the Synod is neither a convention, nor a 'parlour,' a parliament nor senate, where people make deals and reach a consensus. The Synod is rather an ecclesial expression, i.e., the Church that journeys together to understand reality.... The Synod is also a protected space in which the Church experiences the action of the Holy Spirit."[24]

At the conclusion of the 2015 synod, Francis posed the question "What will it mean for the Church to conclude this Synod devoted to the family?" He answered,

> Certainly, the Synod was not about settling all the issues having to do with the family, but rather attempting to see them in the light of the Gospel and the Church's tradition and two-thousand-year history, bringing the joy of hope ... not about finding exhaustive solutions for all the difficulties and uncertainties which challenge and threaten the family, but rather about seeing these difficulties and uncertainties in the light of the Faith."[25]

Affirming existing teaching, Francis added, "It was about urging everyone to appreciate the importance of the institution of the family and of marriage between a man and a woman, based on unity and indissolubility, and valuing it as the fundamental basis of society and human life" while also "trying to view and interpret realities, today's realities, through God's eyes, so as to kindle the flame of faith and enlighten people's hearts in times marked by discouragement, social, economic and moral crisis, and growing pessimism."[26]

Francis also noted the richness brought about by a global gathering and emphasized the importance of conscience:

> And—apart from dogmatic questions clearly defined by the Church's Magisterium—we have also seen that what seems normal for a bishop on one continent, is considered strange and almost scandalous—almost!—for a bishop from another; what is considered a violation of a right in one society is an evident and inviolable rule in another; what for some is freedom of conscience is for others simply confusion. Cultures are in fact quite diverse, and every general principle—as I said, dogmatic questions clearly defined by the Church's magisterium—every general principle needs to be inculturated, if it is to be respected and applied.[27]

Moving beyond doctrine was a pervasive theme. As Francis noted, the synod "was about bearing witness to everyone that, for the Church, the Gospel continues to be a vital source of eternal newness, against all those who would 'indoctrinate' it in dead stones to be hurled at others." The synod, he added, "also made us better realize that the true defenders of doctrine are not those who uphold its letter, but its spirit; not ideas but people; not formulae but the gratuitousness of God's love and forgiveness."[28]

In these remarks as elsewhere, Francis highlighted the role of the conscience in moving beyond dogmatic laws toward an applied theology in the contexts of individuals and cultures. This focus on conscience was echoed again by the 2015 synod's final report. James T. Bretzke, SJ, notes that "conscience more than doubled its appearance in the 2015 Synod Final Report (FR), going from three to seven instances."[29]

In his homily at the concluding mass, Francis cautioned against "falling into a 'scheduled faith'" and encouraged openness to inspiration, referring to "the search for the paths which the Gospel indicates for our times so that we can proclaim the mystery of family love."[30]

That same day, October 25, 2015, the *Relatio finalis* was promulgated. It noted the challenges of communicating church teaching and was expectedly controversial, especially regarding the pastoral care for the divorced and remarried, persons in nonmarital sexual relationships, and same-sex relationships both with and without children.[31]

In the end, three notable paragraphs out of sixty-two total did not receive the two-thirds majority necessary for inclusion. Their topics covered admitting those who are divorced and remarried to Holy Communion, further theological exploration of pastoral practice for such persons, and a clarification that those in same-sex relationships need to be "received with respect and sensitivity."[32] Despite lacking supermajority consensus at the 2014 synod, these topics had remained in the documents and discussions in 2015. As Father Federico Lombardi, director of the press office for the Holy See, had explained the previous year, though the paragraphs lacked sufficient support for inclusion in the 2014 final report, they "'cannot be considered as dismissed, but primarily as paragraphs that are not mature enough to gain a wide consensus of the assembly.'"[33]

## INTERPRETATION

The 2015 *Relatio finalis* reveals the initial results of an extended synodal process in the church's attempts, under Francis, to speak to the needs of families in the contemporary world. The report emphasizes pastoral care and the need to adapt pastoral practice. Through this focus, local contexts become important for consideration and the movements of and decisions by individual consciences, informed by love, to guide the application and transmission of this contextualized teaching. The document's emphasis on following the model of Jesus highlights compassion over legalism:

Seeing things as Christ would see them inspires the Church's pastoral care for the faithful who are living together or who are only married civilly or who are divorced and remarried. From the vantage point of divine pedagogy, the Church turns with love to those who participate in her life in an imperfect manner: she seeks the grace of conversion for them, she encourages them to do good, to lovingly take care of each other and to serve the community in which they live and work.[34]

This is followed by support for discernment that involves people in the life of the community.

Paragraph 54 surfaces themes related to the divorced and civilly remarried, cohabitating couples, and, arguably, same-sex couples. It notes that "a couple in an irregular union" that is stable, public, and "characterized by deep affection, responsibility towards the children and the ability to overcome trials" may provide an opportunity "to lead the couple to celebrating the Sacrament of Matrimony." However, many "persons live together without a desire for a future marriage. . . . Civil marriages between a man and a woman, traditional marriage and, taking into account the difference due, even cohabitation are emerging phenomena in many countries" (*RF* 54). In this case, the church must offer "'a fraternal and attentive welcome, in love and in truth, of the baptized who have established a new relationship of cohabitation after the failure of the marital sacrament; in fact, these persons are by no means excommunicated'" (*RF* 4). This statement is drawn from a general audience delivered by Francis shortly before the synod that appears to have expressed his developing insights during the synod preparations.

The section regarding respect for homosexual persons and those in same-sex relationships clarifies that "the Church's attitude is like that of her Master, who offers his boundless love to every person without exception [cf. MV, 12]. To families with homosexual members, the Church reiterates that every person, regardless of sexual orientation, ought to be respected in his/her dignity and received with respect, while carefully avoiding 'every sign of unjust discrimination'" (*RF* 76). The section then distinguishes between same-sex unions and "God's plan" for marriage. Repeating the Congregation for the

Doctrine of the Faith's judgment from 2003, it states, "Regarding proposals to place unions of homosexual persons on the same level as marriage, 'there are absolutely no grounds for considering homosexual unions to be in any way similar or even remotely analogous to God's plan for marriage and family.'"[35]

Same-sex parenthood is acknowledged in a later section on reproductive technology, stating that "human life and parenthood have become a modular and separable reality, subject mainly to the wishes of individuals or couples, who are not necessarily heterosexual and properly married" (*RF* 33). The topic emerges again in a section on adoption and foster parenting that emphasizes sexual complementarity as an essential aspect of parenthood. "Continuity in the relationships of parenting and upbringing, by necessity, is based, as in procreation, on the sexual difference of a man and a woman.... The best interests of the child should always underlie any decision in adoption and foster care. As noted by Pope Francis, 'children have the right to grow up in a family with a father and a mother'" (*RF* 65).[36]

The final report conveys that much of church teaching on the family is countercultural and needs to be communicated so as to "make people experience the Gospel of the Family as a response to the deepest longings of the human person, a response to his/her dignity and a response to complete personal fulfilment in reciprocity, communion and fruitfulness." In so doing it must announce "the grace which provides the ability to live the goods of the family ... to communicate the beauty of love in the family and make people understand the meaning of terms such as self-giving, conjugal love, fidelity, fruitfulness and procreation" (*RF* 56).

Interestingly, the document clearly acknowledges that this type of proclamation—in light of the gospel and focusing on grace and beauty—is not being fully realized. There is a need for more effective language for conveying teaching on sexuality to young people, and "many parents and people who are involved in pastoral work have difficulty finding an appropriate yet respectful language to bring together

the biological and complementary natures of sexuality which enrich each other through friendship, love and the self-giving of a man and a woman" (*RF* 56). Francis' postsynodal exhortation, *Amoris laetitia*, carries this further, explaining—and some say developing—teaching on marriage and the family through a contextual approach in continuity with his conviction, evidenced throughout the synodal process, that teaching is to be applied and communicated in the context of lived experiences.

## NOTES

1. Francis, "Address at Ceremony Commemorating the 50th Anniversary of the Institution of the Synod of Bishops" (October 17, 2015), https://www.vatican.va/content/francesco/en/speeches/2015/october/documents/papa-francesco_20151017_50-anniversario-sinodo.html.
2. See Appendix 1 of this volume for a reproduction of the original letter obtained by the author.
3. Synod of Bishops, III Extraordinary General Assembly, "Pastoral Challenges to the Family in the Context of Evangelization: Preparatory Document" (November 5, 2013), https://www.vatican.va/roman_curia/synod/documents/rc_synod_doc_20131105_iii-assemblea-sinodo-vescovi_en.html.
4. Synod of Bishops, III Extraordinary General Assembly, "Pastoral Challenges to the Family in the Context of Evangelization: *Instrumentum Laboris*" (June 16, 2014), https://www.vatican.va/roman_curia/synod/documents/rc_synod_doc_20140626_instrumentum-laboris-familia_en.html.
5. Synod of Bishops, "*Instrumentum laboris*" (2014).
6. Author's note: In my role as director of content and programming for the 2015 WMOF, I was provided most of the reports submitted by the episcopal conferences, some of which had been made public. These summarized the results of the consultation questionnaires. They were fascinating and surfaced sometimes surprising priorities of different locales around the world. Concerns raised by the Association of Member Episcopal Conferences in Eastern Africa, for example, exemplified themes not noted as priorities for the United States in the list of "polygamy, poor parenting, economic problems, impact of education systems, the distortion of the meaning of

marriage, gender violence and other abuses that negatively affect the family." See also Cardinal Robert Sarah's discussion of issues for African families, including forced marriage, underage marriage, a view of wives as property, and "the influence of pagan cultures, for example polygamy, and the harmful effects of poverty on family life." Deborah Castellano Lubov, "Cardinal Sarah: Crisis of Today's Families Is How Concepts of Marriage, Family Have Changed," Zenit, October 23, 2014, https://zenit.org/2014/10/23/cardinal-sarah-crisis-of-today-s-families-is-how-concepts-of-marriage-family-have-changed/.

7. Francis, "Address of His Holiness Pope Francis during the Meeting on the Family" (October 4, 2014), https://www.vatican.va/content/francesco/en/speeches/2014/october/documents/papa-francesco_20141004_incontro-per-la-famiglia.html.

8. Francis, "Address of His Holiness Pope Francis during the Meeting on the Family."

9. Francis, "Homily at the Mass for the Opening of the Extraordinary Synod on the Family" (October 5, 2014), https://www.vatican.va/content/francesco/en/homilies/2014/documents/papa-francesco_20141005_omelia-apertura-sinodo-vescovi.html.

10. Francis, "Homily at the Mass for the Opening of the Extraordinary Synod."

11. Francis, "Address for the Conclusion of the Third Extraordinary General Assembly of the Synod of Bishops" (October 18, 2014), https://www.vatican.va/content/francesco/en/speeches/2014/october/documents/papa-francesco_20141018_conclusione-sinodo-dei-vescovi.html.

12. See Francis, "Homily by Pope Francis at the Closing Mass of the Extraordinary Synod on the Family and Beatification of the Servant of God Paul VI" (October 19, 2014), https://www.vatican.va/content/francesco/en/homilies/2014/documents/papa-francesco_20141019_omelia-chiusura-sinodo-beatificazione-paolo-vi.html; and Synod of Bishops, III Extraordinary General Assembly, "The Pastoral Challenges of the Family in the Context of Evangelization: *Relatio Synodi*" (October 18, 2014), https://www.vatican.va/roman_curia/synod/documents/rc_synod_doc_20141018_relatio-synodi-familia_en.html.

13. Francis, "Address for the Conclusion of the Third Extraordinary General Assembly."

14. Some of what is recounted here is from the author's experience as an invited delegate. For a

brief summary of the event, see Ann Schenible, "Sex Complementarity Is the 'Human Experience,' Not a Political Agenda," *Catholic News Agency*, November 20, 2014, https://www.catholicnewsagency.com/news/30967/sex-complementarity-is-the-human-experience-not-a-political-agenda.

15. Francis, "Address to Participants in the International Colloquium on the Complementarity between Man and Woman," *Congregation for the Doctrine of the Faith*, November 17, 2014, https://www.vatican.va/content/francesco/en/speeches/2014/november/documents/papa-francesco_20141117_congregazione-dottrina-fede.html.

16. Francis, "Address to Participants in the International Colloquium."

17. Francis, "Letter of His Holiness Pope Francis for the 8th World Meeting of Families" (December 9, 2014), https://www.vatican.va/content/francesco/en/letters/2014/documents/papa-francesco_20141210_lettera-incontro-mondiale-famiglie.html. The online version is slightly revised from the original, which, as noted above, can be found in Appendix 1 of the volume.

18. Francis, "Letter of His Holiness Pope Francis for the 8th World Meeting of Families."

19. Synod of Bishops, *Instrumentum laboris* (2014).

20. Synod of Bishops, XIV Ordinary General Assembly, "The Vocation and Mission of the Family in the Church and the Contemporary World: *Instrumentum Laboris*" (June 23, 2015), https://www.vatican.va/roman_curia/synod/documents/rc_synod_doc_20150623_instrumentum-xiv-assembly_en.html.

21. Charles Chaput, "How to Read the Vatican Family Gathering," *Wall Street Journal*, October 15, 2015, https://www.wsj.com/articles/how-to-read-the-vatican-family-gathering-1444948185.

22. Chaput, "How to Read the Vatican Family Gathering." Cf. chapter 3 of this volume for Ford's explanation of the tensions between two syntheses of natural law in which moral norms variously precede or follow experience.

23. Nontando Hadebe, "'Not in Our Name without Us'—The Intervention of Catholic Women Speak at the Synod of Bishops on the Family: A Case Study of a Global Resistance Movement by Catholic Women," *Theological Studies* 72, no. 1 (2016): 8.

24. Synod of Bishops, "Introductory Remarks by His Holiness Pope Francis" (October 5, 2015), https://www.vatican.va/content/francesco/en/speeches/2015/october/documents/papa-francesco_20151005_padri-sinodali.html.

25. Francis, "Conclusion of the Synod of Bishops: Address of His Holiness Pope Francis" (October 24, 2015), https://www.vatican.va/content/francesco/en/speeches/2015/october/documents/papa-francesco_20151024_sinodo-conclusione-lavori.html.

26. Francis, "Conclusion of the Synod of Bishops."

27. Francis, "Conclusion of the Synod of Bishops."

28. Francis, "Conclusion of the Synod of Bishops."

29. James T. Bretzke, SJ, "Symposium on the 2015 Synod of Bishops on the Family–Conscience and the Synod: An Evolving *Quaestio Disputata*," *Journal of Moral Theology* 5, no. 2 (2016): 168. Bretzke's examination of "three instances on Generative Responsibility which actually seem to expand the treatment in the *Instrumentum Laboris*, no. 137," is worth particular attention.

30. Francis, "Homily of Pope Francis at the Mass for the Conclusion of the Synod" (October 25, 2015), https://www.vatican.va/content/francesco/en/homilies/2015/documents/papa-francesco_20151025_omelia-chiusura-sinodo-vescovi.html.

31. Synod of Bishops, XIV Ordinary General Assembly, "The Vocation and Mission of the Family in the Church and in the Contemporary World: The Final Report of the Synod of Bishops to the Holy Father" (October 24, 2015), https://www.vatican.va/roman_curia/synod/documents/rc_synod_doc_20151026_relazione-finale-xiv-assemblea_en.html (hereafter cited as *RF*).

32. Synod of Bishops, XIV Ordinary General Assembly, "The Vocation and Mission of the Family in the Church and in the Contemporary World," 53.

33. "Synod's Final Report Shows Nuance on Homosexuality, Remarriage," *Catholic News Agency*, October 18, 2014, https://www.catholicnewsagency.com/news/30753/synods-final-report-shows-nuance-on-homosexuality-remarriage.

34. Synod of Bishops, XIV Ordinary General Assembly, "The Vocation and Mission of the Family in the Church and in the Contemporary World," 53.

35. Synod of Bishops, XIV Ordinary General Assembly, "The Vocation and Mission of the Family in the Church and in the Contemporary World," 76. Cf. Congregation for the Doctrine of the Faith, "Considerations Regarding Proposals to Give Legal Recognition to Unions between Homosexual Persons" (July 31, 2003), 4, https://www.vatican.va/roman_curia/congregations/cfaith/documents/rc_con_cfaith_doc_20030731_homosexual-unions_en.html. See also chapter 19 in this volume.

36. The quote is from Francis's address at the Humanum colloquium.

# 23

## *Amoris Laetitia*

TERESA DELGADO

## CONTEXT

On November 11, 2022, Pope Francis received James Martin, a Jesuit priest, for a private meeting at the Vatican. This was the second audience Francis held with the author of *Building a Bridge: How the Catholic Church and the LGBT Community Can Enter into a Relationship of Respect, Compassion, and Sensitivity*.[1] It is interesting to note that this meeting came six and a half years after the publication of *Amoris laetitia* and during a period of tremendous suffering and struggle for communities and families across the globe, exacerbated by the COVID-19 pandemic, the ecological crisis, forced migration, war and conflict, and growing inequality. *Amoris laetitia* is Francis's most significant contribution to Catholic Family Teaching and was published thirty-four years after John Paul II's apostolic exhortation *Familiaris consortio* (1981)[2] and following the documents of the Congregation for the Doctrine of the Faith that clarified the Catholic Church's response to homosexuality and same-sex relationships from 1986 to 2003.[3] *Amoris laetitia* further draws upon the work of two synodal gatherings, the Extraordinary General Assembly of 2014 and the Ordinary General Assembly of 2015, both devoted to the family and evangelization.

Like many of its predecessors in this documentary tradition, *Amoris laetitia* has provoked much debate and discussion since its release, particularly regarding its stance on adultery, same-sex unions, and sex, to name a few controversial topics. Despite this, Francis's apostolic exhortation and Martin's book hold a similar intention, reflected in Martin's commentary on *Amoris laetitia*. In this document, he explains, Francis seeks "to meet people where they are, to consider the complexities of people's lives and to respect people's consciences when it comes to moral decisions. The apostolic exhortation is ... the pope's reminder that the church should avoid simply judging people and imposing rules on them without considering their struggles."[4]

As a Puerto Rican Catholic theologian, I would like to begin where Francis does in the apostolic exhortation itself. That is, he chose to ground *Amoris laetitia* in the challenges facing families around the world and devotes an extensive second chapter to this reality titled "The Experiences and Reality of Families."[5] As one who affirms the embodied *locus theologicus* of Black and brown bodies, I begin with a reading of this document through a womanist lens that foregrounds the survival and flourishing of Black and brown people, our *gente*, and our families, our *familias*. I begin with a story.

## COMMENTARY

In 2017, Jeanette Vizguerra was living in Denver, Colorado. She was an undocumented immigrant, a mother of four, and a longtime leader in the immigrant and labor movements in Colorado who had resided in the United States for approximately twenty years. She entered the United States from Mexico in 1997 and was living free from any legal difficulty until 2009, when she admitted to using a falsified (not stolen) social security number to gain employment. By then she had three of her four children in the country and was granted a stay, since she was not considered a high priority based on her clear record. According to the *Denver Post*, Vizguerra stayed despite having been ordered to leave the country because she received several deportation postponements from the courts. She was also actively seeking a visa and was being supported by the mayor of Denver as well as members of Colorado's congressional delegation.[6] Vizguerra was required to check in with Immigration and Customs Enforcement on February 15, 2017, but, given the Trump administration's stance regarding undocumented persons, she was concerned that she would be deported this time. She calculated correctly. Instead, she took refuge in the basement of the First Unitarian Church in Denver with the three of her four children who were citizens of the United States. Vizguerra continued to live there with her children under the threat of deportation, as Immigration and Customs Enforcement officials had yet to serve her notice.[7] She was finally granted a stay of deportation in December 2021 by the Biden administration. While this was not a permanent solution, Vizguerra was able to emerge from the sanctuary of the Colorado church committed to working on a pathway to citizenship for many undocumented immigrants like her who have lived in the shadows and in fear for many years.[8]

Jeanette Vizguerra's story recounts many of the challenges and the hopes of families from the margins of society who are identified in the second chapter of *Amoris laetitia*. Here, Francis outlines the burdens of families in the context of migration in both its causes and consequences:

> Forced migration of families, resulting from situations of war, persecution, poverty and injustice, and marked by the vicissitudes of a journey that often puts lives at risk, traumatizes people and destabilizes families.... Migration is particularly dramatic and devastating to families and individuals when it takes place illegally and is supported by international networks of human trafficking. This is equally true when it involves women or unaccompanied children who are forced to endure long periods of time in temporary facilities and refugee camps, where it is impossible to start a process of integration. Extreme poverty and other situations of family breakdown sometimes even lead families to sell their children for prostitution or for organ trafficking. (*AL* 46)

Francis goes on to identify conditions of poverty facing families:

> If a single mother has to raise a child by herself and needs to leave the child alone at home while she goes to work, the child can grow up exposed to all kind of risks and obstacles to personal growth. In such difficult situations of need, the Church must be particularly concerned to offer understanding, comfort and acceptance, rather than imposing straightaway a set of rules that only lead people to feel judged and abandoned by the very Mother called to show them God's mercy. Rather than offering the healing power of grace and the light of the Gospel message, some would "indoctrinate" that message, turning it into "dead stones to be hurled at others." (*AL* 49)

Finally, Francis also names the reality of violence against women:

> I think particularly of the shameful ill-treatment to which women are sometimes subjected, domestic violence and various forms of enslavement which, rather than a

show of masculine power, are craven acts of cowardice. The verbal, physical, and sexual violence that women endure in some marriages contradicts the very nature of the conjugal union. I think of the reprehensible genital mutilation of women practiced in some cultures, but also of their lack of equal access to dignified work and roles of decision-making. (*AL* 54)

Each of these moments of what Jon Sobrino names "a fidelity to the real" reflects a recognition that forced migration, poverty, and gender violence compromise the mere possibility of love, joy, and, yes, even sex (if one understands sex as an occasion of love's generativity, broadly speaking).[9] How can a person begin to speak of the joy of the family, the joy of sex, the joy of love when one's reality is circumscribed by fear above all else, as in the case of Jeanette Vizguerra? Where is the joy as she is faced with the possibility of being separated from the family she loves and who loves her? These questions raise yet another: How does God's love encounter us in such a precarious situation as Jeanette's, and where is the church as the mediator of God's love in such conditions especially for those most vulnerable in our world?

*Amoris laetitia*'s nine chapters, each with a focus on a specific aspect of family life, seek to respond to these very questions. Francis begins the exhortation with "In the Light of the Word," grounding the life of family in the revelation of the biblical text as a source of insight and inspiration. The second chapter, "The Experiences and Reality of Families," communicates Francis's understanding of the contemporary challenges faced by families around the world and for which the church must demonstrate compassion. The third chapter, "Looking to Jesus: The Vocation of the Family," centers Jesus as the exemplar of love and kindness to be mirrored in family life, even in the midst of the aforementioned challenges. The fourth chapter, "Love in Marriage," provides a multifaceted understanding of the ways love is enfleshed and embodied—sexually and otherwise—in married life, understood as the sacramental union between a woman and a man. In

the fifth chapter, "Love Made Fruitful," Francis reflects on the generativity of marital love through children (born and adopted) as well as through engagement with and for the community. The sixth chapter, "Some Pastoral Perspectives," offers guidance for those ministering to married persons and families, informed by feedback from the synods of 2014 and 2015. The seventh chapter, "Toward a Better Education of Children," advocates for the family as the pastoral site of moral development, faith formation, and catechesis of children. In the eighth chapter, "Accompanying, Discerning and Integrating Weakness," Francis provides a nuanced approach to the multiple examples of family life and the good that exists within them while reasserting the church's stance on the definition of marriage and family. The ninth and final chapter, "The Spirituality of Marriage and the Family," offers a prayer for the family, as imperfect as it may be, in its inward expression toward married couples and children and its outward expression as a source of transformation in the world.

Based on the reactions from various voices since its publication (clerical and lay alike), it seems that there is less concern about *Amoris laetitia* mediating God's love and more concern about mediating what is understood to be God's law. Specifically, the main concerns over this document are centered on its presumed divergence from doctrine around love, sex, and marriage. The first major controversy *Amoris laetitia* swirled around was a perceived nod toward same-sex unions, focusing on Francis's statement in the second chapter that "we need to acknowledge the great variety of family situations that can offer a certain stability, but de facto or same-sex unions, for example, may not simply be equated with marriage" (*AL* 52).

Critique has also been leveled against the seeming affirmation of sexual expression that attends to the unitive dimension without proper attention to the procreative dimension as the end goal of all sexual expression in the fourth chapter. Francis states, "A healthy sexual desire, albeit closely joined to a pursuit of pleasure, always involves a sense of wonder, and for that very reason can humanize the impulses. In no way, then, can we consider the erotic dimension of love simply as a permissible evil or a burden to be tolerated for the good of the family" (*AL* 151–152). Francis is not rejecting doctrine on procreative openness; instead, he is offering a contextual approach to moral decision-making around sexual ethics that considers the many factors impacting sexual expression. Using the example of Francis's response to a question on whether the Catholic Church's stance on the use of condoms should be reconsidered given the HIV/AIDS crisis, Lawlor and Salzman highlight the way *Amoris laetitia* privileges what they describe as

> the principle of responsible parenthood as interpreted and acted upon by the married couple's conscience in their particular circumstances [that] is the basis for making responsible decisions to regulate their fertility ([*AL*] 68, 167, 222). This shift from a deductive, act-focused morality—every act of artificial contraception in marriage is immoral—to an inductive, principle-focused morality, responsible parenthood, which takes into consideration the couple's discerning consciences in light of their particular social, economic, and relational circumstances, opens up the possibility for using artificial contraception to regulate fertility or prevent the spread of HIV/AIDS for serodiscordant couples.[10]

Even more vociferous critiques have converged around the possibility of civilly divorced and remarried Catholics receiving communion. Several prominent Catholic leaders have claimed that the ambiguity of the exhortation in this regard suggests a shift in church doctrine on adultery and the indissolubility of marriage.[11] Matthew Levering asserts that while Francis stresses compassion through pastoral care, notably in the eighth chapter, he does not advocate the dissolubility of marriage.[12] Far from it, Francis stresses the importance of *acompanimiento*, especially through suffering. *Amoris laetitia* states,

> It is a matter of reaching out to everyone, of needing to help each person find his or her

proper way of participating in the ecclesial community and thus to experience being touched by an "unmerited, unconditional and gratuitous" mercy. No one can be condemned for ever [*sic*], because that is not the logic of the Gospel! Here I am not speaking only of the divorced and remarried, but of everyone, in whatever situation they find themselves. (*AL* 297)

In response to these critiques, I ask myself this question: Why are these not the pressing issues for me in my reading of *Amoris laetitia*? Why do I not share the frenetic outrage over this document even as some have called for its retraction? I turn back to the womanist theological lens that privileges and foregrounds the reality of those Black and brown bodies who are suffering the absence of joy and love. I hear their stories and I feel their pain not only within the context of their respective families to which this document turns our attention but also, more importantly, in the context of a church that often does not treat its members as family. In other words, through my view from the underside, I read this exhortation as a prophetic call to the ecclesial community itself to be self-reflective and to examine itself honestly, directing inward the following question: Are we attending to our own family members—our Catholic sisters and brothers—with love and joy and generativity in the way that we are asking families to attend to themselves? As Francis notes, "Many people feel that the Church's message on marriage and the family does not clearly reflect the preaching and attitudes of Jesus, who set forth a demanding ideal yet never failed to show compassion and closeness to the frailty of individuals like the Samaritan woman or the woman caught in adultery" (*AL* 38).

Pope Francis's use of the gospel of John's account of the woman caught in adultery is instructive as a means of communicating God's mediating love as the primary concern, as opposed to mediating what is understood to be God's law. I would like to spend some time with Jesus's encounter with the woman accused of adultery in this gospel as an example of an "inductive, principle-focused morality," to employ Lawlor and Salzman's phrase. This story of the scribes and Pharisees trying to create a gotcha moment for Jesus, as John 8:1–11 has commonly been read and interpreted, revolves around a woman captured and condemned to death for adultery.[13] Given their antagonistic relationship with Jesus throughout the gospel, I am struck by the way our interpretive imagination (or lack thereof) has assumed that what the scribes and Pharisees are claiming is true: that this is in fact a woman caught in the act of adultery who deserves the shame and fear of being dragged to the temple, placed in the middle of a crowd of people, and condemned to the death. The line has been drawn in the sand, a border, "a dividing line, a narrow strip along a steep edge."[14] Based on our assumption about this unnamed "adulterous" woman, we have read the story as a border logic between human sinfulness and divine forgiveness, of the grace that transcends judgment and condemnation. From this view it is a morality tale of what not to do (do not commit adultery, do not condemn others) followed by the conclusion "go and sin no more" (John 8:11). We know what we must do to stay on one side of the border; we know what must be done to keep others from entering our side of the border.

I hear something very different in this story; something tells me this is not the whole story. The timing of this story seems significant, happening just after the chief priests and Pharisees had sent guards to arrest Jesus the day before (John 7:32). It is also not long before Jesus, an innocent man, would be handed over to the Roman authorities on false pretenses to die by crucifixion, a public death reserved for the "criminal" and intended to terrorize others to stay in their place. He had just spent the night on the Mount of Olives before coming back to the temple in the early morning to teach the people.[15] It does not seem mere coincidence that the only ones who accuse the woman of adultery are the same men who are also trying to entrap Jesus with his response. Jesus is the object of their scorn and displeasure; the woman is the objectified means to a calculated end. Both Jesus and this captive woman function as scapegoats in the classic sense.

The reader does not hear from the woman until the end of this account, only after Jesus asks her a direct question. What if we were to hear from her earlier in the story? Would she say that she had not done what she was accused of doing? What if she were an innocent victim of sexual assault, blamed for a violation against her? Would she have been believed in her own day? Would she be believed in our day? Does the contextual emphasis of *Amoris laetitia* compel a different reading?

We are told that she was caught "in the act of adultery," but where was her partner who, according to the law, would be condemned to the same death?[16] Was she set up—entrapped—by the same men who sought to entrap Jesus by his response? And what if it were true that she was caught in the act of adultery, of having sex with someone outside of bounds of the law? Is such a transgression deserving of public shaming and public execution?

These are the gaps, the silences, that I hear in the story. As I consider the questions that the silences provoke, the story is opened up as a radical reimagining of power and privilege, of women's subjectivity against a world of objectification, of Jesus's accompaniment and solidarity, and of the compassion and mercy Pope Francis's apostolic exhortation describes. The story is opened up as borderland where, as Gloria Anzaldúa describes, "the only 'legitimate' inhabitants are those in power. . . . Tension grips the inhabitants of the borderlands like a virus. Ambivalence and unrest reside there and death is no stranger."[17] As a borderland story, with Jesus and the woman as the central figures, we are invited to consider the multiple truths existing and in tension simultaneously and Jesus's refusal to reinscribe the border logics of condemnation and judgment. Instead, he is willing to entertain the messiness of the borderlands, trusting in a God who enacts justice with mercy and grace, mediated through love of neighbor, stranger, and enemy alike.

In this telling, I cannot help but think about the lives of undocumented migrants, used as pawns to prove a point. I cannot help but think about the women dragged into the square for a public shaming in our own day, based on assumptions of their sexuality, and how women of color and trans women, for example, are hypersexualized in our society. They are portrayed in ways that underscore the supremacy and purity of white women, of cis women, to the inferiority and "sinfulness" of Black and brown women's bodies while our society goes to great lengths to protect that dichotomy, that border logic.

We are flooded by examples of such public shaming, maiming, and killing. Regina "Mya" Allen, a Black trans woman, was shot at point-blank range in Milwaukee in August 2022; before succumbing to her fatal wounds, she called the police and described the assailant, who was arrested several weeks later.[18] The United States is not alone in this. In Brazil in 2017 another trans woman, Dandara dos Santos, was beaten, tortured, shot, and then her head was crushed. The horrific crime was filmed and distributed on social media.[19] In Mexico, with one of the highest rates of trans murders in the world, Saray Atenea, age thirty-one, was killed in 2021, and her body thrown in a canal that officials say is often used by members of organized crime.[20]

According to the research organization Transrespect versus Transphobia Worldwide:

- 375 trans and gender-diverse people were murdered in 2021, 7% more than in the TMM [Trans Murder Monitoring] update 2020; . . .
- 96% of those murdered globally were trans women or transfeminine people;
- 58% of murdered trans people whose occupation is known were sex workers;
- Murders of trans people in the United States have doubled from last year; people of colour make up 89% of the 53 trans people murdered;
- 43% of the trans people murdered in Europe were migrants;
- 70% of all the murders registered happened in Central and South America; 33% in Brazil;
- 36% of the murders took place on the street and 24% in their own residence;

- The average age of those murdered is 30 years old; the youngest being 13 years old and the oldest 68 years old.[21]

In this telling, I cannot help but think about countless other women caught in wars waged by men and used as objects to take other men down in their vying and positioning for power. We also know all too well how rape is used as a weapon of war. The Independent International Commission of Inquiry on Ukraine issued a report that details war crimes, including the summary rape of girls and women ranging from ages four to eighty.[22]

Some Christian theologians, including Calvin, explain away the "scandal" that Jesus enacts no punishment, no condemnation, for an "adulterous" woman, that he just lets her go. In fact, many since have asserted that "although Christ remits our sins, He does not subvert the social order."[23] But why is it not equally scandalous that the religious power structures of the time may have accused an innocent person and condemned her to death just to prove a point? Even accepting her guilt, how are we not scandalized by the absence of her partner or the extreme punishment exacted by religious authorities without any indication of her reasoning, circumstances, or even the basic value of her life? What responsibility do we have in undoing the systems and structures that make it all too easy to drag a vulnerable person to the middle of the square to be stoned, lynched, or raped for all to see and participate in such a spectacle?

I worry that our anxieties—about this story and about *Amoris laetitia*—have been misdirected.

Have we become so desensitized to the borders we have constructed between us because we are so much more focused on shaming "the squint-eyed, the perverse, the queer, the troublesome, the mongrel, the mulatto, the half-breed, the half dead; in short, those who cross over, pass over, or go through the confines of the 'normal'" rather than dismantling the structures that make such shaming all too easy?[24] The angry accusations against *Amoris laetitia* on the grounds of its perceived rejection of orthodoxy seem to be doing the same.

The stories of Jesus and the woman accused of adultery are strikingly similar, as they are bound together by a border logic that seeks to drive a deep wedge between worlds, *una herida abierta*. The real scandal exists in the manner they were treated by men in power, so ready to be handed over and sacrificed for the supremacy of their systems, religious and legal. Maybe we too are complicit in the scandal if we choose to read from the story only Jesus's response toward a "sinful" woman; perhaps we too are complicit in the scandal if we choose to read from *Amoris laetitia* only Pope Francis's response toward "sinful" people. In taking a step back, we can see the scandal of the structures and powers that limit our capacity to love.

Recalling the key themes articulated at the onset of *Amoris laetitia*, namely "to persevere in a love strengthened by the virtues of generosity, commitment, fidelity and patience" and "to encourage everyone to be a sign of mercy and closeness wherever family life remains imperfect or lacks peace and joy" (*AL* 5), I believe that Pope Francis is making a move even bolder than the perceived affronts to orthodoxy. He is challenging the church, as the prophet Micah reminds us, "to act justly and to love mercy and to walk humbly with [our] God" (Mic. 6:8). This is an exhortation to ecclesial justice, mercy, and humility, to live into a new way of being in communion with one another that refrains from the crucible of perfectionism and accepts people as they are in their suffering and frailty and even in their aspirations in spite of it all. This is a subtle indictment of the church of the Global North, with its power, privilege, and self-proclaimed moral perfection, while turning to the Global South, where God is found in the earthen vessels of *lo cotidiano*, the everyday stuff of life, challenging the power centers of a church whose actions often reflect the dismissal that "nothing good comes out of Nazareth."

## INTERPRETATION

As much as the pages of *Amoris laetitia* speak of the ways families interact with and for their members, mothers, fathers, children,

grandparents, aunts, uncles, and all of the relationships reflected therein, it also speaks to the church itself to be less about passing judgment and more about showing mercy. The encyclical speaks less about admonishing wrongdoing and more about understanding difficult circumstances. It is less concerned about rejecting those who do not pass the morality litmus test and more concerned about accompanying each other in our frailty toward our better selves. It seeks to engage less in tearing down by critique and more in building up with affirmation. It is not caught up in the exclusive access to the inner sanctum of sacramental life and is more centered on welcoming the stranger, the foreigner, the sinner into the Eucharistic celebration. It seems to reject the criteria of personal piety and is more aligned with breaking bread in imperfect communion. *Amoris laetitia* communicates a desire to be less about controlling how we initiate our engagement with the holy and more about allowing the grace of the holy to pour over us, unmerited and free. This is how God's love is encountered in our present reality of family life, as immediate, extended, and in the larger church family. This is how the church can be a mediator of God's love. This is, I believe, what *Amoris laetitia* is calling us to do.

A note of personal disclosure: I am ever the skeptic when it comes to anything official emerging from the hierarchy of the Roman Catholic Church. I reserve the same caution with Pope Francis, to be sure. But I am encouraged—my courage is animated—because in the intention of this document, I see a word of hope and promise for Jeanette Vizguerra and so many other people like her who are seeking refuge and sanctuary in a church that is not dismissive of wrongdoing but does not allow that wrongdoing to stand in the way of God's unconditional embrace of love, generativity, and joy. The underlying foundation of this document is an abiding belief that "all have fallen short of the glory of God," and yet God loves us regardless. What would it mean if this "inductive, principle-focused morality" animated the way of the church in the world? If it were so, we would understand the true gift and blessing of solidarity, of being with each other just because we are. In the words of esteemed Catholic womanist theologian Shawn Copeland, solidarity is nothing less than the "healing of a 'body of broken bones' unto the mystical body of Christ"; it is the very gift of grace.[25]

I am not worried as are so many others about the impact of *Amoris laetitia* on the future of the church. I am not calling for it to be clearer than it already is or more focused on a direct affirmation of doctrine gone before. Instead, I am happy that it has caused so much controversy and disagreement over the past six years. I am delighted that it has forced clergy and laypeople to respond. To me, this ambiguity is a "borderland" experience of which I am familiar, a reflection of a third space, as Anzaldúa describes. *Amoris laetitia* has thus shone a light on the church itself—what it wants to be, what it is called to be—illumined by the life of Jesus, the Jesus who turned over the tables at the temple, the Jesus who allowed a woman to bathe his feet in oil and caress them with her hair, the Jesus who scandalously forgave the woman accused of adultery while reminding those gathered that the one who is without sin shall cast the first stone, the Jesus who was crucified as a criminal and forgave another on the cross, the Jesus who was part of a family. This is the spirit of *Amoris laetitia*. And if this provides us with a glimpse of the future of the church, I am hopeful.

## NOTES

1. James Martin, SJ, *Building a Bridge: How the Catholic Church and the LGBT Community Can Enter into a Relationship of Respect, Compassion, and Sensitivity* (New York: HarperCollins, 2017).

2. John Paul II, *Familiaris consortio* (November 11, 1981), https://www.vatican.va/content/john -paul-ii/en/apost_exhortations/documents/hf_jp-ii _exh_19811122_familiaris-consortio.html.

3. See Congregation for the Doctrine of the Faith, *On the Pastoral Care of Homosexual Persons* (October 1, 1986), https://www.vatican.va/roman_curia /congregations/cfaith/documents/rc_con_cfaith_doc _19861001_homosexualpersons_en.html; Congregation for the Doctrine of the Faith, *Some Considerations Concerning the Response to Legislative Proposals on the Non-Discrimination of Homosexual Persons* (July 23, 1992), https://www.vatican.va/roman_curia /congregations/cfaith/documents/rc_con_cfaith _doc_19920724_homosexual-persons_en.html; and Congregation for the Doctrine of the Faith, *Considerations Regarding Proposals to Give Legal Recognition to Unions between Homosexual Persons* (June 3, 2003), https://www.vatican.va/roman_curia/congregations /cfaith/documents/rc_con_cfaith_doc_20030731 _homosexual-unions_en.html.

4. James Martin, SJ, "Top 10 takeaways from 'Amoris Laetitia,'" *America Magazine,* April 8, 2016, https://www.americamagazine.org/faith/2016/04 /08/top-10-takeaways-amoris-laetitia.

5. Pope Francis, *Amoris laetitia* (March 19, 2016), https://www.vatican.va/content/dam/francesco /pdf/apost_exhortations/documents/papa-francesco _esortazione-ap_20160319_amoris-laetitia_en.pdf (hereafter cited as *AL*).

6. "Jeanette Vizguerra Seeks Sanctuary and Justice," *Denver Post,* February 16, 2017, https://www .denverpost.com/2017/02/16/jeanette-vizguerra -seeks-sanctuary-and-justice/.

7. Julie Turkewitz, "Immigrant Mother in Denver Takes Refuge as Risk of Deportation Looms," *New York Times,* February 15, 2017, https://www.ny times.com/2017/02/15/us/an-immigrant-mother-in -denver-weighs-options-as-deportation-looms.html.

8. "Jeanette Vizguerra Ready for More Permanent Solution as She Leaves Sanctuary," December 29, 2021, https://www.cbsnews.com/colorado /news/vizguerra-colorado-deportation-solution/.

9. Jon Sobrino, *Spirituality of Liberation* (Maryknoll, NY: Orbis Books, 1988 [English trans.]), 14–20.

10. Michael G. Lawler and Todd A. Salzman, "Pope Francis and *Amoris Laetitia*: Reform of Catholic Sexual Ethics?," *Journal of Religion and Society,* Supplement 18 (2019): 153.

11. See Edward Pentin, "Full Text and Explanatory Notes of Cardinals' Questions on 'Amoris Laetitia,'" *National Catholic Register,* November 4, 2016, https://www.ncregister.com/blog/full-text -and-explanatory-notes-of-cardinals-questions-on -amoris-laetitia.

12. See Matthew Levering, *The Indissolubility of Marriage: Amoris Laetitia in Context* (San Francisco: Ignatius, 2019), chap. 3.

13. For a comprehensive account of the patriarchal (mis)reading of this text, see Gail R. O'Day, "John 7:53–8:11: A Study in Misreading," *Journal of Biblical Literature* 111, no. 4 (Winter 1992): 631–40.

14. Gloria Anzaldúa, *Borderlands/La Frontera: The New Mestizo* (San Francisco: Aunt Lute Books, 1987), 3.

15. For more information on the historical addition of this story in later antiquity, see Frederik Wisse, "The Nature and Purpose of Redactional Changes in Early Christian Texts," in *Gospel Traditions in the Second Century: Origins, Recensions, Text, and Transmission*, ed. William L. Petersen, 39–53 (Notre Dame, IN: University of Notre Dame Press, 1989).

16. See Leviticus 20:10 and 18:20.

17. Anzaldúa, *Borderlands/La Frontera*, 3–4.

18. Jax Miller, "Milwaukee Man Charged with Murder of Black Transgender Woman Who Described Her Shooter to Police," Oxygen, October 6, 2022, https://www.oxygen.com/crime-news /clayton-hubbird-charged-regina-mya-allen-murder.

19. Dom Phillips, "Torture and Killing of Transgender Woman Stun Brazil," *New York Times*, March 8, 2017, https://www.nytimes.com/2017/03 /08/world/americas/brazil-transgender-killing-video .html.

20. Alex Cooper, "Trans Woman Tortured to Death, Her Body Dumped in Canal," *Advocate*, December 17, 2021, https://www.advocate.com /crime/2021/12/17/trans-woman-tortured-death -her-body-dumped-canal-saray-atenea.

21. "TMM Update TDoR 2021," Transrespect versus Transphobia Worldwide, November 11, 2021, https://transrespect.org/en/tmm-update-tdor-2021/.

22. "A/77/533: Independent International Commission of Inquiry on Ukraine—Note by the Secretary-General," United Nations, October 18, 2022, https://www.ohchr.org/en/documents/reports /a77533-independent-international-commission -inquiry-ukraine-note-secretary.

23. Quoting E. C. Hoskyns, *The Fourth Gospel*, in Gail R. O'Day, "John 7:53–8:11: A Study in Misreading," *Journal of Biblical Literature* 111, no. 4 (Winter 1992): 631–40.

24. Anzaldúa, *Borderlands/La Frontera*, 3.

25. M. Shawn Copeland, *Enfleshing Freedom: Body, Race, and Being* (Minneapolis: Fortress Press, 2010), 90.

# 24

*Christus Vivit*

MARY M. DOYLE ROCHE

## CONTEXT

The Catholic Church began holding World Youth Day (WYD) during the papacy of John Paul II. The celebration, which occurs every few years, brings young people from across the globe together for a few days that include a papal visit. Akin to a global pilgrimage, it is touted as "an expression of the universal Church and an intense moment of evangelization for the youth world" as well as a "laboratory of faith, a place of birth for vocations to marriage and consecrated life, and an instrument for the evangelization and transformation of the Church."[1] Importantly, young people are considered the "protagonists" of WYD, the primary agents, accompanied by those in other generations, in an experience of a global church. A light is trained on the exuberance of young participants as a sign of the church's ongoing vitality and hope for the future.

WYD has for decades provided a unique and visible opportunity for many young people to be recognized by the pope and the whole church. Francis has attended three WYD gatherings, in 2013, 2016, and 2019. Since the beginning of his papacy, he has also been vocally committed to increasing ecclesial expressions and understanding of synodality as an essential process in the life of the church.[2]

In the fall of 2018, these two emphases came together as Francis convened the XV Ordinary General Assembly of the Synod of Bishops on the theme "Young People, the Faith and Vocational Discernment." The following spring *Christus vivit*, the apostolic exhortation arising from the synod, was released.[3] The synodal process provided a crucial mechanism for young people to have their voices heard in not only a celebration of faith but also raising awareness of the challenges they face and in determining ministerial practices and priorities. To date, the document is the second of three postsynodal apostolic exhortations issued during Francis's papacy, following *Amoris laetitia*, the "Post Synodal Apostolic Exhortation on Love in the Family" of 2016.

Notably, Francis's exhortation defines young people as those between the ages of sixteen and twenty-nine years.[4] This age range approximates the range used by the United Nations for statistical purposes: fifteen to twenty-four. The United Nations defines children as those fourteen years old and younger. While there are moments in *Christus vivit* that seem to blur the lines between children and youths, the document is primarily addressing adolescents and younger adults who are in the process of completing education, finding work, discerning vocations, founding families, and raising children. The exhortation navigates a tension between young people as vulnerable to exploitation and even manipulation but also as informed leaders of social and ecclesial change.

In one current social construction of youth, these years are to be full of promise and the realization of the potentials of childhood. Youth injects energy and innovation into the spaces where it is welcomed, including the church. For the church and any institution of civil society to have a future, it must reckon with and embrace the needs and desires of younger generations. The biological and social sciences have demonstrated that these years are full of continued, growth as bodies and brains are still developing in their capacity to navigate the world of human relationships and responsibilities. Young people, some of whom are already parents themselves, are still actively cultivating important foundational values and virtues as they mature in late adolescence and the early years of adulthood. The synod provided a key opportunity for ecclesial leadership to influence that process and, at the same time, learn from young people who are immersed in a world dominated by technological advances and rapid communication, for better and for worse.

In one sense, the time is always right for an exhortation to young people who are learning, working, building and sustaining families, voting, and otherwise experiencing individual development while assuming increasing social responsibilities. Like many of the documents in Catholic Family Teaching and, more broadly considered, Catholic Social Teaching, *Christus vivit* is also responding to a social and historical moment. While there are many variations across countries and cultures, three intersecting elements might be considered as particularly pertinent: demographic shifts related to young people; the increasing agitation of young people for justice at every level of social organization, including families; and the prevalence of technology that, when left to its own devices, can undermine human dignity and harm human relationships.

First, a snapshot of some demographics. According to the United Nations, over 70 percent of the population of sub-Saharan Africa is under the age of thirty, making children and young people the key to development and flourishing in that part of the world.[5] Over 60 percent of the word's young people live in the Asia-Pacific region (approximately 750 million).[6] In contrast, the percentage of people aged fifteen to twenty-nine in the European Union is only about 16 percent and is expected to decline in the coming decades.[7] The average age for people marrying and having children is also rising in many parts of the world. For example, the US Census Bureau reports the age at first marriage at over twenty-eight years for women and over twenty-nine years for men.[8] The Centers for Disease Control and Prevention in the United States reports the mean age for first childbirth at over twenty-six years for women,[9] while men who enter fatherhood are typically two and a half years older.[10] In some European countries, people are well into their thirties on average when they marry or have children, while some countries in Africa have average ages for these life events remaining in the teens. Birth rates in many countries across the globe have also been in steady decline, which will result in fewer young people of working and both child-rearing and elder-caring age. The decisions that young people are making today about family and work, to the extent that they are able to make decisions, stand to have a profound impact on the future.

The Catholic Church is also cognizant of the demographics of religious disaffiliation. Occasions such as WYD and the 2018 synod on young people bear witness to the vibrancy of young people of faith, indicating that even the church grapples with rising rates of disaffiliation, especially among young people. For example, in the United States, researchers from the Pew Research Center found that 48 percent of disaffiliated Catholics left the church before the age of eighteen. Reasons for disaffiliation vary and include drifting from the church because they do not connect matters of faith and worship with their everyday lives and experiences, loss of faith in the context of suffering and injury, dissenting from particular church teachings, and tensions around the church's role in politics.[11] Regardless of the reasons for disaffiliation, it can no longer be taken for granted that young people will return to active membership in the church when they marry and have children. The participation of young people in the life of the church will require a concerted effort at evangelization. The synodal process under Francis is one way in which the institution has allowed young people to be heard so that their experiences are permitted to have an influence on the church's processes of discernment for teaching and ministry.[12]

Many of today's young people grew up steeped in the world of social media and adapt to innovation more quickly than their elders in a rapidly changing technological landscape. Catholic magisterial documents have long been cautious of technological advances. Among the concerns is that they may facilitate a "throwaway culture" in which many things and even some people are seen as disposable. Social media may lead to shallower relationships and more fragile social connections. It can also distort facts in favor of propaganda. For young people in particular, it can undermine self-esteem, exacerbate feelings of loneliness and isolation, facilitate bullying and manipulation, and reduce them to consumers of mindless entertainment.

Their technological savvy with social media and other forms of media communication has also meant that many young people are able to form wider social networks and organize themselves in support of causes that are important to them. Any number of examples could be offered: young people mobilizing for political change in their home countries; standing in solidarity with women and girls who face discrimination and harassment at work, in school, and in politics; documenting, in word and image, the violence perpetrated on young Black and brown bodies; and raising the alarm about the destruction of the environment. Young people, who are often told that the future stretches out before them, full of possibility, are now painfully aware that time is short for many of the world's youths and indeed is running out for all of us. They are able to make what the late US civil rights leader John Lewis called "good trouble."[13]

## COMMENTARY

It is in the midst of this global context and a world church still reeling from the scandal of the sexual abuse of children and young people that the Synod on Young People took place and gave shape to the content of the ensuing exhortation. *Christus vivit* unfolds in nine chapters and is marked by Francis's pastoral sensibilities, ability to speak plainly, and enthusiasm for the difference that a personal relationship, a friendship, with Jesus Christ can make in a young person's life. There are notes of Ignatian spirituality and practices of moral discernment (*ChV* 70). The text devotes significant space to reflection on scripture, beginning with a meditation on young people as figures in both the Hebrew Bible and the New Testament. *Christus vivit* highlights numerous examples of the crucial roles that young people, as young people, have played in salvation history and throughout the history of the church. The second chapter continues this trajectory and focuses on the person of Jesus as a young person in history and "ever young" in a theological sense. While the biblical record of Jesus's childhood and early adolescence is limited, Francis invites young people to consider that Jesus himself is just emerging from youth as he enters his public ministry and to encounter him in this light.

Claiming that young people are the "Now" of God, Francis grounds his message in "three essential truths." First, God is love, and all people are infinitely loved by God. Young people are significant and have worth in God's eyes (*ChV* 115). God is not waiting for the maturity of older age to initiate a deeply personal relationship (*ChV* 135). God welcomes the questions and the arguments that the young raise when facing life's challenges (*ChV* 117). Second, Jesus sacrificed himself in order to save us: "The Lord's love is greater than all our problems, frailties and flaws. Yet it is precisely through our problems, frailties and flaws that he wants to write this love story" (*ChV* 120). God forgives again and again, and young people are called to trust in God's mercy and allow themselves to be saved again and again. The implication is powerful and straightforward. Citing his message given at the synod itself, Francis proclaims, "You must repeat this always: I am not up for sale; I do not have a price. I am free!" (*ChV* 122). Finally, Jesus is alive, present to us when we are young and throughout our lives, and Jesus is "overflowing with joy." Young people are called to share in this joy and indeed to transmit this joy to elders who may have become worn down by life. Francis exhorts young people to seek the guidance of the Holy Spirit in experiencing this message anew with each day. In a conversational tone, Francis writes that if what you desire is love and a rich emotional life, "Why not? You have nothing to lose" (*ChV* 131). God is the giver of youth, which is to be accepted with gratitude by not only the young but also the church itself. It is a gift that can easily be squandered. He later adds,

> Take risks, even if it means making mistakes. Don't go through life anaesthetized or approach the world like tourists. Make a ruckus! Cast out the fears that paralyze you, so that you don't become young mummies. Live! Give yourselves over to the best of life! Open the door of the cage, go out and fly! Please, don't take early retirement. (*ChV* 143)

Without lofty language or theological abstraction, *Christus vivit* conveys the strong need that the church and the world have for young people. For Francis, youth is a time of dreams and decisions, a thirsting for experience and relationship, growth, and commitment to change for the better, all of which demand tremendous courage for which young people are rarely given credit.

What is less clear is the nature of the "cages" that are entrapping young people and preventing them from living fully in this moment, knowing that they are loved by God and by the people in their lives. One cage is surely rampant consumerism that measures a person's worth in the possession of material goods, values competition over cooperation, and promotes a distorted cult of youth. Yet, we might also ask about families who form cages around their members and churches that discourage

young people from living into their freedom if that path places them in conflict with established teaching or practice. We might ask about the cages of poverty, violence, racism, and gender inequality (to which the church has contributed) that limit the present and the future possibilities of so many of the world's young.

Francis's cultural critique is most pointed in chapter 6, "Young People with Roots." There are forces in the world, in politics and the economy, that require "the young to be shallow, uprooted and distrustful" so that they can be more easily manipulated and exploited. He is wary of ideologies that "need young people who have no use for history, who spurn the spiritual and human riches inherited from past generations, and are ignorant of everything that came before them" (*ChV* 181).

> These masters of manipulation also use another tactic: the cult of youth, which dismisses all that is not young as contemptible and outmoded. The youthful body becomes the symbol of this new cult; everything associated with that body is idolized and lusted after, while whatever is not young is despised. But this cult of youth is simply an expedient that ultimately proves degrading to the young; it strips them of any real value and uses them for personal, financial or political profit. (*ChV* 182)

Francis's enthusiasm for the young ought not be mistaken for this "cult of youth" that discards what is old or losing its luster. In its encouragement of young people to claim their place in the world, *Christus vivit* attempts to resist the kind of intergenerational conflict that can accompany such change. Youth is a valued stage in life but no more or less than infancy, childhood, or advanced age. Growth happens in every stage of life. The vision is one of intergenerational solidarity, as "young and old journey together." The phrase "make a ruckus," like that of "good trouble," acknowledges the tensions that inevitably arise between generations but trains our eyes on the common good of all people at every age. Francis's criticisms do not overwhelm the joyful core message of

*Christus vivit*. Recalling his 2019 WYD message, Francis writes,

> Jesus can bring all the young people of the Church together in a single dream, "a great dream, a dream with a place for everyone. The dream for which Jesus gave his life on the cross, for which the Holy Spirit was poured out on the day of Pentecost and brought fire to the heart of every man and woman, to your heart and mine. To your heart too, he brought that fire, in the hope of finding room for it to grow and flourish. A dream whose name is Jesus, planted by the Father in the confidence that it would grow and live in every heart. A concrete dream who is a person, running through our veins, thrilling our hearts and making them dance." (*ChV* 157)

*Christus vivit* also includes a chapter dedicated to the pastoral care of the young and youth ministry focusing on outreach and growth in an ongoing experience of friendship with Christ. Francis implicitly acknowledges that without the active engagement of young people, ministry to young people may fall flat. For example, he says,

> I trust that young people themselves know how best to find appealing ways to come together. They know how to organize events, sports competitions and ways to evangelize using social media, through text messages, songs, videos and other ways. They only have to be encouraged and given the freedom to be enthused about evangelizing other young people wherever they are to be found. (*ChV* 210)

It is important to note here that young people are evangelizing from their authentic experience; they are not merely in charge of the social media accounts.

Francis calls youth ministers, including the young among them, to seize the opportunity created by an encounter with Jesus and resist the tendency to follow on these experiences with programs that focus on "doctrinal and moral issues, the evils of today's world, the church, her social doctrine, chastity, marriage, birth control and so on" (*ChV* 212). He admonishes, "Rather than being too concerned with communicating a great deal of doctrine, let us first try to awaken and consolidate the great experiences that sustain the Christian life" (*ChV* 212). The call emphasizes allowing young people their freedom and accompanying them on that journey.

As young people discern their various vocations in the church and the world, the call that unites them is the call to friendship and service. Choices around work and family, which are both worrying and exciting (*ChV* 258), are expressions of this fundamental invitation. And in the context of limited options for many young people due to social and economic constraints, Francis encourages, "Keep seeking at least partial or imperfect ways to live what you have discerned to be your real calling" (*ChV* 272).

The questions of discernment resist the temptations of competition and wealth and ask instead,

> Do I know myself, quite apart from my illusions and emotions? Do I know what brings joy or sorrow to my heart? What are my strengths and weaknesses? These questions immediately give rise to others: How can I serve people better and prove most helpful to our world and to the Church? What is my real place in this world? What can I offer to society? Even more realistic questions then follow: Do I have the abilities needed to offer this kind of service? Could I develop those abilities? (*ChV* 285)

The questions are practical and rooted in our lived experiences, with all their limits and possibilities.

*Christus Vivit* departs in significant ways from earlier addresses to young people, particularly in its attempt to recognize the changing context of their lives in the present global context and particular contexts of their lived experiences. For example, although Pius XII was speaking to a very similar age demographic in his addresses to newlyweds roughly three generations earlier, the context has shifted so dramatically that the papal approach is substantially different.[14] Though official teachings about sex, gender, and marriage have not changed during Francis's papacy, *Christus vivit* does not reinforce a patriarchal view of marriage and highly gendered social roles or assume a largely socially scripted life course. Both Francis and Pius XII aimed to support the vocations of young people, and especially the institution of marriage, in their own times. For Francis, all young people are called primarily to friendship with Christ and, if anything, are implored to consider more egalitarian marriage, family, and parenthood as potential expressions of that friendship and signs of hope in an age of anxiety about the future.

## INTERPRETATION

*Christus vivit* exemplifies Francis's pastoral approach. It does not dwell on many of the usual moral admonitions aimed at young people with regard to sexual debut, birth control, gender complementarity, and patriarchal marriage. Young people, at least in the United States if not worldwide, are leaving the church over these very questions. Young people who are affiliated with the church are more likely to participate in the synodal process and benefit from its outcomes. These young people will need to make common cause with young people who have left precisely because their minds and hearts are trained on social justice, on an end to poverty, violence, gender and racial discrimination, and environmental devastation.

The exhortation closes with these words:

Dear young people, my joyful hope is to see you keep running the race before you, outstripping all those who are slow or fearful. Keep running, "attracted by the face of Christ, whom we love so much, whom we adore in the Holy Eucharist and acknowledge in the flesh of our suffering brothers and sisters. May the Holy Spirit urge you on as you run this race. The Church needs your momentum, your intuitions, your faith. We need them! And when you arrive where we

have not yet reached, have the patience to wait for us." (*ChV* 299)

It is a hopeful message, and there is much in *Christus vivit* that can buoy the faith of the young as well as those who parent, educate, and minister to them. This message cautions older Catholics who may be slow to change and fearful of the loss of the privilege and power that comes with age. Relationship with young people is a precious opportunity for the people of God. But like many of those who agitate for change in society and the church, young people are encouraged to be patient, to wait as their elders catch up. While these may be considered words of prudent advice, they also betray the limits set on prophetic leadership among young people. It is the comfort of older generations that continues to set the pace of change. Racism, sexism, clericalism, and homophobia are somehow more understandable in the old, and so real transformation may not come quickly. One might recall Martin Luther King Jr.'s admonition that "wait" often means "never." "Wait" exploits the myth of time in which its simple passage yields progress.[15]

As a teacher of young people, primarily those between the ages of eighteen and twenty-two years, in a Catholic college animated by the charism of Saint Ignatius of Loyola, some of whom identify as Catholic and some who do not, I find much to welcome in *Christus vivit*, perhaps most importantly an invitation to greater freedom in this work. I am not naive; the pastoral approach that gives us room to listen, to explore, to accompany, and to be changed has not been matched by the kinds of doctrinal development that many young people and their allies long for, which may be especially true of those who accompany young women and LGBTQ+ persons. Progressive in many ways, Francis often reaffirms established teachings and patterns of thought on issues of gender and sexuality, especially in doctrinal considerations. Nevertheless, his actions and personal encounters with particular LGBTQ+ persons and their allies are prophetic and may eventually be transformative for others who hold teaching power in the church.

I interpret *Christus vivit* from a place of privilege that allows me to act on its best wisdom and advice. By virtue of being enrolled in a well-resourced liberal arts college, my students enjoy many of the freedoms hoped for in this document even though they hail from a range of social locations. Many of my students also enjoy the privileges that come with wealth, whiteness, US citizenship, and their families' intergenerational social capital. I have the freedom that comes with tenure and a position that is valued and relatively well remunerated. My charge is not catechesis or apologetics but rather the critical exploration and evaluation of Christian theologies and ethics. I have a unique opportunity to accompany young people as they "make a ruckus," challenging ideas old and new on our campus and in the world. I am often entrusted with their most profound questions and doubts. Many of my students will have the freedom to express their vocation in work that they choose and that will provide them a livelihood. They can take intellectual and spiritual risks enveloped in a community dedicated to their well-being. Their social and economic standing will not be shaped exclusively by their state in life whether that be as a spouse, a parent, a partner, a single person, or a member of a religious community. They have time to mature into the kinds of relationships and commitments that other young people take on much earlier. And one of the greatest surprises of teaching is that one stands to learn so much from young people each day in the process of handing on an intellectual tradition.

And yet, much of Francis's worry is also borne out in my experience. I witness loneliness, depression, anxiety, exhaustion, and substance abuse on an epidemic scale. My students are worried about economic security (let alone prosperity), uncertainty about founding families in a culture that has at once idealized that process and offered little social support to sustain it, and the specter of an "uninhabitable earth."[16] I also fear that the sense of possibility and empowerment we strive to impart will be diminished after college, stifled by those in authority including and perhaps most especially the Catholic clergy they encounter in parishes.

*Christus vivit* offers hope to young people, to those with vocations in education and youth ministry, and to all people who want to draw on the enduring graces of youth no matter their age. For Francis, vocational discernment to work and family life is no longer a merely aspirational exercise limited to an existing range of possibilities. It is, as theologian Cole Arthur Riley notes, also and perhaps primarily discerning what is *already* true of young people whose dignity is the *now* of God in families and faith communities.[17] *Christus vivit* provides leverage to demand now a new world and a new church characterized by an intergenerational solidarity with roots that extend back to our ancestors and branch out toward future heirs. Families as domestic churches have a crucial role in handing on the traditions of faith, but this is not unidirectional from elders to the young. Dynamic intergenerational solidarity honors wisdom born of experience but also imagines family as a space where the young can bring traditions that may have ossified back to life in new ways. Intergenerational solidarity in families and churches requires that living traditions be shared, received, and reformed by the young and old together both in God's image and as friends in Christ.

## NOTES

1. World Youth Day Lisbon 2023, https://www.lisboa2023.org/en/about (accessed February 4, 2023).

2. See Francis, "Ceremony Commemorating the 50th Anniversary of the Institution of the Synod of Bishops: Address of His Holiness Pope Francis" (October 17, 2015), https://www.vatican.va/content/francesco/en/speeches/2015/october/documents/papa-francesco_20151017_50-anniversario-sinodo.html. Cf. International Theological Commission, "Synodality in the Life and Mission of the Church," (March 2, 2018), https://www.vatican.va/roman_curia/congregations/cfaith/cti_documents/rc_cti_20180302_sinodalita_en.html#_edn2.

3. Pope Francis, *Christus vivit* (March 25, 2019), https://www.vatican.va/content/francesco/en/apost_exhortations/documents/papa-francesco

_esortazione-ap_20190325_christus-vivit.html (hereafter cited as *ChV*).

4. *Christus vivit*'s inclusion in the documents of Catholic Family Teaching owes to its audience being in an age range in which many persons are beginning to create new independence from their families of origin or are beginning to plan or begin new families of their own. However, the exhortation also remains something of an outlier within Catholic Family Teaching due to its unique concerns and the social situation in which these are now expressed. Appendix 2 of this volume lists the document under the theme "Children & Education" despite the limitations of this categorization. Time will tell if it marks a new trajectory in Catholic Family Teaching or if it will remain a thematic outlier.

5. "Young People's Potential, the Key to Africa's Sustainable Development," United Nations, https://www.un.org/ohrlls/news/young-people's-potential-key-africa's-sustainable-development (accessed February 4, 2023).

6. Economic and Social Commission for Asia and the Pacific, "Regional Overview, Youth in Asia and the Pacific," United Nations, https://www.un.org/esa/socdev/documents/youth/fact-sheets/youth-regional-escap.pdf (accessed February 4, 2023).

7. For statistical data provided by the European Union, see https://ec.europa.eu/eurostat/.

8. "Number, Timing and Duration of Marriage and Divorces," United States Census Bureau, April 22, 2021 (updated October 8, 2021), https://www.census.gov/newsroom/press-releases/2021/marriages-and-divorces.html.

9. T. J. Mathews and Brady E. Hamilton, "Mean Age of Mothers Is on the Rise: United States, 2000–2014," Centers for Disease Control and Prevention, NCHC Data Brief No. 232, January 2016, https://www.cdc.gov/nchs/products/databriefs/db232.htm.

10. Differences in the age ranges sampled can produce significant variability in the estimates produced. However, the general trend for both men and women in the United States has been a decades-long upward trajectory of the median age of both first marriage and first childbirth, with an increasingly narrow gap between these events. For younger Americans these ages are both increasingly beyond thirty years of age; however, significant variability remains across demographic groups. See, e.g., Anne Morse, "Fertility Rates: Declined for Younger Women, Increased for Older Women," United States Census Bureau, April 6, 2022, https://www.census.gov/library/stories/2022/04/fertility-rates-declined-for-younger-women-increased-for-older-women.html?utm_campaign=20220406msacos1ccstors&utm_medium=email&utm_source=govdelivery; and Quoctrung Bui and Claire Cain Miller, "The Age That Women Have Babies: How a Gap Divides America," *New York Times,* August 4, 2018, https://www.nytimes.com/interactive/2018/08/04/upshot/up-birth-age-gap.html.

11. "Leaving Catholicism," Pew Research Center, April 27, 2009 (updated February 2011), https://www.pewresearch.org/religion/2009/04/27/faith-in-flux3/.

12. Robert J. McCarty and John M. Vitek, *Going, Going, Gone: The Dynamics of Disaffiliation in Young Catholics* (Winona, MN: St. Mary's Press, 2018).

13. See Mary M. Doyle Roche, "Cultivating Resistance: Youth Protest and the Common Good," in *Sex, Love & Families: Catholic Perspectives*, ed. Jason King and Julie Hanlon Rubio, 293–303 (Collegeville, MN: Liturgical Press, 2020).

14. See chapter 10 in this volume.

15. Martin Luther King Jr., *Why We Can't Wait* (New York: Harper & Row, 1964).

16. Borrowed from David Wallace Wells, *The Uninhabitable Earth: Life after Warming* (New York: Tim Duggan Books, 2019).

17. Cole Arthur Riley, *This Here Flesh: Spirituality, Liberation, and the Stories That Make Us* (New York: Convergent, 2022).

# CHAPTER

# 25

## Male and Female
## He Created Them

SHARON A. BONG

## CONTEXT

Gender theory lies at the heart of the Catholic Church's teachings on the human body, sexuality, relationships, and the family. Ironically, documents such as the 2019 "'Male and Female He Created Them': Towards a Path of Dialogue on the Question of Gender Theory in Education" by the Congregation for Catholic Education (CCE) allude to gender theory as extraneous and mostly inimical to faith-based documents.[1] This chapter's commentary on "'Male and Female He Created Them'" seeks to explain why such a positioning of gender theory and posturing by the church is strategic albeit problematic and potentially harmful for bodies, sexualities, relationships, and families that go beyond "the order of nature" (MF 23).

There are consequently three dualisms set up in "Male and Female" that need to be interrogated, each containing a hierarchical and oppositional pairing. The first is the church's eternal teachings versus faddish secular (or postmodern) theories from the prism of gender theory that permeates both faith-based and secular-based texts. The second dualism lies in the primacy of reciprocity rather than inclusivity in the configuration of the family. The ethos of "Male and Female" in engendering a *"fully human and integral ecology"* (MF 35) among all

creation, beginning with the human, warrants closer scrutiny, as reciprocity that is founded on "sexual difference" does not necessarily entail gender and sexual inclusivity. Third, the "path of dialogue" as opposed to "ideologically-driven approaches" is a fittingly Christian pedagogical tool with regard to sexuality education, but its formulation within the document is neither comprehensive nor deeply engaged with sexual and reproductive health and rights practitioners globally (MF 52, 55).

## COMMENTARY

### Gender Theory

At the outset, "Male and Female" positions gender theory as an external threat that has precipitated an *"educational crisis, especially in the field of affectivity and sexuality"* in Christian education (MF 1). This dangerous ideology

> denies the difference and reciprocity in nature of a man and a woman and envisages a society without sexual differences, thereby eliminating the anthropological basis of the family. This ideology leads to educational programmes and legislative enactments that promote a personal identity and emotional

intimacy radically separated from the biological difference between male and female. Consequently, human identity becomes the choice of the individual, one which can also change over time. (MF 2)

The encompassing sphere of influence of gender theory—anthropological, familial, educational, ideological, legal, and political—renders it potentially extremely harmful. Citing Pope Francis's 2017 exhortation, *Amoris laetitia,* the CCE warns that gender ideologies have become "absolute and unquestionable, even dictating how children should be raised" (MF 6). Such alarm-raising is reactionary, as gender theory is seen as infringing on the first privilege and duty of parents and the church in the formation of children and young adults, especially in matters of "affectivity and sexuality." This directly impinges on the sanctity of the family premised on sexual difference as a precondition of procreation as well as authentic "reciprocity." What is particularly insidious about gender theory, especially in its "most radical forms," is that it "speaks of a gradual process of denaturalisation" with an "anything goes" ("post-modern") effect, resulting in a downward spiral of sexual identities and the family that are marred by "'liquidity' and 'fluidity'" and "a confused concept of freedom in the realm of feelings and wants" (MF 19). One becomes insensible, almost without a moral compass, in being "generally opposed to . . . truths of existence."

Such "truths of existence" are of course those dictated by the authoritative teachings of the church. Here the CCE's standpoint is indefatigable, not least because so much of Catholic Family Teaching hinges on an essentialist, binary, and complementarian distinction between two genders. The CCE does not stand alone in its zeal against the perceived malaise of gender theory. Similar sentiments are also found in the dangerous rhetoric of political and religious fundamentalists aimed at curbing young people's universal access to sexual and reproductive health and rights services.[2] However, "Male and Female" is not simply reactionary and backward-looking; it is demonstrably cognizant of the wealth of scholarship on gender theory. Yet, to what extent is this cautionary positioning of gender theory defensible, given the document's argumentation and the wider realm of gender scholarship?

Gender theory, in its "most radical forms" is, in fact, transformative, as "it speaks of a gradual process of denaturalisation" whereby the categories of "sex," "gender," and "sexual orientation" (which includes sexual desire, "the realm of feelings and wants") are not always neatly aligned in a gender binary and heteronormative fashion and in fact can be unaligned with each other (MF 19). The fundamental question is whether moral acceptance of this diversity draws us further from or further into true knowledge of the nature of persons.

Here, the work of feminist postmodernist thinker Judith Butler, beginning with her seminal text *Gender Trouble,* is instructive:

I use the term *heterosexual matrix* throughout the text to designate that grid of cultural intelligibility through which bodies, genders, and desires are naturalized . . . to characterize a hegemonic discursive/epistemic model of gender intelligibility that assumes that for bodies to cohere and make sense there must be a stable sex expressed through a stable gender (masculine expressed male, feminine expressed female) that is oppositionally and hierarchically defined through the practice of compulsory heterosexuality.[3]

Butler makes visible the gender work involved, that is, gender theory and its underlying ideology that must be operationalized to align particular "bodies, genders, and desires" as natural, fixed, and lawful (in the eyes of God and "man"). In doing so, she debunks the naturalization of "sex" (male or female), "gender" (identities and expression), and, by extension, "desire" (sexual orientation). This occurs in two ways: by asserting, first, that these categories are "stable," and, second, that they must be "oppositionally and hierarchically defined."[4] A "stable sex" as framed by "hegemonic discursive/epistemic models," such as John Paul II's "theology of the body," refers to the dualism of being either male or female (not both-and). A "stable gender" refers to the dualism of being either masculine or feminine (not both-and). A "stable sex" is aligned with a "stable gender," as one's gender identity and expression must align with the sex assigned at birth; if one is born male, one ought to be gendered masculine and, conversely, if one is born female, one ought to be gendered feminine. The economy of dualisms is that each term is "oppositionally and hierarchically defined": male/female and masculine/feminine where male is not female and female is not male. Moreover, the first terms (male and masculine) are positioned as dominant over the second terms (female and feminine), which are derivative and subordinate.[5]

What cements "gender intelligibility" is the further regulation of bodies and sexualities through the "heterosexualization of desire" that "requires and institutes the production of discrete and asymmetrical oppositions between the 'feminine' and 'masculine,' where these are understood as expressive attributes of 'male' and 'female.'"[6] Heterosexuality becomes (rather than is) the norm. It is "the effect of regulatory practice," that is, consistent socialization from the womb to the tomb. Coercion is also involved in such gender work as "compulsory heterosexuality" and is sustained by rewards for compliance (e.g., the right to marry and start a family) and sanctions for noncompliance (e.g., being deprived of the right to marry and start a family as well as access to corresponding sacraments of the church). Not going beyond "constitutive male-female sexual difference," as "Male and Female" puts it (MF 25), is what Butler terms the "heterosexual matrix." The "heterosexual matrix" is constructed for the majority as the foundational basis of not only one's sex, gender identity, and sexual identity but also one's very personhood. Becoming heterosexual and either recognizably male (and properly gendered masculine) or female (and properly gendered feminine) consolidates "the principle of otherness" that is summed up as sexual difference, which the CCE claims "is a condition of *all cognition*" (MF 27). This is akin to what Butler terms "gender intelligibility."

Butler's work offers a paradigm shift in the way that we conceptualize and understand sex/gender dualism. She writes, "It would make no sense, then, to define gender as the cultural interpretation of sex, if sex itself is a gendered category."[7] Gender theorists previously conceptualized "a natural sex" as "prediscursive, prior to culture" (fixed and immutable) and gender as a social construct (culturally determined based on a "pregiven sex").[8] Butler unhinges "the construction of sex as the radically unconstructed."[9] What this means is that "sex" is not a natural category but instead is a construct, as is "gender." This leads to her oft-quoted concept of "gender performativity" in which "gender proves to be performative—that is, constituting the identity it is purported to be. In this sense, gender is always a doing."[10]

Undoing gender displaces sex/gender/desire as "stable" and "oppositionally and hierarchically defined." Undoing gender is embodied by the following examples: one who is born male, gendered feminine, and desires the same sex; one who is born female, gendered masculine, and desires the same sex; one who is born intersex, is gendered nonbinary, and desires women; and one who is born female, has transitioned to male, is gendered masculine, and desires who they desire.[11] Butler's concept "gender performativity" accounts for these "bodies [that] cohere and make sense," that exist.[12] These bodies transgress and transcend boundaries that are set up by a "hegemonic discursive/epistemic model of gender intelligibility" that seeks to erase not only the existence but also the legitimacy of such bodies, sexualities, and persons.

Gender theories when deployed by feminist and queer theorists, activists,[13] and theologians recuperate these "unruly bodies."[14] These bodies are made sacred even as others (not excluding the Catholic Church) deem them profane. This transgression of existing norms is fundamentally why gender theory is maligned by the CCE. On the one hand, "Male and Female" condemns "all expressions of unjust discrimination" and extols the "*equal dignity of men and women*" (MF 15). And it acknowledges "accusations of a sort of masculinity mentality" (MF 15) (read: toxic masculinity) that is upheld by the church and finds full expression in clericalism. Nonetheless, its admonition "*to respect every person* in their particularity and difference" comes with the proviso that what counts are "legitimate expressions of human personhood" as stipulated by the church (MF 16). This yields a deep ambiguity between the church's insistence on "sexual difference," presented as an inviolable "order of nature" (MF 23), and the admonition against "unjust discrimination." Moreover, the church's claim to the moral high ground via its knowledge of the authentic natural order is gravely undermined by its insistence on supporting "*equal dignity*" without acknowledging "*equal value.*" Such hedging is not present in secular ideologies (e.g., Yogyakarta Principles and YP+10) that advocate "for [the *equal dignity* of] the different identities [as they present] them as being of completely *equal value* compared to each other" (MF 21). These differences have significant implications for how families and their members are understood in terms of being rightly acknowledged and protected.

### Reciprocity and Inclusivity within Families

The CCE insists on the naturalness and fixity of "sexual difference" because it underpins the procreative principle of creation that is epitomized in the generation of the human family. Gender theories that call to question such a construct of sexual difference—by insisting on the "*equal value*" and thus "*equal dignity*" of the human person in going beyond the "*heterosexual matrix*"—are framed in "Male and Female" as excessive, even wanton.

The economy of the two sexes, aligned with the two genders, is presented as the biblical basis of Christian anthropology that becomes "moral law, which is inscribed into our nature" (MF 30). At the beginning of creation, the CCE reminds, "'God created man in his own image . . . male and female he created them' (Gen. 1: 27)" (MF 31). From this, an unapologetic institutionalizing of sex/gender dualism follows: "The *self* is completed by the one who is *other than the self.*" Authorized by a masculinized Creator, sexual difference becomes the basis of reciprocity: "both [sexes and genders]

have a point of encounter forming a dynamic of reciprocity which is derived from and sustained by the Creator" (MF 31). The CCE extols "the need to reaffirm the metaphysical roots of sexual difference, as an anthropological refutation of attempts [fueled by gender theories] to negate the male-female duality of human nature, from which the family is generated" (MF 34).

Anomalies that are not contained by the "heterosexual matrix" or male/female dualism are singled out in "Male and Female," namely transgender, intersex, and queer persons. Gender theories that accord legitimacy to these nonbinary and heteronormative subjectivities are depicted as excessive. "Male and Female" defines "queer" as encompassing "dimensions of sexuality that are extremely fluid, flexible, and . . . nomadic[,] . . . [culminating] in the complete emancipation of the individual from any *a priori* given sexual definition . . . seen as overly rigid" (MF 12). Theoretically, the term "queer" defies labeling; it "should *not* be an identity," as Butler opines, "but should name something of the uncapturable or unpredictable trajectory of a sexual life."[15] However, in practice, such "complete emancipation of the individual" as intimated in "Male and Female" is often unrealized. Bridging this gap between theory and practice, aspiration and reality, requires reflexivity even within the queer movement in holding itself accountable to (un)conscious biases and genderized hierarchies that are leveled, in particular, at trans persons of color. Fueled by the ethos of inclusivity, trans advocates "have argued that queer is exclusionary . . . for being presumptively white and classist[,] . . . [and] 'queers of colour' [seek to] expose and oppose its exclusionary limits in the context of a broadening struggle," to "democratize its potential" for all.[16]

This contrasts with the lack of inclusivity in "Male and Female," as its tone slides from objective to hostile:

> The *process of identifying sexual identity* is made more difficult by the fictitious construct known as "gender neuter" or "third gender," which has the effect of obscuring the fact that

a person's sex is a structural determinant of male or female identity. . . . This oscillation between male and female becomes, at the end of the day, only a "provocative" display against so-called "traditional frameworks," and one which, in fact, ignores the suffering of those who have to live situations of sexual indeterminacy. Similar theories aim to annihilate the concept of "nature." (MF 25)

The CCE's stance amounts to gender-based discrimination and violence directed at intersex ("gender neuter") and trans ("third gender") persons. Both negate the church's favored ideology of either-or sex/gender dualism: in the case of intersex persons, they are *naturally* both male and female (e.g., genitals, reproductive organs, chromosomes, etc.), and in the case of trans persons, they *naturally* proliferate two genders as a "third gender" (e.g., male-to-female trans person, female-to-male trans person).

The church's backlash is stark. Nonbinary identities are derided as a "fictitious construct." Their process of becoming, which involves but is not limited to the "*process of identifying sexual identity*," is deemed frivolous for supposedly flaunting a "'provocative' display . . . of sexual indeterminacy." Their process of becoming is also trivialized as mere "oscillation between male and female."

The one true note amid so many false notes is the recognition of "suffering of those who have to live situations of sexual indeterminacy." For the intersex person, sex reassignment or corrective surgery in infancy is a violation of their right to choose: surgeons determine the "true sex" of infants based only on observable physiology, "frightened parents of ambiguously sexed infants" comply, and infants "of course offer no resistance whatever."[17] As Cheryl Chase concludes, corrective surgery is "essentially a destructive process."[18]

For the trans person, their lifelong process of becoming man or woman may or may not involve (often prohibitively expensive) gender-affirming surgery and hormonal therapy. Transphobia, "a hostile response to perceived violations of gender norms and/or to challenges to the gender binary,"[19] relegates many trans persons as social and sexual outcasts within the family and the church (in the way that "Male and Female," for instance, is overtly transphobic) and is the main cause of their "suffering." Transphobia intersects with other axes of power, such as "sexism, racism, classism, ableism,"[20] and points to systemic marginalization of trans persons by legal, social-cultural, and various other institutions.

After deriding persons of "sexual indeterminacy," the CCE next directs its homophobic misgivings to unions that fall outside the heteronormative construct and their offspring. The CCE renders both these persons and their relationships ontologically different and, in effect, nonexistent (they cannot exist theoretically within the boundaries of the operative gender ideology and therefore do not exist at all). Aspersions are cast on gender theories that, if left unchecked, have the capacity to derail the "natural" family and all creation: "But if there is no pre-ordained duality of man and woman in creation, then neither is the family any longer a reality established by creation. Likewise, the child has lost the place he had occupied hitherto and the dignity pertaining to him" (MF 34). "Male and Female" reinstates the church's idealized construct of sexual difference as the "unity of body and soul" (MF 32) and a "unified totality [that] integrates the vertical dimension (human communion with God) with the horizontal dimension constituted by the interpersonal communion that men and woman are called to live" (MF 33). Evidently, happy are those who identify as cisgender (for whom gender identity and expression align with the sex assigned at birth), for theirs is the kingdom of God on Earth. But what of queer-identifying persons who are in intimate partnerships with persons of the same sex, for instance, where "I" is not essentially distinguishable "from the 'thou' and from the 'you'"? Are such persons not ontologically "created for dialogue, for synchronic and diachronic communion" with the other and their Creator? What is the basis for according nonheteronormative bodies and sexualities "*equal dignity*" if they are found wanting physiologically, psychologically, ontologically, anthropologically, and theologically? If all are created *imago Dei*, how are some regarded as inherently lacking and the families that they beget flawed or false as well?

Gender theories beyond the paradigm employed by the CCE thankfully and humanely offer counternarratives against the CCE's construct of sexual difference in two ways. First, they make visible the reductionism entailed as a form of gender-based discrimination and violence. Second, they herald new ways of becoming whereby "*equal dignity*" is premised on "*equal value.*"

Sexual difference is reductionist for two reasons. According to feminist theorist Elizabeth Grosz,

> Biologism is a particular form of essentialism in which women's essence is defined in terms of biological capacities. Biologism is usually based on some form of reductionism . . . [and] ties women closely to the functions of reproduction and nurturance. . . . Biologism is thus an attempt to limit women's social and psychological capacities according to biologically established limits.[21]

Predictably, "Male and Female" extols the "*values of femininity*" (MF 17), just falling short of referencing women's "feminine genius,"[22] which elsewhere[23] is deployed to glorify women's singular contribution as embodying "*affective, cultural and spiritual motherhood*" (MF 18). Such romanticization of women's capacities as divinely ordained almost masks the reductionism of biologism that "ties women closely to the functions of reproduction and nurturance."

### Reciprocity and Inclusivity in Education

The reductive and dualist gender theory driving "Male and Female" also produces clear implications for Christian-based sexuality education. The CCE's vision is premised on a "pre-ordained duality of man and woman in creation" and "the full original truth of masculinity and femininity" (MF 34, 35). The construct of sexual difference, naturalized by the dominance of the first terms in male/female and masculine/feminine dualisms, becomes the basis of reciprocity or gender complementarity: "Therefore, in the light of a *fully human and integral ecology*, women and men will understand the real meaning of sexuality and genitality in terms of the intrinsically relational and communicative intentionality that both informs their bodily nature and moves each one towards the other mutually" (MF 35). These heterosexualized bodies and sexualities that are biologically determined by sexually different "genitalia" (which outlaws intersex, trans, and nonbinary persons) are then conferred the right to found families. The heterosexual family is entrusted with the "primary right . . . [and] most grave duty" to not only beget offspring but also socialize them in the heterosexualized "light of a *fully human and integral ecology*" (MF 37). It is easy to infer that nonheteronormative expressions of personhood—that is, queer bodies, sexualities, unions, and their offspring—are neither "*fully human* [nor part of an] *integral ecology.*" The violence of exclusion and diminishment is thus intergenerationally perpetuated by a heteronormative insistence on only a highly reductionist binary appreciation of human sexual differences. The CCE writes, "It is precisely within the *nucleus of the family unit* that children can learn how to recognise the value and the beauty of the differences between the two sexes, along with their equal dignity and their reciprocity" (MF 38).

From this perspective, the "*nucleus of the family unit*" risks becoming the locus of sexism, homophobia, and transphobia, as it extends what Sara Ahmed, a feminist-queer and postcolonial theorist, terms "the politics of the straight line." As she explains, "Considering the politics of the straight line helps us rethink the relationship between inheritance (the lines that are given as our point of arrival into familial and social space) and reproduction (the demand that we return the gift of the line by extending that line)."[24] Queer persons and their families may inherit these "lines," but they choose to not reproduce them by living out their diverse sexual orientations, gender identities, and expressions of sex characteristics even as many are bereft of fundamental rights, including the right to found a family. The disruption of the "politics of the straight line" more faithfully realizes a faith-based vision of a "broader framework of an education for love, for mutual self-giving" (MF 37).

## INTERPRETATION

### Needed Critique

A feminist critique (within gender theories) enables one to call out the naturalization of sex/gender dualism that is premised on biologism or biological determinism (not every woman desires to mother or to do so within a heterosexual familial context). In doing so, one accrues cultural capital in having the language to contest the church's truth claims regarding the nature of women. Put simply, there is no natural essence or essential nature of woman. The women-centered conventions that reinstate women's unbounded capacities transcend "biologically established limits" and offer a counterpoint to the binary constructs that are the linchpin of the church's theory of gender/sexuality.[25] It is imperative to critique the church's insistence on the inviolability of sexual difference as it is weaponized to reinforce sexism disguised as gender complementarity (which effectively reinstates the primacy of the male and masculine over the female and feminine) and the exclusivity of the male priesthood.

A feminist-queer critique affirms the generation of queer families and parenting that flows from undoing gender. I term this as "doing family,"[26] based on the lived experiences of narratives of resilience and resistance of families with LGBTQ+-identifying fathers, mothers, daughters, and sons.[27] In "Male and Female," nonheteronormative families and parenting are disqualified from rightful existence, as they do not meet the "physiological *complementarity* of male-female sexual difference [that] assures the necessary conditions for procreation" (MF 28). Simply put, penile-vaginal penetration literalizes "the Way, the Truth, and the Life" (John 14:6). "Male and Female" discounts queer couples' recourse to reproductive

technology, as "it is not a replacement for natural conception" (MF 28). In contrast, practitioners of sexual and reproductive health and rights identify the multisectoral players and complex circumstances involved in so-called transgressions whose blame the CCE places especially on queer persons.[28] These include "the manipulation of human embryos, the fragmentation of parenthood, the instrumentalization and/or commercialization of the human body as well as the reduction of a baby to an object in the hands of science and technology" (MF 28). Despite the church's moral condemnations, when heterosexual married couples utilize reproductive technologies they are heavily cautioned (e.g., on respect for human embryos) but not comparably derided by such a list of offenses.[29]

Gender theorists and practitioners recognize that queer families and parenting are "united by a free and fully conscious *pact of conjugal love*" and embody the family as "'an anthropological fact, and consequently a social, cultural fact'" (MF 36). Whereas sexual difference in "Male and Female" is touted as the path to reciprocity, the affirmation of queer families in terms of parenting as having the right to realize their sexual orientation, gender identity and expression, and sex characteristics and start a family show how inclusivity is the bedrock of not only "*equal dignity*" but also "*equal value*."[30] In fact, there can be no "*equal dignity*" without "*equal value*." This seemingly irreconcilable difference sets up a third dualism between the CCE's vision of sexuality education and comprehensive sexuality education. In the former, the primacy of reciprocity (exclusively founded on sexual difference) takes precedence over the primacy of inclusivity (not exclusively founded on sexual difference).

### Inclusive and Comprehensive Christian Sexual Education

A promising rebuttal to the CCE's reductive and exclusionary vision of authentically Christian sexual education may be offered by comprehensive sexuality education (CSE) defined as a rights-based approach to education on sexuality, which discusses not just sex, but also provides young people with skills to be sexually responsible, [and have] positive attitudes, values and essential life skills. It helps young people to acquire the skills to negotiate relationships and safer sexual practices. CSE includes looking at sexuality as a broad issue, including emotional and social development, beyond just the provision of information to young people, and includes diversity and sexual orientation, violence, relationship, pleasure, SRH [sexual and reproductive health] rights and others.[31]

A "rights-based approach" to CSE goes beyond "a laudable desire to combat all expressions of unjust discrimination" (MF 15) in providing young persons and their formators (including peer educators) an inclusive framework of social justice, as it begins from an ethos of *"equal dignity"* and *"equal value."* CSE advocates claim the right and responsibility to educate young persons *"to respect every person* in their particularity and difference, so that no one should suffer bullying, violence, insults, or unjust discrimination" (MF 16). It is CSE that affirms and welcomes all persons without restriction to only "legitimate expressions of human personhood" (MF 16). The International Conference on Population and Development's Youth Bali Declaration calls on multisectoral partnerships among governments, nongovernmental organizations, civil society, the private sector, and the international community to provide CSE for young persons that is "non-discriminatory, non-judgmental, rights-based, age appropriate, gender-sensitive health education including youth-friendly, evidence based comprehensive sexuality education that is context specific."[32]

A CSE founded on equality, mutuality, reciprocity, and justice celebrates a *"fully human and integral ecology."* It realizes the CCE's "call to love" (MF 3) more fully than the contortions and contradictions of "Male and Female" are able to convey. When integrated with a rights-based framework, CSE can potentially be the "path of dialogue" and the antidote to the violence of silencing, deriding, and reducing those whom we so often refuse to recognize.

## NOTES

1. Congregation for Catholic Education, "'Male and Female He Created Them': Towards a Path of Dialogue on the Question of Gender Theory in Education" (February 2, 2019), http://www.educatio.va /content/dam/cec/Documenti/19_0997_INGLESE .pdf (hereafter cited as MF).

2. On ethnoreligious nationalism as a barrier to realizing universal access to sexual and reproductive health service, see Sivananthi Thanenthiran, "Universal Access to SRH and Universality of SRR: Achieving the Impossible?," *ARROWs For Change* 23, no. 2 (2017): 2–5, http://arrow.org.my /wp-content/uploads/2017/08/AFC-23_2_2017 -WEB-2.pdf.

3. Judith Butler, *Gender Trouble: Feminism and the Subversion of Identity*, 2nd ed. (New York: Routledge, 2006), 208.

4. Butler, *Gender Trouble*, 208.

5. Butler, *Gender Trouble*, 208.

6. Butler, *Gender Trouble*, 24.

7. Butler, *Gender Trouble*, 10.

8. See Chris Beasley, *What Is Feminism? An Introduction to Feminist Theory* (London: Sage, 1999), Judith Lorber, *Paradoxes of Gender* (New Haven, CT: Yale University Press, 1994); and Jack Halberstam, *Female Masculinity*, 20th anniversary ed. (Durham, NC: Duke University Press, 2018).

9. Butler, *Gender Trouble*, 10.

10. Butler, *Gender Trouble*, 34.

11. These are four of sixteen research participants from my own study on reconciling one's sexuality and religiosity or spirituality as queer-identifying persons. See Sharon A. Bong, *Becoming Queer and Religious in Malaysia and Singapore* (London: Bloomsbury Academic, 2020).

12. Butler, *Gender Trouble*, 208.

13. See the Yogyakarta Principles and its ten-year review, "Yogyakarta Principles plus 10 or YP+10," https://yogyakartaprinciples.org/, which are arguably the most comprehensive documents on international standards of advancing sexuality rights that are founded on universal human rights with clear

definitions of how sexual orientation, gender identity and expression, and sex characteristics rest on a spectrum and are mutually constitutive.

14. Saskia Wieringa, "Marriage Equality in Indonesia? Unruly Bodies, Subversive Partners and Legal Implications," *Equal Rights Review* 10 (2013): 97–110, https://www.equalrightstrust.org/ert documentbank/ERR10_sp2.pdf. On Asian queer theologies, see Joseph N. Goh, *Becoming a Malaysian Trans Man Gender, Society, Body and Faith* (Singapore: Springer Singapore, 2020); and Joseph N. Goh, *Living Out Sexuality and Faith: Body Admissions of Malaysian Gay and Bisexual Men* (New York: Routledge, 2018).

15. Sara Ahmed, "Interview with Judith Butler," *Sexualities* 19, no. 4 (2016): 489.

16. Ahmed, "Interview with Judith Butler," 490.

17. Cheryl Chase, "Hermaphrodites with Attitude: Mapping the Emergence of Intersex Political Activism," *GLQ* 4, no. 2 (1998): 191.

18. Chase, "Hermaphrodites with Attitude," 192.

19. Talia Mae Bettcher, "Transphobia," *Transgender Studies Quarterly* 1, nos. 1–2 (2014): 249.

20. Bettcher, "Transphobia," 250.

21. Elizabeth Grosz, *Space, Time and Perversion: Essays on the Politics of Bodies* (New York: Routledge, 1995), 48.

22. I offer a more robust argument here in Sharon A. Bong, "Feminine Genius: Revisiting Gender Complementarity Today," in *Towards Just Gender Relations: Rethinking the Role of Women in Church and Society*, ed. Gunter Prüller Jagenteufel, Sharon Bong, and Rita Perintfalvi, 137–45 (Vienna: Vienna University Press, 2019).

23. Building from the gender constructions of John Paul II, Pope Francis says that "the grandeur of women includes all the rights derived from their inalienable human dignity but also from their feminine genius. . . . Their specifically feminine abilities—motherhood in particular— . . . entails a specific mission in this world." Pope Francis, *Amoris laetitia* (March 19, 2016), 173, https://www.vatican.va/content/dam/francesco/pdf/apost_exhortations/documents/papa-francesco_esortazione-ap_20160319_amoris-laetitia_en.pdf. See also chapter 22 in this volume.

24. Sara Ahmed, "Orientations: Toward a Queer Phenomenology," *GLQ* 12, no. 4 (2006): 555.

25. These conventions include the 1979 United Nations Convention on the Elimination of All Forms of Discrimination Against Women, the 1994 Programme of Action of the International Conference of Population and Development, and the 1995 Platform for Action of the United Nations Fourth World Conference on Women.

26. Sharon A. Bong, "Negotiating Resistance/Resilience through the Nexus of Spirituality-Sexuality of Same-Sex Partnerships in Malaysia and Singapore," *Marriage & Family Review* 47, no. 8 (December 2011): 662.

27. LGBTQ+ is used across this volume; however, I prefer the more capacious LGBTIQAP+, which refers to lesbian, gay, bisexual, transgender, intersex, queer or questioning persons, asexual, pansexual, plus others (e.g., nonbinary persons).

28. There is the intersectionality of poverty and gender-based discrimination that is amplified in the culture of son preference in much of Asia. See Amrita Pande, "Commercial Surrogacy in India: Manufacturing a Perfect Mother-Worker," *Signs: Journal of Women in Culture and Society* 35, no. 4 (Summer 2010): 969–92.

29. See Congregation for the Doctrine of the Faith, *Instruction on Respect for Human Life in Its Origin and on the Dignity of Procreation Replies to Certain Questions of the Day* (February 22, 1987), https://www.vatican.va/roman_curia/congregations/cfaith/documents/rc_con_cfaith_doc_19870222_respect-for-human-life_en.html.

30. Yogyakarta Principles, Principle 2, The Right to Equality and Non-Discrimination, and Principle 24, The Right to Found a Family.

31. Rachel Arinii Judhistari, Shubha Kayastha, and Suloshini Jahanath, "Definitions," *ARROW for Change* 18, no. 2 (2012): 27, https://arrow.org.my/wp-content/uploads/2015/04/AFC-Vol.18-No.2-2012_Youth-SRHR-Movements.pdf.

32. International Conference on Population and Development, *ICPD Review Bali Global Youth Forum Declaration*, para. 2.12, https://www.unfpa.org/sites/default/files/resource-pdf/Bali%20Declaration%20English.pdf.

# CONCLUSION

# The History and Future Trajectory of Catholic Family Teaching

JACOB M. KOHLHAAS AND MARY M. DOYLE ROCHE

## SO WHAT?

Our exploration of the tradition of Catholic Family Teaching has been set against the backdrop of admittedly recent history, emerging at the end of the nineteenth century and living into future possibilities. Even within this short history, the story has been turbulent. Families the world over have weathered the suffering and separation brought on by the seismic changes of industrial and technological revolutions as well as war and violence on local, national, and global scales. Families have been impacted by genocide, economic upheaval, debt and structural adjustment policies, political instability and disenfranchisement, environmental devastation and climate change, globalization, migration and internal displacement, and the pernicious phenomena of poverty, racism, sexism, and xenophobia of every stripe. Families have also persistently made their way in the world even when other institutions have either failed or actively undermined them, such as through corporate policies and practices that destabilize the conditions for flourishing families, governments that abdicate their responsibilities to this "first cell" of civil society, and religious and ecclesial communities that impose heavy burdens resulting in exclusion rather than community.

Alongside these struggles, recent generations have witnessed profound improvements, on average, to personal health, safety, and well-being. Since the mid-twentieth century, the global poverty rate has fallen precipitously, and despite the world population tripling, the real number of persons living in poverty has fallen significantly as well. Life expectancy has also increased at an average rate of over four months per year since 1960, adding more than two decades to the average person's life. Child mortality, maternal mortality, and deaths by infectious disease have all seen drastic global decreases as health care access and access to vaccines have improved. Deaths resulting from war have followed an uneven but clear downward trend, and while civil conflicts are up, conflicts between nations are down. Education has also improved lives as literacy rates, access to education, and female educational achievement have all seen remarkable gains in the last century. Despite the profound challenges of countless particular situations, the average family in the world today enjoys greater gender equity, social stability, and well-being for its members than at any previous point in human history.

Some of these improvements to family well-being have been supported by the teaching, activism, and pastoral outreach of the Catholic Church. Through both social and family teaching, the church has supported rights to property and living wages to ensure the financial stability of families. Since the mid-twentieth century, the Vatican has taken a larger role in international organizations and has advocated for humane treatment of immigrants and refugees while calling for the world to recognize the horrors of war and the profound threat of global climate change. Through a global network of parishes, religious orders, and charitable organizations, Catholic institutions have also provided food, shelter, and assistance to countless families in need.

Other developments represent missed opportunities in which the Catholic Church might have been a vanguard for change but was instead brought along reluctantly. The church lagged behind Western social advancements in coeducation, women's social rights, ecumenical and interreligious engagement, environmental concerns, and several other notable areas, only to latter concede and in some cases even become a significant global voice in advocating for these very social changes.

The journey through this heritage also calls us to reckon with the repeated inconsistencies in the church's ability to live up to the best of its own teaching and, more importantly, the heart of the gospel. The Catholic Church, staunch defender of "the family," has paradoxically also been a weak ally and at times actively antagonistic to the needs of many actual families. Within only the last two centuries, Catholic institutions and many among the Catholic faithful enslaved other human beings and sundered their families in this practice. Catholic institutions constructed safe houses and then exploited the vulnerability of "unwed" mothers, forcing them to relinquish their children to others deemed worthy of rearing children. Catholic institutions separated indigenous children from their families and subjected many to terrible abuse in residential schools while attempting to eradicate languages, cultures, and valued traditions. Large swaths of the Catholic faithful as well as Catholic leaders often stood on the sidelines or even opposed advancements in women's rights and civil rights. Priests and bishops covered up the systemic sexual abuse of children by clergy and other people with power in ecclesial communities, while many of the lay faithful shunned those who raised questions. In some countries, the Catholic Church has lobbied for policies that disqualify some families, based on structures declared "irregular," from accessing key goods and services, including welcoming children, exercising responsible parenthood, gaining legal access to accompany loved ones in illness, and transmitting resources from one generation to the next. The church's relations with LGBTQ+ persons and communities remains a key area of social contention whereby vulnerable persons and populations are far too frequently identified as threats to church and society. In these pursuits, the church and its representatives have followed a narrow moral agenda that often so prioritizes moral norms related to sex, gender, and reproduction that it negates parallel moral commitments to social justice, supportive human relationships, and individual well-being.

At times, voices outside or even in opposition to the Catholic Church identified issues with a moral clarity that Catholic leaders struggled to find. These same leaders often continued to push their efforts well after the social tide had shifted. When moral understanding within the church has developed significantly in light of changing social and contextual knowledge, the church often seems to devote more effort to explaining away or misremembering its earlier position than facing its moral shortcomings with honest memory, open repentance, and an earnest commitment to learn from this history.

This all raises the question of whether so many families have survived and flourished due to being buoyed by the support of the tradition of the church's family teaching or have done so simply alongside or even in spite of these ecclesial pronouncements. That is, concerning Catholic Family Teaching, is there a baby in this bathwater, or are these documents so distorted by the influences of patriarchy, misogyny, white/European supremacy, and clericalism as to be of little value for the future of the church? Can we, for example, legitimately say that the history of family separation is merely a series of isolated incidents carried out by sinful individual actors (the proverbial bad apples in the bushel) while ignoring the systemic connections and historical duration of such practices? Given such checkered moral awareness in the past, why listen now? What claims do these documents actually place on families today or on theological reflection in our contemporary lived experiences?

Contributors to this volume have read and reflected on the documents with care, generosity, and from informed critical vantage points. Offering commentary and interpretation from various geographical, social, and disciplinary locations, they are keenly attentive to the intrinsic dignity of persons and families and the biblical witness to both inclusion and hard choices. They have come to this work through their families of origin and their ministries to families, and many are counted among an increasing number of theologians who are married, parenting children of various ages and abilities, or who shoulder the primary responsibility for the care and provision of vulnerable family members. Many of them teach young people who are actively discerning their role in the church and the world, the kind of work they will do, and the role that family will play in a life well lived.

While many have called the documents and the church itself to account for inadequacies, missed opportunities, and failings, they have all written with hope. The world church, this family of families, can indeed do what families of all shapes and sizes do best: provide for and welcome one another; seek and offer forgiveness; navigate the claims of self-care, fidelity, and justice; educate for solidarity with the vulnerable; reach across differences; and hand on the stories and practices that shape persons and communities from generation to generation. The church, the People of God, the Body of Christ, is happening. It arises in families, around kitchen tables, beside sickbeds, on the dangerous routes of migration, in moments of celebration and loss, and in so much daily muddling through. Most of the time the People of God are witnessing, welcoming, and celebrating Christ in the world and in one another without ever reading a papal document. They do this by

relying on the sources with which this volume begins: the scriptural narrative of salvation history, the support of faith communities for both material and spiritual well-being, lived experiences of love and suffering, and their relationship with God.

Despite several decades of explicitly being offered to the whole People of God, these documents (particularly as they recede into history) are generally read by those who hold academic titles or positions of leadership in the church. They are read by those who have taken up professional ministry and religious life; they are read by those who teach and those with the power of the pulpit. The documents have also met with varying degrees of reception. Some documents or parts of documents have been embraced and acted upon by both clerical leadership and "the people in the pews," while others have been severely criticized or simply ignored. As we moved through the twentieth century and into the twenty-first, the speed with which documents are promulgated and then accessed has also increased dramatically. Social media and other technological innovations mean that news and commentaries (whether expert, biased, or ill-informed) spread quickly, often much quicker than individuals are capable of adequately digesting and reflecting upon a document's contents. These advances have brought both greater access and transparency but also the possibility for sound bites to distort the conversation and foster misunderstanding and division.

Our access to information and, we might say, movements for fuller and more democratic participation in social life generally is raising the expectations of many of the faithful to fuller participation in the life of the church and in its governing and teaching functions. Documents drafted in what appears to be the isolation or seclusion of their writers and paradoxically claim an objective "view from nowhere" while purportedly speaking for everyone are increasingly vulnerable, and rightly so, to gathering dust. In the context of family teaching in particular, documents drafted exclusively by a celibate male clergy with limited consultation will continue to struggle to rally convincing authority and find meaningful impact in many quarters.

The vision of synodality espoused by Francis offers grounds for hope in this collection. Synods have been convened not only precisely on family life and the vocation of young people but also on the synodal process itself. Such an emphasis on our common need to walk together in discernment holds great promise. Though the depth of consultation has been uneven across dioceses, the synods have begun with an invitation to the faithful, to the family of families, to raise their voices and to share their experiences, challenges, and, crucially, their wisdom about life in the world as well as life in the Spirit. The faithful have been given (or have seized?) a more public and transparent platform from which to speak. The heart of the matter now is whether church leadership is really listening and open to transformation and whether the process can become ever more inclusive and not limited to only those willing to blindly cheerlead for the church or offer rationalizations for flawed authoritative assertions. When documents are the fruit of genuine egalitarian collaboration across experiences of difference, guided by the Spirit in love and mercy, we might expect to discover a richer theological anthropology and a wider prophetic vision that will inspire personal, social, and structural transformation in every sphere of life.

We hope that the context, commentary, and interpretation offered by this diverse group of theologians will spark further critical inquiry into the tradition of family teaching and its dynamic interactions with Catholic Social Teaching more broadly conceived. We also hope that an ever more diverse guild will take up this research and shape the theological and moral discourse that will inform the drafting of future documents and their reception. The Catholic Church has global reach and influence. Its organizations and institutions provide for the needs of many families for spiritual sustenance, food and shelter, children's education, adoption services, access to basic health care, and due process before the law. Held accountable to the claims of its own documentary heritage and to the gospel by a fully engaged community of faithful, these organizations and institutions can atone for the violations of past and present and act decisively to make the path to flourishing easier for all families. With or without this commitment, families of faith will certainly continue to make their own way wherever two or more are gathered.

# APPENDIX 1

LETTER OF THE HOLY FATHER FRANCIS
TO THE PRESIDENT OF THE PONTIFICAL COUNCIL FOR THE FAMILY
ON THE EIGHTH WORLD MEETING OF FAMILIES

[PHILADELPHIA, SEPTEMBER 22–27, 2015]

To my esteemed Brother,
Archbishop Vincenzo Paglia,
President of the Pontifical Council for the Family

At the close of the Seventh World Meeting of Families, Pope Benedict XVI announced that the next gathering would be hosted in the City of Philadelphia in the United States. I have confirmed that choice on several occasions, and I look forward with confidence and hope to this grace-filled event, which, God willing, I will attend.

The Meeting will take place between September 22 and September 27, 2015, and its theme will be "Love is Our Mission: The Family Fully Alive."

Today as in the past, the mission of the Christian family is to proclaim God's love to the world through the power of the Sacrament of Holy Matrimony. From this proclamation itself, life-filled families are born and built up, and the center of their human and spiritual dynamism is a loving hearth and home. If it is true that, in the words of St. Irenaeus of Lyons, "Human life is God's glory" *(Adv. Haer.,* IV, 20, 7), it is also true that families give glory to God when, relying on His grace, they live their vocation and their mission to the full.

The Church recently held a Special Assembly of the Synod of Bishops on the subject of "The Pastoral Challenges to the Family in the Context of Evangelization." In an exercise of synodality, we identified the most pressing questions that affect the family in our pluralistic society. Basically, "We cannot put the family into ideological categories, we cannot speak of a conservative family and a liberal family. Family is family!" (*Address to the Participants in the International Colloquium on the Complementarity between Man and Woman*, November 17, 2014). The values and virtues of the family—its essential truths—are the family unit's strengths and are not open to challenge. Rather, it is our own way of life that we must re-examine. It runs a continual risk of being "infected" by worldly attitudes—individualist, consumption-driven, sensual—but our people's task is to keep to the high road, where they live out, and are examples of, the beauty of Holy Matrimony and of the joy of being and forming a family.

The direction given by the Final Report of the recent Synod, as well as that which is guiding the way toward the Ordinary Assembly to be held in October of 2015, invite us to continue our commitment to preaching the Gospel of Holy Matrimony and the family, and to testing pastoral initiatives against the social and cultural context in which we live. The challenges of that context will move us to make increasingly more room for that faithful love which is open to life, to communion, to mercy, to sharing and to solidarity. Accordingly, I urge husbands and wives, priests and parish communities, and the movements and association as well, to let themselves be led by the Word of God, which is the foundation of the holy edifice that is the family—the domestic Church, the family of God (cf. *Con. Oecu. Vat. II, Cost. Dogm. De Eccl. Lumen Gentium*, 6:11).

I appreciate the generous cooperation and organizing commitment that the Archdiocese of Philadelphia is contributing to the Universal Church and to families from the several Continents. I ask the Lord to reward this beloved Local Church, even now, with abundant heavenly blessings.

Invoking the intercession of Our Lady of Guadalupe and Aparecida, I am pleased to bestow upon you, dear Brother, and on the staff of your Council, my Apostolic Blessing, which I gladly extend to all who are working on the preparations for the Meeting. And I ask you please to pray for me.

Fraternally,

Francis

Vatican City, December 9, 2014

# APPENDIX 2

Timeline of Documents and Themes of Catholic Family Teaching

| Gender & Sexual Morality | Marriage & Family Life | Children & Education | Social Mission & Support of Families |
|---|---|---|---|
| | **1880:** *Arcanum divinae sapientiae* Christian marriage | | |
| | | **1885:** *Spectata fides* Christian education | |
| | | | **1891:** *Rerum novarum* Conditions of labor |
| | | **1905:** *Acerbo nimis* Christian education | |
| | | **1919:** *Paterno iam diu* Charitable care for children after the war | |
| | | **1920:** *Annus iam plenus* Continued charitable support for children | |
| | | **1929:** *Divini illius magistri* Christian education | |
| | **1930:** *Casti connubii* Christian marriage | | |
| | | | **1931:** *Quadragesimo anno* The social order |
| | | **1946:** *Quemadmodum* Care for children after the war | |
| | | | **1965:** *Gaudium et spes* The church in the modern world |
| | | **1965:** *Gravissimum educationis* Christian education | |
| | **1968:** *Humanae vitae* Birth regulation and Christian marriage | | |
| **1975:** *Persona humana* Sexual morality | | | |

| Gender & Sexual Morality | Marriage & Family Life | Children & Education | Social Mission & Support of Families |
|---|---|---|---|
| | | | **1981:** *Laborem exercens* — Human work |
| | **1981:** *Familiaris consortio* — The Christian family | | |
| **1986: Letter to the Bishops** — Care of homosexual persons | | | |
| **1988:** *Mulieris dignitatem* — The dignity and vocation of women | | | |
| **1989:** *Redemptoris custos* — The person and mission of St. Joseph | | | |
| | | | **1991:** *Centesimus annus* — 100th anniversary of *Rerum novarum* |
| **1992: Some Considerations** — Discrimination and homosexual persons | | | |
| | **1994: Letter to Families** | | |
| | | **1994: Letter to Children** | |
| **1995: Letter to Women** | | | |
| | **2003: Considerations Regarding** — Legality of same-sex unions | | |
| | | | **2009:** *Caritas in veritate* — Truth, love, and social teaching |
| | | | **2011:** *Africae munis* — The church in Africa |
| | **2016:** *Amoris laetitia* — The Christian family | | |
| | | **2019:** *Christus vivit* — Young people | |
| **2020: Male & Female He Created Them** — Education and gender theory | | | |

# APPENDIX 3

## ADDITIONAL NOTABLE PAPACIES AND DOCUMENTS

The chapters of this volume represent an initial framework for understanding Catholic Family Teaching (CFT) as a historically developing documentary heritage. The selection of chapters prioritized authoritative documents of the universal magisterial while building a representative timeline of developments in CFT. For those interested in further study, this appendix offers brief summaries of additional papacies and documents not directly included in the preceding commentaries.

### Pius X

Pius X is remembered largely for his personal holiness, revision to the age of first communion, and authorship of the "Oath against Modernism" in 1910, to which Catholic clerics and academics were required to swear allegiance until 1967.[1] Many of his encyclicals offer apocalyptic presentations of contemporary social conditions. For example, *Pascendi dominici gregis* proclaims that "it must be confessed that the number of the enemies of the cross of Christ has in these last days increased exceedingly, who are striving, by arts, entirely new and full of subtlety, to destroy the vital energy of the Church, and, if they can, to overthrow utterly Christ's kingdom itself."[2] Pius X found enemies of the church both externally and internally while utilizing excommunication as a weapon against dissent.[3] The same document moves toward conspiratorial thinking as it presents the intellectual threats against the church as not only craven but also concerted and organized.[4]

Unsurprisingly, Pius X's encyclical on Christian education, *Acerbo nimis* of 1905, offers a gloomy assessment of its social context. The church is presented as declining and besieged by the Devil, while the faithful lack both commitment and knowledge.[5] *Acerbo nimis* identifies priests as primarily responsible for the religious education of both children and adults.[6] The document enacts several parish regulations including one hour of catechetical instruction for children every Sunday, sacramental preparation for young people (with a minimum of daily instruction throughout Lent for those preparing for first communion), a Confraternity of Christian Doctrine in every parish, and religious education classes for students in public schools.[7] These same propensities colored Pius X's interventions on behalf of Christian marriage. Like many of his predecessors, Pius X discouraged marriages between Catholics and other Christians,[8] and he also disdained secular political authorities who encroached upon the church's singular right to regulate many aspects of marriage.[9]

Pius X's *Quam singulari* set the age of first communion lower than widely established practice. The document recounts the historical diversity of first communion, ranging from infant communion upon baptism to more recent prohibitions up to the age of fourteen, which he presents as an abuse of conciliar teachings.[10] Rather than legislating a particular age, Pius X emphasized the ability to make rational distinctions as central to a child's preparedness, a capability usually achieved by "about the seventh year."[11] *Quam singulari* is also notable for emphasizing the irrational innocence of childhood in contrast to adulthood, which is inherently beset with moral danger. The limited transitional period between these appears stark to a contemporary reader.

Interestingly, *Quam singulari* makes no direct mention of motherhood. In accord with the *Roman Catechism*, responsibility for discerning if an individual child is sufficiently mature to receive communion belongs to the father and the parish priest.[12] The decree offers the slight adaptation: "the father, or the person taking his place." This makes room for maternal discernment (assisted by a priest) in the absence of a father but generally upholds the traditional association of men with leadership and rationality to the exclusion of mothers.

### Benedict XV

World War I and its aftermath consumed Benedict XV's papacy. Pius X died in the consequential month of August, 1914. Only three weeks earlier, Austria-Hungary had declared war on Serbia, and the onslaught of invasions coupled with declarations of war and alliance had already set the stage for bloody conflict. Amid this turmoil, Benedict XV assumed the papacy on September 3, 1914. He quickly declared neutrality for the Holy See and repeatedly attempted to broker peace between the warring factions.

Benedict XV's first encyclical, *Ad beatissimi apostolorum*, called for a peaceful resolution to conflict and lamented the horrors of the three-month-old war. "There is no limit to the measure of ruin and of slaughter; day by day the earth is drenched with newly-shed blood, and is covered with the bodies of the wounded and of the slain. Who would imagine as we see them thus filled with hatred of one another, that they are all of one common stock, all of the same nature, all members of the same human society?"[13] Despite his ineffective political efforts, Benedict XV's humanitarian concerns established a precedent for future wartime papacies.

Following the war, Benedict XV authored an encyclical on peace and reconciliation[14] and two encyclicals appealing for the charitable care of children affected by the war. The first of this pair, *Paterno iam diu* of 1919, acknowledges the work of "save the children" societies begun in England that same year. Only seven years earlier, Pius X had clarified that Catholics were not permitted to participate in religiously mixed worker's unions, as these touched the "sphere of religion and morality." For the integrity of their faith, Catholics were only permitted to participate in organizations founded on the "commandments and precepts of the Catholic Faith."[15] In contrast, Benedict XV raises no sectarian qualms about the "save the children" associations and simply endorses their social moral mission.[16]

The second encyclical, *Annus iam plenus*, explicitly calls upon children as agents of charity for their distant peers.

> Yes, We call on all who have hearts of kindness and pity to make a generous offering, but in particular we turn to the young children who dwell in the more prosperous cities of the world, to those who can with comparative ease stretch out a helping hand to their poor little brothers in Christ. Is not the birthday of Christ Jesus, in an especial manner the feast of the young? See then how the desolate children of those scattered districts strain suppliant hands to those other happier children, and seem to point to the cradle where the Divine Infant cries in helplessness![17]

Like his predecessor, Benedict XV generally portrays children as innocent, and although it may be largely rhetorical and intended to move parents to action, his direct appeal to children uniquely engages them as responsible moral agents. Both Benedict XV and Pius X occasionally recognized capacities for spiritual longing and moral obligations at relatively young ages. This complicates the innocence that otherwise tends to guide their views of childhood.

## 1917 Code of Canon Law

The *Code of Canon Law*, initiated in the first year of Pius X's papacy with the 1904 bull *Arduum sane munus*,[18] was completed under his successor, Benedict XV, in 1917 and promulgated with the bull *Providentissima mater*.[19] The regulations of the code have several implications for thought on marriage and the family, particularly in its description of marriage as a contract, the ordering of the ends of marriage, and the failure to create a meaningful place for love between spouses.[20]

The concept of marriage as a contract was informed by previous and ongoing contentions with civil authorities over the regulation of marriage. Because the Catholic Church understood itself as the divinely appointed arbiter of marriage, popes argued that the contract itself was essentially and inseparably bound to the sacrament of marriage, in contrast to civil claims that distinguished the contract from the religious ceremony.[21]

Leo XIII had also presented marriage as a contract in *Arcanum*;[22] however, the *Code of Canon Law* reaches a new level of specificity. Canon 1081.2. states, "Matrimonial consent is an act of the will by which each party gives and accepts perpetual and exclusive rights to the body, for those actions that are of themselves suitable for the generation of children." The following canon, 1082, states, "In order that matrimonial consent be considered [valid], it is necessary that the contractants at least not be ignorant that marriage is a permanent society between a man and woman for the procreation of children." Subsequent canons

directly address impediments to validly contracted marriages based on this formal juridical definition.[23]

The *Code of Canon Law* was compiled precisely to provide order to the church's juridical norms such that it offers only a minimal and legalistic definition of marriage with little theological context. The definition functions well in securing the basic analytical framework to which the subsequent canons relate. Marriage in Catholic canon law is sacramental and irrevocable and ordered toward the procreation and education of children. The preponderance of canons regarding marriage clearly refer back to these central features.

Education of children comes up repeatedly as an obligation of marriage, particularly education in the Catholic faith. Canon 1112 states, "Parents are bound by the most grave obligation to take care as far as they are able for the education of children, both religious and moral, as well as physical and civil, and of providing them with temporal goods." Indeed, this obligation is so serious that failure on the part of one spouse to educate children in the Catholic faith constitutes grounds for separation from common life.[24]

Nonetheless, juridical definitions are a poor substitute for theological reflection on the fuller dimensions of marriage and family life. The church believes as it prays, not at is legislates. Consequently, the stature this reductive account came to occupy in theological and pastoral perspectives became problematic, as it represented a reversal of theological priorities. This incompleteness was addressed through Vatican II's use of the more commodious concept of covenant.

## John XXIII

John XXIII had a monumental impact on the Catholic Church by calling the Second Vatican Council but did not compose any significant documents on the family as such. His two social encyclicals, *Mater et magistra* (1961) and *Pacem in terris* (1963), both address numerous issues affecting the well-being of families and in so doing demonstrate the rich interconnectedness between the traditions of Catholic Social Teaching (CST) and CFT.

John XXIII's understanding of the family generally coincides with that of his predecessors. This is exemplified in repeated themes including the family as the foundation of society, the obligations of society to the family, the primary right and obligations of parents in the education of their children, and the importance of stable marriages and families.[25] His social encyclicals developed existing themes of CST related to family well-being, such as family wages,[26] protections for immigrants,[27] and the needs of those who make their living as artisans or through farming.[28]

The most notable shift in John XXIII's writings is his affirmation of women's changing social roles. "Women are gaining an increasing awareness of their natural dignity. Far from being content with a purely passive role or allowing themselves to be regarded as a kind of instrument, they are demanding both in domestic and in public life the rights and duties which belong to them as human persons."[29] This statement is remarkable, as Leo XIII's *Arcanum divinae* and Pius XI's *Casti connubii* had firmly established the primacy of husband over wife and the primary and nearly exclusive obligation of women to the home and family.[30] John XXIII still affirms women's unique calling to motherhood and understands motherhood primarily as work within the home, but this is no longer cast as inevitably in conflict with greater social freedoms and involvement in public life. Moreover, this change of view is explicitly identified as a product of women's own experience. Predictably, *Pacem in terris* does not call attention to how women's own insights have revised established authoritative papal teaching. Two years later, *Gaudium et spes* further developed John XXIII's affirmation,[31] and the postconciliar church followed the council's lead. The question of women's social rights was redefined as the noninherently conflictual task of appropriately balancing women's primary vocation and obligations in motherhood with recognition of female dignity, equality, and rightful claims to equitable inclusion in public life.

## Theology of the Body

In November 1979, less than a year after becoming pope, John Paul II began delivering catechetical instruction through a series of papal audiences that became known as the Theology of the Body. The first set of addresses, "Catechesis on the Book of Genesis," laid the foundations for a personalist anthropology that ultimately supported the normative moral claims of *Humanae vitae*. The second series provided a catechesis on the Sermon on the Mount. In these, lust acquires central importance for understanding the postlapsarian human, who has become "the man of lust."[32] The fall brought about the human capacity to objectify other persons and desire to dominate them, which stands in direct contradiction to the personalist moral norm.[33]

Although these addresses were no more authoritative than the nearly forgotten addresses of Pius XII three decades earlier, they quickly acquired a significant level of influence in Catholic thought that has been both hailed and contested ever since. The Theology of the Body has been popularized and embraced in many forms even though many of the Catholic faithful remain unaware or uninterested in its content. Among academics, some have strongly supported John Paul II's perspective as a nearly inviolable explication of true doctrine, while others have sharply questioned its methodology, motivations, and conclusions.[34]

The speeches do provide supplemental explanatory support for authoritative teaching, and despite not holding a high level of authority as addresses alone, some of their elements were quickly incorporated into more authoritative documents. These include the norm that moral sexual relations are characterized by a mutual self-gift and that men and women are complementary in their persons, specifically as a function of gendered differences. Already by 1994, merely fifteen years after being posited by John Paul II, these ideas were included in the *Catechism of the Catholic Church*.[35]

## NOTES

1. Pius X, "The Oath against Modernism," Papal Encyclicals Online, 1910, https://www.papal encyclicals.net/pius10/p10moath.htm. The oath appears in Latin under the section titled "Iurisiurandi Formula" in Piux X. *Sacrorum Antistitum* (n.d.), https://www.vatican.va/content/pius-x/la/motu_proprio/documents/hf_p-x_motu-proprio_19100901_sacrorum-antistitum.html.

2. Pius X, *Pascendi dominici gregis* (September 8, 1907), 1, https://www.vatican.va/content/pius-x/en/encyclicals/documents/hf_p-x_enc_19070908_pascendi-dominici-gregis.html.

3. Pius X, *Pascendi dominici gregis*, 2; and Pius X, *Praestantia scripturae* (November 18, 1907), 1–5, https://www.papalencyclicals.net/pius10/p10prasc.htm. (This version of *Praestantia scripturae* does not contain internal paragraph numbering. Latin and Italian texts are available at vatican.va).

4. Pius X, *Pascendi dominici gregis*, 4. A comparative rhetorical study of Pius X's antimodernist social analysis and more recent documents dealing with sexual and gender diversity could well elucidate reoccurring conceptual patterns in CFT.

5. Pius X, *Acerbo nimis* (April 15, 1905), 1, https://www.vatican.va/content/pius-x/en/encyclicals/documents/hf_p-x_enc_15041905_acerbo-nimis.html.

6. Pius X, *Acerbo nimis*, 9–12.

7. Pius X, *Acerbo nimis*, 19–24.

8. See chapter 4 of this volume; Gregory XVI, *Summo iugitar studio* (May 27, 1832), https://www.papalencyclicals.net/greg16/g16summo.htm; and Gregory XVI, *Quas vestro* (April 30, 1841), https://www.papalencyclicals.net/greg16/g16quasv.htm. Both of the works by Gregory XVI are available in Italian at vatican.va.

9. Pius X, *Afflictum propioribus* (November 24, 1906), in the Benedictine Monks of Solesmes, *Matrimony*, trans. Michael J. Byrnes (Boston: St. Paul Editions, 1963), 204 (available in Latin at vatican.va). This took the form of enforcing the Council of Trent's prohibition of clandestine marriages, in this case marriages contracted between consenting parties without a priest and at least two witnesses present. Pius required Catholics to follow the canonical form of the sacrament but allowed for the validity of Protestant marriages contracted outside of this form. See Pius X, *Provida sapientique* (January 18, 1906), in the Benedictine Monks of Solesmes, *Matrimony*, 202. Cf. Pius X, *Ne temere* (August 2, 1907), in The Benedictine Monks of Solesmes, *Matrimony*, 205.

10. Pius X, *Quam singulari* (August 7, 1910), 1–7, https://www.papalencyclicals.net/pius10/p10quam.htm.

11. Pius X, *Quam singulari*, 14, 21.1.

12. Pius X, *Quam singulari*, 21.4, 18.

13. Benedict XV, *Ad beatissimi apostolorum* (November 1, 1914), 3, https://www.vatican.va/content/benedict-xv/en/encyclicals/documents/hf_ben-xv_enc_01111914_ad-beatissimi-apostolorum.html.

14. See Benedict XV, *Pacem, Dei munus pulcherrimum* (May 23, 1920), https://www.vatican.va/content/benedict-xv/en/encyclicals/documents/hf_ben-xv_enc_23051920_pacem-dei-munus-pulcherrimum.html.

15. Pius X, *Singulari quadam* (September 24, 1912), 4, https://www.vatican.va/content/pius-x/en/encyclicals/documents/hf_p-x_enc_24091912_singulari-quadam.html.

16. Save the Children was founded in 1919 by the sisters Eglantyne Jedd, an Episcopalian, and Dorothy Buxton, a Quaker.

17. Benedict XV, *Annus iam plenus* (December 1, 1920), 2, https://www.vatican.va/content/benedict-xv/en/encyclicals/documents/hf_ben-xv_enc_01121920_annus-iam-plenus.html, 2.

18. Pius X, *Arduum sane munus* (April 14, 1904) https://www.vatican.va/content/pius-x/la/motu_proprio/documents/hf_p-x_motu-proprio_19040414_arduum-sane.html. This text is available only in Latin.

19. Benedict XV, *Providentissima mater* (May 27, 1917), https://www.vatican.va/content/benedict-xv/it/bulls/documents/hf_ben-xv_bulls_19170527_providentissima-mater.html. This text is available in Italian and Latin.

20. Salzman and Lawler view the code largely as innovative within the tradition, whereas García de Haro sees it as continuous with the developing thought of canonists. Both see the code's description of marriage as incomplete but disagree on whether it constitutes a divergence from or clarification of the larger tradition. See Todd Salzman and Michael

Lawler, *The Sexual Person* (Washington, DC: Georgetown University Press, 2008), 37–38; and Ramón García de Haro, *Marriage and the Family in the Documents of the Magisterium*, trans. William E. May (San Francisco: Ignatius, 1993), 95–97.

21. Leo XIII wrote letters concerning the relation of civil and ecclesial authority to Piedmont, Italy, as well as to France, Peru, and Hungary. Pius X wrote a similar letter to Bolivia.

22. Leo XIII, *Arcanum divinae* (February 10, 188), 23–24, https://www.vatican.va/content/leo-xiii/en/encyclicals/documents/hf_l-xiii_enc_10021880_arcanum.html.

23. 1917 *Code of Canon Law*, 1081.2, 1082.

24. 1917 *Code of Canon Law*, 1131.1. Canon 1132 acknowledges the possibility of non-Catholic spouses assuming responsibility for the education of children in the Catholic faith should their partner fail in their duties.

25. See John XXIII, *Mater et magistra* (May 15, 1961), 193–95, https://www.vatican.va/content/john-xxiii/en/encyclicals/documents/hf_j-xxiii_enc_15051961_mater.html; and John XXIII, *Pacem in terris* (November 4, 1963), 16–17, https://www.vatican.va/archive/hist_councils/ii_vatican_council/documents/vat-ii_const_19651207_gaudium-et-spes_en.html.

26. John XXIII, *Mater et magistra*, 13, 33; and John XXIII, *Pacem in terris*, 20.

27. John XXIII, *Mater et magistra*, 45. Cf. John XXIII, *Pacem in terris*, 25, 105–8.

28. John XXIII, *Mater et magistra*, 85–90, 123–27, 131–46.

29. John XXIII, *Pacem in terris*, 41.

30. See Leo XIII, *Arcanum*, 11; and Pius XI, *Casti connubii* (December 31, 1930), 74–75, https://www.vatican.va/content/pius-xi/en/encyclicals/documents/hf_p-xi_enc_19301231_casti-connubii.html.

31. Vatican II, *Gaudium et spes* (December 7, 1965), 52, 60, https://www.vatican.va/archive/hist_councils/ii_vatican_council/documents/vat-ii_const_19651207_gaudium-et-spes_en.html.

32. John Paul II, *Blessed Are the Pure of Heart* (Boston: Pauline Books & Media, 1988), 36.

33. John Paul II, *Blessed Are the Pure of Heart*, 79.

34. Hogan and LeVoir describe this as a unique methodological achievement in uniting the important yet dangerously subjective insights of phenomenology with the objective truths of moral teaching through the use Genesis, which communicates "objective truth which is at the same time central to human experience." Richard M. Hogan and John M. LeVoir, *Covenant of Love: Pope John Paul II on Sexuality* (Garden City, NY: Doubleday, 1985), 4.

35. *Catechism of the Catholic Church*, 2nd ed. (Vatican City: Libreria Editrice Vaticana, 1994), 2333, 2337, 2346, https://www.usccb.org/sites/default/files/flipbooks/catechism/.

# CONTRIBUTORS

**Sharon A. Bong, PhD,** is a professor of gender studies at the School of Arts and Social Sciences, Monash University Malaysia (Bandar Sunway). She has authored *Becoming Queer and Religious in Malaysia and Singapore* (2020) and *The Tension between Women's Rights and Religions: The Case of Malaysia* (2006) and coedited *Gender and Sexuality Justice in Asia* (2020). She was a forum writer for Catholic Theological Ethics in the World Church and a member of the board of editors and board of directors for *Concilium*, the international journal for theology.

**Maria Elisa A. Borja, PhD,** is an assistant professor at the Ateneo de Manila University (Quezon City, Philippines), where she received her PhD in moral theology. She teaches marriage, family, and vocation. She recently published "The Ties That Bind: Filipino Female Transmigration and the Left-Behind Family as Domestic Church of the Poor through the Lens of the FABC" in the book *Catholicism in Migration and Disapora,* edited by Gemma Tulud Cruz (Routledge, 2023), and "Catholic Families in Asia: Living the Eucharist as the Domestic Church of the Poor" in the journal *Loyola Papers* (2022).

**Teresa Delgado, PhD,** is the dean of St. John's College of Liberal Arts and Sciences at St. John's University (Queens, New York). Previously, she served as director of the Peace and Justice Studies Program and professor and chairperson of the Religious Studies Department at Iona College (New Rochelle, New York). She received her doctorate from Union Theological Seminary (New York City) under the guidance of the trailblazing womanist theologian Dr. Delores S. Williams. Delgado has published on topics including diversity in higher education, transformational pedagogies, constructive theology and ethics, and justice for racially, ethnically, and sexually minoritized persons.

**Mary M. Doyle Roche, PhD,** is an associate professor of religious studies at the College of the Holy Cross (Worcester, Massachusetts), where she teaches courses in Christian ethics and Catholic moral theology. She is the author of *Children, Consumerism, and the Common Good* (Lexington, 2009) and *Schools of Solidarity: Families and Catholic Social Teaching* (Liturgical Press, 2015) and editor of "Children and Youth: Forming the Moral Life," special issue of *Journal of Moral Theology* (January 2018).

**Craig A. Ford Jr., PhD,** is an assistant professor of theology and religious studies at St. Norbert College (De Pere, Wisconsin) and serves on the faculty at the Institute for Black Catholic Studies at Xavier University of Louisiana (New Orleans), the only Catholic Historically Black College or University in the United States. He earned his PhD at Boston College (Massachusetts) and writes at the intersection of queer theory, critical race theory, and the Catholic moral tradition.

**Eric Marcelo O. Genilo, SJ,** is an ordained minister and a member of the Society of Jesus, Philippine Province. He is a professor of moral theology at the Loyola School of Theology at Ateneo de Manila University and a formator of diocesan seminarians at San Jose Seminary in Quezon City, Philippines. He earned his licentiate and doctoral degrees at Weston Jesuit School of Theology (Cambridge, Massachusetts).

**Julie Hanlon Rubio, PhD,** is Shea-Heusaman Professor of Christian Social Ethics and Associate Dean at the Jesuit School of Theology of Santa Clara University (Berkeley, California). Her research focuses on Catholic social thought, family, feminism, and politics. She has published seven books, including *Family Ethics: Practices for Christians* (Georgetown, 2010); *Sex, Love, and Marriage: Catholic Perspectives* (Liturgical Press, 2020), which she edited with Jason King; and *Can You Be a Catholic and Feminist?* (Oxford University Press, 2024).

**Jason King, PhD,** is Beirne Chair and director of the Center for Catholic Studies at St. Mary's University in San Antonio, Texas. He received his PhD from the Catholic University of America (Washington, DC). He currently serves as editor emeritus of the *Journal of Moral Theology.* His publications include *Faith with Benefits: Hookup Culture on Catholic Campuses* (Oxford, 2017) and the coedited volume *Sex, Love, and Families: Catholic Perspectives* (Liturgical Press, 2020) with Julie Hanlon Rubio.

**Jacob M. Kohlhaas, PhD,** is an associate professor of moral theology at Loras College (Dubuque, Iowa), where he teaches a range of courses in theology, ethics, and general education. His research centers on theological anthropology, ethics, and relationships. His work has been published in *Theological Studies,* the *Journal of Religious Ethics,* the *Journal of Moral Theology, America,* and *US Catholic.* He is the author of *Beyond Biology: Rethinking Parenthood in the Catholic Tradition* (Georgetown University Press, 2021).

**Michael G. Lawler, PhD,** is the Amelia and Emil Graff Professor Emeritus of Catholic Theology at Creighton University (Omaha, NE).

He served as Dean of the Graduate School at Creighton and previously held faculty appointments in Dublin and Nairobi. He earned his PhD at the Aquinas Institute of Theology (St. Louis, Missouri). He is the author of twenty-five books, among them *Marriage in the Catholic Church: Disputed Questions* (Liturgical Press, 2002), *The Sexual Person: Toward a Renewed Catholic Anthropology* (Georgetown, 2008), and *Pope Francis and the Transformation of Health Care Ethics* (Georgetown, 2021), the latter two coauthored with Todd A. Salzman.

**Claudia Leal, PhD,** is an ordinary professor at the Pontificio Istituto Teologico Giovanni Paolo II for the study of marriage and family (Rome, Italy). She previously served on the faculty of theology at the Pontificia Universidad Católica de Chile (Santiago) from 2012 to 2022 and earned her doctorate in moral theology from the Accademia Alfonsiana (Rome, Italy). Her research interests include conscience and faith, narrative ethics, and Christian sexual ethics.

**Léocadie Lushombo, i.t.,** is an assistant professor of theological ethics at the Jesuit School of Theology of Santa Clara University (Berkeley, California). She obtained her PhD in theological ethics from Boston College (Massachusetts) and holds master's degrees in theological ethics from Catholic Theological Union (Chicago), in sustainable development from the Universidad Pontificio Comillas (Madrid, Spain), and in economics and development from the Catholic University of Central Africa (Yaoundé, Cameroon). She has worked extensively as a researcher and consultant-trainer in justice, peace, and gender issues in Africa and Latin America and is the author of *A Christian and African Ethic of Women's Political Participation: Living as Risen Beings* (Lexington, 2023).

**Andrew Massena, PhD,** is an assistant professor of biblical studies at Loras College (Dubuque, Iowa), where he teaches courses in scripture, comparative religion, and general education and serves as the director of the Archbishop Kucera Center and as a faculty coordinator for the Interfaith Leaders Program. He earned his doctorate from Boston College (Massachusetts) in 2020, where he wrote his dissertation on rabbinic and patristic exegesis of the Decalogue.

His publications have appeared in such journals as the *Journal of Scriptural Reasoning* and *Studies in Christian-Jewish Relations.*

**Emily Reimer-Barry, PhD,** is an associate professor in the Department of Theology and Religious Studies at the University of San Diego (California). She teaches courses in theological ethics utilizing feminist and antiracist pedagogies. Her research explores themes in fundamental moral theology, including the role of experience in theological method as well as topics that probe the relationship between social justice and sexuality, including HIV prevention, birth control, gender justice in marriage traditions, and reproductive justice.

**Richard N. Rwiza, PhD,** is a Catholic priest from the Archdiocese of Arusha, Tanzania, and an associate professor of moral theology and dean of the Faculty of Theology at the Catholic University of Eastern Africa (Nairobi, Kenya). He holds a licentiate in moral theology from the Catholic University of Eastern Africa and both a master's and a doctorate in moral theology from the Katholieke Universiteit Leuven (Belgium). His publications include *Formation of Christian Conscience in Modern Africa* and *Environmental Ethics in the African Context.*

**Todd A. Salzman, PhD,** is the Amelia and Emil Graff Professor of Catholic Theology at Creighton University (Omaha, Nebraska). He has authored eleven books and over 150 scholarly articles on ethical method, virtue ethics, sexual ethics, biomedical ethics, and ecclesiology and ethics including *What are They Saying about Catholic Ethical Method?* (Paulist Press, 2003), *The Sexual Person* (Georgetown University Press, 2008), and *Introduction to Catholic Theological Ethics* (Orbis, 2019), the latter two coauthored with Michael G. Lawler. Salzman and his wife, Katy, have three children: Ian, Aaron, and Emily.

**Annie Selak, PhD,** (she/her/hers) is an expert in feminist ecclesiology who teaches feminist theology in the Department of Theology and Religious Studies at Georgetown University (Washington, D.C.) and serves as director of Georgetown's Women's Center. She earned her doctorate in systematic theology at Boston College (Massachusetts). Her research

has appeared in *Modern Theology*, the *Journal of Catholic Social Thought*, the *Washington Post*, and *National Catholic Reporter*. In *The Wounded Church*, to be published by Fordham University Press, she analyzes moments where the church fails to live into its mission through a feminist vision.

**Angela Senander, PhD,** is a theologian who served as chair of the Department of Systematic and Moral Theology at Washington Theological Union and a research fellow at Georgetown University's Berkley Center for Religion, Peace and World Affairs (Washington, DC), where she wrote *Scandal: The Catholic Church and Public Life* (Liturgical Press, 2012) as well as "Beyond Scandal: Creating a Culture of Accountability in the Catholic Church," *Journal of Business Ethics* (2017). She now serves as system director of formation in a Franciscan health care system.

**Matthew Sherman, PhD,** serves as the director of campus ministry and as an associate professor of theology at Holy Cross College in Notre Dame, Indiana. His work and teaching involve the intersection of theology and ministry, the role of ethics in historical theology, and connections between sacramental and moral thought. Sherman earned his doctorate from Boston College (Massachusetts) and teaches courses in fundamental morals, bioethics, marriage and family, and Catholic Social Teaching.

**Wilhelmina Uhai Tunu, LSOSF,** is a Catholic nun from Tanzania with the Religious Institute of the Little Sisters of St. Francis. She is currently based in Uganda and serves as a member of the General Council of her institute in the Socio-Pastoral Ministry Desk and also lectures at the Queen of Apostles Philosophy Center (Jinja, Uganda). She holds a master's and a PhD in theology with specialization in moral theology from the Catholic University of Eastern Africa (Nairobi, Kenya).

**Paul Turner, STD,** is pastor of the Cathedral of the Immaculate Conception (Kansas City, Missouri) and director of the Office of Divine Worship for the Catholic diocese of Kansas City–St. Joseph. He holds a doctorate in sacred theology from the Collegio Sant'Anselmo (Rome, Italy). His publications include *Ars*

*Celebrandi: Celebrating and Concelebrating Mass* (Liturgical Press, 2021), *In These or Similar Words: Praying and Crafting the Language of the Liturgy* (World Library Publications [now GIA], 2014), *Whose Mass Is It? Why People Care So Much about the Catholic Liturgy* (Liturgical Press, 2015), and dozens of other titles.

**Ellen Van Stichel, PhD,** is an assistant professor of Christian social and political ethics in the Faculty of Theology and Religious Studies at KU Leuven (Belgium) and the coordinator of the Centre of Catholic Social Thought. Her research interests and publications include topics such as (global) inequality, poverty, social exclusion, macroeconomic ethics, the link between social and ecological justice, and the role and importance of political emotions from the perspective of Christian social thought. Recently she coauthored "Rethinking Catholic Social Thought and Practice in a Context of Crisis," special issue of *Journal of Catholic Social Thought* (2023).

**Kate Ward, PhD,** is an associate professor of theological ethics at Marquette University (Milwaukee) and earned her doctorate from Boston College (Massachusetts). Her book *Wealth, Virtue, and Moral Luck: Christian Ethics in an Age of Inequality* (Georgetown University Press, 2021) explores the ethical problem of inequality and the role of economic status in the pursuit of virtue. She is currently completing a book on work in Catholic social thought.

**Mary Beth Yount, PhD,** is an associate professor of theological studies at Neumann University (Aston, Pennsylvania) and was the director of content and programming for the World Meeting of Families and the visit of Pope Francis to Philadelphia in 2015. Yount has published more than twenty articles, book chapters, and reviews and is a two-time Catholic Press Association awardee. She has also consulted for the United States Conference of Catholic Bishops, six Vatican dicasteries (congregations) and papal visit teams, and various universities, dioceses, and nonprofits.

# INDEX